THE BEST PLAYS OF 1959–1960

THE
BURNS MANTLE
YEARBOOK

from "Toys in the Attic"

Illustrated with photographs, and with
drawings by HIRSCHFELD

THE BEST PLAYS
OF 1959–1960

EDITED BY LOUIS KRONENBERGER

DODD, MEAD & COMPANY

NEW YORK · 1960 · TORONTO

EDITOR'S NOTE

IN editing this forty-third volume in the *Best Plays* series, I find myself once more under very pleasant obligations. Once more my wife, Emmy Plaut, has provided help that is more fairly called collaboration. For editorial assistance I must thank Garrison Sherwood and Barbara Kamb. I must also thank, for the use of photographs, the Editors of *Life* Magazine and Doris O'Neill, and for the use of its tabulation of Hits and Flops, *Variety* and Mr. Abel Green. Particular thanks are due, for their reports, to Miss Cassidy, Mr. Hobson and Mr. Hewes, and for very kindly granting the use of their sketches, to Will Steven Armstrong, Howard Bay, Alvin Colt, William and Jean Eckart, Roger Furse, David Hays, Ruth Morley, Oliver Smith and Miles White. And, as always, it is a great pleasure to be associated in this project with Mr. Hirschfeld.

It is also pleasant to refer to two inclusions in this year's text. In choosing *The Thurber Carnival* as one of the Ten Best, doubtless we include what is even less a "play" than a number of musicals that have qualified for the honor; but a kind of delightful individual revue that constitutes the work of a single highly creative mind is surely to be welcomed whenever it exists. The second inclusion, which I think is to be welcomed also, is some representative passages from Mr. Hewes' choice of the best Off Broadway play of the year, *The Connection*.

LOUIS KRONENBERGER

CONTENTS

x CONTENTS

SUMMARIES OF THE SEASONS

THE SEASON ON BROADWAY

NO Broadway season can be summed up in an adjective, nor would I bring one to bear on the season now past. But in attempting to characterize 1959-60, the key phrase must surely have less to do with what the season achieved than with what it aspired to. The key phrase, that is to say, would have less to do with successes than with standards. No matter how depressing one would find a season plagued by bad plays that wanted to be good ones—and 1959-60 had, surely, its quota of these—one would feel none of the resentment or indignation induced by a season rich in trash that just hoped to make money. (Over some of this trash I shan't even put a tombstone, but simply ignore it in this chronicle.) And there was something else about 1959-60 on Broadway—the fact that it offered every variety of theatre piece, adaptation or stunt as a substitute for original plays; the fact that even commercial-minded creativeness seemed on the wane, and that much that was bad was at the same time largely borrowed.

If this is to put the season's worst foot forward, it is because it drags its other one. Certainly 1959-60 offered its very real good things and its bright rewards. Add to the better plays some first-rate acting and performing, whether in Shakespeare at one end or in a two-man revue at the other, and those who would champion the theatre at all costs, who would cry "Our theatre, right or wrong!" could make out a fair case of a kind. But a much stronger case, I fear, can be made on the opposite side; I fear that the general lack of aspiration dwarfs the specific sense of achievement, and that time and again even had the plays that ignominiously failed been sufficiently better to succeed, they would only have ignominiously succeeded. We have entered, as is all too well known, a new Broadway era—an era of high costs that makes for a theatre of hits or flops, with little room for what lies between, and with part of its attitude shaped by the belief that anything *avant-garde* or highbrow or special should seek success Off Broadway. But there is perhaps something further involved in this new era—the sense of ignorant and ill-qualified producers crashing the Broadway scene, their standards as low as their tastes are loutish, to produce the sort of stuff Broadway once provided in late spring, during the "silly season." These people are helping to create a third kind of theatre that can only be called Sub-Broadway.

3

In any case, the past season was one in which a fifth of the plays closed within a week of opening, and a good third of the plays within two weeks. Since it was a season never rich in good things, and till late in February half-starved for them, such a casualty rate cannot be explained on the theory that the going was too strong. The going, as a matter af fact, could hardly have been weaker, and so many plays quickly threw in the sponge not because—with rare exceptions—they weren't good or entertaining enough to meet the competition, but because they weren't good or entertaining at all. What was really remarkable about the season was that from start to finish it didn't produce, even at a popular level, a single really good comedy; that the successful plays that boasted comic qualities —such as *The Tenth Man* and *The Best Man*—were strongly compounded of other qualities as well; and that anyone in search of rewarding light entertainment, with nothing else added, had to go for it to *At the Drop of a Hat* or *The Thurber Carnival* or *Fiorello!*

Fortunately, there was a fairly decent showing on the more serious or dramatic side—things as newsworthy, in one way or another, as *Toys in the Attic*, *The Miracle Worker*, *The Andersonville Trial*, *Five Finger Exercise*, *The Tenth Man*, *Caligula*, *The Deadly Game*, *Duel of Angels*. But even there—and without, I think, being cranky —one must point out that it was the serious side of *The Tenth Man* that fell short; that *The Miracle Worker* is far from deft as playwriting, and that both it and *The Andersonville Trial* are to a considerable extent documentary; and that *The Deadly Game* was made over from a TV play that had itself been dramatized from a novelette. But if the creative spirit prospered painfully seldom during 1959-60, there were compensatory blessings by way of acting and direction, and consolatory oases during desert-dry evenings. The season had its good things to remember, however many more things there were to forget.

During 1959-60, drama—which normally comes off better than comedy—did so to a most abnormal degree. The season's drama started off professionally, if not impressively, with the first of many stage works taken from real life—with Jerome Lawrence and Robert E. Lee's play about President Harding called *The Gang's All Here*. Their portrait was a largely familiar one of a genial, poker-playing mediocrity who was hoisted into the White House, who politically was not so much a Republican as a know-nothing, whose cronies were crooks whom he turned into Cabinet members, and on whose strong right claws he leaned for support. At the end, the authors portrayed a Harding who commits suicide—but not till he has been roused, by what he unwillingly learned, to responsible action.

Arthur Hill, Fred Stewart, Bernard Lenrow, E. G. Marshall, Yvette Vickers, Melvyn Douglas and Bert Wheeler in "The Gang's All Here"

The authors, using simple strokes and sure-fire commonplaces, and in every case working from the outside out, gave their play a certain measure of story interest and shock value, while Melvyn Douglas, with a finely managed impersonation, won sympathy for their protagonist. But wherever the play's pull was not purely factual it seemed flagrantly fictional, most of all during a weak last act. *The Gang's All Here* brought no insight to any of the questions it asked, it got beneath none of the skins it flayed; nor, furthermore, did it always jibe with the facts—Harding, inside the party, was no such Convention dark horse as he was made out to be, nor was he quite such a babe in the wood.

Chéri was the first of two plays adapted from Colette novels; and a pretty empty play it proved to be. The story of an overindulged, sexually precocious, humanly immature young man—the son of a *grande cocotte* who had brought him up to make a rich marriage—it pivoted on his affair, before marriage, with a cocotte twice his age. Life, for both of them, was over at the end of Act I; and so was the play. Thereafter they could only mope while apart, come uneasily together, then part once more. Meeting, they talked too much, wept too much, moralized too much; between their meetings, the play offered pictures of demireps who proved dismal conversationalists. Chéri's mistress, at sixty, managed to reach the age of content, but Chéri could only kill himself. Fairly interesting while chronicling its love affair, the play thereafter fell apart, with no more wit to its frivolous scenes than depth to its sober ones.

The season quickened with what remained its great human-interest story, William Gibson's *The Miracle Worker*. The tale of Annie Sullivan's clenched, turbulent, finally triumphant grappling with the child Helen Keller took on new and affecting reality in stage form. The tremendous force of the play's crucial scenes could not have derived from the facts alone, or from Mr. Gibson's use of them; it needed the magnificent teamwork of Anne Bancroft and young Patty Duke and, behind them, the brilliant direction of Arthur Penn.

The Boston Irish girl whose first job was as nurse and teacher to the deaf, blind, mute Helen, had herself known blindness as well as squalor. In encountering an ungovernable small animal who, denied sight and speech, could only flail and thrash about with her arms and legs, Annie was fortunately stubborn, hardheaded and wryly humorous: mere pity for Helen, she realized, would be all wrong. There consequently ensued between teacher and child a Homeric tussle, a kind of barbaric ballet, a literal knockdown-and-drag-out fight that, Annie felt, could not be won by commanding obedience-without-understanding of Helen; there had to be comprehension and communication when Helen through her fingers could signal to her mind.

The Miracle Worker ended with that communication made, when what for Helen had been a mere finger game turned into a vital language. The key to Annie Sullivan's method—her militantly unsentimental attitude—proved a saving thing for the play itself. It set the play's tone, it kept it from being more than an occasional tear-jerker, it let humor and heroism constantly jostle each other. As playwriting, as a work that involves some knotty Keller family relationships and some eerie Sullivan family memories, *The Miracle Worker* is all too often makeshift and on occasion quite clumsy. But perhaps the flat family scenes provide a useful letdown, in contrast to the tense, brawling, fist-flying, plate-smashing, blind-rage struggles that proved, in the hands of two remarkable actresses, a form of unforgettable theatre.

The season's big basketful of disappointments was added to once again with *The Warm Peninsula,* in which Julie Harris and June Havoc alternated their heart throbs. First Miss Harris, a plain girl who wore glasses and wanted a man, would chat with the audience; then Miss Havoc would come on, an out-of-work nightclubber who wanted a man she could like. Julie soon fell in love with a painter who, it turned out, was kept, while June fell in love with an athlete who, it turned out, was married. As a penny-plain-and-tuppence-colored combine of the wistful wallflower and the rueful tramp, the play seemed designed for the slightly retarded matinee trade, who could revel at the sight of two cups running o'er, one lightly spiced, one nice and sugary. The play itself was all of a piece with no jangling false notes, there being no true ones to jangle against.

Flowering Cherry, by an English playwright, Robert Bolt, brought little variation to the familiar theme of the inept blusterer, the insecure braggart, under whose deadweight a whole household is genteelly sinking. Mr. Bolt could write neatly enough about inflated nullity, he could make characters recognizable in a rather dusty mirror, he could suggest what life looks like through smoke-colored glasses. But if nothing in the play seemed grossly contrived or distorted, nothing, either, seemed really created or alive. There was none of the sudden bite, or comic lustiness, or tragic undertow with which, from *Juno and the Paycock* and *The Show-Off* to *A Touch of the Poet* and *The Entertainer,* the fourflusher as family man had been portrayed. Moreover, in applying some empurpled staging to so much good gray realism, Frith Banbury flyspecked the play's one real virtue—its honesty.

Dore Schary's *The Highest Tree* was a downright disaster of good intentions. The author of *Sunrise at Campobello* was writing in protest: he is one of the many people who, aware of the danger of strontium-90 in the air, want further bomb-testings abolished. The play's central figure, Dr. Aaron Cornish, was a famous atomic scientist stricken, very possibly because of his atomic activities, with acute leukemia. After soul-searching, he determined to spend whatever time remained to him urging an end to nuclear bomb tests. He spent much time conferring with his doctor and arguing the dangers of nuclear-testing with a contrary-minded colleague. This, if dull, was at least pertinent; much oftener Dr. Cornish was visited by a variety of relatives. In they would come with their little domestic problems, and out they would go; back they would come, and out

they would go again. Few plays have combined so little action
with so many needless people and such endless talk. But the worst
trouble wasn't that the play was all talk; it was that it was never
talk. It was a flow of stilted professorial speech and editorial-writer
rhetoric. As his own director, furthermore, Mr. Schary only stressed
what was wooden or hammy; he never seemed aware that there is
an art to preaching, or that to plead the cause of humanity you
should yourself seem human.

Against such deadness, Paddy Chayefsky's *The Tenth Man* had
the vividness of a genuine theatre piece. It equally drew upon life
and departed from it; and by means of visual and atmospheric ef-
fects, of lacing fantasy with reality and prayers with wisecracks, it
created its own heightened world. Part of Mr. Chayefsky's purpose
in all this was to cast light on the world of reality, to establish sym-
bolisms and inspire speculation. At this more serious level, his play
noticeably failed. But as a theatre piece, well staged by Tyrone
Guthrie and often well acted, it was striking and enjoyable.

Mr. Chayefsky's "tenth man" is a young lawyer, with no faith
in religion or in life itself, who is yanked off the streets into a shabby
Orthodox-Jewish synagogue to complete a quorum for morning
prayers. Actually, except for an aged rabbi, even the elderly Jews
who show up lack faith; they come out of habit or boredom, and as
to a club where they can argue and gossip and gag. One of them
now brings his eighteen-year-old granddaughter, a schizophrenic
who has been in and out of institutions and who, he thinks, is possessed of an evil spirit that must be exorcised. Amid prayer and
prattle, amid the girl's infatuation with the lawyer, the lawyer's in-
volvement with his analyst and the old rabbi's communings with
his God, the synagogue prepares for the exorcism ceremonies. In
the confusing midst of them, it is the lawyer who keels over, exorcised of an inability to love, after which he and the girl sally forth
to face life together. In what it juxtaposes and contrasts—surreal-
ism and photography, insanity and farce, demonology and Freud—
The Tenth Man is sharp theatre. And Mr. Chayefsky has an
equally good ear for the colloquial speech of his characters and for
their dialectical pomposities. Unhappily, in spattering its theatrical
vignettes with philosophic question marks, *The Tenth Man* took on
obligations it refused to meet. Far from elevating its fantasy into
a real vision, it failed to save it from sentimentality. Not only were
all the people in the play uniformly nice, but exorcism was used
merely as a miracle drug to provide a sleazy happy ending; and the
blithely vanishing young couple suggested the schizophrenia of playwrights who would give meaning to their words, yet eat them too.
In certain ways *The Tenth Man* recalled the fine stories of the Jew-

ish fantasist Bernard Malamud; but in the ways that really count, it fell far short of them.

Having transferred Warren G. Harding to the stage in *The Gang's All Here*, Messrs. Lawrence and Lee now told Harry Golden's story, using Mr. Golden's own title of *Only in America*. The stage difficulties involved were immediate and persistent; there was little from Mr. Golden's book to adapt beyond his genially hard-hitting personality, which really needed the first person, and his egalitarian philosophy of life, which seemed both pious and blatant when acted out. Accordingly the authors had to blow up into two hours of theatre what was not only ill-suited to the theatre but what, even in book form, came off much the best in ten-minute draughts. Thus they could only bring Golden to North Carolina, introduce him around, plant him in front of his typewriter, and festoon him with homely metaphors, Yiddish phrases, and good, bad and indifferent jokes. They showed him slowly winning the hearts of all his white, Southern, Gentile neighbors. But in his game of hearts there lurked a menacing queen of spades—the unsuspected fact that Mr. Golden had once gone to prison. It overhung his life until it finally broke out in headlines, only for all who knew him not just to rally to his defense but to pay him homage. That the adapters should so magnify what everyone in the play is quick to minimize is proof of how desperately they needed dramatic material, of how Golden's queen of spades was their one ace in the hole. And indeed, despite lively moments and amusing details, the play constantly stretched its already flimsy materials. Clearly, *Only in America* should never have been a play; and only on Broadway, with its headlong opportunism, could it ever have become one.

In *A Loss of Roses*, William Inge once more went back to the Middle West of a generation ago, once more portraying troubled, torn, anonymous lives. This time he treated the jangled relationship between a widow and her twenty-one-year-old son, and what happened when an out-of-work tent-show dancer, who had once been their maid, came to stay with them. The mother, whom the son resented from being too much drawn to her, had for the boy's sake not married again; and aware of her own dangerous feelings toward him, had tackled their relationship wisely but not too well. When the pathetically buffeted dancer arrived, the son deluded himself that the way out lay not just in an affair with her but in marriage, only for him to leave her high and dry and then, as a way out for himself, to leave his mother.

In seeking to probe one of the most tangled of relationships, Mr. Inge achieved his familiar sharp little vignettes and touching muffled cries; he achieved, too, in the mother, an interesting variation on a type. His general failure seemed due partly to method and partly to mood. The dancer's role got on top of the main story and kept it from breathing. Into a short play Mr. Inge further tossed irrelevant comedy bits and a too farcical bed-hopping scene. Hence, mother and son never got deeply probed. A big moment, again—such as the mother's refusing her son's anniversary gift—too much sacrificed character to plot. The silver cord never really bound Inge's story, which remained too distant from its materials, too much given to mood.

From England, with Peter Shaffer's *Five Finger Exercise*, came help for Broadway. Though it had the look of one more mousy English country-house play, it became more and more cat-and-mousy. The Harrington family proved somewhat non-U and wholly non-unified. Father was a self-made manufacturer, all the more defensively philistine because of his snobby, culture-climby wife and his sniffing, muddled mama's-lapdog of a son. Into their divided, deluded midst, as tutor to a cheery teen-age daughter, came a quiet young German, hating the land of which his brutal Nazi father seemed a symbol, and eager for a friendly English home. Perceptive about the Harringtons, he—who had known real horror —tried to prevent their inflicting needless horror on themselves. But in sounding the alarm bell, he merely fed the fire, and soon accusations and recriminations flared up all around.

Mr. Shaffer can write dialogue that, sharp in itself, is also characterizing; and he can cunningly build up atmosphere and tension. These gifts, joined to a vivid production, created a generally good evening that at its best was engrossing. The play had, certainly, its contrived moments and false notes, the family life its reminiscent commonplaces, and the young German served too many convenient purposes to come off quite whole. But in view of England's gulf between classes and generations and its often tight-lipped family tactics, there was a measure of truth to the play, along with a generous portion of theatre.

In *Silent Night, Lonely Night* Robert Anderson told of two people in a New England inn on Christmas Eve. Strangers in adjacent rooms—the woman has a son in a neighboring prep-school infirmary, the man a wife in a sanitarium "up the hill"—they come together out of loneliness and become increasingly autobiographical. They look back on marriage that has come to grief, they resist pity while revealing self-pity, they talk of love and resist sex. In the end they go to bed together, then she goes back to her unfaithful husband, and he to the wife he has played a part in driving insane. What Mr. Anderson wrote was a kind of Elegy in a Country Bedroom, an unburdening of troubled hearts and a sluicing of wistful memo-

ries. Much of it was honesty evocative and well-expressed, but as
it suffered as a play from all lack of movement, so it did as a conversation piece from badly overstretching a mood. It grew monotonous, it came to seem watered and then sugared. But it was perhaps not so much its undramatic subject-matter as its form that
condemned it; as a longish one-acter it might have lyrically chronicled a meeting and sustained a mood. As anything longer, it could
only be less.

Jean Anouilh's *The Fighting Cock* revealed an Anouilh more balanced than bitter in mood, and much more effective as a *philosophe*
than as a playwright. His play was at times a witty variant on
a persisting theme—one all the more persistent for posing an in-
soluble question. *The Fighting Cock* concerns a retired general
disgusted by a world filled with "cheats" and lost to honor, who
would start a movement to get rid of the "maggots." Against this
befuddled, testy idealist rooted in the past Anouilh sets people who
accept the way of the world, sometimes with an eye to the future.
Radical laborers and reactionary aristocrats, pretty young wives
and clever young men assail the general, not because he dreams but
because all his dreams are out of fashion.

The play pleasantly balances its blunderer from the age of chiv-
alry against the more efficient citizenry of an age of compromise.
It is a highly Anouilhan balance, in that it finds much to be said
against both sides. But where Anouilh shows a certain contempt
for riders on bandwagons, for his knight riding full tilt in the wrong
direction his mockery is compassionate. And where, in earlier work,
Anouilh set his version of Molière's surly misanthrope against a too
complaisant world, his hero in *The Fighting Cock* comes closer to
Cervantes' cracked Don. Anouilh retains here his gift for little
dialectical monologues and variety turns. There are bright remarks
enough; but instead of a sense of fermentation beneath the foam,
there is considerable dramatic flatness. It is not just that the play
finds no destination; it fails no less to dramatize the very lack of
one. Almost predestined to an intellectual stalemate, the story
needed greater emotional leverage and a more vibrant charge than
it ever got. Whether it was the part's fault or the player's, Rex
Harrison never made the general expressive enough. And whether
it was the production's fault or the play's, Peter Brook's staging
never achieved a right blend of the aromatic and the astringent.

Jolly's Progress concerned a wild, quick-witted young Alabama
Negro housemaid who, having been seduced by her employer and
sent packing by his wife, found sanctuary with an enlightened writer.
While the writer plays Prof. Higgins to the girl's Liza, the town
assumes he is playing Don Juan; soon preachers rail and hooded

figures threaten. A play in which the racial angle might have breathed chill realism on Shavian comedy, *Jolly's Progress* was so gagged up with the crude and the stereotype that whatever was not *Pygmalion* was tatterdemalion.

Saul Levitt's *The Andersonville Trial* was based on a famous real-life military trial—that of Henry Wirz, the Civil-War superintendent of Andersonville prison, where some 40,000 Union soldiers lived in unutterable filth and where a third of them died. The first half of Mr. Levitt's play consists, indeed, of witnesses' accounts of the unspeakable conditions and the unthinkable treatment. But, as the testimony piles up, it emerges that Wirz was rather the brutal agent than the inhuman author of what went on, that he was actually carrying out orders from higher up.

Against all this, a conscience-pricked judge advocate argues that Wirz was morally obligated to disobey such monstrous military orders—a ticklish thesis to propound before a military court. But after Wirz insists on personally taking the stand, the judge advocate wrests permission to raise the moral issue; and the trial thereupon erupts into something beyond cross-examination or even debate. On the judge advocate's side, the trial becomes an indictment that by-passes the law; on Wirz's it becomes a mine-not-to-reason-why defense that side-steps morality. In all this Mr. Levitt makes very good use of two strong natural assets—of a stormy trial, always a virtual synonym for lively theatre; and—behind the trial—of what remains one of the great mass-horror stories of history. Upon these two things he raised, with discernible modern overtones, a large moral problem of guilt. The play offered an evening that had much in its favor in both theme and treatment, that had both effective bursts of eloquence and genuine bouts of theatre. At the same time the play lacked a certain cleanness of impact; it pounded too hard in places, it stretched things out too long, it did not altogether plumb its moral issue or its chief actors; and by mixing dialectics into its histrionics, it rather forfeited much of the straight realistic fascination of a trial. All this helped show why it is no accident for trials to be good theatre: theatre minds and legal minds equally highlight and softpedal to a purpose, equally employ shock and diversionary tactics, can equally breed doubts in the very act of showing dexterity. Vivid in so many of its parts, the play did not altogether satisfy as a whole.

A sadly uneven play about a sadly unbalanced household, Katherine Morrill's *A Distant Bell* was yet not without interest. Concerned with a mother who has been in and out of mental homes and is shunned by the community, and with her three edgy, repressed young-lady daughters, the play told how one daughter got to know

*Arthur Treacher, Rex Harrison, Natasha Parry, Roddy McDowall,
Gerald Hiken, Alan MacNaughton and Jane Lillig in "The Fighting
Cock"*

a young newspaperman who liked her and accepted the household,
only for a younger sister to win him away with janglingly tragic
consequences. Handling ticklish material in her own undaunted
way, Miss Morrill created, not another Freudian blueprint, but a
kind of disconcerting watercolor. It was an honest try with fitful

rewards, but it all too often seemed as unfocussed and out-of-touch as its heroine; as ill-equipped to cope with crises, as fancy of language, as given to repeating itself. It seemed most effective when it was a genre study of a household, a sort of cracked-*Glass Menagerie*.

The Deadly Game, adapted from a Friedrich Duerrenmatt novelette by James Yaffe, caught the author of the bitterly sardonic *The Visit* in a rather more playful mood. To be sure, his playfulness involved the gallows, as his retort on men's love of money was to put a price on their heads. On this occasion, his people play Murder. A brash, coarse, well-heeled American salesman, seeking a snowy night's lodging in a Swiss chalet, finds gathered there a retired judge, a retired prosecutor and a retired defense lawyer who meet regularly to dine well and then stage "trials" of various living or historical characters. Invited to stand trial for murder, the American, equally sure of his innocence and of his adroitness at games, accepts. Under steady grilling, he makes more and more admissions while growing more and more angry, till it becomes clear that he so much coveted his boss's job as half-consciously to bring about his boss's death.

As another of Duerrenmatt's pessimistic, wormwood-flavored judgments on mankind, *The Deadly Game* had both its moral and its theatrical merits. Tried at a Duerrenmatt "court of the Unconscious," few men would escape whipping; indeed, in the Unconscious of the very men who stage the trials there may well lurk as much blood-lust as love for law. They, with their icy, refined, half-mad sense of justice, and the American with his coldhearted, dog-eat-dog view of life, face one another in contrasted inhumanity. The play has a parlor-game brittleness and bite, and in its best scenes a thrusting theatricality. Less happily, Mr. Yaffe's adaptation needs half an evening of Won't-you-walk-into-my-parlor? before being ready for its parlor game; and is perhaps a little too ready to let the American convict himself, to create another death of a salesman. *The Deadly Game* stood in need of greater impact, partly because it was not a well-rounded play; here again, as with *Silent Night, Lonely Night*, a long, intense one-acter is what really seemed called for. But here again, if on a diminished scale, was the sardonic, macabre quality of *The Visit*.

From the Continent, too, in a neat translation by Justin O'Brien, came Albert Camus' *Caligula*, wherein one of the most searching of modern minds had pondered one of the most nefarious rulers of history, a ruler whose one excuse for being a monster is that he was almost certainly a madman. But though Camus wrote *Caligula* in 1938—an ominous time of madmen and monsters—even then his play was not in any usual sense tendentious. His Caligula was no self-made, power-mad Red or Brown or Black-shirted dictator, but someone born to the purple. Endowed with unlimited power, he came—out of disillusion with life—to thirst after unlimited "freedom." The Caligula of Camus would have the impossible; would dispense with love, friendship, reason, with every bond that unites humanity; would as passionately destroy as other men create; would claim to be a god that he might act the beast. With inverted logic and suppurated sensibility, Caligula degrades, tortures, murders, rapes those about him; alternates appalling melodrama with grisly farce; becomes now a kind of rancidly self-communing Hamlet, now Venus in a gold wig. But the more inhumanly homicidal his acts become, the more inherently suicidal is his mood, boundless egotism shatters into nihilism, limitless freedom festers into self-imprisonment, until Caligula's assassination is in truth an assignation with death.

Camus' attempt to hold a monster up to nature and draw a sane moral from a mad career produced a startlingly simple moral—in Camus' own words, "One cannot be free at the expense of others." In extracting, from such sick and vast-scaled violence, mere copybook wisdom, there is perhaps something at once overelaborate and insufficient. Caligula himself, in any case, is pathologically fascinating but not in the deepest sense truly interesting—which may explain why the play had its provocative writing, its brilliant bursts of theatre, its explosive moments of action, its lightning-flashes of revelation, and yet failed of sustained drama. Though strikingly staged by Sidney Lumet, it suffered in the theatre from playing in a barnlike musical-comedy house and seeming overproduced. But, however stimulating, it remains on its own terms underdramatized: partly because its dehumanized hero is surrounded, in morality-play fashion, by flat allegorical types; partly because his dreams, just for being so unfettered, grow paradoxically one-dimensional. By mixing theatricality and intellectualism, *Caligula* seems at times too vivid a stage piece, at times too pallid a one.

As midseason hastened toward spring, there were a number of minor debacles in the drama of violence, most of them no sooner opened than closed. *Cut of the Axe,* laid in a small-town jail and concerned with vagrants held for a murder that it turns out the police chief had committed, preached morality in the language of melodrama, and both of them in terms of stereotypes and clichés. *The Cool World,* exposing a Harlem world of Negro juvenile delinquency—indeed a kind of teen-age hero-worship of vice—never did justice to its subject-matter. *The Long Dream,* which Ketti Frings had adapted from a novel of Richard Wright's, differed from most Southern-Negro dramas in centering on a Negro named **Tyree Tucker** who is well-off—and has got that way by acting the "good" Negro, by cringing, sashaying, and working in cahoots with a corrupt police chief. Trouble starts when the young son, for whose future's sake Tyree has partly dirtied his hands, learns about his father; trouble mounts when Tyree and the police chief clash and create a spiral of tragic melodrama that ends with the son's death. The moral plight of Tyree, of the social victim who sells his soul to save his family's and to nourish their bodies, is familiar enough; the twist in *The Long Dream* was that—so great were the pressures —Tyree's defense went beyond mere rationalization when he cried out: "I can't be corrupt, I'm a nigger!" But his being a slight variant on a type was as close as the play came to something really new and valid. For though it told an often terrible, and a sociologically buttressed, story, *The Long Dream* was too often a poor play. Inherent truth seemed itself corrupted, here with melodramatic staples, there with declamatory clichés, and with a glaringly false final curtain.

Horror and violence persisted in *There Was a Little Girl*, the kind of play where everything needs to be done right, and where almost nothing was. Concerned with a well-brought-up eighteen-year-old girl who is assaulted by two hoodlums and raped by one of them, it thereafter offered dribbling scenes that never came close to justifying what had given rise to them. Along with wobbliness of stagecraft went a gossipiness of tone: perhaps the key to the play's level of taste was the between-the-scenes music that blared forth the mixed sentimentalism and sensationalism of a vastly-in-need-of-soap opera. *Semi-Detached* concerned the occupants of a two-family Montreal house—a house divided by prejudice, by the sniffiness and anti-Catholicism in an English-speaking family, by the rigidity and fear of worldly ways in a French-speaking one. It required tragedy to bring the families together and choke them with fellow-feeling. But by then the play itself was choked with clumsy staging, clumsier plotting, and well-meant pleas for tolerance. The tragedy, moreover, seemed as ill-founded as the bigotry, and a few sharp stage moments seemed lathered into one more example of soap opera.

Of all the quick-closing shows, Beverley Cross's *One More River* promised the most for half an evening; promised, indeed, well. It got vigorously—if rather reminiscently—under way with a crummy freighter, a dead captain, a viciously tyrannizing mate, a respected bosun, a peppery resentful crew. When it was revealed that the mate had thrown boiling water into a deck boy's face and blinded him, the crew was itself so boiling mad that, but for the bosun's insistence on a proper trial, it would have strung the mate up. The trial itself involved sensational charges, and the mate's defense got into the deeper and murkier waters of character. At this point the play also got into deeper and murkier waters, where it eventually drowned: disbelief came to nose out tension and playwriting mishaps to outnumber maritime dangers. Mr. Cross's using desperate measures to keep melodrama afloat spoiled what started off as a good realistic thriller and what was given, moreover, a good naturalistic production. The raciness of the dialogue aroused hopes for what, at a vibrant popular level, Mr. Cross might write next.

Coming at this turn of time, Lillian Hellman's *Toys in the Attic* slapped a slumped, lethargic season into awareness. The reason was not just the sense of tautness, insight and power that the play displayed, but the very sense, so to speak, of playwriting. *Toys in the Attic* constituted a dramatic journey, with a destination; and not a mere series, however vivid, of theatrical way stations. And it so palpably reached its destination that its finest moments were its concluding ones. Laid in New Orleans, it pivoted on thirty-four-year-old Julian Berniers, a weak, likeable ne'er-do-well who had been protectively kept going by two adoring old-maid sisters. Recently he had married an odd, unbalanced heiress who was possessively happy with him only when they were hard up. When Julian mysteriously got hold of a lot of money and showered everyone with presents, everyone, far from being jubilant, was distressed. They all knew that they had lost him, now that he himself had found his feet; they all became aware that his ungrown-up dependence on them had constituted their happiness. They became aware, too, of much about themselves—of one sister's incestuous feelings toward Julian, for example. It is she, acting through the simple-minded wife, who viciously contrives to get him back with them on the old terms. Only they are not the old terms. Blindman's Buff has become I Spy; nursemaids have proved false, toys been broken, children hurt.

The play suffered from an action that seemed intricate and talky in getting under way, and that turned melodramatic enough to seem too manipulated. But even so, it was an action in the service of a theme. Miss Hellman's old mordant power was in evidence again and again, and was combined with a broadened sense of humanity. Always sharp at characterization, the author of *The Little Foxes* became more probing and wide-ranging about character. She passed from human greed to something at times no prettier but far more universalizing—to human need, to the ego's fierce need to be needed and be loved, and hence its ugly need, when foiled, to hurt or betray or destroy. In *Toys* it isn't vixen teeth that bite, but human lips denied a kiss. Generally well-acted and extremely well-staged by Arthur Penn, the play went on to win the Critics Circle award.

Felicien Marceau's Paris hit, *The Good Soup,* which Garson Kanin adapted for Broadway, constituted, even to the form it took, the reminiscences of a coldly successful French cocotte. (In the theatre, Ruth Gordon played the middle-aged Marie-Paule, with Diane Cilento acting out her younger self.) From prostitution in "half-hour hotels," Marie-Paule had gone on to living grubbily with men, and then to being kept, and then to marriage and motherhood and expanding her husband's business. When, at length, she tumbled from affluent respectability, it was ironically for just once blundering through compassion. Told in revue-skit-sized flashbacks, the play used a good deal of material that was theatrically very reminiscent. Its scenes were oftener familiar and hardheaded than lighthearted and novel so that, regarded as light farcical entertainment, it needed sass and zest. But, with the story it had to tell, there was no need to see it only as something frothy as champagne or French as snails; it could also be as French as money. Marie-Paule was never girlishly rueful or gallantly raffish; she was cynical and hard. She wasn't ruined or misled—the one time love came to her it was wholly physical; and her regret was not for being calculating but for once miscalculating; not for her tarnished youthful past, but for its passing. In spite of her jauntily presented, and even half-parodied, experiences, hers was a real portrait; and despite its being too often fashioned of clichés, hers—like that in Restoration comedy—was a real attitude. But just as Restoration comedy can grow tiresome in constantly pursuing sex for pleasure, *The Good Soup* flagged from constantly pursuing it for pay. For the light touch to triumph over the spotted truth, Marie-Paule's career needed more amusing variety, or she herself a sense of humor, or M. Marceau a brighter wit. Yet *The Good Soup* had its own kind of interest for succeeding with the ice rather than the champagne.

Gore Vidal's *The Best Man* was Broadway's salute to an election year: a lively theatre piece laid at a fanciful 1960 national convention, and concerned with a fierce struggle between two would-be nominees. Former Secretary of State William Russell was cultivated, intellectual and endowed with scruples; Senator Joseph Cantwell was self-made, self-obsessed, and swollen with ambition. At the outset, a tough, cynical old pro of an ex-President could almost surely play kingmaker; but when he refused, Cantwell planned to knock out Russell by reviving a forgotten mental breakdown; and if Russell would stoop, he in turn could bring up an old Army scandal.

From there on till very near the end, *The Best Man* chronicled a pretty traditional sort of struggle between a set hero and a set villain, and much of the play's interest lay in the sheer simplicity of this. Despite its special election-year coloring, *The Best Man* was very much a hardy perennial in the way it contrasted ethics with opportunism, statesmanship with careerism, light with darkness. To be sure, many topical references and real names were introduced, and dinner parties were enlivened as to who was who, or half who, among Mr. Vidal's cast of characters. But Mr. Vidal was always aware that, to sustain a whole evening, storytelling must count for more than anecdote-mongering, and a protagonist than a prototype. *The Best Man* offered little about smoke-filled rooms and even less about current issues or rival parties; the play, indeed, all but obliterated the idea of there being any second party. If a modern-angled morality play, *The Best Man* at the same time always remembered that bad politics are a prime source of good theatre, that stage tricks pall beside political ones.

Two famous French writing names brought the dramatic season to a close. *A Second String,* which Lucienne Hill adapted from a novel of Colette's, concerned the home life of an egocentric French playwright-philanderer. Dashing imperiously in and out on his wife, his son, and the secretary who is also his mistress, he at last makes his wife a sufficiently impatient Griselda to force a showdown over him with the mistress, only for the two women to find confederacy more sensible than civil war. Whatever wit or wisdom the original Colette story may have possessed was all but boiled out of it by turning French into English and a novel into a play. What was technically a drama of situation became in practice a thin conversation piece, with the same topics and têtes-à-têtes recurring over and over, and with the talk itself seldom bright.

In *Duel of Angels,* the last play he wrote before his death in 1944, the wittily ironic, aromatically pessimistic Jean Giraudoux offered a suavely chill farewell—a glass of iced champagne held in almost as cold a hand. In the Aix-en-Provence of 1868, Giraudoux offers variations on the old Roman story of Lucrece. The play opens in the best Giraudoux style of artificial high comedy: the ultra-pure wife of Aix's over-righteous new Judge, by cutting dead everyone involved in sexual intrigue, even the innocent deceived mates, is rocking the town with scandal. When one decent husband's eyes are opened, his fond if promiscuous wife first berates the prude and then drugs her—plotting with a procuress to make the virtuous lady believe that while unconscious she was violated by the town rake. As the itself-violated Lucrece theme sounds louder chords, as the pure lady bids the rake kill himself, as the righteous Judge rejects the wife he thinks was raped and she takes poison, rejecting life itself, Giraudoux's artificial story remains scrupulously behind glass. But gusts of realistic rain or melodramatic sleet beat against it— with Giraudoux cleverly letting his characters concede how tragedy is jostling farce, or drama encroaching on comedy. But the play, as it plunges over rapids in which both men and women are hurt and virtue and vice are drowned, is just kept between banks by its ironic tone and wit. By the end, the champagne perhaps seems more like Pernod, and the last word goes significantly to the procuress.

In Giraudoux's duel of attitudes, the play's blood thins as its plot thickens, and the evening yields not so much a sharp intellectual meaning as a plaintively cynical mood. The old generalities jut up: Must sensuality grow so coarse, or purity so prudish, or life itself so punishing? But though limited in substance, *Duel of Angels* has considerable style. Christopher Fry, moreover, adroitly conveyed Giraudoux's gloved and scented prose, and in an otherwise undistinguished production, Vivien Leigh's errant lady was conceivably the best performance of her career.

Though any number of the season's plays had strong comic and satiric elements, there were—as I said earlier—curiously few outright comedies, and none of any value. When Broadway sets out to amuse, and only to amuse, it is more and more at a dangerously popular level. This is not a matter of how broad the situations are, or how farcical the treatment, but rather of how needlessly hoked up so much of it seems, how brassy the tone, how incessant—and indifferent—the wisecracks. A farce called *Roman Candle* was an apt example of all this. It concerned an Army scientist pursued by a girl possessed of extrasensory perception; the pursuit, taking place in back-to-back Washington apartments, involved launching missiles in Alaska and unloosed endless gags about the Army and the Navy, horseracing and Eisenhower golf, martini-making and love-making. The whole thing was one of those mechanized gag-farces with good gags here and there, but tired and dead ones strewing the distance between; with vaudeville-turns in the road and broken-down scene writing. It was all clankingly commercial, not least for portraying its hero as marvelously indifferent to money. Another farce called *The Golden Fleecing* had to do with three U. S. Navy men in Venice, who plot to win fortunes at roulette by making use of their ship's mechanical computer. The fault was that—despite admirals and their winsome daughters, signalmen who passed out, couples who dove into canals, Venetian glass and Venetian gangsters—matters were never farcical enough. The show was well into its second act before it ever exploded into laughter; and things expired again in the third. The author, Lorenzo Semple, Jr., was too laborious tying his yarn in knots, too predictable in untying it.

George Axelrod's *Goodbye Charlie* opened very well, with a satiric picture of a weirdly conducted memorial service for a lecherous Hollywood heel. But Charlie, who had been killed by a vengeful husband, did not stay dead: he came back to earth in the form of a woman—of, for that matter, Lauren Bacall—to do penance for his sins against womankind. He had great trouble adjusting to his new role; his old pal, for whom he now began to palpitate, had greater trouble; and Mr. Axelrod had the greatest trouble of all. The kind of Hollywood taste that, in his opening scene, he had made his target now seeped into his treatment. A situation that from the outset was dangerous eventually turned dull as well. Mr. Axelrod was as stuck with his leering joke as though it were gum on his shoe; it was all *la même chose* without any *plus ça change*. Miss Bacall did well, and Mr. Axelrod did well as his own director; but in such a situation, the incidental brightnesses could only seem negligible.

Broadway, during '59-'60, was more mindful of the classics than during most recent seasons: it offered, indeed, one play by William Shakespeare and one by George Bernard Shaw. Moreover, it had done all this before the end of October, and thereafter could piously fold its hands and look virtuous for the rest of the season. Both productions had their very rewarding side. *Much Ado About Nothing,* a comedy whose main plot could not be drearier, or subplot at its best more delightful, had John Gielgud and Margaret Leighton playing Benedick and Beatrice. The "main plot" was as tedious and improbable as ever; but Sir John and Miss Leighton brought juice and bite to their prickly-pear romance. Wearing their hearts on their fingernails while moving blindfolded toward the altar, they seemed perfectly matched at sparring, brilliantly mated at witty detail. A certain added tribute went to Miss Leighton for her sustained hoity-toityness and verve. The stars' side of the evening made the dismal side worth putting up with.

Shaw's *Heartbreak House* was bestrewn with stars; and the production, like the play itself, was periodically brilliant rather than everywhere right. It has always had its advocates as one of Shaw's most important works, and certainly Shaw himself meant it to be important. But increasingly this Shavian *Cherry Orchard,* this portrait of "cultured, leisured Europe" before World War I, seems to mingle largeness of conception with looseness of treatment, and size with sprawl. As Shaw's characters explain themselves and react on one another, in an evening-long, often brilliant, conversation piece, something now veers toward tragedy, something else explodes as farce, here fireworks light up the scene, there flummery disfigures it. Rather too often the play drifts just as its people do and seems to reflect their languor. Its characters, moreover, are all so busy explaining what they suffer from that, though they convey a forcible sense of diagnosis, they give off only the feeblest sense of disease. But *Heartbreak House* is full of marvelous bits and pieces and has, at its best, a kind of special Shavian magic. And though the production had its real limitations, it offered notable performances by Pamela Brown, Diana Wynyard and Alan Webb.

As one effort to redress the Broadway balance, the Phoenix Theatre offered a number of classics in repertory. Opening its season with its one twentieth-century play, *The Great God Brown,* it could only reveal that however originally exciting O'Neill's drama might have been as an experiment, in itself it is now hopelessly dated. In drawing on Freud and the Unconscious, in embracing expressionism and the unrealistic, O'Neill wrote scenes with theatrical force; but he seemed to be working, not in a living world, but sometimes in a laboratory and at other times in a void. The Phoenix next offered Ibsen's *Peer Gynt* which, with its poetry killed off in translation, seemed a vast, dull allegorical sprawl. From *Peer Gynt* the Phoenix went on to *Lysistrata* and the wonder is that—indulging in the sort of arty vulgarity that far outdoes the commercial kind—it did not go under. Happily the Phoenix went on next to a rewarding *Henry IV,* Part I in which Eric Berry showed a talented Englishman's ability to play Falstaff with nimbleness and verve, and in which Stuart Vaughan's staging maintained a happy balance between tankard humor and martial heroics. The success of Part I led the Phoenix to offer, with equal success, Part II. This, as much the less played of the two Parts, was not only a small event in itself, since it has splendid merits; but it enabled playgoers to witness, in the two Parts taken together, something vastly and variedly Shakespearean. Mr. Berry was once again an engaging Falstaff, there were several other good performances, notably John Heffernan's as Shallow; under Mr. Vaughan's direction the comedy scenes kept their blend of rust and magic; and the Phoenix ended its once-shabby season in happy form.

The 1959-60 season perhaps came off best in a field that defies being captioned—in the field of specialities, of one-man or two-man shows, of dolled-up recitation, of nightclubbing in disguise. Here indeed there were no distressing failures at all, and there were two of the season's most unusual and attractive successes.

Hurd Hatfield, Micheal MacLiammoir, John Gielgud, Margaret Leighton, Donald Moffat and George Rose in "Much Ado About Nothing"

At the start of the season the French singer, Yves Montand, was greeted rapturously for a three-week Broadway engagement. With his repertory of gay and sentimental, amorous and satiric songs, his way of garnishing them with dance steps or pantomime, and his engaging personality, M. Montand was a most welcome entertainer. He had, too, that something extra that derives from something individual. Whether he is more than a very accomplished popular entertainer seems to me in some doubt: his personality is a little too neatly combed and carefully parted, his use of a microphone gives a kind of set stance and technique to his show, and the ideal set-up for him is perhaps not a theatre but a night club, and not twenty songs but six or eight. But there is no questioning his appeal.

Following this one-man show from France came a two-man show from England—*At the Drop of a Hat*—that for sheer gaiety was not bettered all season. The two men were Michael Flanders, who was vivacious and bearded and sailed about in a wheelchair; and Donald Swann, who was mousy and bespectacled and stayed put at the piano. Flanders wrote the words for the songs they sang, Swann the music; and Flanders also did the incidental patter. The two men are both very British but very much themselves; casual, informal, yet with the timing of the solar system and the teamwork of the Lunts. Sharply satirical one moment, they were whimsically gay the next; their tone was urbane, their joking educated; and they were often most lively when most deadpan, and most deadly when most daft. But their success lay in their total effect. Delightful as their best songs were, the evening might have got becalmed without Flander's patter. And bright as his patter was, it might have proved wearisome but for his technique—the lines he threw away, the jokes he held his nose at, the changes of pace, the changes of face, the alarming sounds in his throat. If Flander's way was to be sinuous, mocking and charming, Swann's way was to play everything straight, then to seem suddenly straight out of Edward Lear.

In *A Lovely Light* Dorothy Stickney held the stage alone, half-impersonating, half-interpreting Edna St. Vincent Millay. Using a minimum of props and commentary, Miss Stickney wove an autobiographical chronicle out of Edna Millay's poems and letters, from her Maine-seacoast youth through her Greenwich Village *vie de bohême* to her married life with Eugen Boissevain and her solitary death at the age of fifty-eight. A kind of tribute from a great admirer of Miss Millay's work, *A Lovely Light* was also a pleasant theatre piece. Mingling pert comment from the letters with the lyrical longings of the poems, Miss Stickney nicely balanced the mockingbird and the nightingale. Unhappily her material was too restricting: only glimpsed through chinks was that mingled poet and woman who during the 1920s crystallized an attitude and epitomized an era. With her gaily illicit valentines and her often vibrant *cris de coeur*, Edna Millay was as much one kind of romantic lead on the stage of the twenties as Scott Fitzgerald was another. In *A Lovely Light*, however, her famous candle burned at one end only, and so ladylike that it could have graced a dinner table. As a result, the gallant, wind-blown, untidy Edna Millay who became a legend was scarcely discernible.

Another lady of legend was brought to the stage in *Dear Liar*, which Jerome Kilty made from the forty-year correspondence between Mrs. Patrick Campbell and Bernard Shaw. What resulted was no play, nor was it meant to be; by intention, Katharine Cornell and Brian Aherne were much less impersonators than dramatic instruments. In form, the whole thing perhaps most resembled a set of verbal duets. Neatly worked out and gallantly acted, *Dear Liar*—despite much that was pleasant and provocative—somehow fell flat as a whole. These, after all, were love letters without any love affair, and with a snarl in them for every coo. Where the temperamental Mrs. Pat was always losing her temper, a didactic G. B. S. was always telling her off, and seemed at his cool calm worst when she was painfully on her uppers. But what limited the evening was less Shaw's deficiencies as a lover than as a letter-writer, a role in which he fell far short of the dramatist. Indeed, things perked up most when the two stars could get their teeth into something theatrical rather than into each other; while they themselves were not really wedded to their parts. The unfailingly gracious Miss Cornell seemed too gentle, while Mr. Aherne seemed too jaunty.

Once again, as with *At the Drop of a Hat,* an evening in a special category became a special treat. *A Thurber Carnival* was a sort of one-mind show, an animated anthology of pen-and-pencil work by the most splendidly mad of modern humorists. The thought of an all-Thurber show, however alluring, could not but cause qualms: how was that unique world of his to stay vaultingly alive inside theatre walls, or to seem superbly demented in a mere three dimensions? But to a notable degree, it did: for one thing because much of Thurber snugly fits into a kind of intimate revue; again, because other Thurber bits extend the horizons of an intimate revue without violating its spirit. Finally, a lot of blown-up Thurber drawings serve the show equally well as sources of its comedy or as members of its cast. With eight pleasant human actors to boot, with sympathetic Burgess Meredith staging and a simple, uncluttered stage, Thurber could shoot straight at his audience, could create a glorious, instructive world in which everyone was to some degree mad. The demonstration began at once, with four dancing couples who suddenly stopped to fling forth wild remarks out of nowhere; it continued with a round of fables, skits, and recitations, some very famous, others new or new-made for the occasion. What the *Carnival* happily proved is that Thurber can be as funny when spoken as when read. There were sketches, to be sure, that sagged considerably, and ideas that spluttered; the low points were much like those in any better-grade intimate revue. But the high points —and they were many—were uniquely wonderful.

It was a busy season for musicals, and a fairly booming one: there were a number of hits. The first of these, *Take Me Along,* set to music Eugene O'Neill's one pleasant, nostalgic play of family life, *Ah, Wilderness,* in which he had traded tragedy for Tarkington, Freud for the Fourth of July, and tomtoms for small-town brass bands. *Take Me Along* retained what was pleasantly nostalgic; retained much the same small-town look, 1910 flavor, and horse-and-buggy pace. Its drinking was confined to a likeable bachelor and a would-be sex-bad boy; its passion consisted of the same boy's book-fed notions of it. Even in its parading, the show did not turn brassy; its tunes were offhand but lilting, and its cast were mostly actors rather than performers in musicals. The one outright performer was Jackie Gleason, and he managed rather more of a vaudeville than a video air; while Walter Pidgeon, Robert Morse, and Eileen Herlie all seemed refreshingly personal, rather than professional, in their way with a song. The show could have done with more dancing, and it rather tended to repeat certain scenes and reprise certain songs. But from the outset this was a musical that put its trust in mood rather than momentum, and that rather than shatter the funnybone, ravish the ear or dazzle the eye, simply left a nice taste in the mouth.

The Girls Against the Boys had a theme—set forth in the title—that seemed promising for a revue; and certainly, in any such comic warfare, Nancy Walker would make a sterling commander on one side and Bert Lahr a doughty generalissimo on the other. But the girls and boys in *The Girls Against the Boys* were forever fighting their material instead of one another, and conveying rather the din of battle than the exploits. The singing and stomping in the show were often as piercingly loud as an unsupervised children's party, and the sketches and jokes were correspondingly leaden. Whenever Miss Walker and Mr. Lahr were allowed to do things instead of compelled to say them, they were their very likeable and skilful selves. But far too often the show either alternated dullness with noise, or combined them.

The most looked-forward-to musical of the season, *The Sound of Music,* proved something less to look back on. With Rodgers and Hammerstein music and lyrics, a Lindsay and Crouse libretto, and with Mary Martin as star, the show understandably had a $2,300,000 advance sale. In accordance with Rodgers and Hammerstein's desire not to repeat themselves, they this time went to Austria for their story, to the famous Trapp Family Singers who dramatically escaped from the Nazis' clutches. Besides Captain von Trapp, there was a young novice from a neighboring abbey who taught his seven children to sing and who married their father. As a musical, *The Sound of Music* thus challengingly combined the cloister and the kindergarten, nursery rhymes and Nazi salutes.

Mr. Rodgers came off best, with a pleasantly versatile if not distinguished score. Elsewhere the show's virtues seemed marred by its weaknesses. For one thing, Rodgers and Hammerstein did repeat themselves—governess, motherless children, and children's papa all suggested, at times, *The King and I.* Moreover, *The Sound of Music* suffered by comparison; it had less swing, less gaiety, less piquancy than *The King and I.* It had indeed a great and pervasive fault: instead of offsetting sweetness with lightness, it turned

Theodore Bikel, Patricia Neway, Mary Martin, the children of the Von Trapp family and Kurt Kasznar in "The Sound of Music"

sticky with sweetness and light. If sometimes attractive, its abbey scenes were pretty-pretty. If sometimes fetching, its children's scenes were far too cute. The milk of human kindness was not enough for *The Sound of Music;* it insisted on the syrup. As a result, much rewarding detail blurred into an all churchbells-and-wedding-bells kind of world. Despite a triangular love story, there wasn't one tantrum; despite seven Trapp children, there wasn't one brat. The show's warmheartedness became, in the end, as cloying as a lollipop and as trying as a lisp.

Very little touted, the season's next musical took title to all sorts of prizes. Winning the Critics Circle musical-comedy award, the Tony award, and the Pulitzer Prize, *Fiorello!* was frequently winning in itself. That irascibly humane fighting gamecock, New York's Mayor La Guardia, displayed in the theatre—as he did in his day on the platform—a naturally theatrical personality. The period, again, through which he moved—roughly 1917 to 1933—had a fine gaudy glamour; and out of a dynamic human being and a razzle-dazzle era came a sometimes uneven, but lively and enjoyable, musical that replaced the usual frills and tinsel with welcome tobacco juice and cigar smoke. Happily it portrayed a crusader without ever adopting the tone of a crusade. While pumping lead into ward politics or Tammany wigwams, it poked fun at

Fiorello's own brandished tomahawk: splendidly played by Tom Bosley, La Guardia was the more engaging for not being too endearing, was the more lively for not being too reasonable. The straight-shooting book by Jerome Weidman and George Abbott wove deftly in and out of the song numbers, and the lower it went for theme, the higher it mounted in effectiveness. Two of the best things in the show were ditties that spoofed graft and the boys in the back room; even more zipful were a rousing electioneering street dance and a fine 1920s high-kicking chorus line. Fine at its best and fun a lot of the time, *Fiorello!* had its flop songs and scenes and its second-act vapors. But with George Abbott to stage it with his feeling for pace and pep, it was never for long in the doldrums.

Saratoga, adapted from Edna Ferber's novel *Saratoga Trunk,* was a gorgeously decked out period musical, moving from a plush New Orleans in the eighties to a palmy Saratoga Springs. But Cecil Beaton's sets and costumes were much the brightest part of the show. Despite some lively Ralph Beaumont dances, some pleasant Harold Arlen music, and some neat bits of Morton DaCosta staging, *Saratoga* had all the animation of a tableau. As so often, the chief trouble was book trouble: the story of a male and female fortune hunter who unromantically join forces to get on in the world but become the victims of romance, *Saratoga* snowed banalities, tripped over its own gaudy furnishings, and interminably prevented a heroine born out of wedlock from entering it. Wholly lacking freshness and zip, the show equally lacked charm and style.

Earlier, *Happy Town,* treating of a Texas town without a single millionaire, had come off a musical without a single merit; nor was there much more merit to a musical about beatniks, *Beg, Borrow or Steal.* Early spring brought *Greenwillow,* with Frank Loesser music—very pleasant some of it, but far from first-rate, and merely providing bright spots in a dull and irritating evening. An off-in-the-distance village, and also an out-of-the-past one, Greenwillow might conceivably have been Rip Van Winkle country—its doings, at any rate, could put you to sleep for twenty years. It offered a woodsy, folksy, pixie world full of scampering rustics, nocturnal rituals, and people who hear the Devil's call to wander; and it indulged in such novelties as folks darting out of portable outhouses. In it, indeed, every day seemed like Arbor Day and every night like Hallowe'en, and its people were of a sort usually encountered on calendars. It offered, moreover, lovers but no proper love story; devils but no improper temptations; and the kind of quaint language that in trying to be folk poetry, turns horrible as

Dick Van Dyke, Susan Watson, Dick Gautier, Chita Rivera, Kay Medford and Paul Lynde in "Bye Bye Birdie"

prose. There were those who found it charming, but anyone with memories of a J. M. Synge could only find its whimsies bogus, while even those with memories of a J. M. Barrie would find its cuteness grim.

Bye Bye Birdie was a sleeper among the season's musicals, and nothing could have proved more lively. If not particularly expert, it did not have to be: it had an infectious bounce, and Gower Champion's exuberant staging. Concerned with an Elvis-Presleyish crooner and his shrieking teen-age worshippers, the show happily found fun lurking in all sorts of things. If this made for a slight untidiness, it also made for freshness and variety; it kept the crooner from being given too much house room, it kept a whole rock-'n-rollcall of teen-agers from becoming oppressive. If the love interest did not altogether make love interesting, it was often brightened with glints of hate and it boasted an amusing roadblock to the altar—the man's mother, a murderously possessive momma who was forever jabbering of self-sacrifice and talking of suicide. Enjoyable, too, was a teen-ager's father trying to assert himself, whether at home or on TV. The best thing of all was a ballet in which Chita Rivera crashed a Shriners' dinner and started a small Keystone-Comedy chase, now around the table, now on it, now under it.   One reason, indeed, why *Bye Bye Birdie* landed successfully on its feet was that it was seldom off them; people were always hurrying in one direction or fleeing in another, fairly often dropping funny remarks as they went.   Musically the show traveled light, once or twice in fact with an empty suitcase.   But it everywhere happily elevated freshness above slickness and playfulness above mere workmanship—a lesson to producers who squeeze the originality and fun out of musicals by making them smooth and "professional" at all costs.

Thereafter, the musical scene straggled to an end.   *From A to Z* was an intimate revue starring Hermione Gingold who at times wrested victory through her leering *grande-dame* methods, but who was most of the time no match for her material.   As the other numbers tumbled out in alphabetical disorder, there were periodic rewards, notably Elliott Reid chattering away as the truffled editor of a $60-a-copy society magazine.   But all too often there were only wispy song-and-dance numbers, or watery skits, or wobbly satires. *Christine,* which brought down the curtain on the 1959-60 Broadway season, was a tedious romantic musical, despite its out-of-the-way romance.   The lady was Irish, the man was both Hindu and the lady's widowed son-in-law.   But even this unhackneyed relationship involved believing that beautiful, young-looking Maureen O'Hara could be a grandmother; and everything else was all too exotically familiar and reminiscently rusty.   Once again East is East and West is West; and Mother-in-law, in the end, knows best. But the end took forever to reach in a prosy, flat, humorless libretto. Sammy Fain's score was only mildly helpful—his Irish and Indian love calls were tuneful but commonplace.   The show's most sustained asset was Hanya Holm's vividly grotesque choreography of cobra dances and plate dances; but it could not save so sober-sided and lifeless a tale.

THE SEASON IN CHICAGO

By Claudia Cassidy

Drama Critic, Chicago *Tribune*

WHAT season in Chicago? Orchestra, opera, concerts, and dance, yes. Theatre continued to dwindle almost into extinction. Counting just about everything countable, the season of 1959-60 brought fourteen shows, and racked up 105 weeks of playgoing in four theatres. Two hopefully and beautifully restored playhouses met defeat. The little Civic, jewel box junior of the Civic Opera house, managed ten weeks' booking, then lapsed into a brooding dusk. The Michael Todd, once the Harris, sighed and settled for *Ben Hur*.

Yet the town was not inhospitable. *The Music Man* extended its stay to fifty-six weeks at the Shubert, grossing more than $3,250,000, which is a good price for corn. *Redhead* dropped in with Gwen Verdon making her first call, and the producers who had polished it up for the occasion must have regretted West Coast contracts that limited the run to four bulging weeks. *Show Business* was a stock name for a haphazard show, yet it ran nine weeks because of the saucer-eyed, long-stemmed chrysanthemum top, Carol Channing.

In quite another realm of playgoing, no shoehorn could have squeezed more customers into the Blackstone for the painfully short three weeks allotted *The Visit,* another Alfred Lunt-Lynn Fontanne illustration of how unresourceful actors are who go stale in a good play when they could use a long run to supreme advantage. The production, with Thomas Gomez and Glenn Anders new in the cast, was even finer than it had been the season before, and the Lunts have not played more superbly.

With Basil Rathbone, Frederic Worlock, and Michael Higgins heading the cast, *J.B.* did everything in its considerable power to retain and project the original impact of the play. In some ways it was less pretentious and more moving. But it had an incalculable loss in the lemon-tart flair of Christopher Plummer's satanic fury.

Dear Liar looked in briefly with Katharine Cornell and Brian Aherne, proving not very much in theatre and rather less than the Shaw-Campbell letters in print. *The World of Carl Sandburg,* a duller world than the name at its best implies, found Gary Merrill a better actor than many suspected, and Bette Davis no actress at all until she reached the inimical world of Elizabeth Umpstead.

31

Early in the season Ralph Bellamy played his memorable F.D.R. in *Sunrise at Campobello,* with Russell Collins as Louis Howe. Much later Geraldine Page was the corrosive magnet of *Sweet Bird of Youth,* with Rip Torn a remarkable Chance Wayne—unfortunately before Tennessee Williams decided to rewrite the second act and do away with or at least diminish Boss Finley.

On the credit side, that was the best of it. *The Pleasure of His Company,* drawing-room comedy with sinking spells, found Cyril Ritchard its most buoyant support. But Donald Oenslager's spacious drawing room also was inhabited by Cornelia Otis Skinner, Leo G. Carroll and Conrad Nagel, and it charmed some nostalgic playgoers, perhaps on the theory of half a loaf.

Major disappointments, for dissimilar reasons, were *West Side Story* and *Look Homeward, Angel.* The musical was the so-called original production with Larry Kert, but it had run down so badly in casting, direction, and lethal brilliance that old friends scarcely recognized it. Oddly, nothing was done to remedy matters. Just as the show was closing, Jerome Robbins crept secretly into town to do some work on it. This disregard of a valuable property cut to fourteen weeks what should have been a full season's run.

The treatment of *Look Homeward, Angel* was the sort of thing that makes you marvel that theatre survives. Almost nothing remained of the production in so many ways the theatre at its best. Into the second city of the land came a trucked version with new producers, director, mostly a new cast, and a cheap variation of Jo Mielziner's setting. Many went to see it, warned of its crudities, because they did not want to be denied so remarkable a play. In its shoestring fashion it was an honest effort, with Miriam Hopkins as the mother and Michael Ebert, son of opera's Carl Ebert, as Wolfe's "myself when young." But the magic, and the word is not too elusive for what it once had, was gone.

In the horror realm came *A Mighty Man Is He,* on Theatre Guild subscription, no less; a broken-down version of *Mary Stuart,* with Eva Le Gallienne and Signe Hasso, which Tyrone Guthrie slipped into town to try to rescue—just before it left; and dispiriting versions of *The Tempest* and *Measure for Measure* by the Arnold Moss Shakespeare Festival Players, who lacked, among other things, scenery, costumes, and actors.

On the sidelines were the Judy Garland show; *The Fabulous Josephine Baker,* oddly booked into the Regal on the south side; Hal Holbrook's *Mark Twain Tonight;* and something by the indelible name of *Kreplach Kapers.* The Goodman school of acting made several disastrous attempts to prove that a guest star is all you need with a student cast. Just about the time it was settled that no such thing could plausibly be done, Eugenie Leontovich came along as star and director of *The Cave Dwellers,* and did it.

In deference to superstition, and woeful experience, no note of optimism will mar these pages. The Great Northern Theatre is crumbling quietly, waiting to be torn down. The Erlanger is threatened by a Civic Center, political not social. Every third door in town seems to open on a little theatre group, and owners of two prosperous night clubs are putting $500,000 into a 300-seater on the near north side to be called "The Happy Medium." It will have a big stage, lounge seats, a bar, and two performances nightly, starting with an unnamed revue. Its manipulators come from Broadway, on and off.

Meanwhile, half a dozen summer theatres continue to thrive and one of them, part of a restaurant promotion on the far southwest side, has maneuvered the "celebrity star" system into staying open forty-two weeks a year. It is called Drury Lane.

For 1959-60, the record:

Shubert Theatre: 44 weeks—*The Music Man,* 40 weeks, 56 in all; *Redhead,* 4 weeks.

Erlanger Theatre: 29½ weeks—*West Side Story,* 14 weeks; *Dear Liar,* 10 days; *Show Business,* 9 weeks; *The Pleasure of His Company,* 5 weeks.

Blackstone Theatre: 22 weeks—*Sunrise at Campobello,* 6 weeks; *A Mighty Man Is He,* 3 weeks; *Look Homeward, Angel,* 3 weeks; *The Visit,* 3 weeks; *J.B.,* 4 weeks; *Sweet Bird of Youth,* 3 weeks.

Civic Theatre: 10 weeks—*Garden District,* 6 weeks, 8 in all; Shakespeare Festival Players, 1 week; *The World of Carl Sandburg,* 1 week; *Mary Stuart,* 2 weeks.

THE SEASON IN LONDON

By Harold Hobson

Drama Critic, the London *Sunday Times* and
The Christian Science Monitor

DURING the season 1959-60 the London theatre was caught neatly in a pincers movement between east and west, and then finally given an exhilarating clip on the jaw from France.

Theatre Workshop, who operate from a base at the Theatre Royal, Stratford, in east London, among Victorian slums and fish-and-chip shops, spreading the gospel of Brecht and Socialism, have the most easterly theatre in London. For ten years after the end of the war this troupe of players wandered up and down the country, living on wages less than could have been earned by selling matches in the gutter. Then, by a series of extraordinary chances, they found themselves representing Great Britain at the Paris Festival of International Theatre. They went to Paris simply because the British Government was too mean to pay the expenses of a conventional company; and Theatre Workshop was the only organization that was willing to go and practically pay its own expenses, the actors carrying their scenery by hand through the customs.

The director of Theatre Workshop is Joan Littlewood, a woman of immense dynamism. Miss Littlewood cares nothing at all for conventional drawing-room drama, or for good clear speech, or for English social manners. The French found this a huge relief. They did not have to bother to listen to what the actors said, which they would have found difficult to understand anyway. Instead of being confronted with a troupe of players practically immobile in the best traditions of English good form, they found actors and actresses who gesticulated wildly, leapt about the stage, poked their faces out at the audience and grimaced, and who generally gave the impression of actually being alive. Theatre Workshop got a tremendous popular and critical acclaim.

In the season just ended they caught the eye of the West End managements, weary of seeking for sly little comedies about the quickest way of getting two people not married to each other into bed. Brendan Behan's *The Hostage,* a play about the I.R.A., Shelagh Delaney's *A Taste of Honey,* which shows London what

34

Frontcloth for "At the Drop of a Hat"

living in Lancashire is like, Wolf Mankiewicz's *Make Me an Offer,*
a musical about a seller of Wedgwood pottery, and Frank Norman's
Fings Aint Wot They Used t'Be have been among the outstanding
productions of the West End; and all of them emanate from Theatre
Workshop. They mingle elements of farce and tragedy, music hall,
slapstick, Left Wing politics, dances, song, vulgarity, vigor, razor-
slashing, violence—all driven together and along by the energy of
Miss Littlewood.

American visitors to these pieces on the whole believe that they
have seen it all before. The Brechtian tricks, the Left Wing propa-
ganda, and the contempt for normal standards of speech and behavior remind them of the American theatre of the thirties. At the
same time, it all comes as relatively new to the British, hitherto be-
sotted in the theatre with interest in the lives and surroundings of the
(often spuriously) elegant. During the 1959-60 season the West
End theatre discovered (what the Industrial Revolution had hidden
from them) that Britain has a working class.

Pretty much the same lesson has been taught the theatre by the
English Stage Company at the Court Theatre, which is as far to the
west as Theatre Workshop is to the east. Aided by preliminary work

by the Belgrade Theatre, Coventry (whose talented director, Brian Bailey, was killed in a motor accident in the spring), the English Stage Company discovered a new, working-class dramatist called Arnold Wesker. Mr. Wesker is a charmingly simple soul, a firm believer in unilateral nuclear disarmament, and a convinced Socialist. He wrote a play, *Roots*, on the theme of the necessity of awakening the underprivileged to a sense of beauty and poetry and culture, which gave the young actress Joan Plowright one of the finest parts of her career. It was a very moving play indeed, for Mr. Wesker conveyed admirably his own deep emotion and sincerity. When it, too, moved into the West End, it was warmly greeted.

Another Court Theatre production, John Arden's *Serjeant Musgrave's Dance*, had less success. A party of deserters came to a cold northern town at the end of the last century. They talked wildly in a local inn, and one of them was killed in a hayloft. The leader was a Bible-thumping Pacifist, horrified by what he had seen of British Imperialism abroad. In the last act a town meeting was called, in which this man led a campaign against war. This scene had considerable theatrical excitement, especially when it was seen that the man was mad. *Serjeant Musgrave's Dance* was taken by the Left as a demonstration of its own theories, and by the Right as an indication that such theories are lunatic. But it was a confused, though in retrospect exciting, play, and it had only a short run.

It seems odd that the West End should now be dominated by Left Wing drama, from Left Wing theatrical organizations, at the very moment when politically the Left in Britain is in very sore straits. Does it mean that the British theatre is behind the times, as Shaw always said it was? Or is it offering a foretaste of the future? It would be rash to guess.

Meanwhile, the English Stage Company has contributed to the West End some plays that are entirely unpolitical. They have produced in the most fashionable theatres in London N. F. Simpson's Lewis Carrollish *One-Way Pendulum*, Peggy Ashcroft's splendid but rather cold *Rosmersholm*, and Noel Coward's adaptation of Feydeau, *Look After Lulu*, in which Vivien Leigh frisked about the stage of the New Theatre in her underclothes for several prosperous months.

Against these achievements, the ordinary West End managements have not had very much to show. Graham Greene's *The Complaisant Lover*, in which a husband in all sincerity proposes that his wife shall have a lover if she wants one, is not among his major pieces. But it has been an enormous success, largely owing to Ralph Richardson's extremely touching performance of the husband, a man infinite both in charity and stupidity.

Michael Redgrave's own adaptation of the Henry James story,

The Aspern Papers, ran long and triumphantly at the Queen's Theatre, American visitors particularly admiring the delicacy of Sir Michael's Boston accent as the hero of the play, who broke the hearts of two women in his determination to find out the secret life of a long-dead poet. Flora Robson in this play gave a subtle performance of a plain woman gradually warming and becoming beautiful in the light of what she took to be love. In another play, John Mortimer's *The Wrong Side of the Park,* at the Cambridge, about a woman plagued with love, and the recollections and misunderstandings of love, Margaret Leighton was equally fine. On the musical—and American—side of the theatre, the Rodgers and Hammerstein *Flower Drum Song* failed to evoke the ecstasies aroused in the two previous years by *My Fair Lady* and *West Side Story.*

From France, however, came conquerors. Marie Bell and her company took the daring step of bringing over three tragedies by Racine—*Phèdre, Berenice,* and *Britannicus.* Racine is a dramatist who has been abused by English critics for three centuries. He is said to be cold, and the rhythm of his Alexandrian lines monotonous. But on this occasion, at the Savoy Theatre, he triumphed. Audiences were large at the opening performances, and then became enormous. The theatre was sold out matinee and evening. The magnificent regularity and power of the Racinian verse came to English audiences as a revelation. Even the supremacy of Shakespeare was a little bit shaken, and France took on a new glory.

OFF BROADWAY

By Henry Hewes

Drama Critic, *Saturday Review*

IN 1959-60 there was an increase in that suspiciously high-minded breed of Off Broadway producers who regard the theatre more as a mission than as a game of roulette played with someone else's money. The happy result was a record number of Off Broadway openings (more than a hundred attractions at some forty locations) and three young American playwrights and six musical-comedy writers and/or composers successfully launched.

At the top of this list was Jack Gelber, whose play *The Connection* established itself as the most original piece of new American Theatre writing in a long, long time. Mr. Gelber, a twenty-seven-year-old Chicagoan who emigrated to New York via a detour through San Francisco's beatnik colony, wrote *The Connection* while vacationing in Haiti. Someone advised him to send it to the Phoenix Theatre, but when he telephoned to ask them to read his script, he received what seemed to him the rather strange reply that the Phoenix was only considering plays by Nobel Prize winners. Then a friend put him in touch with the Living Theatre, and within two weeks his play was read and accepted. This proved most fortunate, for had the play been produced by an ordinary Off Broadway playhouse, it would never have survived the excoriating reviews it received from the second-string reviewers of the leading New York newspapers. However, because it could be nursed along in repertory with another play, it was able to hang on until the magazine critics could give it more enthusiastic appraisals. They did, and *The Connection* not only became a solid hit, but also won a Vernon Rice award and an Obie as the best full-length new American play Off Broadway. It even collected two ballots (Tynan, *The New Yorker;* Hewes, *Saturday Review*) in the Drama Critics Circle Award voting for the best American play to be produced anywhere in New York City this season.

Borrowing its form from jazz, where the individual soloists take turns improvising upon an agreed-upon theme, *The Connection* follows a group of dope addicts through two phases of their existence: the irritable waiting for the man with the heroin to show

up, and the only slightly happier temporary peace that follows
their injections.   To give his stage hipsters something to punch
against, Mr. Gelber invades their privacy with a few "squares,"
and because language can never really be as hip as music, he leaves
spaces for three jazz musicians to play their spontaneous responses
to the situations.   In its determination never to be phony, it deliberately avoids the structural clichés which would make it fit the
specifications of what we have come to think of as "a play."   That
is, it has no hero, it doesn't send us home with a message, and it
indicates no resolution of the problems that face its troubled characters.   Rather, it is a new form of theatre in which honest ex-
ploration arranged in meaningful proportion and pattern is enough.

Of equal promise was another new writer, Edward Albee, whose
short play *The Zoo Story* was produced on the same bill with
Samuel Beckett's *Krapp's Last Tape* by a new producing organization called "Theatre 1960."   The thirty-one-year-old playwright,
who was born and raised in New York City, took the long way
around with *The Zoo Story*.   A friend in Florence sent it to a
Swiss actor, who made a tape of it, which he forwarded to a Frank-
furt publishing house, which published it in German and persuaded
the Berlin Festival to produce it on the same bill with *Krapp's
Last Tape*.   Its success there led to the New York production.

The Zoo Story begins with a beatnik annoying a mild-natured
conformist in Central Park.   But gradually we sense the fact that
this beatnik is driven by an urge to arouse a human soul out of its
modern lethargy and into an awareness of the real world.   This
leads to violence, and the beatnik succeeds in his compulsive mission only at the cost of his own life.   The melodramatic ending
is somewhat less effective than the earlier portion of the play where
the beatnik recites "The Story of Jerry and the Dog."   In this
parable, Jerry, faced with a dog that tries to bite him every time
he returns to his boardinghouse, attempts to solve his problem
first with kindness and then with cruelty.   The result is an even-
tual compromise in which they neither love nor hurt, because they
no longer try to reach each other.   Mr. Albee was also represented
later in the season with a short sketch titled *The Sandbox*, which
had fun when a cantankerous old grandmother, dumped into a
sandbox by her dull, middle-aged grandchildren, retaliates by throwing sand at them while they pretend not to notice.

The third playwright to receive auspicious baptism Off Broadway
was twenty-four-year-old Jack Richardson, whose play *The Prodigal* was written while in Germany on an Adenauer Philosophy Fel-
lowship.   It sought to retell part of the Orestes legend in terms of
an angry young man (indeed Orestes was played by an actor who

had played Jimmy Porter in last season's revival of *Look Back in Anger*). While it lacked a great deal in production finesse, we were here and there caught up in the author's insights and wit.

Other new American playwrights who made their debut this season included: Frank Duane (*Guitar*), Bronson Dudley (*The Piano Tuner*), Robert Duncan (*Faust Foutu*), Miss B. F. Dunn (*The Snow Maiden*), Philip Freund (*The Brooding Angel*), Francis Gallagher (*Vincent*, with Leonard Cimino as Van Gogh), Fred Laurence Guiles (*Song for a Certain Midnight*), William Guthrie (*The Ignorants Abroad*), Catherine Hughes (*Madame Lafayette*), Philip Lewis (*Which Way the Wind*), H. B. Lutz (*The Chip*), Sam Robbins (*Answered the Flute*), J. I. Rodale (*The Goose*), John Duff Stradley (*Alley of the Sunset*), Jay Thompson (*The Bible Salesman*), Charles Williams (*Cranmer of Canterbury*), and Norton Cooper and Nat Pierce (*Ballad of Jazz Street*).

The growing willingness of more experienced playwrights to allow their work to be premiered Off Broadway continued. Since there is a rather drastic difference between the hundred or so dollars in weekly royalty from an Off Broadway hit and the two thousand odd dollars Broadway authors can collect, it must be assumed that the reason for working Off Broadway was still largely the difficulty of persuading Broadway producers to accept plays that did not seem to have smash hit potential.

William Gibson, with two hits in two Broadway tries, logged a vacation cruise with his cosmic fantasy *Dinny and the Witches*. Despite an amusing performance by Julie Bovasso as a "nitwitch" and a lovely song ("Don't Know What I'm Here For"), the play took much too long to find a simple answer to the song's question.

Sam and Bella Spewack had less luck over here with *Under the Sycamore Tree* than they had in London. This satire on human foibles, in which we watch an ant colony try to solve its problems both vs. other ants and vs. human beings, was entertaining in spots but wore a little thin over the course of the evening.

Similarly George Tabori's *Brouhaha*, which was drastically rewritten to make the leading male role suitable for Viveca Lindfors, failed to achieve even the limited run it had in its British presentation. There were flashes of wit and a moment of ingenious theatricality when David Hurst, as a Russian ambassador, has presumably stalemated his American opponent (played by Russell Nype) in a game of diplomatic strip poker. Mr. Nype wins the day by shedding his spectacles. There was also the suggested message that peaceful poverty may be preferable to a prosperity that owes its existence to the threat of war and the use of violence.

But the satire exasperated with its random pursuits, and the tiny Middle-Eastern country in which it took place lacked even the tenuous charm of the Middle-European principality Peter Ustinov created for *Romanoff and Juliet.*

Three "established" playwrights who have yet to register their first hit failed to do so in second outings. Aldyth Morris's *The Secret Concubine* proved an interesting Chinese fable in which a hitherto heirless emperor's concubine gives away the male baby she bears him. Her motive is to create a future in which the emperor will not be able to sacrifice his men to war or slavery for fear that he may be hurting his own new anonymous son. Eva Stern gave a lovely lyrical portrayal in the title role and Israeli actor, Michael Shillo, as the emperor, exhibited a disciplined talent in his American debut. But the play resisted the complexity of its production.

In an effort to present an accurate picture of the temper of Modern American life in *Come Share My House,* Theodore Apstein ended up with too many dull situations. However, in the leading role of an uneducated Mexican girl who ends up helping the American student who had to marry her, Elisa Loti gave a fascinatingly concentrated performance, to emerge as the best new dramatic actress of the season.

At the end of May, Lionel Abel, America's answer to Jean-Paul Sartre, came along with a thinking-man's play called *The Pretender.* It laid bare the incredible unpracticality of intellectuals by drawing for us a Negro writer whose actions are always based upon their validity as pure ideas. These included living in Mississippi out of respect for the aristocracy of the old South, and avenging the rape of his wife by organizing a Negro posse for the purpose of lynching the white man responsible for the crime. Unfortunately, the play was wrongly cast and Mr. Abel's interesting play never overcame the inherent difficulty of making intellectual decisions dramatic.

Other "established" playwrights represented in the 1959-60 season included Rock Anthony (*Courtyard*), Paul Goodman (*The Cave at Machpelah*), and Louis Lippa (*The Breaking Wall*).

If the experienced playwrights were not successful, one experienced adaptor was. Paul Shyre, who is responsible for the wonderful adaptations of Sean O'Casey's autobiographies, was represented by his stage version of John Dos Passos' *U.S.A.* Originally performed two seasons ago on the Theatre Matinee Series, it was produced with the utmost professional finish on an open stage at the Martinique. This "See It Now" of America from 1890 to 1929 effectively illuminated the contradictions and hypocrisies in the American tradition, and was beautifully performed by a small cast, with Sada Thompson supplying a particularly memorable solo as she told the story of Isadora Duncan.

In the Autumn of 1959, a New York television station, WNTA-TV, courageously began to produce (for seven video-taped performances each) recent full-length plays, most of which had not been hits on Broadway. Thus it usurped to some degree one of Off Broadway's main functions. While many such revivals were still attempted, only three had any appreciable success. Best was Alan Schneider's vigorous production of *Summer of the Seventeenth Doll.* This Australian version of *Sweet Bird of Youth* benefited from the high degree of humor and honesty that performers Louise Latham, Rae Allen, Leon Janney, Dana Elcar and Margaretta Warwick provided.

Robert Penn Warren's *All the King's Men,* which in 1948 had been staged at the New School Dramatic Workshop by Piscator, was produced in a revised version, with Clifton James giving a powerful performance as the Huey Long-type politician, and John Ragin bringing a troubled sensitivity to the role of the idealistic young journalist. But the author's desire to show complexity was negated by the audience's predisposition simply to despise the ruthless governor.

Director Gene Frankel evoked a disciplined performance from his cast in Sophie Treadwell's *Machinal* to present it as a clear picture of how the individual could be destroyed by social forces. While this was not terribly moving, Vincent Gardenia's portrayal of a gross American businessman was an amazingly skilful and penetrating characterization. A revival of Tennessee Williams' *Orpheus Descending* was generally conceded to be an improvement on the unsuccessful Broadway production, but José Quintero's attempt to give new life to *Camino Real* failed to make Mr. Williams' stage nightmare fly.

Classical playwrights received normal attention but subnormal success. David Ross returned Chekhov's *The Three Sisters* to the Fourth Street Theatre, and while it remained effective it was somewhat inferior to his former revival of the same play. Vladimir Sokoloff gave an excellent performance in a mixed-style production of Tolstoy's *The Power of Darkness,* which failed to make the infanticide either credible or moving. *Shakuntula* merely proved the inadvisability of attempting a folk classic with a motley group of actors. And perhaps the most ludicrous evening of the season was the revival of Daudet's *Sappho,* in which at one point a supposedly enamored young man answered an invitation to bed with a beautiful woman by protesting that it might adversely affect his studies.

Without question the best classical production of the year was the Piccolo Theatro di Milano's *The Servant of Two Masters*. This company, considered by many as the finest repertory company in the world, played the Goldoni comedy in Italian at the City Center. However, even those of us who cannot follow the quickly spoken language were excited by the sense of style unapologetically enjoyed by the performers, and by the sort of inventiveness only achievable in a company that keeps working on the same plays over a period of years. Giorgio Strehler's bold direction and Marcello Moretti's hilarious antics as Arlecchino stood out.

Off Broadway turned its attention to minor Shaw with one company presenting in repertory *Getting Married, The Shewing Up of Blanco Posnet, Buoyant Billions, Overruled, The Dark Lady of the Sonnets,* and *Passion, Poison, and Putrefaction.* While the intention was excellent, the company merely succeeded in adding their poverty of talent and inadequate production resources to plays that were already quite poor enough. But at the Grolier Club, director Eli Rill and a cast that included Michael Flanders, Viveca Lindfors, and Kevin McCarthy delightfully presented for one performance a discarded section of *Back to Methuselah,* titled *A Glimpse of the Domesticity of Franklin Barnabas.*

Other revivals at Off Broadway playhouses included *Antigone, The Hasty Heart, Kataki, La Ronde, Tobacco Road,* and *Waltz of the Toreadors.* The Equity Library Theatre featured mostly revivals at its Lenox Hill Playhouse with *Hotel Paradiso, Noah, Escape Me Never, The Beautiful People, Hamlet* (played by Neil Vipond), *The Women, Time Limit, Tiger at the Gates, Carousel, The Member of the Wedding, Hell-bent for Heaven, Summer and Smoke, Ring Round the Moon,* and *Dark of the Moon.*

Although there were short-lived revivals of *The Tempest, Henry VIII,* and *Measure for Measure,* Shakespeare was pretty much left to the Phoenix and to the summer festivals, some of which were Off Broadway in spirit. The American Shakespeare Festival Theatre at Stratford, Connecticut, began its sixth season with a sub-par *Romeo and Juliet* that regarded the play's poetry as a hurdle rather than as an asset. But there was an improvement with an entertaining *The Merry Wives of Windsor,* featuring Larry Gates as a quick-witted Falstaff instead of the usual bumbling fool. And the season was topped with an excellent *All's Well That Ends Well,* which allowed director John Houseman to end his five-year tenure at Stratford gloriously.

A little further Off Broadway (or, if you wish, Off-Tremont Street) the Metropolitan Boston Arts Center erected a huge new tent theatre across the river from Harvard University, where it presented a spotty production of *Twelfth Night,* but aroused great controversy with a *Macbeth* that starred Jason Robards, Jr. and Siobhan McKenna and was directed by José Quintero. While Mr. Robards revealed his greatness in sudden, inventive, deeply felt moments, and Miss McKenna was magnificent in the later scenes of remorse, the total production lacked shape and often lost Shakespeare's vocal music. Meanwhile, back in New York, Joseph Papp, after beating down Park Commissioner Moses' stand on charging admission to Central Park Shakespeare, had just enough energy left to present an indifferent production of *Julius Caesar* directed by Stuart Vaughan.

The production of modern foreign authors, which has always been a fruitful activity for Off Broadway, surpassed even last season's distinguished crop. *Krapp's Last Tape* revealed to us a new and more human facet of Beckett's writing. In this short solo we see an old man revisiting not his actual past but his past as recorded in short retrospect on spools of tape. The language is rich, reminding one of James Joyce and Dylan Thomas, and the final stage picture of Krapp clutching at the heat of life (symbolized by the tape) with an appreciation that has grown in inverse proportion to his powers to experience it is unforgettable.

Jean Genet's *The Balcony* emerged as the most profound and most poetic play of the season and received two votes from the Drama Critics Circle as the best foreign play of the season. *The Balcony* takes place in a special kind of brothel, where men indulge their illusions by performing the rituals of archbishops, generals, judges, etc. Outside the brothel a revolution is going on, and through the action of the chief of police the ordinary people inside the brothel subvert the revolution and in actuality take over the public offices they have previously held only in their imaginations. But the plot is less important than the allusions, the ironies, and the sense of contact with the human subconscious Mr. Genet achieves. And much of all this was preserved in José Quintero's only partially fulfilled production of a most difficult play, which was at a disadvantage in the too-close quarters of Circle-in-the-Square's newly renovated theatre-in-the-round.

A second French playwright provided New York with the most thought-provoking play about the world's present state of affairs since *The Cave Dwellers* two seasons ago. Eugene Ionesco's *The Killer* introduces his version of the modern hero. He is M.

Bérenger, a timid soul naive enough to believe in morality, public responsibility, friendship and marriage, and Christian enough to give every other human being the benefit of the doubt. The play follows the dream life of Bérenger through the pleasant phase of an antiseptic welfare-state utopia and into the anxiety of concern about a killer who symbolizes Bérenger's fear of death, and his despair about taking any effective action about matters which should be settled by a responsible citizenry. Unfortunately, the production here became over-inventive, so that the building horror of Bérenger's dream was vitiated with distracting elements. Nevertheless, it was clear that M. Ionesco had taken a significant step on his way from theatrical innovator to major playwright.

A third import was the American professional premiere of Chekhov's *A Country Scandal*, written when he was twenty-one. This play, never produced in Russia, turns out to be more modern and more vital than his later masterpieces. Its protagonist, Platonov, is the prototype of a John Osborne cad-hero. We see him seducing women, insulting his wife, and driving himself to destruction in a farcical and purposeless society. Platonov says, "When we're born we cry because we've entered the madhouse. Women are my only escape." The production here with little-known actors went rapidly, thanks to bold cutting, and accented the humor so that the audience could achieve the tragi-comic perspective from which Chekhov's intentions are best seen. One could quarrel with the heart-attack ending chosen by adaptor Alex Szogyi as preferable to Chekhov's alternate one in which Platonov is ineptly and grotesquely shot by a crazed woman. One could criticize the cutting, which made the many vignettes of Russian country life seem incomplete. But one had to admit that the result was highly entertaining and faithful to the spirit of Chekhov.

Of the other imports, perhaps the most interesting was British playwright Ronald Duncan's *The Death of Satan*. The play takes place in the British rather than the Italian version of Hell, where punishment consists of the boredom of listening to those who have committed sins similar to one's own. While unsuccessful in homogenizing its facetious parody, its awkward scenes of amorous activity by a Don Juan on sabbatical, and its metaphysical poetry, the play nevertheless contains stirring and caustic speeches about the desperate state of a world that in its worship of man and mediocrity has lost stature and capacity for passion.

Another British playwright, John Whiting, similarly caught the present-day climate of man's estate in an exasperatingly obscure play titled *Marching Song*. In this, Kevin McCarthy played a returning European general, whose lapse into human feeling cost his country a war victory, and Brooke Hayward, daughter of Margaret Sullavan (who died during this play's short run), made her professional debut as a beat-generation prostitute who falls in love with him.

Two of Italy's best modern dramatists were presented with mixed receptions. Ugo Betti's *Time of Vengeance*, a Pirandelloish drama about the exercise of absolute justice in a hypothetical Italian town, contained some challenging situations, and Diego Fabbri's *Between Two Thieves*, which presented a trial to re-examine the facts and the real responsibility for Jesus's crucifixion, intrigued many. Justice was also the subject of *The Jackass*, a rambling adaptation of an old Friederich Duerrenmatt radio script which took much too long to prove that sometimes it is better to accept a small loss than to risk becoming involved with lawyers, judges, and thieves. Jean Anouilh's old play *Jeannette* was given its American premiere by director Harold Clurman in his first official Off Broadway venture. Although Mr. Clurman wrote a brilliant program note to show how well he understood the play, hardly anything that went on on stage bore much relation to his analysis. Then, at the season's end, New York was treated to its first glimpse of the highly regarded twenty-eight-year-old exiled Spanish playwright, Fernando Arrabal, whose spoof of war, called *Picnic on the Battlefield*, seemed rather ordinary, but whose other playlet, *The Executioners*, penetrated deep into the heart of modern indifference and the dehumanizing effect a "self-sacrificing" mother can have on her children.

Other foreign playwrights whose work was premiered Off Broadway included Henri de Montherlant (*Pert-Royal*, starring Uta Hagen), François Mauriac (*The Egoists*), Eugene Ionesco (*The New Tenant*), and Franz Spencer (*The Villa of Madame Video*).

Since the present increasingly fractionized and pressurized methods of construction of a Broadway musical are hostile to new talents, it is particularly important that these talents be able to find themselves in more peaceful precincts. And, happily, this season new musical attractions began to flourish Off Broadway as never before. First there was *Billy Barnes Revue*, a disarming patchwork of topical sketches and songs that introduced Patti Regan, a sour-faced comedienne of promise, and proved so attractive that it moved to Broadway for many weeks before returning to conclude its run Off Broadway. (While *Lend an Ear* was revived with some skill, the revue field was otherwise undistinguished—with *Parade*, *Misguided Tour*, and *Follies of 1910* failing to make much impression.)

Then along came *Little Mary Sunshine*, which will go down in history as the first successful original musical comedy in Off Broadway history. The show, written by newcomer Rick Besoyan, is a spoof on the *Rose Marie* sort of operetta. Because it is performed with great style and fun by a cast headed by Eileen Brennan, one readily forgives the somewhat tedious elaboration of the same joke over the whole evening. Its catchiest song, "Look for a Sky of Blue," parodied the absurd optimism of yesterday's musical, and yet sent patrons home humming the tune, which was an unexpected bonus in this era of heavily laden musicals.

More original still was *The Fantasticks*, which introduced the writing talent of Tom Jones and the composing talent of Harvey Schmidt. Loosely basing their plot on Rostand's *Les Romantiques*, they arrived at a truly delightful creation, which tells a childishly simple romance with an air of knowing at one and the same time its blessedness and its absurdity. The first act follows the boy and girl through some lighter-than-air escapades that end in rosy illusion-filled love. Act II exposes this romance to life's harsher realities, which drive the innocents away from and then back to each other and their uncomplicated happiness. The songs are lovely and filled with ingenious humor. "They Were You," with its compelling insistence, seemed to have a good chance to become the year's most popular show tune. And director Word Baker (whose last show *The Crucible* closed earlier in the season after establishing a new record of 571 performances for an Off Broadway play) kept the whole volatile business precise and formful without losing an iota of its fancy.

A somewhat less distinguished though quite entertaining musical comedy, *Ernest in Love* owed more to its performances of sections of Oscar Wilde's *The Importance of Being Ernest* than it did to its songs. However, Anne Croswell and Lee Pockriss's score was pleasant and clever and gave audiences an excuse to taste Wilde's great comedy again.

Less felicitous was *Miss Emily Adam*, a musical by James Lipton and Paul E. Davies based on Winthrop Palmer's *Rosemary and the Planet*. Cherry Davis started out promisingly as a child who rebels against parental misunderstanding with a song which includes the amusing line, "I'd go to court, but I'm too short." Unfortunately, there was not enough time for similar charm in the rest of the book, which catapulted her through a brave new world satirizing both the societies of joyless obedience and of decadent free will.

In *The Crystal Heart*, Broadway playwright William Archibald tried to write a delicate musical comedy in collaboration with the lovely music of Baldwin Bergerson, but even with Mildred Dunnock in the leading role, the whole concoction seemed remote and precious and failed to engross us at all.

The vogue of reviving old musical comedies with tongue in or out of cheek continued. Under Larry Carra's stylish direction, *Leave It to Jane*, the old P. G. Wodehouse, Guy Bolton, Jerome Kern musical about dear old Siwash, survived mixed notices to establish itself as a steady attraction now going into its second year. Particularly enchanting was Kathleen Murray's deliciously mannered performance in the title role. Less fortunate was a revival of Cole Porter's *The Gay Divorcee* despite a tenaciously droll comic stint by Beatrice Arthur. And while *Oh, Kay* reminded us of the strength of the old Gershwin score and was agreeably performed by a good cast that included one of Broadway's best dancers, Eddie Phillips, it seemed more of a museum piece than a still effective theatre work.

The City Center brought back three Broadway musicals. Its revival of *Finian's Rainbow* overwhelmed audiences who hadn't remembered the strength of the Harburg-Lane score, and the production was moved to Broadway. *The King and I* also gained new respect in a revival starring Barbara Cook and Farley Granger. And as part of its opera season, City Center staged Marc Blitzstein's *The Cradle Will Rock*, which seemed dated in its pro-labor passion but still very funny in its shafts of social satire. Furthermore, it served to showcase the rising musical-comedy talent of Tammy Grimes, who sang her role with a Lotte Lenya kind of authority. Also in the revival category, Dorothy Raedler brought her troupe of American Savoyards back to Jan Hus House for another extended run of the ever-popular Gilbert and Sullivan canon.

Meanwhile, Mr. Blitzstein's adaptation of *The Threepenny Opera* continued to attract audiences at the Theatre De Lys, where it registered its 1966th consecutive performance on May 31st and seemed to have an excellent chance of supplanting *Oklahoma* as the longest running musical of all time.

There were three productions of mime theatre, of which the most distinguished was that of Etienne Decroux and a group of students in what amounted to a demonstration rather than an attempt to entertain. M. Decroux is the world's purest exponent of the art of mime, and he and his company achieved many exciting abstractions of life's natural processes, the best of which featured four mimes as a cluster of trees in the process of growth. The others were Shai K. Ophir, accompanied by the season's prettiest performer, Barbara Loden, in *41 in a Sack,* and Lionel Shepard in *The Mime and Me,* which received more acclaim for an accompanying guitar-ist-singer, James Gavin, than it did for its star.

Finally, there was the Greater New York Chapter of ANTA's Matinee Theatre Series, which in its fourth season of operation at the De Lys offered five programs. The first, *Shakespeare in Harlem,* a series of vignettes of Harlem life taken from Langston Hughes's poem of the same name, later moved uptown for a short run at the Forty-first Street Theatre. The second gave a professional premiere to Tennessee Williams' early poetic play, *The Purification,* and to William Inge's short *The Glory in the Flower.* Mr. Williams' haunting play of violence in New Mexico required a little more feeling of dance synchronized with word music than the actors were able to give. And Mr. Inge's sketch of a too selfishly romantic girl in love with a cheap seducer suffered both from not having enough time to develop its theme and from lack of focus. Then came Robert Frost's *A Masque of Reason,* written in a Shavian tone, with God thanking Job for having relieved him of the responsibility of rewarding good and punishing evil, and shamefacedly admitting that his reason for making Job suffer was "just showing off to the Devil." On the same bill another Job expert, Archibald MacLeish, supplied *This Music Crept by Me upon the Waters.* The latter, in an atmosphere of cocktail-party talk, neatly demonstrates modern human beings' failure to grasp the incredible happiness and ecstasy around them. This bill was followed by Ionesco's *Victims of Duty* and Dostoevsky's *Notes from Underground.* Then, in an effort to present an unestablished writer, the series offered Jack Dunphy's *The Gay Apprentice* and *Too Close to Comfort* with an extremely diverse reception. For its final production of the season, director Robert Glenn, who did so well with *Shakespeare in Harlem,* returned to stage Sean O'Casey's *Time to Go* and Paul Vincent Carroll's *The Coggerers* with such success that the production was invited to tour to Washington. It should also be noted that three of the "lost plays" of Eugene O'Neill (*Abortion, The Movie Man,* and *The Sniper*) were given a premiere production that failed to raise them above the low esteem in which the late playwright himself held them.

Off Broadway added several "new" playhouses. Circle-in-the-Square, after ten years of operation in Sheridan Square, was forced to move to new quarters. It took the old Amato Theatre on Bleecker Street and remodeled it to approximately the same sort of theatre-in-the-round it had before, except that now there were no impeding pillars in the center of the acting area, and the back wall was made more adaptable. Furthermore, it approached the problem of making "scene changes" mechanically by providing a system where objects could be lowered and raised from the area directly above the stage. In one building on West Forty-second Street two conventional small theatres were constructed. On the ground floor was the plush Maidman Playhouse. And upstairs the Institute for Advanced Studies in Theatre Arts had themselves a studio theatre where three distinguished foreign theatre artists staged productions. (From Western Germany, Dr. Willi Schmidt staged Schiller's *Love and Intrigue;* from France, Jacques Charon produced Molière's *The Misanthrope;* and from the USSR, Yuri Zavadski directed scenes from Chekhov's *The Cherry Orchard.*) Lastly, at a remote address deep in the Lower East Side, the bright new 175 East Broadway Playhouse was fitted into an old building.

In both quantity and quality this was the most satisfactory Off Broadway season to date. Less than ever did it seem a showcase for actors aspiring to Broadway careers, or for producers training themselves for subsequent big killings uptown. Indeed, the trend seemed to be in the other direction—with discouraged Broadwayites anxious to refind themselves under more relaxed Off Broadway conditions. And several of the very few commercially successful Broadway producers were reported considering the possibility of acquiring Off Broadway outlets for productions they felt worth doing for special audiences. But perhaps the greatest virtue of this season was that so many of its top achievements could only have incubated in a non-Broadway culture, and that the promise inherent in these was one that seemed more apt to be realized in future Off Broadway productions than in Broadway spectacles.

THE TEN BEST PLAYS

THE TENTH MAN

A Play in Three Acts

By Paddy Chayefsky

[Paddy Chayefsky *was born in New York's Bronx 36 years ago. After graduating from DeWitt Clinton High School and CCNY, he went into the Army. He wrote a musical, "No T.O. for Love," which was produced by Special Services. He helped with the writing of "True Glory," an award-winning documentary. Later he worked on a script for Universal Pictures and was a gag writer for Robert Q. Lewis. Elia Kazan used him for film rewrites and he wrote many hour-long TV plays, among them "Holiday Song," "Marty," "Middle of the Night," and "The Catered Affair." "Marty" was the first TV script to be successfully made into a motion picture, and it won an Academy Award. The film version of "Bachelor Party" was a U.S. entry at the Cannes Film Festival. His first Broadway play, "Middle of the Night," ran almost two years and was then made into a film by Chayefsky's own company. It was chosen as the official American film for the Cannes Film Festival.*]

A DAPPER "old Jew" displaying a Van Dyke beard, a homburg hat at a jaunty angle, and a cashmere coat, comes out briefly to explain two things before the play begins. "A dybbuk," he says, "is simply a demon that possesses the body of a live human being . . . That's a dybbuk." And a "minyon"—a minyon is a quorum of ten Jewish men over the age of thirteen which is necessary for just about anything connected with Jewish religion—"You simply must have ten Jews to do anything. . . ." Smiling graciously, he then departs and the play begins.

The synagogue of Hodresh Shel Bochar is merely a shabby, dusty, converted store. There are no pews for its congregation: folding chairs are used when needed. Only the Holy Ark and lectern on the railed platform give the synagogue its identity. At one side of the room a Rabbi's study has been created by partitioning off a corner; heat for the congregation comes from an archaic metal heating unit, and light is provided by unshaded bulbs.

Very early on this cold winter morning, an old, intensely devout Jew is at his prayers. A white prayer shawl covers his shoulders as he prays silently from a prayer book that rests against the rail of the altar. Apparently faint, and clutching at the rail to steady himself, he pauses; regaining his strength, he continues as before.

Three other old men hurry into the synagogue out of the cold. One of them, the Sexton, bustles about. Flicking on the hall switch, he next fusses with the heater, while the other two oldsters, Schlissel and Zitorsky, shuffle towards the radiator.

Seeing the old man at his prayers, Schlissel figures that Hirschman slept in the synagogue again. Rubbing his hands together for warmth, Schlissel sighs: "So how goes it with a Jew today?"

ZITORSKY—How should it go?

SCHLISSEL—Davis won't be here this morning. I stopped by his house. He has a cold. His daughter-in-law told me he's still in bed.

ZITORSKY—My daughter-in-law, may she grow rich and buy a hotel with a thousand rooms and be found dead in every one of them.

SCHLISSEL—My daughter-in-law, may she invest heavily in General Motors, and the whole thing should go bankrupt.

ZITORSKY—Sure, go have children.

Still at his chores, the Sexton sees if Hirschman is all right, then goes to unlock the Rabbi's office. Thawing out near the radiator, Schlissel adds that Foreman won't be here either. Today is the day that Foreman's granddaughter is being sent back to the institution. Schlissel states as a fact that the girl is incurable: she's been in and out of mental institutions since she was eleven years old. When visiting Foreman last week, Schlissel met the psychiatrist and did not hesitate to discuss the whole business with him. Evelyn Foreman is a schizophrenic with violent tendencies. Considering this diagnosis for a second, Zitorsky sighs: "Ah, may my daughter-in-law eat acorns and may branches sprout from her ears." Schlissel tops him: "May my daughter-in-law live to a hundred and twenty, and may she have to live all her years in *her* daughter-in-law's house."

The dapper old Jew, Alper, who introduced the play, now makes a chanting, praying entrance, his voice zooming to a shrill incantation and an abrupt amen, which is echoed by Schlissel and Zitorsky.

As Alper joins the other two, the Sexton uses the Rabbi's phone to hustle up a quorum. "Hello, Harris," he cries, "this is Bleyer, the

Sexton. Come on down today, we need you. Foreman won't be here. Davis is sick. We won't have ten men if you don't come down. Services start in twenty minutes. Hurry up. . . . Wear a sweater under your coat. . . . All right." Hanging up, the Sexton consults a large ledger.

Huddling near the radiator for warmth, the three men talk sporadically. Looking at Hirschman at the altar, Schlissel calls him a pious humbug. Alper at once defends old man Hirschman's devotion and erudition. Schlissel scoffs at his show of orthodoxy. He says that it is a very profitable thing: two old ladies, convinced that Hirschman is a saint, are paying for his room and board. "That can't come to very much," argues Alper; "he's been fasting the last three days." Schlissel persists: "And the reason he sleeps in the synagogue so frequently is because his landlady does not give him heat for his own room in the mornings." "Ah," sighs Zitorsky, "go be an old man in the winter."

ALPER—I must say, I really don't know what to do with myself on these cold days.

ZITORSKY—You know what would be a nice way to kill a day? I think it would be nice to take a trip up to Mount Hope Cemetery and have a look at my burial plot. A lovely cemetery. Like a golf course, actually. And quite a nice trip, well over two hours. One has to take the Long Island Railroad to Manhattan, a subway to the Bronx, and then an amiable bus ride to Yonkers. By the time one gets there and comes back, the whole day has been used up. Would you like to come? I'll pay both your fares.

ALPER—Why not? I have never been to Mount Hope. I have my burial plot on Mount Zion Cemetery.

ZITORSKY—Oh, that's a beautiful cemetery.

ALPER—Yes, it is. My wife wanted to buy plots in Cedarlawn because her whole family is buried there, but I wouldn't hear of it.

ZITORSKY—Oh, Cedarlawn. I wouldn't be buried in Cedarlawn.

ALPER—It's in such a bad state. The headstones tumble one on top of the other, and everybody walks on the graves.

ZITORSKY—They don't care in Cedarlawn. My wife once said, she should rest in peace, that Cedarlawn was the tenement of cemeteries.

ALPER—A well-turned phrase.

ZITORSKY—She had a way with words, God grant her eternal rest.

ALPER—I'd like you to come to Mount Zion sometimes, see my plot.

ZITORSKY—Maybe, we could make the trip tomorrow.

SCHLISSEL—Listen to these two idiots, discussing their graves as if they were country estates.

ALPER—At seventy-two, what should we discuss—our mistresses?
ZITORSKY—Where are you buried, Schlissel?
SCHLISSEL—Cedarlawn.

Tactfully adding that Cedarlawn has many lovely spots, Alper
urges Schlissel to join them on their outing. Having nothing else
to do, Schlissel accepts.

Removing prayer shawls and phylacteries from velvet praying
bags, each reciting the accompanying prayers in his own way and
at his own pace, the three old men prepare for the morning service.
It is obviously a highly individual matter. As Hirschman, still un-
mindful of the others, huddles near the altar, a dim, yellow, Rem-
brandt-like light falls on prayer shawls, old men's faces, and the
cracked walls of the synagogue.

All this while, the Sexton plugs away at the telephone: "Hello?
Mr. Arnold Kessler, please. . . . How do you do? This is Mr.
Bleyer, the Sexton at the synagogue. Perhaps you recall me. . . .
Did I wake you up? I'm terribly sorry. As long as you're up, according to my books, your father died one year ago yesterday, on
the eleventh day in the month of Elul, may his soul fly straight to
the Heavenly Gates, and how about coming down with your brother
and saying a memorial prayer in your father's name? . . . Let me
put it this way, Mr. Kessler. We need ten men for a quorum. If
you and your brother don't come down, we won't be able to say the
morning prayer. . . . As a favor to me . . . Kessler, may your
children be such devoted sons, and bring your brother. You are
doing a good deed. Peace be with you. Hurry up. . . ." Totaling
up on his fingers the results of his efforts, the Sexton scowls.

As the men continue at their prayers, the Sexton bustles out of the
office and, going to the front door, says to no one in particular:
"Listen, I'm going to have to get a tenth Jew off the street some-
wheres. I'll be right back."

The murmur of prayers fills the synagogue as a distracted wisp
of a man pokes his head in the door, then disappears to return immediately with a young girl. Pushing her quickly into the Rabbi's office, he closes the door and waits for Alper to finish. Seeing old
Foreman, Alper heads his way. Chanting, ". . . and, it shall be
for a sign upon thy hand, and for frontlets between thy eyes; for
by strength of hand the Lord brought us out from Egypt. Amen!"
Alper greets Foreman. So agitated that he finds it hard to speak,
Foreman confesses that, having slipped his granddaughter out of the
house when her parents weren't looking, he has brought her here.
Sinking into a chair, he says faintly: "Alper, I have seen such a thing
and heard words as will place me in my grave before the singing of
the evening service." Suddenly espying Hirschman, Foreman de-

cides he must speak to the Cabalist. Alper asks him to compose himself and tell why he has brought the girl here. As an old friend from the Seminary in Rumni in the Province of Poltava, and sympathizing with Foreman's tenderness for the girl, Alper tries to talk sense to him. He asks him to make peace with this unhappy situation. But all Foreman does is whisper that his granddaughter is possessed of a demon: there is a dybbuk in her. It spoke to him this morning.

Foreman relates that when he entered Evelyn's room early this morning to console her, she was lucid and aware of being sent back to the institution. A minute later, however, she fell into a swoon, and the face she turned to her grandfather was twisted and hideous. Though her lips never moved, a voice came from her that was not her own. It addressed Foreman and he recognized it. "David Foreman, son of Abram," spoke the voice, "this is the soul of Hannah Luchinsky, whom you dishonored and weakened in your youth, and the gates of Heaven are closed to me. . . ." Fascinated by this recital, Alper is not averse to inquiring further: "Who did the dybbuk say she was?" "Hannah Luchinsky," answers Foreman. "You remember Luchinsky, the sexton of the Rumni seminary with his three daughters? Hannah was the handsome one, who became pregnant, and they threw stones at her, called her harlot, and drove her out of the city." "Oooohh—" remembers Alper. "I was the one who debased her," says Foreman. Finding this hard to believe, Alper says: "You? You were such a nose in the books, a gentle and modest fellow. Dear me. A dybbuk. Really! What an extraordinary thing. Schlissel, you want to hear a story?"

Though small, frail, and in a highly nervous state, Foreman repeats that Evelyn is possessed by a dybbuk, but as quickly warns Schlissel: "Now please, before you go into one of your interminable disputations on the role of superstition in the capitalist economy, let me remind you that I am a follower of Maimonides and . . ." True to form, Schlissel asks what this nonsense is.

Alper wonders whether Foreman is sure about his statement. Foreman asks indignantly if they think he is a superstitious peasant, he who has argued with Hirschman about the Cabala and who was a teacher of biology in the Hebrew Theological Seminary for thirty-nine years. A follower of the great Ramban who scoffed at sorcerers, Foreman reports only what he sees. His anger disappearing as quickly as it came, Foreman confesses this is just as hard for him to believe as it is for his friends.

SCHLISSEL—A dybbuk. Sure. Sure. When I was a boy in Poland, I also heard stories about a man who lived in the next town who was possessed by a dybbuk. I was eight years old, and one day after school, my friend and I walked barefoot the six miles to the next town, and we asked everybody, "Where is the man with the dybbuk?" And nobody knew what we were talking about. So I came home and told my mother: "Mama, there is no man with a dybbuk in the next town." And she gave me such a slap across the face that I turned around three times. And she said to me: "Aha! Only eight years old and already an atheist." Foreman, my friend, you talk like my mother who was an ignorant fishwife. I am shocked at you.

FOREMAN—Oh, leave me be, Schlissel. I have no patience with your pontificating this morning.

ALPER—Don't let him upset you, Foreman. The man is a Communist.

FOREMAN—He is not a Communist. He is just disagreeable.

SCHLISSEL—My dear fellow, I have never believed in God. Should I now believe in demons? A dybbuk. This I would like to see.

Foreman proposes furiously to illustrate what he has been talking about. Leading the old men into the Rabbi's office, he cries out to his terrified granddaughter: "Dybbuk! I direct you to reveal yourself."

After a blood-curdling scream that sends the old men to safer, distant ground, Evelyn's voice tells Foreman that she is Hannah Luchinsky, the whore of Kiev, the companion of sailors, who, while the pleasure of five wealthy merchants on a yacht, was lost at sea. Since then her soul has wandered until it reached Evelyn's body. Foreman now pleads that the dybbuk leave her. "I have wandered in Gilgul many years," says the voice, "and I want peace. Why do you plague me? There are among you those who have done the same as I and will suffer a similar fate. There is one among you who has lain with whores many times and his wife died of the knowledge." Zitorsky cries out aghast. Laughing, Evelyn's voice says: "Am I to answer questions of old men who have nothing to do but visit each other's cemeteries?" Zitorsky not only is convinced of the dybbuk but terrified.

Evelyn now sprawls wantonly in the Rabbi's chair, apparently finished with the interview. Closing the door behind them, the four old men retreat into the synagogue. "Well, that's some dybbuk, all right!" exclaims Zitorsky. "The girl is as mad as a hatter and fancies herself a Ukranian whore," answers Schlissel; "this is a dybbuk?" But to Alper, the whole thing has an authentic ring. Quickly dismissing any such idea, Schlissel insists that over the years Foreman has stuffed the girl with all the superstitions of the Russian pale. She is a lunatic who should be packed off to an asylum.

A gentleman and diplomat, Alper first asks Schlissel to consider poor Foreman's condition; then he asks that Schlissel, out of simple courtesy, try to be silent. Besides, he argues, what have they better to do today? "Ride two and a half hours to look at Zitorsky's tombstone? When you stop and think of it," continues Alper, "this dybbuk is quite an exciting affair. Really, nothing like this has happened since Kornblum and Milsky had that fistfight over who would have the seat by the East Wall during the High Holidays." Since it is put to him in this fashion, Schlissel yields, and wants immediately to tackle the problem. Now that they have this dybbuk, what are they going to do with it?

Alper suggests a ritual, a form of exorcism to deal with the dybbuk. Zitorsky suggests telling their Rabbi. Schlissel at once turns thumbs down on Zitorsky's suggestion: they can't have a young rabbi fresh from the seminary handle a matter of this importance. Feeling they need a rabbi of real standing, Schlissel proposes the Korpotchniker Rabbi of Williamsburg. Alper now suggests his candidate: the Bobolovitcher Rabbi of Crown Heights. A fight brews, but Alper yields quickly to Schlissel's Korpotchniker, just as Zitorsky belatedly comes to and suggests the Lubanower Rabbi of Brownsville. He is squelched, as usual. His man having won, Schlissel now informs them that the Korpotchniker's secretary may take weeks before he can arrange an audience. In that case, feeling the need for someone immediately accessible, Alper suggests sensibly that they consult Hirschman, the Cabalist, for advice.

Having finished his prayers, old Hirschman shuffles towards the men. Before anyone can stop him, Foreman cries out that his granddaughter is possessed of a dybbuk. After a moment of horror, the Cabalist asks if the dybbuk was the soul of a woman wronged in her youth: waking last night for his midnight devotions, Hirschman had heard the whimpering of a woman's soul; but having fasted for three days, he had dismissed the sound of this dybbuk as a fantasy of his weakened state. "For," says Hirschman, "only those to whom the Ancient One has raised his veil can hear the traffic of dybbuks. Is this a sign from God that my penitence is over? I have prayed for such a sign. . . ." As Hirschman considers this possibility with wonder, Alper breaks in: "Actually, Hirschman, all we want to know is if you knew the telephone number of the Korpotchniker Rabbi. We are not quite sure what to do with this dybbuk now that we have her." Brought down to earth, Hirschman says that the Korpotchniker is his cousin, and he will call him.

Alper is awed; Schlissel finds Hirschman creepy; and Zitorsky follows after him with a dime for the telephone. While waiting for his number, Hirschman advises the old men that they were wise to go to the Korpotchniker, "a Righteous one among the Righteous

Ones." On the phone, Hirschman says in gentle tones: "Is this Chaim, son of Yosif? . . . This is Israel, son of Isaac . . . And peace be unto you . . . There is a man here of my congregation who feels his granddaughter is possessed by a dybbuk and would seek your counsel from my cousin. . . . He will bless you for your courtesy. Peace be unto you, Chaim son of Yosif." Hanging up, the Cabalist asks for a pencil and paper, which seems more difficult to produce than the Korpotchniker. Finally someone finds an envelope and someone else a pencil stub. Giving Foreman the Korpotchniker's address, Hirschman repeats the Korpotchniker's secretary's message—that Foreman must hurry to the Korpotchniker's home, where he will be received after the morning services.

Foreman is immensely grateful, but the others start arguing how Foreman is to get to Williamsburg.

ZITORSKY—Oh, Williamsburg. That's quite a ride from here.

SCHLISSEL—What are you talking about? You take the Long Island Railroad to Atlantic Avenue Station where you go downstairs, and you catch the Brooklyn subway.

ALPER—Maybe I should go along with you, Foreman.

FOREMAN (regarding the door to the Rabbi's office)—You don't have to go along with me.

ALPER—A simple fellow like you will certainly get lost in the Atlantic Avenue Station which is an immense conflux of subways.

SCHLISSEL—What you do, Foreman, is you take the Long Island Railroad to the Atlantic Avenue Station, where you take the Double G train on the lower level . . .

ALPER—Not the Double G train.

SCHLISSEL—What's wrong with the Double G?

ALPER—One takes the Brighton Train. The Double G train will take him to Smith Street, which is a good eight blocks walk.

SCHLISSEL—The Brighton Train will take him to Coney Island.

Worried about leaving Evelyn, Foreman concedes that in his final despair he may be clutching at the thought of dybbuks as less painful than an institution. "Now in the sober chill of afterthought," confesses Foreman, "it all seems so unreal and impetuous. And here I am bucketing off to some forbidding Rabbi to listen to mystical incantations." After warning Alper to hide Evelyn from the police who by now must be looking for her, Foreman goes to say good-bye to the girl.

Immeasurably cheered, Schlissel crows: "So the girl is a fugitive from the police. The situation is beginning to take on charm." "Look at Schlissel, the retired revolutionary," says Alper; "as long as it's against the law, he believes in dybbuks." "I believe," says Schlissel, "in anything that involves conspiracy."

Ignoring Zitorsky's "Have we got something to tell you!", the Sexton burst in with his own news: "I've got a tenth Jew!" The tenth man thus ushered into the synagogue is fine-looking, though scowling and troubled. His name is Arthur Carey, and from his unshaven face and the state of his clothes it is obvious that he has been on a bender. The Sexton gives Carey a skullcap; then, finding out that his eighth and ninth men haven't appeared, he grumbles: "Sure, go find ten Jews on a winter morning!" and dashes out again.

As Foreman goes off on his big adventure, his friends are all agog at the approaching exorcism. Schlissel assumes a blasé attitude. "Oh, I don't know," he says, "you've seen one exorcism, you've seen them all." Without needing to be prodded, Schlissel reports on the exorcism he witnessed as a youth in Poland. To Alper this sounds like a marvelous ceremony but Schlissel, sure that they no longer exorcise dybbuks the way they used to, finds today's religion so pallid that it is hardly worth-while being an atheist.

Old Harris finally arrives. Taking off his overcoat, he reveals a numeraled sweater, the possession of a younger member of his family; then nodding to the others, he hurries to put on his shawl and phylacteries.

Alper offers to help Carey with his preparations for the services. Turning down shawl, phylacteries, and even prayer book, Arthur Carey says: "Look, the only reason I'm here is some man stopped me on the street, asked me if I was Jewish, and gave me the impression he would kill himself if I didn't come in and complete your quorum. I was told all I had to do was stand around for a few minutes wearing a hat. I can't read Hebrew and I have nothing I want to pray about, so there's no sense giving me that book. All I want to know is how long is this going to take because I don't feel very well and I have a number of things to do." Reassured that he will be out in fifteen or twenty minutes, Carey puts on his cap absentmindedly and sits scowling, while Alper bemoans the state of modern Jewry. At this point, having to make a very personal telephone call, Carey heads for the Rabbi's office.

SCHLISSEL—Well, look about you, really. Here you have the decline of orthodox Judaism graphically before your eyes. This is a synagogue? A converted grocery store, flanked on one side by a dry cleaner's and on the other by a shoemaker. Really, if it wasn't for the Holy Ark there, this place would look like the local headquarters of the American Labor Party. In Poland, where we were all one step from starvation, we had a synagogue whose shadow had more dignity than this place.

ALPER—It's a shame and a disgrace.

ZITORSKY—A shame and a disgrace.

While in the Rabbi's office, Arthur eyes Evelyn sourly, and asks for privacy. She, unhearing, stares at the floor.

Schlissel sums it all up: "Where are all the Orthodox Jews? They have apostated to the Reform Jewish Temple, where they sit around like Episcopalians listening to organ music." Finding this an interesting subject for disputation, Alper is concluding that—along with Gentiles who live goodly lives—Reform Jews are not so terrible, when he remembers Evelyn and races towards the office. As the three old men enter the office, Arthur glares at them so fiercely that they back out again and hover nervously outside.

ARTHUR (*shading his face, and keeping his voice down*)—Hello, Doctor, did I wake you up? This is Arthur Carey. . . . Yes, I know. Do you think you can find an hour for me this morning? . . . Oh, I could be in your office in about an hour or so. I'm out in Mineola. My ex-wife lives out here with her parents, you know. And I've been blind drunk for—I just figured it out—nine days now. And I just found myself out here at two o'clock in the morning banging on their front door, screaming . . . (*The girl's presence bothers him. He leans across the desk to her and says*)—Look, this is a very personal call, and I would really appreciate your letting me have the use of this office for just a few minutes.

EVELYN (*hollowly*)—I am the whore of Kiev, the companion of sailors.

ARTHUR—Boy, Doc, there's a real weird broad sitting here. . . . No, I'm all right. At least, I'm still alive. I've got to see you, Doc. Don't hang up on me, please. If my analyst hangs up on me, that'll be the end, I'll tell you that. Just let me talk a couple of minutes. . . . I'm in some damned synagogue. I was on my way to the subway. Oh, my God, I've got to call my office. I was supposed to be in court twice last week. I hope somebody had the brains to get a continuance. So it's funny, you know. I'm in this damned synagogue . . . Doc, I'll be down in about an hour. . . . No, I'm all right. . . . I'll see you in about an hour.

Pulling himself together, Arthur comes out of the office and reports to the worried old men that there is a strange girl inside who maintains that she's the whore of Kiev. A telephone call from Evelyn's father on top of this convinces the old men that they had better move her quickly to a safer hiding place. They choose Alper's basement.

Wishing to get Evelyn away before the Sexton's return, Alper takes her by the arm. Her resulting shrill screams electrify everyone except old Hirschman, who is oblivious of everything. Zitorsky escapes into the street. Arthur wants to know what they're doing to the girl. Alper tries his diplomatic best to explain: "My dear fellow," he says to Arthur, "you are of course understandably confused. The girl, you see, is possessed by a dybbuk." "Yes, of course," answers Arthur, "well, that explains everything." As Alper continues, Zitorsky peers nervously into the synagogue and approaches warily. Arthur inquires after the girl's mother and father, or whoever is responsible for her. Getting nowhere, he goes back to the Rabbi's phone just as the Sexton ushers in the reluctant Kesslers.

As the Sexton hurriedly prepares for the services, Arthur puts in another call to his analyst. This time it concerns helping Evelyn, a psychotic girl who should be in an institution. "But there are three weird old chaps here," says Arthur, "who insist she's possessed by a demon. . . . Yes, a demon. . . . I don't know what I'm talking about myself. I can't even remember how I got out to Mineola in the first place. All I know is there's this psychotic girl here. . . . She apparently has a long schizophrenic history. . . . No, right here in the office . . . not ten feet away from me. . . . Look, Doc, let me see if I can organize this story for you from the beginning . . ."

By the time Arthur has finished his tale, the Rabbi finally strides into the synagogue. Young, brisk, efficient, the Rabbi nods quickly to the members of his congregation. Removing his coat as he heads for the altar, he hears that they have ten men today. "Good. Then let's start the services," he answers.

Having been told to refer his latest problem to the Rabbi, Arthur hangs up. Sitting a moment, Arthur watches the immobilized girl. When he goes out into the synagogue proper, prayers have begun.

Having hurried Mr. Harris and the Kesslers, the Sexton rushes through his own preliminary prayers, while the others make individual statements at the top of their lungs.

ALL—He is the Lord of the Universe, who reigned ere any creature yet was formed! . . . (*Now each goes about his individual prayers, mumbling, walking, occasionally raising his voice to signify beginnings and ends of paragraphs, so that as the curtain slowly comes down, we hear many fragments of prayer.*)

ACT II

The services proceed. The splendid Torah, removed from the Ark, is uncovered and placed on the lectern as Zitorsky reads the day's prayers and the congregation gives its responses. Leaning against the wall of the Rabbi's office, listening to the solemn ritual, Arthur is obviously impressed; while inside the office Evelyn, hearing the prayers, finds peace.

Reading from the Torah, Zitorsky sings out: "Blessed be he who in his holiness gave the Law unto his people Israel. The Law of the Lord is perfect."

CONGREGATION (*scattered response*)—And ye that cleave unto the Lord your God are alive every one of you this day.

ALPER (*at the lectern*)—Blessed is the Lord who is to be blessed for ever and ever.

CONGREGATION—Blessed is the Lord who is to be blessed for ever and ever.

ALPER—Blessed art Thou, O Lord our God, King of the Universe, who hast chosen us from all peoples and hast given us Thy Law. Blessed art Thou, O Lord, who givest the Law.

CONGREGATION—Amen!

Going into the synagogue proper, Evelyn speaks amiably to Arthur about the service and inquires for her grandfather. Reassured that he will return soon, Evelyn says in a spritely way: "I think all synagogues should be shabby because I think of God as being very poor. What do you think of God as?" "I'm afraid," cracks Arthur, "I think of God as the Director of Internal Revenue."

Laughing brightly at this, Evelyn as quickly complains of being tired, and wishes Arthur to go back to the office with her. Following her warily, he is rather attracted by this newly discovered ingenuousness. Seating herself in the Rabbi's swivel chair, Evelyn whirls around like a little girl. She rattles off her medical history, with all the attendant technical terms and psychiatric jargon. Listening, Arthur merely smiles in response. Frowning briefly, Evelyn now asks: "Did my grandfather say when he would be back or where he was going?" Then brightening, she rattles on: "Oh, well, I'm sure he'll be here. He is the dearest man in the world. I'm much closer to him than I am to my own father. I'd rather not talk about my father if you don't mind. It's a danger spot for me. You know when I was nine years old, I shaved all the hair off my head because that is the practice of really orthodox Jewish women. I mean, if you want to be a Rabbi's wife, you must shear your hair and wear a wig. That's one of my compulsive dreams. I keep dreaming of myself as the wife of a handsome young Rabbi with a fine beard down to his waist and a very stern face and prematurely grey forelocks on his brow. I have discovered through many unsuccessful years of psychiatric treatment that religion has a profound sexual connotation for me. Oh, dear, I'm afraid I'm being tiresome again about my psychiatric history. Really, being insane is like being fat. You can talk of nothing else. Please forgive me. I am sure I am boring you to death." "No, not at all," says Arthur. "It's nice to hear somebody talk with passion about anything, even their insanity." Actually Arthur is delighted with Evelyn's youthful effusiveness. Staring at her, he finds it hard to believe that she's psychopathic and asks her if she is very "advanced." "Pretty bad," says Evelyn. "I'm being institutionalized again. . . ." She's apt to slip off any minute, says Evelyn matter-of-factly, adding that he must deal very realistically with her in such a case: harsh reality being the most efficacious way to deal with schizophrenics.

Evelyn now tells Arthur that she is very fond of him and that he must visit her in the asylum. As she describes the place, her face takes on a vacuous expression and her words become confused. Arthur harshly breaks in on this flow of inanity. Shocked into reality, Evelyn begins to cry and throws herself into his arms. As he caresses her gently, she cries: "Oh, I can't bear being insane!" For Arthur this is something of a revelation. In the past it almost seemed to him that the worlds created by the insane were more pleasurable than the real world, from which he had attempted flight through suicide. Having no talent for suicide, Arthur had thought that insanity might be his solution. "I always thought life would be wonderful," says Evelyn, "if I were only sane."

ARTHUR—Life is merely dreary if you're sane. It is utterly unbearable if you are sensitive. I cannot think of a more meaningless sham than my own life. My parents were very poor, so I spent the first twenty years of my life condemning munitions manufacturers for my childhood nightmares. Oh, I was quite a Bernard Barricade when I was in college. I left the Communist Party when I discovered there were easier ways to seduce girls. I turned from reproaching society for my loneliness to reproaching my mother, and stormed out of her house to take a room for myself on the East Side. Then I fell in love—that is to say, I found living alone so unbearable I was willing to marry. She married me because all her friends were marrying somebody. Needless to say, we told each other how deeply in love we were. We wanted very much to be happy. Americans, you know, are frantic about being happy. The American nirvana is a man and his wife watching television amiably and then turning off the lights and effortlessly making the most ardent love to each other. Television unfortunately is a bore and ardent love is an immense drain on one's energy. I began to work day and night at my law office, and besides becoming very successful, I managed to avoid my wife until I could honestly say I was too tired for anything but sleep. For this deceit, I was called ambitious and was respected by everyone including my wife, who was quite as bored with me as I was with her. We decided to have children because we couldn't possibly believe we were that miserable together. I took up with one mistress after another for no other reason than I wanted to feel guilty towards my wife. I could find no other way to be kind to her. I contrived to get through each day only by the most exhausting self-reproach, scolding myself for despising my work and for disliking my children. All this while I drove myself mercilessly for fear that if I paused for just one moment, the whole trembling sanity of my life would come crashing down about my feet without the slightest sound.

As Evelyn listens attentively, Arthur spills out everything from his dreadful feelings of nightmarish isolation to his visits to the psychoanalyst, his drinking bouts, and his death wish. Evelyn finds him wonderfully wise and he in return finds her amazing. But embarrassed by her unabashed sudden fondness, he goes to the door of the office and watches the ceremony from there.

As Evelyn decides that she wants to give Arthur a wonderful Cabalistic volume that old Hirschman had given her, Schlissel beckons Arthur to join them. Outside, shaking his head over Evelyn, Arthur tells Schlissel it is utter nonsense that a lovely girl like that is possessed by demons. He advises Schlissel to call her father. To Schlissel this only means that there would be no exorcism, which he has looked forward to. As the Sexton shushes them, Arthur stares at Schlissel in disbelief.

Called on by the Sexton, the trapped Kessler boys read their memorial prayer with no idea of what they are reading. In the midst of it, old Foreman, more harassed than ever, bursts into the synagogue. Schlissel rushes to find out what happened. Foreman, it turns out, couldn't even find the Long Island Railroad. Schlissel promises condescendingly to take him there himself as soon as the service is over. As the Sexton once more asks for quiet, Foreman automatically joins in the service, and Evelyn, unnoticed by everyone, walks calmly out of the synagogue.

Huddled together, Schlissel, Alper, Zitorsky, and Foreman rattle through the last prayer: ". . . and with my spirit, my body, also; the Lord is with me, and I will not fear. Amen." "Amen," says Alper, "what happened?" Schlissel says that he is going to take Foreman directly to the Korpotchniker, but while he is gone, he wants them to keep Arthur, who wants to talk about the girl, away from the Rabbi. "Take the Long Island Railroad to Atlantic Avenue Station," warns Alper, "then take the Brighton train." "Oh, for heaven's sake," answers Schlissel, "are you presuming to tell me how to get to Williamsburg?"

As the service ends, everyone disperses. The Sexton busies himself with putting away shawls and phylacteries, while Harris, somewhat slower than the others, takes a long time removing his shawl and putting on his coat. With horror, Alper and Zitorsky watch Arthur waylay the Rabbi. Brushing Arthur aside, saying he'll see him in a minute, the Rabbi strides into his office, where he puts in a long-distance phone call to another rabbi. As he waits, the Rabbi sees Alper poke his head into the room, and then, after a look around, go away.

"Harry, how are you, this is Bernard here," says the Rabbi on the phone. "I'm sorry I wasn't in last night, my wife Sylvia said it was wonderful to hear your voice after all these years. How are you, Shirley and the kids? . . . Oh, that's wonderful, I'm glad to hear it. Harry, my wife tells me you have just gotten your first congregation and you wanted some advice since I have already been fired several times. . . . Good, how much are you getting? . . . Well, five thousand isn't bad for a first congregation, although I always thought out-of-town paid better. And what is it, a one-year contract? . . . Well, what kind of advice can I give you? Especially you, Harry. You are a saintly, scholarly, and truly pious man, and you have no business being a rabbi. You've got to be a go-getter, Harry. When I came to my present post here almost three months ago, believe me, I found Judaism in absolute shambles. But I've got things moving now. I've started a Youth Group, a Young Married People's Club, a Theatre Club which is putting on its first production next month, *The Man Who Came to Dinner*. I'd like you to come, Harry, bring the wife, I'm sure you'll have an entertaining evening. And let me recommend that you organize a Little League Baseball Team. It's a marvelous gimmick. I have sixteen boys in my Sunday School now. . . . Harry, listen, what did I know about baseball?" Wishing to spare his friend pain, the Rabbi explains that the youth of this rocket age consider God nothing more than a retired mechanic. As a matter of personal survival, the Rabbi organizes bazaars and raffles, and obtains licenses to conduct Bingo games. He too wished only to bring the word of God to his first congregation, but he soon found that he had no congregation. The Rabbi concludes this conversation with the statement that he now doesn't care if they believe in God just so they come to temple. ". . . of course, it's sad," says the Rabbi, as he offers his friend his good wishes.

Arthur finally gets a word in as the Rabbi leaves the office. Mentioning the insane girl inside, Arthur informs the Rabbi that the old men are determined to rid her of demons by performing an exorcism. Confused and trying to be patient, the Rabbi finally assumes that what Arthur has been saying is that he wants to get married. For a moment Arthur wonders if he is really awake; then he tries again as the Rabbi watches Zitorsky search up and down the synagogue. "Mr. Zitorsky," cries the Rabbi, "what are you doing?" "Well," says Zitorsky to Arthur, "have you ever seen such a thing? The girl has vanished into thin air." After a quick examination of the Rabbi's office, Arthur says that Evelyn has probably just walked out the door. By this time the Rabbi asks Zitorsky for an explanation.

Delighted to oblige, Zitorsky embroiders a fine fantasy about Evelyn's dybbuk who spoke to them as fire flashed from Evelyn's mouth, and as she (like some Chagall heroine) rose into the air. Trying to tone down these details, Alper still feels bound to admit that it was quite an experience. The girl has now disappeared into thin air, exactly as her grandfather has disappeared into Brooklyn.

Puzzled by the tale, the Rabbi is impressed when he hears that Foreman has gone to see the Korpotchniker Rabbi, who is their own Mr. Hirschman's cousin. However, he advises the men to call Evelyn's father to see if she has come home. "Thank God," says Arthur, "for the first rational voice I've heard today."

Glancing at his watch and feeling no longer needed, Arthur says he'd better be on the way to his analyst. "Peace be unto you," says the Rabbi. Amused, Arthur pauses at the door: "Peace be unto you, Rabbi."

THE RABBI—Who was that fellow?

ZITORSKY—Who knows? The Sexton found him on the street.

THE RABBI—Well, I have to be down at the printer's. A dybbuk. Really. What an unusual thing. Is Mr. Foreman a mystical man? By the way, Mr. Alper—Mr. Zitorsky—you weren't at the meeting of the brotherhood last night. I think you should take a more active interest in the synagogue. Did you receive an announcement of the meeting? Please come next time. (*Heads for the door.*) I would like to know what the Korpotchniker said about this. Will you be here later today? I'll drop in. Let me know what happens. You better call the girl's family right away, Alper. Good morning. Peace be unto you."

Alper and Zitorsky go to the Rabbi's phone prepared to do his bidding, but then with Talmudic reasoning, Alper talks himself out of informing the family. And not wanting to trouble "the immense machinery of the law," the two old men, deciding roguishly to look for Evelyn themselves, dart out into the street.

Out of the hollow hush of the empty synagogue Hirschman's voice chants in religious ecstasy, as Evelyn returns, clasping a large, handsome book. Panicky at first because no one is around, she whirls about as Arthur rushes in. "I went home to get this book for you," she says. Arthur, it seems, couldn't leave till he knew she was all right. A moment later, Evelyn flings herself into his arms, crying that she loves him. As they stand locked in an embrace, Hirschman's voice chants: "For Thy salvation I hope, O Lord! I hope, O Lord, for Thy salvation. O Lord, for Thy salvation I hope! . . ."

SCENE II

Around noon, old Hirschman suddenly ends many hours of quiet with Hallelujahs and paeans of joy. He has had a dream in which *his* father called *him* "Rabbi," and had asked him for *his* blessing. This is the sign that Hirschman has long prayed for: since his father has told him that his soul is now cleansed and he has found a seat among the righteous, his years of penitence are over.

Still filled with wonder at his dream, Hirschman calls joyfully: "Where is the wine, Sexton? The wine! There was a fine new bottle on Friday! I have been given a seat among the righteous! For this day have I lived and fasted! I have been absolved! Hallelujah! Hallelujah! . . ." And passing around honey cakes that he had brought with him in memory of his father, he laughs and cries: "I shall dance before the Ark! Sexton! Sexton! Distribute the macaroons that all may share this exalted day! The Lord has sent me a sign, and the face of my father smiled upon me!"

Alper is touched and happy for Hirschman; Zitorsky is delighted at having a party. As the Sexton brings the wine, Zitorsky cries out: "I tell you, Bleyer, if you have a little whiskey, I prefer that. Wine makes me dizzy." "Where would I get whiskey?" says the Sexton. "This is a synagogue, not a saloon." Arthur is drawn into this little group, which shortly changes into a gay, stomping, chanting circle of Chassidic dancers. Hirschman and Zitorsky, in wonderful spirits, start the formless Chassidic pattern. Next, clapping their hands, Alper and the Sexton stomp along with the others until the four old men are whirling about as if they had danced right out of an oil painting by Max Weber. They collapse momentarily; then not wanting to call it quits, they start in all over again. At last, they come to a halt completely winded. It has been sixty years since the Cabalist danced this way.

Awakened by their romp, Evelyn has been a delighted witness to the scene; Zitorsky, catching sight of her, now whirls her into a dance. Hirschman orders him to let the girl rest. Instead, whirling away herself, Evelyn dances in an increasingly wanton fashion, that is proof to Hirschman that she is struggling with the dybbuk. He stops her: "Lie down, my child. Rest." Suddenly faint, Evelyn sinks to the floor. According to Hirschman this is because the dybbuk has weakened her. Giving Evelyn wine to revive her, Arthur suggests that she is weak from having had nothing to eat all day.

Helping Evelyn into the Rabbi's office, Arthur is determined to notify her family. An equally determined Hirschman insists on taking Evelyn to the Korpotchniker himself. "Please, gentlemen," says Arthur, "I really don't think it's wise to pursue this whimsy any longer." The mild-mannered Cabalist, suddenly turned man of authority, demands that Evelyn "be brought to a righteous man among righteous men, clothed in the whitest of linen. And the righteous man shall plead with the dybbuk, and, if necessary, proceed against the dybbuk with malediction and anathema."

The tug of war continues. Hirschman issues orders for the girl's coat and a taxicab; Arthur insists on notifying the girl's parents. Telling Alper to give Arthur her parents' telephone number, Hirschman prophesizes that there'll be no one at home because everyone, assuming Evelyn to be safe with her grandfather, will have gone about his business.

As Arthur waits for an answer to his call, Hirschman wonders why Arthur doesn't believe in dybbuks. Alper expounds philosophically on the symptoms of the times, and when Arthur hangs up, Alper sums up that "whenever a man is unhappy he seems to have a compunction to write his misery down in the form of philosophy."

CABALIST—Is that true, young man, that you believe in absolutely nothing?

ARTHUR—Not a damn thing. Life is an unimpeachable fraud, a desolate moment in time which somehow we clever mortals have contrived to stretch into seventy or eighty years of petulant pain.

CABALIST—There is no truth, no beauty, no infinity, no known, no unknown?

ARTHUR—Precisely.

CABALIST—The passions of men are illusions with which we convince ourselves we are alive? Love, faith, God and the devil are all social contrivances, ballasts which we strap on our belts to keep ourselves from flying off into insignificance?
ARTHUR—Yes.
CABALIST—Young man, you are an utter ass.

That sets Arthur off. Having read the Cabalistic book that Evelyn gave him, he says: "Any disciple of this abracadabra is presuming when he calls anyone else an ass." Frowning, Hirschman says that one does not *read* the Book of Zohar. Entombed in it for sixty years, he has only but "sensed a glimpse of its passion." Since Arthur is possessed only by the tangible, he would be wiser to believe in dybbuks than nothing at all. At this point Arthur informs Hirschman that in ten minutes a psychiatrist could strip and lay bare this man of God as a man of guilt who has invented a God so as to be forgiven.

"Well," says Alper, as Arthur next dials the police, "what can anyone say to such bitterness?" "One can only say," shrugs Hirschman, "that the young man has very little regard for psychiatrists."

Confusion grows when Schlissel and Foreman, by now complete wrecks, return from hours of subway riding. They have taken every train that the transportation system provides; twice they got off just to see daylight, and both times they found themselves in New Jersey. By now Schlissel is convinced that there is no Williamsburg, much less a Korpotchniker Rabbi.

As Evelyn suddenly screams to be saved, Foreman stands aghast and Alper begs Hirschman himself to save the girl: "You have had your sign from God," he pleads, "you are among the righteous. Save her." Arthur rushes to Evelyn's side as she gasps and screams about "the dybbuk." When she slumps into Arthur's arms, he calls out for a doctor; then, suddenly cracking, he tells Hirschman: "For God's sake, perform your exorcism or whatever has to be done. She's dying."

With quiet authority Hirschman instructs the Sexton: "It may be necessary to cast the final anathema. We shall need two black candles, the ram's horn upon which you blow Tekiah, praying shawls of white wool, and there shall be ten Jews for a quorum to witness before God this awesome affair." As always for the Sexton, everything is simple except the ten Jews. Hurrying into his coat, the Sexton scurries out, as Alper comforts Foreman. A pall hangs over the synagogue.

ACT III

The Sexton is still trying to drum up ten men by phone. He is able to rope in old Harris again though at first he is loth to tell him why he is needed. "Hirschman is going to exorcise a dybbuk from Foreman's granddaughter," he finally says. "I said Hirschman's . . . a dybbuk. . . . That's right; a dybbuk. . . . Right here in Mineola. . . . That's right. Why should Mineola be exempt from dybbuks?" But having only eight men counting Harris, the Sexton is frankly at the end of his resources. Putting on his overcoat, he doesn't relish the thought of dragooning two strangers from the street: "I will have to stop people on the street, ask them if they are Jewish—which is bad enough—and then explain to them I wish them to attend the exorcism of a dybbuk. . . . I mean surely you can see the futility of it."

At this eleventh hour, Hirschman makes a final effort to rid Evelyn of the dybbuk through quiet persuasion; when he fails, he leaves the frightened girl as Arthur steps in to comfort her. Arthur's bleak notion of consolation is to tell Evelyn that his analyst approves of the exorcism as a form of shock therapy that might well lead to a cure. Evelyn has ideas of her own: she pours out her love for Arthur, her desire to marry him, her certainty that he would be happy with her. This is enough to make Arthur judge her mad on all counts.

She doesn't insist that he have faith in dybbuks, or God, or the exorcism; she wants him to have faith in her. Despite his protests, it is becoming clear that Arthur can't help being attracted to her. Nevertheless, he expostulates bitterly on the utter falseness of love, convincing Evelyn that he has a love-destroying dybbuk of his own. Turning on his heel, Arthur discovers that he must run a gantlet of old men who have been eavesdropping on every word. "My dear fellow," says Alper, "how wonderful to be in love." "I love nothing," cries Arthur. Then more in control of himself, he adds: "Don't you think it's time to get on with the exorcism?"

The Sexton, at this point, bursts into the synagogue with ominous news. Although the Rabbi, decently enough, has promised to make their ninth man, the whole question of a quorum has become academic. Two strapping, burly policemen are parked right outside the door. Assuring the nervous old men that the police won't interrupt a religious ceremony, Arthur urges him to start immediately. On Hirschman's order, two black candles are produced. "We do not have a quorum," worries Alper. "Will this be valid?" "We will let God decide," Hirschman answers.

Led by Hirschman, the old men sweep their white shawls over their heads, face the opened Ark, and begin a wailing, primitive recital of their sins. Arthur finds this savage ritual frightening, but as Hirschman intones the same phrases over and over and the men repeat their responses again and again, the cumulative effect sweeps him along with the others. Tension builds, and as the repetition reaches a climax Evelyn is brought forth clothed in white, and stands in sullen silence while the Sexton, ram's horn in hand, waits for Hirschman's word. Instead a large policeman, opening the synagogue door, asks brusquely for the Rabbi and then for Evelyn Foreman.

ALPER—You are interrupting a service, Officer.

POLICEMAN—I'm sorry. Just tell me, is that the girl? I'll call in and tell them we found her.

SCHLISSEL—First of all, where do you come to walk in here like you were raiding a poolroom? This is a synagogue, you animal. Have a little respect.

POLICEMAN—All right, all right, I'm sorry. I happen to be Jewish myself.

ALPER—Sexton, our tenth man!

Unaware of the true nature of the ceremony he is witnessing, the Policeman agrees to stay for ten or fifteen minutes while the Rabbi, out of his depth in these mystical matters, arrives to take his place simply as an observer. "But it would please me a great deal," he says, "to believe once again in a God of dybbuks. I fear I had come to think of him as the account executive for IBM. . . . Well, we are ten."

In the ominous dark, in the shadows cast by the candles, Evelyn listens unmoved to the eerie blasts of the ram's horn. "Sexton," commands Hirschman, "blow the Great Tekiah, and, upon the sound of these tones, Dybbuk, you will be wrenched from the girl's body and cast into Gilgul."

Evelyn remains unchanged; but suddenly from another direction, there is a horrible atavistic scream and Arthur falls heavily onto the floor. "My God," cries Alper, "I think what has happened is that we have exorcised the wrong dybbuk."

Coming back to life, Arthur finds to his surprise that he has a hunger for life and that he wants not only to live, but to love, cherish and heal Evelyn. He declares to all those present that if God won't exorcise Evelyn's dybbuk, he will himself. "Well," says Schlissel, "what is one to say? An hour ago he didn't believe in God; now he is exorcising dybbuks." "He still doesn't believe in

God," Alper answers. "He is simply in love." "Is there any difference?" asks the Cabalist, as he turns once more to his prayers.

Aware that Arthur may have had a sign from God, Foreman yet feels compelled to warn him that a marriage between a suicide and a schizophrenic is something to be thought of less impulsively. "These are forlorn times, Mr. Foreman," answers Arthur. "The suicidal and the insane are all that is left to make a better life."

FIVE FINGER EXERCISE

A Play in Two Acts

BY PETER SHAFFER

[PETER SHAFFER *was born in Liverpool, England, and attended St. Paul's School in London, where he won a scholarship to Trinity College, Cambridge. In 1951, when he was 25, he came to the United States and worked in the Acquisitions Department of the New York Public Library. During this time he wrote "The Salt Land," presented on British TV. Later he returned to England and wrote "The Prodigal Father" and "Balcony of Terror," both done by the BBC. In 1958 "Five Finger Exercise" was presented in London, where it has played continuously since; a new cast replaced the original one in September, 1959.*]

THE week-end cottage of the Harrington family is like an aggressive signpost to Mrs. Harrington's taste. There is more in it of town than of country, and a little too much of everything in every style. The living room-dining room brick wall has a raised fireplace with the usual andirons plus a vase of leaves. A window seat under the dining room casement windows has been converted into a sideboard covered with china and plants. The garden door is next to the casement window; the kitchen door is in the brick wall.

At the living room end is a sofa and coffee table; a comfortable chair and a side table serve to divide the room; against the back wall stands a lamp, a commode with crystal candelabra, a tray with a whiskey decanter, a pitcher of water and glasses. More green leaves are nearby in a china umbrella stand.

The entrance hall has the usual country cottage accumulation of hats and coats on wall pegs. The staircase leads out of this hall to a landing with a glimpse of a bedroom, as well as a corridor leading to other bedrooms and a bath. A few more steps lead up to Pamela

Harrington's littered schoolroom. Mrs. Harrington has made this room very feminine, and Pamela has added her own girlish touches.

At the breakfast table this Saturday morning in September, good-looking Louise Harrington, a bit too stylishly dressed for the country, sits pouring coffee. Stanley Harrington, a forceful, well-built man in middle age, smokes his pipe, reads his paper, and waits impatiently for their son to make his appearance.

When Clive does appear, his father greets him gruffly: "Good afternoon. What do you think this place is—a hotel?" As Clive apologizes, Louise, merely to spite Stanley, gushes over Clive and offers to make a fresh batch of eggs. This Clive turns down and, changing the subject, asks about his sister. Happy about the surprise she has in store for him, Louise announces that Pamela is out walking with her tutor. Pleased with herself, Louise pours Clive's coffee and explains: "You know—the German boy I engaged in London to come in every morning and give Pamela her lessons. Well, he's going to live with us. As part of the family." Delighted with her effect, Louise says that Pamela's mad about the idea, and Clive will be, too. "He's terribly nice," Louise continues, "and anyway, it's time you had some well-bred friends for a change. He's marvelously educated and has the most divine manners. I always say it takes a Continental to show us just how ignorant we really are." She goes into the ktichen.

Clive exclaims that this idea of his mother's is ridiculous and unnecessary.

STANLEY—Your mother thinks different. Apparently, the Best People have private tutors, and since we're going to be the Best People whether we like it or not, we're going to have a tutor too. We don't send our daughter to anything so common as a school. Oh, well, I can afford it. What's money after all? We have a town place, so we simply got to have a country place. (LOUISE *enters from the kitchen with toast for* CLIVE.)

LOUISE—You always said you wanted a country place!

STANLEY—I meant a little week-end cottage. Not a damn great fancy place like this. However, now we've got a country place, we've simply got to have a tutor.

LOUISE—Now look, Stanley. This is Walter's first day down here and I want everyone to be very sweet to him. So just keep your ideas to yourself. We don't want to hear them.

STANLEY—We? Clive agrees with me.

LOUISE—Do you, Clive?

CLIVE—Well, yes; I mean well, no. Isn't it a bit early for this kind of conversation?

STANLEY—You just said you thought a tutor was ridiculous.

CLIVE (*unhappily*)—Well, not really ridiculous . . .

Irritated, Stanley rounds on Clive and asks why he was so late last night. Clive answers nervously that he had promised to review a play for a magazine; in fact, he himself had asked to do the piece. Stanley asks whether the play was any good. When Clive becomes enthusiastic over the performance of *Elektra*, Stanley says: "What's that?" In exaggerated surprise, and with much hand fluttering, Louise exclaims: "Really, Stanley, there are times when I have to remind myself about you—actually remind myself." "Suppose you tell me, then," says Stanley quietly. "Go on . . . educate me." Loftily dumping this into her son's lap, Louise comes back on cue when Clive says it's Greek: "Who was in it, dear? Laurence Olivier? I always think he's best for those Greek things, don't you? . . . I'll never forget that wonderful night when they put out his eyes—I could hear that scream for weeks and weeks afterwards, everywhere I went. There was something so *farouche* about it. You know the word, dear: *farouche?* Like animals in the jungle." It is obvious that if this is culture, Stanley regards it dimly. As Louise rubs it in that Stanley wouldn't appreciate such poetic drama, Stanley says: "And this is what you want to study at Cambridge, when you get up there next month?" "Yes, it is, more or less," Clive admits. Stanley wonders whether Clive considers this the most useful thing he can do with his time; that, for Clive, has nothing to do with the matter.

STANLEY—You don't seem to realize the world you're living in, my boy. When you finish at this university which your mother insists you're to go to, you'll have to earn your living. I won't always be here to pay for everything, you know. All this culture stuff's very fine for those who can afford it; for the nobs and snobs we're always hearing about from that end of the table— (*Indicating* LOUISE.) But look here . . . if you can't stand on your own two feet, you don't amount to anything. And not one of that pansy set of spongers you're going around with will ever help you do that.

CLIVE—You know nothing about my friends.

STANLEY—Oh, yes I do. I've seen them. Arty-tarty boys. Going around London, giggling and drinking and talking dirty; wearing Bohemian clothes . . . Who did you go with last night for instance?

CLIVE—Chuck.

STANLEY—Chuck? Oh, yes, the fellow that never washes. Sings in cafes and wants to stay in school till he's thirty, living on government grants. Such a dignified way to go on.

LOUISE (*sharply*)—I should have thought it was a sign of maturity to want to become more educated. Unfortunately, my dear, we were not all born orphans; we didn't all go to grammar schools or build up a furniture factory on our own by sheer will power. We can never hope to live down these shortcomings, of course, but don't you think we might learn to tolerate them? We just didn't have the advantage of your healthy upbringing in the tough world outside.

Picking up his golf clubs, Stanley issues a half-hearted invitation that Clive walk around the golf course with him. He knows it won't be accepted, and it isn't. Muttering that he'll never understand his son, Stanley leaves the house.

"Breakfast as usual," says Clive. Louise at once asks Clive to side with her in the matter of this house, and to promise that he will not let her down. Rising, saluting Louise, Clive crosses and kneels in front of her: "*Votre Majesté,*" he cries. "My Empress!" Allowing her hand to be kissed, Louise answers: "*Levez!*" And with other flirtatious bits of play-acting, Louise extracts Clive's promise to be happy. "Darling. My darling Jou-Jou," she cries, and they embrace fondly.

That attended to, Louise removes her rings and bracelets in preparation for dishwashing. Arguing that housework is no longer beneath them because today everyone does it, Louise coaxes Clive to the kitchen.

Dashing into the house, Pamela races up the stairs to the schoolroom, all the while calling back to Walter, who follows at a slower pace. A perky fourteen and singularly without problems, Pamela is so gay that even her serious, reserved German tutor finds himself gay and at ease in her company. For his part, Walter almost exerts enough influence to make Pamela serious. Settling down to the day's French lesson, Pamela manages one conjugation successfully, but then, unable to concentrate further, says: "Oh, phooey to French. I hate it really."

WALTER—Why?

PAMELA—Because the French are a decadent nation. Personally I think we all ought to study Russian and American.

WALTER—But American is the same as English.

PAMELA—Oh, no, it isn't. . . . When they say "dame" they mean young girl, and when we say "dame" we mean old girl. But when we call someone "old girl" we really mean what they call a dame. So you see . . .

Pamela's information about the American language comes straight from her friend Mary. Mrs. Harrington may consider Mary common, and object violently to her, but Pamela finds her delightful, even to her shocking-pink socks, her habitual expression "Drop Dead," and her boyfriend in the American Air Force. "How old is she?" asks Walter. "Sixteen," says Pamela, "but that's all right; they like them young. I don't think they actually . . . well, you know. . . . Sometimes, she gets decked up in her black jeans and goes off to some sexy club in Ipswich under a Polish restaurant. But her mother doesn't like her going round the streets looking like that, so she has to sneak off when no one's looking." To Walter this suggests witches sneaking off to their Sabbath. "When they used to worship the Devil," says Walter, "they used to sneak off just like that. It was the same thing like your English Teddy Boys. You make yourself very excited, then people give you a bad name and start being afraid of you. That's when you really do start worshipping the Devil." With another "phooey," Pamela says teasingly that it sounds as if Walter had actually seen the Devil. Walter replies very seriously that he *has* seen the Devil—in the place he was born. Unable to shake Pamela off, Walter continues that he does not miss that place, nor is it his home. When she persists that there must be some things in Germany that he misses, Walter confesses to remembering with pleasure skating under the stars amid the happy, torch-lit Christmas crowds. Swept along by Walter's description, Pamela is all for having him give her a quick course in German so that he can take her to Germany at Christmas. Her sudden zeal for acquiring another language is dampened by Walter's refusal to teach German.

A passionate admirer of England where he has lived these last five years, Walter is now in line for citizenship. Since he will admit to no German ties or German family, Pamela offers him her own, and asks him to repeat after her: "My family lives at 22 Elton Square, London, and 'The Retreat,' Lower Orford, Suffolk." Walter repeats this dutifully. One moment giving him full marks, the next she ruffles his hair, hops up, and runs shouting down the stairs. Walter catches her at the landing and returns her to the schoolroom and to her history book.

As Louise calls for him, Walter continues down to the living room, where Clive waits to direct him to his mother's music room—a place behind the kitchen and happily at a distance, since Stanley Harrington does not care for music.

Clive takes kindly to Walter because Walter likes his sister. But he warns him about this—his first family. "This," says Clive, "*isn't* a family. It's a tribe of wild cannibals. Between us we eat everyone we can. You think I'm joking?"

WALTER—I think you are very lucky to have a family.

CLIVE—And I think you're very lucky to be without one. . . . I'm sorry. Actually we're very choosy in our victims. We only eat other members of the family.

WALTER—Then I must watch out. Your sister thinks I'm almost a member already.

CLIVE—Pam? You know I don't like the way she's growing up at all. She wants to include people all the time. She doesn't seem to want to exclude or demolish anybody.

WALTER—Perhaps that's because she takes after her mother.

CLIVE—Well, of course, a girl who took after my father would be almost unthinkable. . . .

Settling himself to chat with Walter, Clive is interrupted by Louise: ready for her music lesson, Louise thinks that Walter should play for her. "You have such beautiful hands," she says. And taking one of Walter's hands in hers, she remembers once shaking hands with Paderewski. "Of course," she is quick to add, "it was many years ago, and I was only a girl, but I've never forgotten it. He had hands almost exactly like yours, my dear boy. Much older of course—but the same bone formation, the same delicacy. . . ."

Listening to his mother's fancy talk and to Walter's courteous answers, Clive improvises some silly answers of his own. "He's being very naughty, isn't he?" says Louise. "Really, Jou-Jou."

Tactfully choosing this moment to present some wild flowers he has picked on his walk, Walter earns Louise's extravagant thanks and a new nickname. As a companion piece to Clive's Jou-Jou, Louise now dubs him Hibou which, translated by Louise, is "owl."

Pamela now bursts downstairs with the excuse that she needs Louise to test her on her history. With lessons of her own to occupy her, Louise has no time for her daughter's, and delegates Clive to carry on, while she goes off with Walter.

Left to their own happy company, Clive and Pamela launch into an act that has probably been running for years. Finishing off impersonations of Old General Harrington and little Daphne, Pamela thinks vaguely of the history she has been studying, but prefers to talk of Walter. She adores him. Showing concern for Pamela's education, Clive rattles off a list of the members of that most uncertain European dynasty, the Perhapsburgs. Delighted with her history lesson, Pamela pounces on Clive and starts to roughhouse. As Clive is about to oblige her with one of his special stories, Walter returns. He had been asked to fetch Louise's handbag. "Stay with us," begs Pamela, "Clive's telling me a story."

WALTER—A story? About history?

PAMELA—About a prison.

CLIVE (*showing off to* WALTER)—Yes, it's going to be brilliant. All Gothic darkness and calamities. It's called "The Black Hole of East Suffolk." Sit down and I'll unfold.

WALTER—No, excuse me. Mrs. Harrington is waiting. (*He gives* CLIVE *a short bow and leaves.* CLIVE *stares after him.*)

PAMELA—What's wrong?

CLIVE—Nothing.

PAMELA—What about the little girl in prison?

CLIVE (*turns and looks at her; he speaks with sudden energy and rather bitterly*)—It wasn't a girl. It was a little boy. A little German boy with blonde hair, who played the piano rather well. He walked straight into the prison of his own free will and shut the door behind him. (CLIVE *leaves through the front door as the piano can be heard.*)

SCENE II

Two months later, returning for his first week-end from Cambridge, Clive finds his family depressingly unchanged. Stanley complains bitterly of the noise Pamela makes practising on the piano; Louise, in return, attacks Stanley sarcastically for his lack of appreciation; and when she retires to the kitchen, Stanley calls Clive to task for a conversation he had had with Stanley's factory manager. Clive was reported to have called his father's furniture grotesque, shoddy, and vulgar.

STANLEY—And I suppose you think that's clever? That's being educated, I suppose; to go up to my manager (LOUISE *enters*) in my own factory and tell him you think the stuff I'm turning out is shoddy and vulgar. . . . Is it?

LOUISE—Just because *you've* got no taste, it doesn't mean we all have to follow suit.

STANLEY—Now listen to me, my boy. You get this through your head once and for all; I'm in business to make money. I give people what they want. I mean ordinary people. Maybe they haven't got such wonderful taste as you and your mother; perhaps they don't read such good books—what is it? "Homes and Gardens"?—but they know what they want. If they didn't want it, they wouldn't buy it, and I'd be out of business. (*Piano stops.*) Before you start sneering again, young man, just remember something—you've always had enough to eat. (*The explosive opening of the Brahms Third Symphony is heard from* WALTER'S *room.*) One stops, the other starts. I'm going out.

Louise asks Stanley not to go out, since his son is with them for his first week-end; then calling upstairs to "Walter dear," she asks him to play his record another time: Mr. Harrington has a headache. Offering Walter fresh coffee and "delicious *petits fours*," Louise asks him to join the family circle, then goes to the kitchen. Aware that he has hurt his father, Clive apologizes for his tactlessness. For his part, Stanley is ready to consider the matter closed. Though trying to communicate, the men still find they are as far apart as always. Stanley is completely at sea about Clive's Cambridge life, and the use he will make of it. Utterly defeated by his son's educational theories, he argues that since Clive is in a privileged position he must make the most of it. People judge a man by the company he keeps, and now is the time for Clive to be making contacts with the right people, people of influence. Clive understands only too well his father's approach to the University. "Good!" says Stanley. "Now you've got a good brain, and I'll see to it you've got enough money. There's no harm in having a few pounds in your pocket, you know. Never be so foolish as to look down on money. It's the one thing that counts in the end." Overhearing this, Louise cries: "Money! Is that all you ever think about? Money!" "You don't have any difficulty spending it, I notice," answers Stanley.

Riled by Louise's condescension, Stanley gets up and asks Clive to join him in a walk. Excusing himself because of reading that he must do, Clive turns down the offer of a drink at the Red Lion, and lets his father leave by himself.

Louise tries to coax Clive out of his "mood" with endearments and the Empress Act: "*Embrasse-moi . . . non?* . . . It's your Empress." As Clive answers half-heartedly, Walter, his mother's Hibou, appears. Walter is courteous and Clive self-conscious as Louise leaves the room. Walter inquires about Cambridge. Clive says it's all right, then bursts out: "No, it's wonderful, really. Like going to a new country. I suppose one of the thrills of travel is hearing people speak a foreign language. But the marvelous thing about this is hearing them speak my own for the first time." Conceding that Pam speaks a few words of it, Clive wonders where Pam is, and then assumes that she has gone for a walk: "A night for walks.

Pam tripping along so gaily . . . Father marching along so . . . rightly. And I should be by his side. Or better still, a pace or two behind. 'Clive to heel, sir. Heel.' Let me introduce myself: Spaniel Harrington." He raises his glass and drains it, and can see that Walter is unhappy about his tone.

WALTER—I think if you forgive me . . .

CLIVE—Well?

WALTER—I think you have a duty to your father.

CLIVE—A duty? What a very German thing to say. I'm sorry, I'm not quite sober.

WALTER—I did not mean duty in that sense. I meant that it seems to me . . . Clever children have a duty—to protect their parents who are not so clever.

CLIVE—Protect?

WALTER—I do not put it very well perhaps.

CLIVE—You know when I was on the train tonight, I was so looking forward to seeing them again. I know I've only been away a few weeks, but so much has happened to me . . . and I thought, I don't know why, they would have changed as much as I have. But everything's exactly the same.

Entering with her tray of coffee and cakes, Louise is delighted that the three of them will have this hour to themselves. Her idea is that Walter should recite some German poetry for their edification. Clive points out that Louise doesn't understand German. This is immaterial to Louise: "It's not the meaning, it's the sound that counts, dear. And I'm sure this boy will speak it adorably. Most people make it sound like a soda syphon, but when you speak it I'm sure I'll feel exactly what the poet wants to say—even more than if I actually knew the language and to cope with all those miller's daughters and woodcutters and little people. It's difficult to explain —but you know what I mean." Emptying his whiskey glass, Clive says: "I don't—I'm going out."

LOUISE—Where?

CLIVE—To the pub.

LOUISE—You can't be serious.

CLIVE—Too vulgar?

LOUISE—Don't be silly, Clive. No, it's just so . . . uncivil, dear. There's plenty of drink in the house if you really need it, though I think you've had quite enough already.

CLIVE—You're right, I have. (*To* WALTER.) Excuse me. I'm sure you recite beautifully.

LOUISE—But your father asked you if you wanted to go to the pub and you said no.

CLIVE—True. (*He goes out.*)

Walter is thoroughly uncomfortable, and Louise's changing the subject doesn't alter the fact. He suggests diffidently that Clive is not very happy. Ignoring Clive's unhappiness, paying no attention to Walter's wish to help, Louise claims that she is not a very happy person either. With a touch of the tragedy queen, she asks Walter to see for himself, and warns him that whatever he does, he must marry a girl who's his equal—*if* he can find one. Launching into the story of her Bournemouth life, spattered with descriptions of her aristocratic little French mother, helplessly extravagant as highborn people so often are, and her father who lost all of his small inheritance in speculation, Louise only interrupts her flow to ask whether Walter understands what speculation is. "Oh, yes," says Walter, "he was a stock broker." "Heavens no—a lawyer!" cries Louise. "Both my parents came from professional people, so naturally they had reservations about marrying me into the furniture business. Still, I was attracted to Stanley. I won't deny it. He had a sort of rugged charm, as they say. Obviously I was interested in all kinds of things like art and music and poetry which he, poor man, had never had time for. But when you're young, those things don't seem to matter. It's only later when the first excitement's gone, you start looking a little closer." Sighing, she continues. "Walter, these past few years have been intolerable." Louise goes to Walter. "There are times," she says, "when I listen to you playing when I go almost mad with sheer pleasure. Year after year I've had to kill that side of myself. Smother it. Stamp it out. Heaven knows I've tried to be interested in his bridge and his golf and his terrible business friends. I can't do it. I'm sorry. I didn't mean to talk like this. I'm embarrassing you."

As Louise creates this sense of intimacy, Walter, not really getting the point, merely offers his deep gratitude. Louise leads the talk into personal channels, only for Walter in his innocence to reroute it. He will not allow her to attribute a lovely Viennese accent to him when it is German. "I am German," Walter maintains. "This is not so poetic." "But Hibou," says Louise, "there's good and bad in all countries—surely?"

WALTER—You are too good to understand. I know how they seem to you, the Germans: so kind and quaint. Like you yourself said: miller's daughters and woodcutters. . . . But they can be monsters.

Chita Rivera and Dick Van Dyke in "Bye Bye Birdie"

JOHN GIELGUD MARGARET LEIGHTON
as Benedick as Beatrice
in "Much Ado About Nothing"

IRENE WORTH
as Albertine Prine
in "Toys in the Attic"

MICHAEL FLANDERS and DONALD SWANN
in "At the Drop of a Hat"

TOM BOSLEY
as LaGuardia
in "Fiorello!"

PAMELA BROWN
as Lady Utterword

DIANA WYNYARD
as Mrs. Hushabye
in "Heartbreak House"

ROLAND CULVER
as Stanley Harrington
in "Five Finger Exercise"

ANNE BANCROFT
as Annie Sullivan

PATTY DUKE
as Helen Keller

in "The Miracle Worker"

LEE TRACY
as Arthur Hockstader

MELVYN DOUGLAS
as William Russell

in "The Best Man"

VIVIEN LEIGH
as Paola
in "Duel of Angels"

ERIC BERRY
as Sir John Falstaff
in "Henry IV, Part I"

GEORGE C. SCOTT
as Lt. Col. Chipman in
"The Andersonville Trial"

Alice Ghostley, Tom Ewell, Paul Ford and Wynne Miller in "A Thurber Carnival"

Anne Bancroft and Patty Duke in "The Miracle Worker"

Albert Dekker and Herbert Berghof in "The Andersonville Trial"

Anne Revere, Jason Robards, Jr. and
Maureen Stapleton in "Toys in the Attic"

Photo by Henry Grossman

Patricia Falkenhain, Eric Berry and Gerry
Jedd in "Henry IV, Part II"

William and Jean Eckart's costume designs for "Fiorello!"

Costume designs by Alvin Colt for "Christine"

Set design by David Hays for "The Tenth Man"

Sketch by Will Steven Armstrong for a set in "Caligula"

Oliver Smith's set design for "Five Finger Exercise"

Set design by Roger Furse for "Duel of Angels"

Howard Bay's set design for "Toys in the Attic"

Sketches by William and Jean Eckart
for sets in "Fiorello!"

Costume designs by Miles White for "Take Me Along"

Design by Oliver Smith for a backdrop in "Take Me Along"

Photo by Friedman-Abeles

Scene from "Bye Bye Birdie";
set design by Robert Randolph

KATE - ACT 1 - SC 1

Ruth Morley's costume designs for "The Miracle Worker"

Jackie Gleason, James Cresson, Robert Morse, Walter Pidgeon and Una Merkel in "Take Me Along"

Scene from "The Tenth Man"

Vivien Leigh and Mary Ure in "Duel of Angels"

Claude Dauphin, Pat Hingle and Max Adrian in
"The Deadly Game"

LOUISE—Really now . . .

WALTER—Yes! . . .

LOUISE—Even in England we're not all angels.

WALTER—Angels to me! Because this to me is Paradise.

LOUISE—How charming you are.

WALTER (*with increasing heat*)—No, I am sincere. You see . . . here in England most people want to do what's good. Where I come from this is not true. They want only power. . . . They are a people that is enraged by equality. They need always to feel shamed, to breathe in shame—like oxygen—to go on living. Because deeper than everything else they want to be hated. From this they can believe they are giants, even in chains. . . . (*Recovering as he sits on sofa.*) I'm sorry. It's difficult to talk about.

LOUISE—Anything one feels deeply is hard to speak of, my dear.

WALTER—One thing I do know. I will never go back. Soon I'll be a British subject.

LOUISE—You really want to stay here.

WALTER—If you had seen what I have, you would know why I call it Paradise.

LOUISE—I can see for myself how you've suffered. It's in your face. (*Extending her hand to him.*) Walter . . . you mustn't torment yourself like this. It's not good for you. You're among friends now. People who want to help you. People who love you. . . . Doesn't that make a difference?

WALTER—You are so good to me! So good, good . . . (*Impulsively he bends and kisses her hands.*)

LOUISE (*suddenly taking his head in her hands and holding it close to her*)—Oh, my dear . . . you make me feel ashamed. (CLIVE *comes in abruptly through the garden door; stares at them fascinated.*) It's been so long since anyone has talked like this to me. (CLIVE *bangs door.*)

Finding it hard to recover her composure under Clive's cold stare, Louise leaves, to check on Pam's whereabouts.

More disturbed than he is aware, and evidently fairly drunk, Clive approaches Walter.

WALTER—Clive, what's the matter? Why are you looking at me like that?

CLIVE—Hair is being worn disheveled this year. The Medusa style. What would have happened if Medusa had looked in a mirror? Are monsters immune against their own fatal charms? Observe, please, the subtle and dialectical nature of my mind. It's the French in me, you understand. An inheritance from my very French, very

aristocratic ancestors.   Perhaps you've been hearing about them.
In actuality, I regret to say, they weren't as aristocratic as all that.
(*He sinks onto sofa.*)   My great-grandpa, despite any impression
to the contrary, did not actually grant humble petitions from his
bedside—merely industrial patents from a run-down little office near
the Louvre.   The salary was so small that the family would have
died of starvation if Helene, my grandmother, hadn't met an English
lawyer on a cycling tour of the Loire Valley, married him, and exchanged Brunoy for Bournemouth.   Let us therefore not gasp too
excitedly at the loftiness of Mother's family tree.   Unbeknownst to
Father it has, as you see, roots of clay.   (CLIVE *pours some coffee.*)
Still, they *are* French roots.   I even have them in me.   For example,
my Mother's name for me—Jou-Jou.   Toy.   More accurately in
this case, ornament.—Being French, Mother imagines she's real
ormulu in a sitting room of plaster gilt.   She suffers from what I
might call a plaster-gilt complex.   If you see what I mean.   To her
the whole world is irredeemably plebeian—especially Father.   The
rift you may detect between them is the difference between the
Salon and the Saloon.   At least that's what she'd have you believe.
. . . I won't deny that she's only really at home in the Salon; but
then where else can you be so continuously dishonest?

Not wishing to listen to this kind of talk, Walter starts to leave
and remarks that had Clive come from Europe and been taken in as
he had been—"Taken in!   Taken in is right," interrupts Clive.
Pushing Walter down on the dining room table, Clive instructs him:
"Taken up!   Like a fashion, or an ornament; a piece of Dresden,
a dear little Dresden owl . . . and believe me, like any other valuable possession, sooner or later you will be used!   I know this family, let me tell you."

As a slammed door signals Pamela's return, and as she streams
upstairs full of the latest hilarity from Mary's lips, Clive abruptly
proposes that Walter come away with him.   As Clive pleads with
him, Walter, though thoroughly startled, manages to be tactful.
Since Christmas is a family time, Walter wishes to be here for Christmas; nor will he be able to leave with Clive immediately after.   He
has been paid for his services through January and feels that he has
an obligation to Clive's mother.   Pacing the room in a frantic kind
of remorse, Clive cries: "This is quite beyond anything, isn't it?   If
you came away with me, it would be for my sake—not yours.   I
need a friend so badly."

WALTER—You are unhappy.   I am sorry.   I really . . .
CLIVE (*the bitterness returning*)—Is that all you can say?   "I'm

sorry." Such an awkward position I put you in, don't I? The poor little immigrant, careful not to offend. So very sensitive. (*With sudden fury.*) When in hell are you going to stop trading on your helplessness—offering yourself all day to be petted and stroked? Just like I do. Okay, you're a pet. You've got an irresistible accent. You make me sick.

Clive tries clumsily to detain Walter as he excuses himself and goes upstairs. Clive goes back to the whiskey bottle as Stanley comes home.

Finding his son drinking guiltily, Stanley says that Clive should have come along with him this evening. There was a jolly crowd at the club. This sitting and drinking alone is silly and not normal. Once again Stanley makes overtures, but the going is rough. Accusing his father of being patronizing, working himself into a rage, Clive hammers home the theme that Stanley not only does not understand him but is proud of it. Stanley listens to this outburst and has nothing to say except that his son is drunk and should be in bed. In a wild tirade, Clive admits to being *himself,* whereas his father thinks only of what he might become: "Yes, I'm drunk. You make me drunk." Half-heartedly he adds: "You and everything."

Frightened and perplexed, Stanley says good-night, starts for upstairs; then, conscious of failure, comes down again. He finds Clive, with Walter's glasses on his nose, crying terribly. Offering sympathy that is ignored, knowing something is wrong but not knowing what, Stanley sees a connection between Walter's glasses and his son's misery. Clive's wretched silence goading him beyond control, Stanley grabs Clive's wrists and demands to know what happened with Walter.

It is Clive's turn to be frightened. Going to the stairs, he slowly turns to face his father. "It was Mother!" he cries. "What?" says Stanley. "I came in and they were there," says Clive, pointing at the sofa. "He was kissing her. She was half undressed. And he was kissing her, on the mouth. On the breasts. Kissing . . ." Stanley hits him. Falling on the sofa, Clive mumbles: "Department of Just Deserts."

ACT II

On that bright, cold Sunday morning, Pamela, in notable contrast to the others, spreads her usual cheer. She tells Walter, who has good reason to be worried about Clive, that the best thing would be to get him married to someone who would pay him a lot of attention. Here no one really pays him any; they only use him whenever they are rowing. "Clive spends his whole time," says Pamela, "not being listened to."

Stanley, who is under considerable strain, refuses all offers of breakfast, and though warming briefly to his daughter, goes into the garden, minus coat or jacket, just to sit and brood.

Pamela next dashes upstairs to wake Clive, who very understandably hates getting up this morning and, even more, fears seeing his parents. When he does come downstairs, he momentarily manages to be sarcastic and cool to Louise, but under her flirtatious coaxing capitulates.

LOUISE (*fondling* CLIVE)—*Mon petit* Cossack . . . Silly boy . . . D'you think I'm so stupid that I don't know what's wrong? D'you think I can't see for myself? We're a little bit jealous, aren't we? As if you didn't always come first. You know that. Don't you? (*He nods, stiff with reluctance.*) Then it's ridiculous, isn't it, to be jealous? And of who? A poor lonely boy with no people of his own to care for him, all by himself in a foreign country. Really, Jou-Jou, you ought to be ashamed. Let's say no more about it. I want you always to be happy—remember? Very, very happy.

Pamela, loaded with picnic and riding paraphernalia for the day ahead, now creates a diversion by falling downstairs. Dashing out of his room, Walter scoops her up into his arms, something that makes her unusually indignant. When Louise, taking over, sees that Pamela has no broken bones, she listens to her daughter's complaint that what Walter did and the way he held her was "soppy." "Because he was worried about you?" Louise asks. "Oh, Mother," says Pamela, rubbing her ankle, "you don't understand anything. . . . It's just so undignified, can't you see? It shows no *respect* for you. . . ." But, a moment later, Pamela confesses that she really finds Walter fresh and beautiful. Involved as she is with her own feelings about Walter, Louise reacts with irritation. When Pamela doesn't immediately add a sweater to the other things she is taking on her ride, Louise, to her daughter's surprise, speaks very sharply to her and leaves the room. Shaking herself together, Pamela gathers up her load and gaily goes off for her outing.

When Walter, coming downstairs piano-music in hand, stops to speak pleasantly to Clive, it is clear that Clive had come to a dog-in-the-mangerish conclusion. Since this possession that everyone has valued and wished to own is not to be his, it must be discarded: Clive advises Walter to leave. Walter, he thinks, would be better off in Germany. "Why?" asks Walter. "Last night you did not want it." "Last night . . . !" cries Clive. "I want it now. I want you to go." Controlling his anger, Clive continues: "For your sake. Only for your sake, believe me. . . . You've got a crush on our family that's almost pathetic. Can't you see how lucky you are to be on your own? Just because you never had a family, you think they're the most wonderful things in the world."

WALTER—Clive . . .

CLIVE—Why have you got to depend all the time? It's so damned weak!

WALTER—You know nothing!

CLIVE—I can see.

WALTER—What can you see? My parents? My father—can you see him, in his Nazi uniform?

CLIVE—But you told me your parents were dead.

WALTER—Yes, I know. They are alive. In Muhlbach. Alive. There was no uncle.

CLIVE—Your father was a Nazi?

WALTER—Oh, yes. He was a great man in the town. Everybody was afraid of him, so was I. . . . When the war broke out, he went off to fight and we did not see him for almost six years. When he came back, he was still a Nazi. Everybody else was saying, "We never liked them. We never supported them." But not him! "I've supported them," he said. "Hitler was the greatest man our country has seen since Bismarck. Even now we are defeated, we are the greatest country in Europe. And one day we will win, because we have to win." Every night he used to make me recite the old slogans against Jews and Catholics and the Liberals. When I forgot, he would hit me—so many mistakes, so many hits.

CLIVE—But your mother?

WALTER—My mother . . . she worshipped him. Even after we found out.

CLIVE—What?

WALTER—That during the war . . . he worked at Auschwitz concentration camp. . . . He was one of their most efficient officers. Once he told me how many . . . (*He stops in distress. His voice is dead with loathing.*) I could have killed him. I could have killed him till he was dead. And she worshipped him—my mother. She used to smile at him, stare at him—as though he owned her. And when he used to hit me, she would just—just look away as though what he was doing was difficult, yes—but unavoidable, like training a puppy. That was my Mother.

In spite of Walter's horrible story, Clive still maintains that he should leave. "For my sake," says Clive, "I want it." Hearing

Louise call Walter's name, Clive almost viciously orders him to answer; then turning on his heel, he leaves the house.

All ready for a cozy, intimate chat, Louise is of no mind to listen to Walter's worries about Clive. Pooh-poohing them, she says airily: "It's just a tiny case of old-fashioned jealousy, that's all."

Deliberately recreating the mood of the previous evening, she says to Walter: "You know, last night held the most beautiful moments I've known for many years. I felt—well, that you and I could have a really warm friendship. Even with the difference . . . I mean in . . . in our ages." "Between friends," answers Walter, "there are no ages, I think." Louise leads him tenderly on.

WALTER—Some things grow more when they are not talked about.

LOUISE—Try anyway. I want you to.

WALTER (*looking away from her*)—It is only that you have made me wonder—

LOUISE (*prompting eagerly*)—Tell me.

WALTER (*lowering his voice still more as he walks toward* LOUISE) —Mrs. Harrington, forgive me for asking this, but do you think it's possible for someone to find a new mother? (LOUISE *sits very still. She stares at him.*) Have I offended you?

LOUISE (*smiles without joy*)—Of course not. I am . . . very touched.

WALTER (*kneeling*)—I'm so glad. That is why I feel I can talk to you about Clive, for example. I am most worried for him. He is not happy now. And I do not think it is jealousy. It is something else—more deep in him—trying to explode. Like the beginning of an earthquake or so.

LOUISE (*with increasing coolness, and rising*)—Really, my dear, don't you think you're being a little overdramatic?

WALTER—No. I mean exactly this. You see . . . that boy . . . It is very difficult for me to explain.

LOUISE (*wryly*)—I appreciate your attempt. . . . But really, I'm sure I know my children a little better than you.

WALTER—Of course. But in this case—with Clive—I feel something which frightens me—I don't know why—

LOUISE (*her temper breaking*)—Oh, for heaven's sake! (WALTER *recoils.*) I mean . . . after all, as you admit yourself, you *are* only a newcomer to the family, remember. (*Sweetly.*) Now why don't you go and play me some of your nice music? (WALTER *looks confused, and lowers his eyes before her strained smile. He exits into the kitchen.* LOUISE *starts to pick up dishes and silverware, but puts them down with a big crash.*)

In the schoolroom that night after supper, Pamela suddenly goes off on a tangent from French verbs: "Oh, phooey . . . You know this is the perfect way to end today. It's been a stinker, hasn't it?" She ticks off the day's peculiarities: Clive's not appearing even for meals, her mother's strange irritability, and her father's surprising quiet.

Downstairs, Louise and Stanley—who has been looking for Clive in every village pub—clash openly. "Your son," says Stanley, "is turning into a drunkard." "The way you've been behaving lately's enough to make anyone drink," retorts Louise. "No one would think he's your son, you treat him so abominably." Stanley finds that her treatment of Clive has turned him into a sniveling little neurotic and mama's boy. As Louise recovers from this shaft, Stanley demands that she listen: all those times he wanted to teach Clive golf or swimming, Louise, maintaining that he was too delicate or had reading to do, interfered. Stanley now gives her full rights to Clive; he no longer considers him *his* son. She has seen to that.

Using the one way she knows for bringing Stanley to heel, Louise exclaims that this limited life with him is more than she can bear. Asked bluntly if she wants a divorce, she lets Stanley answer his own question. Knowing that it's too late for him to start over again, Stanley does not want a divorce that might also harm Pam. Louise, taking umbrage, asks why he didn't mention Clive. Stanley points out that Clive is no longer a child.

Hoping for a fresh start, Stanley suggests that the two of them go away alone together to Monte Carlo. "You know," says Louise, "I can't stand the place."

Pamela, coming down for her good-night, kisses Stanley and, going away, leaves in her wake a somewhat softened atmosphere. "Well," says Stanley, "it's worth a try, isn't it, Louise?" Louise agrees, but, profiting by the moment, asks Stanley to do her a favor. Since Pamela has developed a crush on Walter, she thinks it wise to get rid of him. "In the most tactful way, of course," she says, "actually the sooner the better."

As Clive barges in drunkenly, Louise sends Stanley upstairs to do her bidding; but, unable to cope with Clive's insolence, she retreats to the kitchen. Bothered by the brightness of the room, Clive turns out the lights, sinks into an armchair, and rests wearily in the dark.

Stanley, in the schoolroom, is not having an easy time. Worried about Clive and his drinking, worried about his own relations with Clive, Stanley never gets to the point of his visit. He asks Walter what he thinks, then violently refuses to listen. Deeply hurt by his son and his wife, Stanley tries to probe the failure of his family life. Walter listens uneasily, answers when spoken to, and as soon as possible escapes.

Coming on Clive sitting despairingly in the dark, Walter determines to help him. Assuring Clive that there is nothing basically wrong with him, that his parents really love him and want to do everything for him, Walter emphasizes that he is not speaking in pity. Nor should Clive pity himself. But since he is like a butterfly impaled on a pin, he should, Walter thinks, go away.

WALTER—You must get off the pin. At the end of term in Cambridge, don't come back here. Go anywhere else you like. Join your friend singing. Go into a factory. The important thing is this—the moment you get out of here, people will start telling you who you are. Clive, what is it you want from life? I could tell you what I want. To live in England. To be happy teaching. One day to marry. To have children, and many English friends. . . . And what about you, Clive?

CLIVE—I think I want . . . to achieve something that only I could do. I want to fall in love with just one person. To know what it is to bless and be blessed. And to serve a great cause with devotion. I want to be *involved*.

WALTER—Then break the glass! Get out of the coffin. Trust everything, not because it's wise, but because not to trust will kill you. Trust me, for instance. I'll see you often. But you must go away from here. Now please, say yes—you will go.

CLIVE—Yes. I'll go.

Overhearing this conversation proves the last straw for Stanley. When Clive goes up to bed, Stanley's rage boils over. Blaming Walter for his son's effeminacy, he suddenly finds himself altogether willing to do Louise's dirty work. Admittedly not believing her reasons for Walter's dismissal, he brings forth a reason of his own that he knows is no truer. "Could it be because you've been trying to make love to my wife?" says Stanley. "You filthy German bastard." Walter reacts sharply, but the blows rain fast. Citing Walter's "pal" as his witness, Stanley says Clive saw Walter with Louise. Wincing as though he had been slapped, Walter tries from the depth of his humiliation to protest. Stanley administers the coup de grâce: "Do you know what we do with people like you in England? Chuck 'em out. I'm going to fix it so you never get your naturalization papers. I'm going to write to the immigration people. I'll write tonight. I'll say—let's see—'Much as I dislike complaining about people behind their backs, I feel it is my duty in this case to warn you about this young German's standard of morality. Whilst under my roof, he tried to force his attentions on my young daughter, who is only fifteen.' Try and get your papers after that. They'll send you back to the place where you belong."

Entering from the kitchen, Louise cries out at the sight of Walter's pain. She berates Stanley for the way he handled the situation. "Was he very brutal, *mon cher?*" she sympathizes. Walter hysterically throws himself at her feet and clings to her. Louise takes his hands away and says how disappointed she is in his behavior. Since her children have always come first with her, and since Walter has been a disturbing influence over them both, he must leave. Then coolly discussing financial arrangements, she signifies that the matter is closed. "Oh, Hibou, don't look so stricken," she says; "it makes it so much more difficult for everybody."

As Walter leaves the room and goes upstairs, Clive, passing him, wonders what is wrong and asks his parents. "If you really want to know," says Stanley, "I told him what you said last night about him and your mother." When Louise insists on knowing what Clive had said, Stanley brushes it aside with the simple statement that he didn't believe it anyway. "Then why did you pretend to Walter just now as if you did?" cries Clive. Stanley merely turns on his heel and goes upstairs.

Accusations start to fly. When Clive feels sorry for Stanley at his mother's hands, and at his own, Louise finds the conversation obscene. She says that his father is upset only because of something she asked him to do. When Clive finds out that this was to dismiss Walter, he is very upset. He protests that Walter can't be sent away. But as music can be heard from Walter's room, Clive now asks coldly: "What was it? Jealousy? Shame, when you saw the innocent together? Or just the sheer vulgarity of competing with one's own daughter?" Her anger turning to sobs, Louise wins Clive's embraces but not his old subservience. For a moment she endures his embrace, then with a gesture of hysteria, shakes him off and turns on him.

LOUISE (*her face terrible*)—D'you think you're the only one can ask terrible questions? Supposing I ask a few. Supposing I ask them! You ought to be glad Walter's going, but you're not. Why not? Why aren't you glad? You want him to stay, don't you? You want him to stay very much. Why?

CLIVE (*in panic*)—Mama!

LOUISE (*harsh, pitiless*)—Why? You said filthy things to your father about me. Filth and lies. Why? Can you think of an an-

swer? . . . Why, Clive? Why about me and Walter? Why?
Why? Why? (*The record in* WALTER'S *room has stuck.*)
CLIVE—Stop it! You're killing . . .

Both at the same moment realize with alarm that something is
wrong in Walter's room. No hand has moved the needle. Dashing
for the stairs, Louise tries Walter's door but can't open it. As she
shouts for Stanley, she smells gas. Stanley crashes in the door,
drags Walter out, and orders Louise to get the doctor. "Oh, God,
let him live," begs Stanley, "let him live!" Downstairs Louise tele-
phones to the doctor as Clive opens the windows in Walter's room.
When Walter begins murmuring in German, Stanley fervently thanks
God. "He's not going to die?" says Clive. "No . . . no . . . he's
coming around," his father assures him.

Aroused by all this excitement, Pamela sleepily puts on her robe
and opens the schoolroom door. Clive rushes to stop her; closing
the door behind them and assuring her that nothing is the matter,
he takes Pamela to her bedroom. "Nothing . . . it's all right,"
says Clive. "Walter fell down and hurt himself. Like you did.
Now go back to bed. Go on." As Pamela retires, Clive crosses to
the hall. "The courage . . . for all of us," he breathes. "Oh, God
—give it!"

THE ANDERSONVILLE TRIAL

A Play in Two Acts

By Saul Levitt

[Saul Levitt *was born in Hartford, Connecticut, and came to New York at the age of three. He is a graduate of New York's City College. "The Sun Is Silent" was his first novel, and his short stories have appeared in "Cosmopolitan," "American Mercury," and "Harper's." He has written considerably for television and for documentary films.*]

IN the sweltering heat of summertime Washington—the year is 1865—a military court has convened to try Henry Wirz, who was in charge of the Confederate prison at Andersonville, Georgia.

Eight generals enter the sparsely furnished courtroom as all present stand at attention. General Lew Wallace, the presiding judge, calls the court to order and inquires of the clerk if all witnesses have reported, if all concerned with these proceedings have signed the oath of allegiance to the government of the United States. He then comments on the absence of the defendant.

Approaching the judges' table, Captain Williams reports an unsuccessful suicide attempt that morning of his prisoner. Having tried to slash his wrists, Wirz is now in the care of the prison doctor, Dr. Ford. "The incident should not have occurred," says General Wallace coldly. "You are charged with custody of the prisoner. You will take the necessary steps so it will not occur again. You say the prisoner is in condition to appear shortly?" "Within a few minutes," Williams answers, and, dismissed, he leaves the room.

Except for the press and a few members of the public seated at one side of the room, the sole civilians are Otis Baker, counsel for the defense, and his assistant. Though preferring that his client could hear the charges against him, Baker submits to the court's ruling that he plead the indictment in absence of Wirz.

Judge Advocate Chipman, a battle veteran of thirty-two, is an angry, aggressive, independent man who endures the yoke of discipline with some difficulty. With his uniformed aide at his side, Chipman presents the government's case:

Charge—Criminal conspiracy to destroy the lives of soldiers of the United States in violation of the laws and customs of war.

Specification—That Henry Wirz who was in charge of the Confederate prison at Andersonville, Georgia, did keep in barbarously close confinement Federal soldiers, up to the number of 40,000, without adequate shelter against the burning heat of summer or the cold of winter and—

Specification—That said Henry Wirz in carrying out this conspiracy did not provide the prisoners of war with sufficient food, clothing, or medical care, causing them to languish and die to the number of more than 14,000.

Specification—That he established a line known as the "deadline" and that he instructed the prison guards stationed on the walls of the prison stockade to fire upon and kill any prisoner who might pass beyond that deadline!

Specification—That he used bloodhounds to hunt down, seize, and mangle escaping prisoners of war, through these various causes bringing about the deaths of about fifty Federal soldiers, their names unknown.

Specification—That through direct order and/or by his own hand he brought about the murder of thirteen prisoners, their names unknown.

Asked how he pleads for the prisoner, Baker, well aware that his objections will be overruled, makes them with dispatch: this military court, now that the war is over, is without proper jurisdiction; and he would like a motion to postpone because potential witnesses are afraid to testify.

CHIPMAN (*with open sarcasm*)—If Mr. Baker's witnesses can in good conscience take the oath of loyalty to the government of the United States, they have nothing to fear.

BAKER—The court is aware of the temper of the times. It is only four short months since Mr. Lincoln was assassinated.

WALLACE (*a clap of thunder*)—We will leave that name out of this trial!

BAKER (*rises*)—Nevertheless, Mr. Lincoln's presence is in this room—his murder is felt in this room—and it swells the charge of murder against the defendant to gigantic size—

CHIPMAN—For which an inhuman cause is responsible. Surely

counsel will not turn Mr. Lincoln's tragic death to advantage here.

BAKER—It is my concern, sir, that the present indictment leaves out Captain Wirz's military superiors, making him the single victim of the national mood of vengeance against the South—

WALLACE (*using gavel*)—That will be all, Mr. Baker. Motion denied. If you have no further motions—

BAKER—I do. As to specifications alleging crime of murder and abetting murder against certain persons, move to strike them since no persons are named.

CHIPMAN (*rising to left of* GENERALS)—Counsel cannot with his motions dispose of the horror of 14,000 unknown dead dumped into unmarked graves at Andersonville. Better records were kept of bales of cotton. Move to deny.

BAKER—Will the judge advocate tell us where accurate prison records were kept during the War? (CHIPMAN *reacts with annoyance*.) The judge advocate owes me common courtesy here. A person accused of crimes punishable by death is entitled to a proper defense.

CHIPMAN—We know what is defended here. Counsel's political motives are well understood.

WALLACE (*banging gavel*)—The exchange will stop.

BAKER—I only remind the judge advocate that he is in a court of law, and no longer on the battlefield. The horror of war is universal. The North had its Andersonvilles.

WALLACE—The government of the United States is not on trial here, Mr. Baker.

BAKER—That remains to be seen.

The court door opens; Captain Williams indicates to the lieutenant in charge that the prisoner is ready to appear. "Prisoner to the court!" cries the lieutenant, as Henry Wirz enters—followed by Dr. Ford with his medical bag—and goes towards his counsel. Baker reminds Chipman of his request that Wirz be allowed to recline on the sofa provided by previous arrangement. Chipman's slurring reference to Wirz's "so-called war wound" causes Wirz to exclaim angrily, in a heavy German accent, that he will not be slandered; he was honorably wounded as a soldier in the line. He wishes to make a statement.

Cutting through these remarks, General Wallace gives Wirz permission to use the sofa, and promises to let him make his statement later. Not heeding the general, Wirz cries out that it was not guilt of conscience that drove him to try to take his life this morning. "If that is all you have to say . . ." says Wallace. "Only a few words more, sir," Wirz rushes on. "I calmly sized up the situation, as a soldier. As I see it I have simply no chance whatsoever, and I decided not to give the government the satisfaction—" "That will be all, Mr. Wirz." "One other matter, sir," adds Wirz. "That will be all!" says Wallace. But Wirz manages to get in a plea on a personal matter. He does not know whether his letters to his family are getting through, and since his children read about him in the newspapers as the Butcher of Andersonville, this is all-important to him. He demands the right to give his side of the case to his children. After a whispered conversation with the generals, Wallace promises that in the future Wirz's letters will go by military packet. Wirz is still not to be silenced. In fawning tones edged with irony, he thanks the court for all its consideration, both in medical care and in spiritual comfort. Suddenly venomous, he adds: "All that is wanted of me is my life. I am not fooled!"

Leading Wirz to the sofa, Baker apologizes to the court for his client's outburst, and runs into Chipman's anger. Baker reminds the judge advocate that normal courtroom behavior calls for at least the assumption that one's opponent is acting in good faith. Refusing to assume this, since Baker stands with those secretly opposed to this government, Chipman asks who pays him for defending Wirz. "Not the government," anwers Baker. And since Chipman has made insinuations about his loyalty, Baker further enlightens him: "I am paid by a committee formed to defend Captain Wirz. I am not involved in this case in the way the judge advocate would wish. I take my cases where I find them, subject to one condition: I must feel there's a shade—the smallest shade of doubt—as to a man's guilt. Regarding my politics in my home city of Baltimore, a city of divided loyalties, some held that I was an enemy to the Confederate side because I felt that slavery was not worth dying for since it was an unworkable institution that was doomed to extinction anyway. And there were the others who suspected me because I was lukewarm on the glorious future that would follow a Northern victory. The colonel might make his own position clearer." Chipman is willing: "I was brought up to believe that slavery was evil. From my home town of Washington, Iowa, I answered Mr. Lincoln's second call for volunteers. It was natural for me to go to war against a cause which wished to perpetuate human bondage. I am here in the service of the Union to secure justice for men barbarously murdered by that Southern cause. I am personally involved here, Mr. Baker, if you are not." "As a lawyer," asks Baker, "or as a clerk under orders to process Wirz through to the hangman?"

As Chipman's aide restrains him, there is a long silence. General Wallace then says: "I take it you gentlemen are through. Under military law we could of course dispense with defense counsel; the defendant would not have to be present. And this case could be heard in a small room. But the government has seen fit to set it here in the Court of Claims and before an audience. Conceding the temper of the times and the emotions of all parties, we intend to hold this trial within bounds. I do not advise further testing the power of the court to maintain order. . . ." Then, getting down to the business of the court, Wallace asks Baker to plead the charge. "The prisoner enters a plea of not guilty to the charge and all specifications," answers Baker.

On the general charge of criminal conspiracy, Chipman summons his witness, Mr. D. I. Chandler. Wirz, in a loud aside, asks Baker if he has all necessary documents and the evidence that he had released young Northern prisoners to pick blackberries? Assured that all this is at hand, Wirz says: "But it will do no good. I must die. Yes . . . I must die. The real crime I have committed, Baker—you understand what it is of course—that I chose the losing side."

Before interrogating the witness, Chipman states the rule of evidence applying in cases of criminal conspiracy: evidence of a common design to which the defendant willingly lent himself.

Chandler is obviously a man of breeding. As a lieutenant colonel in the Army of the Confederacy, he had been assigned to "the war office on military prisons maintained by the Confederacy"; and because of civilian complaints forwarded to Richmond, he had gone, in the course of official duty, to Andersonville, Sumter County, Georgia, and had remained there for two weeks.

There is a large schematic map of the Andersonville stockade mounted on a stand near the judges' table. Pointer in hand, Chandler, at Chipman's request, explains that the whole camp covered some sixteen acres which were originally part of a pine wood. Completely cleared of trees, these sixteen acres had no shade or shelter of any kind in a country whose temperature ranged from over 100 degrees in summer to near freezing in the rainy winter. The stockade was topped by a platform for the sentries, and within its walls and parallel to them, at approximately a distance of twenty-five feet, ran the "deadline" beyond which prisoners could not go without being shot. Bordered on both sides by a swamp, a stream which hardly could have been more than a yard wide ran through the camp. The only buildings were a cookhouse and a "Dead House" outside the stockade.

When he was at Andersonville, Chandler found it so overcrowded that each man had about the equivalent of a six-foot cell. "There was an insufficiency," he testifies, "of water, shelter, and food." Under further examination by Chipman, it turns out that the stream supplied all the water available to 40,000 men for drinking and washing, while being the sole repository of cookhouse waste and human excretion.

Living on the bare ground summer and winter, the men had only the clothes they arrived with, and when these were gone, no others. Their food consisted of unbolted meal that cut their insides like a knife, plus now and then some maggot-ridden meat. Under further questioning, Chandler admits that the men had in some cases been driven in desperation to cannibalism. "And if I were now to sum up Andersonville as a pit," says Chipman, "an animal pit in which men wallowed—the sick, the dying, the insane wallowing among the dead—would I exaggerate the picture of the place?" "No," answers Chandler.

Chipman submits in evidence the report that Chandler had drawn up recommending that all prisoners be transferred to other prisons without delay, and that Andersonville be at once shut down.

CHIPMAN—And that report was ignored, was it not?—Ignored, disregarded, the condition allowed to continue—?

CHANDLER—I did not agree to come here to indict the leaders of the cause for which I fought, as plotting the murder of defenseless men.

CHIPMAN—The report revealing how Winder and Wirz were operating that camp was ignored—

CHANDLER—I have told you I could not endure Andersonville. You people act as though you were better human beings than we were.

CHIPMAN—No, but our cause was. Your report was ignored!

CHANDLER—Due to the crisis—the bitterness—the disorder—with General Sherman marching through Georgia burning his way—

CHIPMAN—It was ignored—

CHANDLER—As your officer would have ignored it, sir, if it had been General Lee marching through Pennsylvania into New York—

Ordered to answer Chipman's questions, Chandler says that General Winder had such hard, bitter feelings toward the prisoners that he maintained if half the prisoners died, there would be twice as much room for the rest. Chipman now bears down hard on Wirz's rules governing the prisoners' attempts to escape: he says these were conforming to Winder's inhuman attitude toward those men. Baker interrupts: "I must ask the judge advocate what he means by that suggestive, ambiguous phrase, *conforming to.*" Chipman withdraws this phrase, but makes the witness concede that the aforementioned rules violated the customs of war and were, besides, cruel and in-

human. "Was Wirz the personal choice of Winder for superintendent of that camp?" he asks. "Yes," says Chandler.

Under cross-examination Baker brings out, and submits as evidence for the defense, Chandler's second report to the war office.
In this report he recommended the dismissal of General Winder, but
not of Wirz. He had observed nothing in Wirz's conduct to justify
his dismissal. "Mr. Chandler," Chipman says after Baker is through
with the witness, "very often, as you know, commanders are fore-
warned of inspection and dress up their commands in advance.
Couldn't that have occurred in your case?" "Possibly," says Chandler. "And isn't it possible," Chipman continues, "that they would
fear the consequences of complaints against Wirz? Those men did
not know you and Wirz would still be in command after you were
gone. And under those circumstances, isn't it very possible that they
would not answer you truthfully?"

CHANDLER—Perhaps. I did the best I could with that Andersonville situation—

CHIPMAN—Did Wirz do the best he could? In spite of Winder's
orders, couldn't he have chosen to . . . There are ways—

BAKER—Ways of doing what? Evading the orders of his superior?
What is the judge advocate suggesting?

CHIPMAN—Withdrawn. That will be all, thank you, Mr. Chandler.

The next witness to take the stand is Dr. John C. Bates, assigned
by the Confederate Surgeon General as medical officer to Andersonville—an assignment he patently didn't care for. His duties consisted of writing prescriptions for unavailable drugs, amputating
gangrenous limbs, and certifying the large number of dead each
morning.

CHIPMAN—Did you in the course of your stay there make any
estimate of the rate of death at that place?

BATES—I did; yes, sir. I had always kept a ledger book covering
the ailments and treatment of my patients in civil life—farmers—
their families—their horses too. . . . And I decided to keep some
sort of a record in that camp . . . because I was deeply shocked by
that place when I came there.

CHIPMAN—Please tell the court what your estimate of the death
rate was.

BATES—In the spring months it averaged fifty, sixty, seventy men
a day . . . in spells of extreme heat during the summer reaching a
hundred men a day. More in May than in April, more in June than

in May, and in July, August, September 3,000 men a month were dying.

CHIPMAN—What were the principal causes for that high rate of death?

BATES—The lack of sanitary facilities—the lack of exercise—the anemia of the men from lack of food rendering them subject to fatal illness from the slightest abrasion or infection—the lack of medical supplies.

CHIPMAN—And, Dr. Bates, in your professional opinion, how many of the thousands who died there would have lived if conditions had at least been sanitary?

BATES—I would estimate—seventy-five to eighty per cent.

When Dr. Bates proposed certain measures to improve conditions, he had met with complete lack of co-operation. Wirz said that Bates had no understanding of the difficulties in running a huge camp. "He was downright incoherent," reports Bates, "damned me for a Yankee sympathizer—" Chipman has only one more question for this witness: "When you spoke to Mr. Wirz and he complained to you that his job was difficult . . . did you understand him to mean his job was difficult administratively or difficult humanly?" "Mr. Wirz dwelt on *his* difficulties," replies Bates, "not the men's."

Cross-examining Bates, Baker refers to the doctor's professionally objective point of view. He wins concessions that it was the Commissary General in Richmond who decided the allotment of food for each prisoner, and that it was the Surgeon General who allotted the amount and type of medical supplies. Focusing on Bates' impression that Wirz was callous toward the condition of the prisoners, Baker gently demonstrates that Bates' first sense of shock at the condition of the camp gradually lessened, so that by September Bates had almost grown accustomed to the idea of 3,000 deaths a month. "Of course you had," says Baker. "Any human being to save his sanity would have had to do that. So Captain Wirz's 'callousness' in that place wasn't so strange after all, was it?"

CHIPMAN—Dr. Bates, do you remember one single instance, in conversing with Wirz, when he expressed any criticism of the orders or disposition of his superior?

BAKER—Objection. I find that a strange question to be asked by a counsel for the War Department, himself a soldier. Is it being held against Captain Wirz that he did not make a public judgment of the motives of his military superior?

WALLACE—The court must agree Wirz was not bound to comment on the orders of his military superior.

CHIPMAN—If the court please, we are concerned here with the frame of mind of a man carrying out his superior's inhuman design. We are bound to explore his thinking when he obeyed those orders—

BAKER—His thinking when he obeyed those orders? And if he did not like those orders what was he supposed to do? Disobey them? If conscience is the measure by which soldiers obey or disobey orders, one can hardly condemn the Army officers who went over to the Confederacy, since they did so on the ground of conscience. (*The gavel comes down.*) On that ground Robert E. Lee deserves a monument—

WALLACE (*obviously perturbed*)—That will be all, Mr. Baker. (*To* CHIPMAN.) I am certain it was not in the mind of the judge advocate to raise the issue of disobedience to a superior officer—

CHIPMAN—Under certain circumstances that issue may require consideration—

WALLACE (*with great deliberation; cueing, ordering, and warning* CHIPMAN *at the same time*)—The court is not, of course, suggesting the line of inquiry the judge advocate is to take here. But the court will say that it is disposed to draw its own inference as to a criminal design from evidence of the defendant's words and acts—and not from an examination of moral factors which can drop us into a bottomless pool of philosophic debate. . . . I am certain the judge advocate will agree and that he will withdraw that question as to whether or not Wirz criticized his superior officer.

CHIPMAN (*flatly*)—The question is withdrawn.

Chipman calls as next witness the owner of a plantation that bordered on the Andersonville camp. Mr. Spencer, the owner, says that once vegetables and grain had supplanted the cotton crop during these war years, there was not only an overabundance but Wirz had been offered supplies and had rejected them. "The proof is," says Spencer, "that without it being solicited, there were people in the vicinity who came forward and made an effort to get food into that camp. In one case a group of women in Americus, including my wife, made that attempt. . . . They had those wagons driven up to the gate of the stockade. Mr. Wirz was at the gate when those ladies arrived. He would not permit the food to be brought in—he cursed those women. He told them they were giving aid and comfort to the enemy—that Yankee soldiers were unlawfully invading—looting the South—that those women were traitors—and worse. He used the violentest and profanest language I have ever heard in a man's mouth. He said if he had his way he would have a certain kind of a house built for those women and he would put them all in there where the Confederate soldiers would teach them loyalty in a hurry and teach it to them in a way they wouldn't forget—" Chipman interrupts to inquire whether, had Mr. Wirz solicited food, Spencer thinks large amounts of it would have been provided. "I am certain," says Spencer, "that the people of Georgia would have responded."

Chipman asks whether Spencer knew the defendant, which he did, and whether he was acquainted with General Winder, which he was. "When he came there once," says Spencer, "Winder said that the Yankees had come South to take possession of the land and that he was endeavoring to satisfy them by giving them each a small plot—pointing to the gravesite." "And did you ever hear Wirz speak along the same lines?" asks Chipman. "I can tell you," says Spencer, "that he boasted he was killing more Yankees at Andersonville than Lee was at Richmond." "You heard those remarks?" Chipman asks. "Yes," replies Spencer; "to wipe out those men. That was the scheme."

Wirz makes a violent outburst against this testimony. As Wallace asks his counsel to restrain him, Wirz cries: "Who will understand? An ordinary man like me—assigned—" Wallace shouts: "Guards!" As the guards and Dr. Ford move toward Wirz, he cries: "The drummer boys I saved—and now—I am surrounded!" When the guards grab his arms, he shrieks in pain and faints.

Baker calls for a postponement. Asked about Wirz's condition by the court, Dr. Ford surmises that it is a fainting spell from which Wirz will recover and that, though he lacks strength and suffers from strain, he will be well enough to continue.

Wallace overrides Baker's plea. "It's no use, Mr. Baker—" he says. Baker cites the open bias of the witness and the bitterness of the times. "We are not empowered to move this trial into the next century. This trial will continue," answers Wallace. "You will make clear to the defendant that should there be another demonstration here he will be tried *in absentia*." "*In absentia*," murmurs Wirz, "Latin for absence. I understand all languages, but the language of this trial—" "The court," interrupts Baker, "has suffered sufficient provocation to send Captain Wirz from this courtroom, but I suggest it does not." Not caring for suggestions from the counsel for the defense, Wallace orders Baker either to cross-examine or step down.

Cross-examining Spencer, Baker has no trouble bringing out that it was actually Winder who ordered the offerings of food not to be brought into camp. He asks why Spencer neglected to mention this fact. "Wirz wouldn't have tried in any case," answers Spencer; "I know that man." "Answer the question," demands Baker. "Why didn't you say so?" "I wasn't asked," says Spencer.

Baker moves to dismiss Spencer's testimony as irrelevant since all it proves is that Captain Wirz carried out a direct order.

CHIPMAN—Move to deny!

BAKER—Will the judge advocate offer a ground for denial? Is he saying that Captain Wirz should have defied that direct order of General Winder's?

CHIPMAN—Will you deny that was an inhuman order?

BAKER—Which he should have disobeyed?

WALLACE—Defense motion is denied.

BAKER—Of course denied. It is now plain enough why Captain Wirz is tried here on a conspiracy charge. On that charge the accused may be convicted without any direct evidence against him.

WALLACE (*rising*)—Mr. Baker!

BAKER—If there is a conspiracy, it is one directed against Captain Wirz. I say now that the motives which bring Wirz to trial here dishonor the government of the United States; and that—contradicting its own military code—the Army will have this man though he was only doing his proper duty.

WALLACE—Are you through, Mr. Baker?

BAKER—I am through!

WALLACE—You have been in contempt since the beginning of that outburst. The court will consider a formal charge against you. You are dismissed from this proceeding forthwith, and will immediately leave this room.

Starting for the door, Baker is all for leaving Wirz without counsel so that this trial can be seen for what it is. Chipman, however, pleads with the court that Baker be allowed to purge himself of contempt, so that no one can say that the defendant was denied counsel of his choice.

Wallace allows Baker to purge himself of contempt by recanting his remarks. "I do so recant," says Baker, "and apologize and give my oath that I will not hereafter impugn the fairness of the court or the motives of the government and Army of the United States."

The trial continues, and Chipman calls his next witness.

SCENE II

Some time later, Chipman has on the stand James Davidson, one of the many former Andersonville prisoners that he has summoned to testify. Interrupting the testimony to ask Chipman if he expects to wind up his case today, Wallace says that, while not wishing to exclude anything pertinent, the court finds it unnecessary to hear

further corroborating facts "alleged" many times over. Assuring the
court that he will conclude this afternoon, Chipman questions the
emaciated witness about a time when he and another escaped prisoner were tracked down by dogs, and his fellow prisoner was destroyed by them.

Obviously under a strain, obviously disliking even to talk about
Andersonville, Davidson says: "Captain Wirz rode up a minute after
that pack of dogs had treed us, yelling 'Get those Yankee bastards'—
beggin' your pardon." "And he was present while those dogs were
tearing your companion?" asks Chipman. "While they were tearing
him, yes, sir," replies Davidson.

Telling of a second incident, Davidson reports that he was an eye-
witness when a man torn by dogs was brought into the stockade.
Again, he says, Wirz was present. "Like I said," repeats Davidson,
"he rode in and this man fell down. Captain Wirz rode around him,
looking down at him, reining in his horse which was skittering and
rearing—that was a horse with a temper—then rode back through
the gate."

In his cross-examination, Baker points out that while Davidson's
companion was allegedly torn by the dogs, this witness was untouched: "Now since you admit those ferocious dogs didn't attack
you, shall I understand you were completely unhurt when you were
brought back to the camp?"

DAVIDSON (*slowly*)—No, sir.

BAKER—You were bruised some, weren't you?

DAVIDSON—Some.

BAKER—Bloodied a bit, too?

DAVIDSON—Some. From all that running and stumbling against
rocks—

BAKER—And from bramble bushes and whipping branches and
dead cypress limbs, some of them as pointed as knives?

DAVIDSON—Yes, sir.

Showing that the second man alleged to have been torn by dogs
might have suffered a different sort of injuries, Baker casts doubt
on this testimony, too.

Watching his witness fall apart, Chipman looses his anger on the
man. Finally Wallace interferes: "Colonel Chipman! I think the
witness is through. Are you now ill, Mr. Davidson?" Stepping
down, Davidson says: "Yes, sir. I got pains—" "You have told
us about that incident as well as you can now recall it, is that correct?" continues Wallace. "Yes, sir," says Davidson. "How old

are you, Mr. Davidson?" asks Wallace. "Nineteen, sir," answers the ravaged figure.

The court wishes that the witness may recover good health and forget what he has endured in war and prison. Chipman adds his abject apology as well. Wallace now addresses himself very deliberately to the judge advocate: "The weather continues hot and we have been at this trial longer than anticipated. I will ascribe tempers to the heat. Call your next witness, Colonel." But then Wallace promptly refuses to allow Chipman's next witness to testify since it means going once more over well-trodden ground.

After a brief confab with his aide, which leads to passing up a witness because "Baker will roast him and toss him back well done," Chipman rejects his aide's advice to call Gray, a witness that Baker won't roast. Instead he calls a punch-drunk ex-prisoner on the specification that Wirz caused the death of prisoners by direct order. Baker makes a fool of this witness, too, and, showing that his testimony may very well be highly embroidered, he asks the court to dismiss all counts under this specification. The "deadline" established by Wirz, states Baker, was a proper military line required for the order and safety of the camp. Rising at once, Chipman argues that this was no purely military line: to get a decent drink of water, men risked their lives by slipping over this deadline. When they succeeded, the guards opened fire.

CHIPMAN—Killing and wounding for a drink of water! And Wirz knew that and he let those men get shot down, didn't he?— And counsel calls that a purely military line. Move to deny defense motion as to that "deadline" in that it was clearly part of the cold, inhuman design of that camp.

BAKER (*rising*)—Inhuman?

CHIPMAN—Yes.

BAKER—Immoral?

CHIPMAN—Yes.

WIRZ—Let me answer!

BAKER (*to* WIRZ)—One moment! Will the judge advocate openly and finally state once and for all his belief that Captain Wirz's duty was to make a moral not a military choice?

CHIPMAN—The *human* choice.

WALLACE—This arguing over an irrelevant issue becomes intolerable—parties are warned. Defense motion denied. The judge advocate will now state the connection between the moral issue and the charge of conspiracy.

CHIPMAN (*sits*)—The judge advocate will not attempt to make that connection.

As the court rules an adjournment until tomorrow, at which time the defense will take over, Chipman breaks in to say that he may want to call further witnesses. "If so," says Wallace, "they will be witnesses bringing in new criminal evidence. I say *new* criminal evidence in the precise legal meaning of the term. I hope that is understood."

The court having adjourned, and the generals having departed, counsel for both sides remain in the room.

BAKER—The choices in this world are bitter, Colonel, aren't they? On the one hand to follow your decent instincts and on the other— Tell me, if you can, Colonel, how does your role in this room differ from Wirz's at Andersonville—seeing that he too did nothing more or less than carry out policy?

CHIPMAN—You compare me to him?

BAKER—You know in your heart that you condemn him only for carrying out the orders of his superior. You have as much as said so. But this court will have no part of that argument. And what then do you do but withdraw it? You obey, as Wirz obeyed.

CHIPMAN—You compare me to him?

BAKER—Oh, of course, you're governed by purer motives. After all, you are on the edge of a brilliant career. You'll walk out of this case the envy of every struggling young lawyer in the country; the successful prosecutor of the one war criminal to be hanged out of this war. Yes, your future's assured . . . if you don't jeopardize it. Shall the government's own counsel at this time preach disobedience to orders? How does it feel to be an instrument of policy, nothing more?

CHIPMAN—God damn you—

BAKER—Get as angry as you wish—that's the truth of it. Good afternoon, gentlemen. (*Exits.*)

Realizing only too well that Baker is twisting things to tempt him into arguing with the government, Chipman cries: "Where do we stand after days of those witnesses we've put on—those sick, broken survivors of that place? I haven't really proved conspiracy and I have not proved criminal acts. I ask you what kind of a case do we bring in?" If he wants a better case, says his aide, put on the redoubtable Gray. "You don't know for a fact he's lying," he says; but Chipman knows he's capable of it.

What sticks with Chipman is the moral issue. "I mean," he says, "if we feel that Wirz should have disobeyed—and if we evade the issue—if we're afraid to raise it—how are we actually any better than that creature at Andersonville?"

Wishing no fight with the government, partisan to his bones, aware of the risk he runs, Chipman still asks: "Am I more of a man than he was? Either I press this court to consider the issue of Wirz's moral responsibility to disobey—or God damn my soul, I'm no better in my mind than he was! I can't go around that." He wishes he could get Baker to put Wirz on the stand, and knows that he can't. His aide's parting advice is to put Gray on the stand to nail down this case: ". . . and you'll have your man, even if it's not in *your* way. The government has a point to make; it struggles to pull together a divided country. Isn't that a worthy, an important thing? At least as important as the purity of your soul?" "You could be right," Chipman answers wrily.

ACT II

The next morning Chipman puts on the stand his surprise witness, Sergeant James S. Gray. This regular army man proves a cool fellow as he matter-of-factly tells how he saw Wirz knock down a man, stamp on him, and shoot him. What's more, Gray provides the man's name—William Stewart; his rank—private; and his regiment —the Ninth Minnesota Infantry. Since this specific information is just what the prosecution needs, Baker at once suspects that it is all false, and Wirz, at his side, confirms his suspicions. When Gray points to Wirz as the man who had committed this murder, Wirz cries: "Look close, Sergeant—make sure! I give you the chance to take back that lie before God judges you!" Gray remains indifferent to this outburst.

Since the defense was unprepared for this witness, Baker wins a few minutes' time to confer with Wirz, who doesn't know who Gray is but knows there never was a Stewart. Under cross-examination Gray proves to be slick and unshakeable in his testimony, but there is one glaring gap: Gray can name no other witness to this murder. "However, fortunately for the prosecution," says Baker, "which until now has lacked for a clear criminal instance, it has dredged you up as the single witness to the murder of a man having at least a name." Bearing down hard, Baker continues: "Sergeant, do you believe in an afterlife and that man's sins, including the sin of lying, will there be punished?"

GRAY—I believe there is such a thing as punishment after death—
BAKER—Have you ever been arrested for a criminal offense?

GRAY—No, sir!

BAKER—I gather you like Army life, seeing that you have re-enlisted?

GRAY—I would say that.

BAKER—After all, the Army feeds you, keeps you comfortable, and, judging by your sergeant's stripes, you are considered by your superiors to be a good soldier, one who knows what he is supposed to do without it being explained to him in so many words.

GRAY—A man gets to know what is expected of him.

BAKER—And if you felt—even if you weren't told—what was expected of you, you would carry it out.

GRAY—Certainly.

BAKER—And if you felt—even if you weren't told—what the Army's real concern was in some situation and if you understood that to mean that you were supposed to lie—

WALLACE—Finish your question along that line, Mr. Baker, and you will be in contempt—

Taking another approach, Baker shows that by Gray's pre-war occupation the man is a rank, unfeeling opportunist. Yet under direct accusation that he's lying, Gray replies coldly: "I saw that happen as I have described it." When Baker is through with the sergeant, Chipman demands to know whether Gray is lying, and receives the same cool answer: "I saw that happen as I described it—sir!" When Gray steps down from the stand, the judge advocate concludes his case.

Rising, Baker says the defense is not only ready, but, since it finds but one charge (that of alleged murder) worth refuting, it will waive its entire list of witnesses and call just one man—Dr. Ford, the physician in charge at the Old Capitol jail. The court is surprised, but Wirz, feeling shortchanged, is so visibly upset that Baker has to quiet his protests.

Through Dr. Ford's testimony, Baker shows that Wirz's arms are so ulcerated and mangled from war wounds that he would be incapable of elevating his whole arm, let alone pull a trigger. On top of this, Baker brings out that Dr. Ford had consulted with the doctor who had examined Wirz at Andersonville, and learned that Wirz's condition was no better in 1864 than it is today. Dr. Ford can't see how Wirz could have knocked down and shot "William Stewart." "He could not have killed him," concludes Baker. "The defense rests. Thank you."

Showing some strain after Baker's performance, Wallace asks harshly of Chipman if he wishes to cross-examine. Chipman has no heart for that, so, thanking the witness, Wallace announces that the court will convene in two days' time to hear government and defense summations.

Glancing at Wirz, who is obviously still upset, Chipman asks a continuance until tomorrow morning; but Wallace signifies that if there is no new evidence, the court will consider matters finished. With one eye on Wirz, Chipman says quickly that he does not feel that the situation at Andersonville has been adequately explained. Wirz explodes into loud agreement. As Wallace raps for order, Chipman invites Wirz to take the stand. On his feet at once, Baker sharply declines this invitation for his client. Wallace warns Wirz to listen to counsel. Baker says loudly: "Are you out of your mind?" Wirz insists that he does not want to die without saying a word in his own behalf. *"Listen,"* demands Baker, "the evidence they've offered is tainted from start to finish. And they know it! Let them bring in their verdict of guilty. But it must then go to the President, who may pardon as he values the reputation of the government. That's your single chance." Heedless of all advice, Wirz is now determined to speak for himself so that in his children's eyes he will seem not a monster but a man.

Wirz is sworn in and takes the stand. Doing his curt best to control him, Baker shows that Wirz came to this country from Switzerland as a young man, worked sporadically and unsuccessfully in Northern cities, went South, and at the outbreak of the war enlisted in the Confederate Army. Promoted because of previous military training abroad, Wirz was wounded at the battle of Seven Pines, and shortly after was offered the job of superintendent by General Winder. Wirz never received special or secret instructions on how to run Andersonville beyond the prescribed regulations for care of prisoners of war. At first there were ample supplies for the camp, but an enormous influx of prisoners some months later was not matched with a sufficient increase in rations. Baker offers in evidence a letter to General Winder in which Wirz pointed out these facts, which Winder answered by coming to Andersonville. "He said," reports Wirz, "that we were taking care of the prisoners just as well as the enemy took care of *our* men in *their* hands. He said he had reports that our men were not well-treated, particularly at a camp at Elmira, New York, where they were dying like flies. He was in a temper and he made it clear *that* closed the subject, and as an inferior officer I felt I could not pursue the matter further. However, I did what was in my power to do there—as about those drummer boys—"

Wirz had requested additional guards so as to keep prisoners from escaping, but when they were not forthcoming, he won Winder's approval of the "deadline." "But that does not mean I didn't consider those prisoners," says Wirz, "as I started to say before about those drummer boys—" Baker allows him to tell how he had permitted sixty or seventy of these youngsters to live on parole outside the stockade to gather blackberries. Trying to channel Wirz's testimony, Baker now asks about Father Whelan, thus giving his client opportunity to say that all priests and ministers were welcome at the camp, and that Father Whelan was permitted to distribute fresh bread. Wirz next is led to explain that General Winder had graciously accepted the women's offer to bring food into the camp until their arrival coincided with bad war news. In a rage at Sheridan's progress, Winder refused the food, and Wirz as an inferior could not countermand his order.

BAKER—Did you try to get relieved?

WIRZ—I have not finished! I was saying that place was entirely on my head and I had there the responsibility to keep order and keep those men from escaping and they kept trying and it was difficult to keep order there since the men kept trying. Naturally they had the right to try and I had my duty to prevent them.

BAKER—But you did try to get relieved of that assignment, did you not?

WIRZ—Yes, sir, I tried to do that. I wrote to General Winder, asking to be assigned to another post, but he informed me he could not relieve me. And, simply—I had there to stay and so it kept on being on my head.

Baker asks that this letter be submitted for the defense.

Concluding, as he thinks, with the denial that there was no William Stewart and that Wirz killed no one, Baker is balked by Wirz's insistence on going on. "Am I not to be asked," he cries, "my conception of my duty?" Baker is reluctantly compelled to ask him. Wirz says: "That one does as he is ordered. That he keeps his feelings to himself. That he does not play the heroic game which some people who are not in his position think he could play. That he obeys. That he does not concern himself with the policies of his superiors—but obeys. That he does his assigned job and obeys. That when the order to charge is given—he obeys. That when ordered to keep prisoners—he obeys. And if in so doing he must die, then he dies!" "Your witness, Colonel," says Baker.

Leading Wirz down the garden path, Chipman makes him admit that his duty consisted equally of keeping his prisoners alive and preventing their escape; that when Wirz asked Winder to relieve him of his post, he had simultaneously tried to be promoted; and in spite of Wirz's realizing that Andersonville was indescribable hell, he

*Herbert Berghof, Albert Dekker, Ian Keith and George C. Scott in
"The Andersonville Trial"*

seems to have shown no mercy except to those frequently mentioned
drummer boys. Referring to Wirz's bringing up his own children
in a devoutly religious home, Chipman says: "And you saw nothing
strange in leaving your family and your grace at meals to go to your
job of overseeing the dying of those men?" Baker objects; Chipman withdraws this last question.

Prowling about Wirz, Chipman would know why he didn't com-
mandeer supplies from Georgia farmers? Wirz answers that it was
not authorized. Why had he not sent out prisoners to collect fire-
wood? They would have escaped. Why not enlarge the stockade?
"Size," says Wirz, "was prescribed." "Let the prisoners among
whom were carpenters, masons, and mechanics of all sorts build the
shelters which would have kept them alive?" demands Chipman.

Repeating that such a thing was not authorized, Wirz admits that it would have saved many lives. "We will say only one!" cries Chipman. "Would you say that one single human life is precious, Mr. Wirz?"

As Wirz puzzles over this odd line of questioning, Baker strongly objects, and the court—seeing no connection between it and the charge of conspiracy—questions Chipman. Chipman asks permission to explore this line at least one step further, and is granted it.

CHIPMAN—Sir, professing religion as you do, would you agree that moral considerations, the promptings of conscience are primary for all men?

WIRZ—Of course I do! I observe that ideal like most men—when I can.

CHIPMAN—When you can. Then you could not observe moral considerations at Andersonville?

WIRZ—That situation was General Winder's responsibility—not mine.

Wirz proclaims that Winder's authority embraced him in all circumstances. Advancing slowly, Chipman asks Wirz if Winder had ordered him to slaughter one of his own children would he have complied? At first refusing to answer such a question, Wirz finally says: "No." "It would be an insane order," says Chipman. "Yes. Insane. Or inhuman. Or immoral. And a man therefore in his heart does indeed make some inner judgment as to the orders he obeys."

WALLACE (using gavel)—The judge advocate will hold. The court has stated more than once, it is not disposed to consider the moral issue relating to soldierly conduct. It has indicated to the judge advocate that we are on extremely delicate ground at any time that we enter into the circumstances under which officers may disobey their military superiors. However, the judge advocate apparently feels he must enter that area. He will now advance some legal basis for that line of questioning or withdraw it.

CHIPMAN—If it please the court—we will endeavor to connect this line—

WALLACE—The judge advocate must in advance furnish a legal basis—

CHIPMAN—The judge advocate respectfully urges—

WALLACE (gavel)—The court must hear some basis for permitting this line of inquiry!

CHIPMAN—If it please the court: military courts judging war crimes are governed by both the criminal code and by the broader, more general code of universal international law. In most cases that come before them, they will judge specific acts in which the nature and degree of offense is determinable without great difficulty. But on rare occasions, cases occur demanding from a court a more searching inquiry. Should the court allow such broad inquiry, it becomes more than the court of record in a particular case; it becomes a supreme tribunal—willing to peer into the very heart of human conduct. The judge advocate respectfully urges that the court does not in advance limit or narrowly define the basis for questioning. Should the court insist on such a basis, then we are through with the witness. (*Sits.*)

WALLACE—Does the judge advocate offer the court alternatives?

CHIPMAN—We did not mean to imply that.

WALLACE—The court is flattered to think it may take on the mantle of a supreme tribunal—however, it is still a military court.

CHIPMAN—If it please the court—

WALLACE—No, Colonel, I'm not through. The court grants that it may be philosophically true that men have the human right to judge the commands of their military superiors, but in practice one does so at his peril.

Wallace would have the peril of that line of reasoning understood, and, underlining how precarious Chipman's position may prove to be, he poses a question of his own. "If," says Wallace, "at the outbreak of the war, the government of the so-called Confederacy had stood on the moral principle of freedom for the black man and the government of the United States had stood for slavery, would a man have been bound on moral grounds to follow the dictates of conscience—even if it led him to the point of taking up arms against the government of the United States?" Unable to sidestep this double-barrelled question, Chipman says that a man would have been bound to follow the dictates of his conscience even to the point of taking up arms against the government of the United States. "The Colonel understands, of course," says Wallace, "that a man must be prepared to pay the penalties involved in violating the—let us say—the code of the group to which he belongs. In other societies that has meant death. In our society it can mean merely deprivation of status— the contempt of his fellows—exile in the midst of his countrymen. I take it the Colonel understands my meaning."

Understanding only too well that he has reached the decisive point in his life no less than in this trial, Chipman eloquently proclaims that he still wants this to be a human victory, a memorial to the 14,000 Andersonville men who were put to death in a "subtle, furtive, hidden manner." Not unmoved by his plea, Wallace allows

Chipman to inquire into the moral issue of disobedience to a superior officer. Baker is incredulous. Declaring that there is no legal case here, he says it is impossible to make a connection between normal obedience to orders and willful conspiracy, and no high-sounding words can possibly conceal this fact. He is overridden.

Wirz, asked why he obeyed if General Winder's authority over him was not absolute, sniffs disaster. Wallace requests him to answer. Wirz answers that he would have been court-martialed for disobedience. Chipman drums away at this question of obedience. Wirz repeats: "As I say for the last time, it was to me a military situation." Pointing out to Wirz that this was *not* a military situation, since these were unarmed, helpless men, Chipman reminds him that Chandler had realized that this was a question of human beings, as had the Southern women also. Where was Wirz's conscience?

Roused to fury, Wirz screams that the people in this room would have done no differently.

CHIPMAN—And if they could not, then we must shudder for the world we live in—to think what may happen when one man owns the conscience of many men. For the prospect before us is then a world of Andersonvilles—of jailers concerned only to execute the commands of their masters. And freed of his conscience—fearing only the authority to which he had surrendered his soul—*might the jailer not commit murder then?*

WIRZ—I did not commit murder!

CHIPMAN (*circles front of* WIRZ)—You did not kill William Stewart?

WIRZ—There was no William Stewart!

CHIPMAN—You were never in a fury with those men—a fury great enough to overcome the weakness of your arms?

WIRZ—It is as the doctors say—

CHIPMAN—To whom do you dare say that? You and I have been on the battlefields. We've seen men holding their bowels in their hands and with their legs broken, still moving forward. You raised your arms—

WIRZ—No!

CHIPMAN—Yes! You were in a fury when you rode out to hunt down those men with that dogpack and when you caught them you raised those two dead arms—

WIRZ—No!

CHIPMAN—Then how did you rein that hard-mouthed horse you rode to the left—and how to the right—and how bring his head down when he reared—if not with those two dead arms? (*He grabs* WIRZ *by the upper arms and pulls him out of the chair.*)

WIRZ—Yes! Possibly!—I raise my arms sometimes! Yes!—but I did not kill any William Stewart because there was no William Stewart, so help me God.

CHIPMAN—We will leave Mr. Stewart aside—but you had to obey orders which you knew were killing men, didn't you?

WIRZ—I had to obey.

Chipman works on Wirz until the man spills over with the horror that had been his job. Feeling everlastingly badgered by Chipman, Wirz tells of his nightmarish duties and how he found the job unendurable. His *idée fixe* had been to prevent the ever-escaping men from escaping. At night he couldn't sleep for thinking about those men endlessly digging "in that hopeless effort to escape—like rats." Pouncing on Wirz's use of the word "rats," Chipman says the men were no longer *men* in Wirz's eyes. "In your mind you canceled them out as men and you made them less than men, and then they might die and one did not have to suffer over that!" Almost gently Chipman now asks: "Why did you try to commit suicide in your cell? —Is it because you feel nothing?" Still Wirz says nothing. "Is it because you have no human feeling left and cannot endure yourself feeling nothing? Is it because in the darkness of your cell you asked your children, 'Should I have done my duty, or should I have given a man a drink of water?' And you heard their answer." Wirz gives a stifled cry. "You wish to die," says Chipman. "I ask you for the last time. Why—inside yourself—couldn't you disobey?" "Simply—I could not," says Wirz, utterly broken. "I did not have that feeling in myself to be able to. I did not have that feeling of strength to do that. I—could—not—disobey." "The government rests," says Chipman.

SCENE II

The following day, the court declares Wirz guilty on all counts and sentences him to die. The guards lead him away.

Left alone in the empty courtroom, the two attorneys meet. Complimenting Chipman for having won on his own terms, Baker still wonders who will really care that he fought to purify the occasion. "Men will go on as they are, subject to powers and authorities. And how are we to change *that* slavery? When it's of their very nature?" Chipman wearily questions this, but has no answer except the one he knows well: "We try." "We redecorate the beast in all sorts of political coats," says Baker ironically, "hoping that we change him, but is he to be changed?" "We try," says Chipman. "We try."

THE DEADLY GAME

A Play in Two Acts

By Friedrich Duerrenmatt

Adapted by James Yaffe

[Friedrich Duerrenmatt *was born in 1921 in Konolfingen, a village near Berne. When he was 13 his father, a parson, took the family to Berne, where young Duerrenmatt went to high school and then to the University. Later he attended the University of Zurich. His first play, "It Is Written," was produced in Zurich in 1947. "The Marriage of Mississippi," his first real success, was produced in Germany in 1952 and later Off Broadway as "Fools Are Passing Through." He has written several plays and radio scripts, one film play, and four novels. "The Visit," produced in 1959 with the Lunts, was a spectacular success.*]

[James Yaffe *is a native of Chicago. He attended Yale University and his professional career began when his first short story appeared in the Ellery Queen Mystery Magazine. Following this he wrote many short stories. Little, Brown published three novels: "What's the Big Hurry," "The Good-for-Nothing" and "Nothing But the Night." He has also done many television scripts. "The Deadly Game" is his first Broadway play.*]

IN the cozy, fire-lit sitting room of an Alpine house, a very old man, dressed in evening clothes, dozes by the fire. Two other elderly men, in dinner jackets, are playing chess.

A table has been set for a buffet dinner in the room's alcove, and while one of the oldsters puzzles his next move, the other—his host—

debates which wine he should choose of the two bottles held out to him by his manservant. Feeling in a festive mood, he decides on the Chambertin.

Suddenly awake, the old man by the fire inquires querulously whether Gustave has arrived, and is alarmed when the brooding chess player says that Gustave will not come tonight. Reassuring the old man that Gustave is simply delayed by the snowstorm that is raging, their host directs the manservant: "Pierre, put the oil lamp outside the door just to be sure. Really, Bernard, you mustn't upset Joseph with your congenital pessimism." And as he tucks a blanket around the legs of his old friend, the doorbell rings.

Reaching the front door, Pierre opens it to encounter a stranger. Covered with snow, and red with cold, the stranger is sorry to barge in on them, but his car has struck a snow drift. "It is a miracle that you saw our lights," says the host. "This road is most treacherous. The house is built on the edge of the mountain." The stranger, introducing himself as Howard Trapp—with two P's—meets his host, Emile Carpeau—with one P; the chess player, Bernard Laroque; and the old man by the fire. Leading Trapp up to the old man, Carpeau says: "And this is the elder statesman of our little group—my respected friend Joseph Pillet. In our hearts we all have a special place for Joseph." Hearing that Trapp is a motorist lost in the storm, Joseph Pillet shows unnatural excitement. "And he's going to join us tonight?" asks Joseph. "I am so happy, *monsieur*. We have been waiting such a long time." Seeing Trapp's puzzled look, Carpeau intervenes smoothly: "Joseph means that we see so few strangers here, we wait anxiously for each new face. Won't you move closer to the fire, Mr. Trapp?"

Remarking on how far Trapp is tonight from his native land, the United States, Carpeau is amused when Trapp wonders how he knew. Not wanting to make too much a point of this, he offers Trapp some brandy although they usually don't start to drink until all the guests have arrived. Having no desire to intrude on their party, Trapp offers to go into another room. "Nonsense," says Carpeau. Emile adds: "Parties are so much more enjoyable when they give us a chance to meet new people." Joseph pleads with Trapp to remain, and Trapp, flattered by all this attention, agrees. "I can see why you look forward to strangers up here," he says, "this place is really out in the middle of nowhere, isn't it?" "That is precisely what I like best about it, Mr. Trapp," answers Carpeau. "Wouldn't satisfy *me*," says Trapp; "I like people, action, places to go."

CARPEAU—Only natural, at your age. When I was a young man, how I loved to surround myself with people! But the years have made me—more selective.

BERNARD—I have never been able to achieve a balanced attitude toward people. Almost seventy years of disillusionment have failed to destroy one bit of my delight in the human race.

TRAPP—With me there's never been any disillusionment. I never had any illusions in the first place.

CARPEAU—I hope you're not a cynic. So many in your type of work are inclined to be cynical.

TRAPP—I'm sorry, but I don't believe I said anything about my type of work.

CARPEAU—Why, you're a salesman, aren't you?

TRAPP—I'll be damned!

CARPEAU—What is the popular expression in English? A "traveling salesman"?

TRAPP—How did you know that?

CARPEAU—My apologies, Mr. Trapp. I've trained myself to notice things. The cut of your clothes, your manner of speaking, of holding yourself—all these things cry out to me, "salesman."

BERNARD—I fear you've stumbled on a nest of trained observers, Mr. Trapp. We are all retired lawyers, you see, and a legal career obliges one to be a student of human nature.

TRAPP—I'm a student of human nature myself. In my business you have to be. You'll never make any sales unless you're able to size a man up and find out his weaknesses. (*Laughs.*) I never had much to do with the law, though. I was brought up in a neighborhood where everybody ran when they saw the law coming. (*He laughs, and the others join in.*)

CARPEAU—Yes, this attitude is most common—even among the law-abiding Swiss.

Observing now that Trapp is tired and wet, Carpeau has Pierre escort him to an upstairs bedroom so that he may get ready for the dinner Carpeau has prepared. "When my friends come to visit me," he says, "I like to preside over the cuisine and make little experiments." "Emile's experiments," adds Bernard, "are the supreme moments of our existence."

As Trapp starts after Pierre, he inquires about a phone. He really should call his wife. "I'm so sorry, Mr. Trapp," says Carpeau, "but I've never felt the need for a telephone." "Well, it isn't important," Trapp replies. "I don't know how I can ever pay you back for your hospitality." "Who knows, Mr. Trapp," says Carpeau with a smile, "we may think of something."

The minute the old men are alone together, the room buzzes with excitement. Joseph worries that it would be too terrible now that they have Mr. Trapp, if Gustave didn't arrive. He pleads with the others to find out if Trapp is "possible." Bernard doesn't think so. Carpeau inquires why not?

CARPEAU—You like everybody the moment you set eyes on them. Do you remember last year? That philosophy professor from the Sorbonne?

BERNARD (*sheepishly*)—Well, yes, I confess that I did go a bit overboard in that instance. He was such a cultured, soft-spoken gentleman.

CARPEAU—I don't criticize you, Bernard. How could we accomplish anything if it weren't for your indestructible faith in people? I merely say that Mr. Trapp may turn out to be more of a possibility than you anticipate.

BERNARD—But what have you got against him?

CARPEAU—You observed his clothes, no doubt. Very expensive material. Our new friend would seem to be a most successful man.

BERNARD—Success is not necessarily incriminating. We established that precedent a long time ago.

CARPEAU—Of course we did. I remember how hard you fought for it in the case of that Italian banker. I simply find Mr. Trapp's success to be a suggestive circumstance, a vague indication—

The doorbell rings, and this time it is Gustave. Apologizing for his late arrival and frowning briefly as he hangs his coat next to Trapp's, Gustave follows Carpeau into the living room. "It's a nightmare outside. I nearly went off the road three times," he says. Carpeau hopes that Gustave will be at the top of his form tonight. Sniffing the delicious smells from the kitchen, Gustave promises he'll do his best as soon as he satisfies his ravenous appetite; but the three cronies tease him that he may not eat until he guesses their secret. With incredible suavity and dash, Gustave delivers: "Very well, my friends—where is he?—the stranger who arrived just before me—the American gentleman." And he checkmates Bernard's chessman. "Bravo!" cries Emile Carpeau. Gustave dismisses his little performance by explaining he had seen a coat of American cut dripping in the hall. Joseph pipes up: "Bernard and Emile disagree about him, Gustave. Bernard thinks he isn't possible, but Emile isn't so sure." "What do you think, Joseph?" asks Gustave. "Well—I think he's possible. He's a traveling salesman, and he has a great deal of money, and he doesn't seem to like lawyers very much, and he drinks cognac as if it were water." Hearing Trapp outside, Gustave promises Joseph to give his opinion.

"I certainly feel a lot better," says Trapp. "Oh, by the way, the cuffs of my pants were soaking wet, and I saw this suit hanging in the closet, so I just borrowed the pants." "Quite all right," says Carpeau, "the suit was left by a guest some months ago."

Introduced to the fourth member of the group, Trapp is drawn out by Gustave on his dislike of lawyers. The others, finding the subject so fascinating that they can't resist joining in, soon take over the conversation. "Gentlemen, gentlemen!" cries Carpeau. "I'm afraid," he tells Trapp, "you'll just have to get used to these little conflicts. Gustave and Bernard have been flying at each other's throats for thirty years. For a long time they were paid to do so." Trapp doesn't understand. "Until my retirement, I was Judge of the Criminal Court of the municipality of Geneva," says Carpeau. "Gustave was our Chief Prosecutor—a terror to the criminal elements for miles around—and Bernard was our Public Defender, for many years the most famous criminal lawyer in Switzerland." But not wanting to talk of themselves, Carpeau suggests that they talk of something more interesting. Taking the hint, Gustave says: "Of course, I forgot myself. Your own profession interests me enormously, Mr. Trapp. I envy your opportunities to travel, see new places, meet all kinds of people."

TRAPP—I've been around, all right. But as far as I can see, people are about the same wherever you go.

GUSTAVE—You feel that we all have a certain common humanity which is more important than our individual differences?

TRAPP—Well, actually I was thinking in terms of sales technique. When you're trying to sell a piece of merchandise, it doesn't matter if the customer is rich or poor, young or old, male or female—there are three things you always have to make him believe. One: that he's getting this product for a lot less than it's worth. Two: that all the people he looks up to in the world have got one. And three: that his best friends are going to burn with jealousy because *he* has one.

GUSTAVE—In short, greed, envy, and condescension—these, in your opinion, are the mainsprings of human conduct?

At the end of this enlightening little talk, Gustave finds that Mr. Trapp is going to provide them with a very stimulating evening. Overjoyed, Joseph can't wait for the dinner so they can get on to more important things, but Carpeau—cook and judge—offers a toast to Mr. Trapp in some rare old wine, which Trapp, Joseph notes, pours down his gullet like water.

As everyone now moves to the buffet table to help himself to dinner, the judge says: "I can heartily recommend the *croustade de champignons*— You know, Mr. Trapp, we weren't always such heavy eaters. A few years ago our appetites were quite feeble—before we started playing our game." Dispensing just a little information at a time, the judge explains that their game has been the re-enacting of famous trials of history. Joseph adds that this occupies them three or four nights a week. The former prosecutor adds that in all seriousness this game has proved more than entertainment, their very lives depend on it.

BERNARD—Gustave doesn't exaggerate. Five years ago, we were forced to retire because of our age. In retirement we soon became physical wrecks. Gustave and I were obliged to watch our blood pressure, the doctors suspected our good friend Emile of having diabetes, and poor Joseph was a martyr to his arthritis.

PROSECUTOR—With nothing to do, no purpose in life, our souls as well as our bodies began to atrophy. Physically and spiritually, idleness was killing us.

JUDGE—In short, a sad collection of old fossils. And then we got the idea of playing this game. It was Gustave's idea.

PROSECUTOR—No, no, you give me too much credit. The idea sprang into our minds at once—as if by a miracle.

ATTORNEY—A strange illogical word to hear from *you*, Gustave—but it *was* a miracle! Would you believe it, Mr. Trapp, our little game turned out to be the fountain of youth. Within a few short months our stomachs, our livers, our pancreases put themselves in order. Boredom disappeared, appetite returned, and I venture to say that today we're the youngest men of our age in all Europe.

PROSECUTOR—Younger, in a sense, than we were in our prime. After grinding away for years in the courts of the outside world, we are finally able to practice law in its purest form.

JUDGE (*with a smile*)—Mr. Trapp, you need some more wine. Good wine is one of life's chief joys, but I think that few people in your country have yet acquired the habit.

TRAPP—Pour away, Judge. One thing I've never had trouble with—acquiring bad habits.

PROSECUTOR—I believe it.

The old men would very much like to have Trapp's reaction to their game. Conceding it might be fun in its way, Trapp plans to be an interested spectator. "But you must play!" cries Joseph. "The whole evening would be ruined without you." "That's right, Mr. Trapp," says the judge. "You see, challenging as it is to re-create the famous trials of history, it is an even greater challenge when we have live material to work with." Trapp asks if they have actually played this way before. "We most certainly have," says the judge. "The last time—to give you an example—was approximately a month ago. We had a snowstorm much like this one, and a former mayor of the province found his way to the house just as we were finishing dinner.

ATTORNEY—It was a delicious meal. The poor man was unlucky to miss it.

PROSECUTOR—Unlucky in other ways too. He was convicted of poisoning his first wife. We sentenced him to hang.

TRAPP (*much amused*)—That would be enough to kill anyone's appetite.

PROSECUTOR—Naturally he was upset. But the law is the law— the sentence could not be set aside. (TRAPP *gives* PROSECUTOR *a sharp look, half amused, half puzzled.*)

TRAPP—But didn't I read somewhere that capital punishment's been abolished in Switzerland?

PROSECUTOR—In Switzerland, yes. Not in our court.

JUDGE—The mayor had the same notion. We tried to make him understand how necessary capital punishment is to the true spirit of our game. But he couldn't seem to grasp the point.

PROSECUTOR—He was generally a confused sort of man. Scarcely worth playing with.

ATTORNEY—Those are his trousers you're wearing, Mr. Trapp. He neglected to take them with him. (TRAPP *roars with laughter.*)

Realizing that they want him for their defendant, Trapp says cheerfully that he's a pretty respectable citizen with no crimes or vices and with a good credit rating. Except for an occasional ticket for speeding, his past is an open book. Though they would be grateful to him if he would play, the judge says that his participation must be entirely voluntary. Trapp is willing, but the prosecutor insists: "No. Don't make a hasty decision, Mr. Trapp. We have certain rigid rules. Once you've agreed to join us, you can't back out." "That's right," says the judge. "Once you place yourself under the jurisdiction of our court, you must submit to that jurisdiction right through to the end of the trial." Grinning and looking around at all the eager old faces, Trapp agrees to take a chance.

Taking Joseph, Pierre, and Gustave with him to the kitchen where he will prepare *crêpes au liqueur*, and leaving the defendant behind for a quiet talk with his attorney, the judge says that the game will start with the dessert.

Taking the precaution of shutting the kitchen door firmly behind the prosecutor so that they can make their plans without being overheard, the defense attorney actually has few thoughts on the subject. Trapp, against his advice, refuses to admit to any small, juicy crime.

ATTORNEY—Mr. Trapp, I'm your attorney. All communications between us are strictly confidential. I've seen abysses open, believe me.

TRAPP (*very good-humored about it*)—I'm sorry. I wish I could open an abyss for you now. But I guess I'm just innocent of any crime.

ATTORNEY—Young man, listen to me—in this world of ours no one is completely innocent. Each of us carries some burden of guilt which troubles him and fills him with self-loathing. I myself, when I was a very young man— (*Breaks off, moved.*) Where would sympathy, mercy, forgiveness come from if not for our common share of human fallibility? Such being the case, it would be very poor tactics to appear before our court without announcing exactly what crime you wish to be charged with.

TRAPP—And what would be good tactics?

ATTORNEY—To stand trial for some crime that isn't particularly shameful, but even rather admirable and charming—like swindling an insurance company, for instance. If the prosecutor *does* happen to stumble on the proof, I may be able to suggest that your guilt has a kind of nobility in it, that you gave the money to a widow or an orphan—robbing the rich to help the poor, so to speak.

TRAPP—That's very clever. The only trouble is, I *haven't* robbed the rich to help the poor. If you knew me better, you'd realize how completely out of character that is.

ATTORNEY—Perhaps so, Mr. Trapp. But you don't know our court. To maintain your innocence from the start, believe me, could easily be catastrophic. You'll be compelled, instead of choosing your own offense, to let one be thrust upon you.

By now Trapp is slightly irritated. "If the prosecutor's so smart," he says, "let him find one!" That, according to the attorney, is a foregone conclusion; giving up with a sigh, he offers Trapp two pieces of advice. First, he must weigh every word he utters, and secondly, he must promise to be very frightened of his dangerous adversary, Gustave Kummer. Trapp indulgently promises.

The judge and his entourage return with the elegant dessert, and wait to hear what the defendant has in store for them. There is a moment of startled silence when they learn that the defendant leaves himself open to any charge the prosecutor may hit upon. Then Joseph murmurs eagerly: "He says that he's innocent? Is it really going to be one of those?" Though it would appear so, the judge seriously advises Trapp to reconsider, and to specify the crime for which he wishes to be tried. The prosecutor breaks in sharply: "Excuse me, Emile, but the defendant *is* over twenty-one. Presumably he knows how to take care of his own interests." "I knew how to do *that* long before I was twenty-one," says Trapp. "If we're going to have a game, let's make it a good one."

Trapp at once finds two things odd about this court: he's not sworn in, and Pierre continues to stand in his immobile fashion by the door.

JUDGE—Pierre is one of our most important players. He's our combination bailiff, sheriff, and chief jailer. Well qualified because of his penal experience.

TRAPP—Penal experience. What penal experience?

ATTORNEY—Pierre spent fifteen years in prison, Mr. Trapp—for manslaughter. He used to have a dreadful temper. He got into a fight one night over a woman.

PROSECUTOR—He was the wronged party, but he *did* strike the fatal blow, and I was obliged to prosecute him.

TRAPP—*You*—?

JUDGE—And I sentenced him, Mr. Trapp.

ATTORNEY—Unfortunately I did not defend him.

TRAPP (*with an uneasy look at* PIERRE)—But under the circumstances—how could you hire him?

JUDGE—I was delighted to get him, Mr. Trapp. We're more than employer and employee—we're friends, we understand each other. Isn't that right, Pierre? (PIERRE *nods*.) Now then, if we might proceed with the questioning.

The prosecutor asks about Trapp's eleven-year marriage, about his seven-year-old son, left behind in New York with a governess, and about Trapp's wife's presence on this trip. "Your wife's company is essential to your pleasure?" "Sure," says Trapp, "she's a good-looking chick." As the prosecutor looks pleased, as if he had scored a point, Trapp continues: "But I begged her to stay in New York with the kid. She was the one who insisted on coming with me. But she's crazy about skiing and Europeans. Well, if you're charging me with child neglect, Mr. Prosecutor, you've got the wrong party."

JUDGE—The storm seems to be growing worse, doesn't it? I'm afraid it's with us for the rest of the night.

PROSECUTOR—Apparently the elements don't bother *you*, Mr.

Trapp. The signs were sinister even this morning, yet you set off on your trip to Geneva anyway.

TRAPP—If you don't take chances you'll never get anything out of life.

PROSECUTOR—A healthy point of view, but I'm sure that your wife was terribly concerned for your safety when you said good-bye to her at the ski lodge.

TRAPP—Oh, she said she was . . . at first. But I told her there was a $5,000 commission at stake, and her concern disappeared fast enough.

Noting with interest this large commission, the prosecutor now follows Trapp's business dealings as exclusive European agent for a new miracle textile. Trapp gives a brash idea of how he handles a customer, and all except the defense attorney show amusement.

The prosecutor forges ahead: on the assumption that Trapp was not always the successful man he is today, he begins to get results. "Careful, careful," warns Trapp's attorney. "Well, he's right about that, you know," says Trapp. "I wasn't born with a silver spoon in my mouth. In his whole lifetime my old man never made as much money as I make in one year. Well, it's a hell of a lot different for *my* boy, I can tell you that." "In short," concludes the prosecutor, "you've worked hard to get where you are today?" Proud of his tough start, of going to work as a youngster, Trapp blandly explains how he began his career as a front in a crooked real-estate racket. Breaking in quickly to plead his client's youthful innocence as excuse for this wrongdoing, the attorney says: "Perhaps this is the crime you'd like to be charged with?" Trapp mockingly agrees, but the prosecutor refuses the bait.

Digging further into Trapp's past, the prosecutor thinks he has come upon a cold-blooded desertion of his mother in her final days, but no matter how rough and cynical Trapp's answers are, it turns out that he was always devoted to his mother.

As the judge asks Pierre to serve the coffee, the attorney warns Trapp against self-confidence. Disregarding this advice and refusing coffee, Trapp, over his attorney's objection, accepts a glass of brandy from the prosecutor. He then sits back and smugly considers his difficult past and fortunate present. "Just between us, my dear sir," says the prosecutor, "you've bulldozed your way up rather quickly, haven't you?" "Damned right I have," says Trapp. "Was it simply diligence and hard work?" asks the prosecutor. "Oh no, it wasn't that easy," Trapp answers with a self-satisfied laugh. "I could've been the most diligent salesman who ever lived, but I still had to get around Foster, and believe me that was tough." Trapp had been chief assistant to Foster, the previous European agent, and he had been stuck in New York lacking chances and an expense account. The prosecutor is curious to know how he got Foster out of the way. Trapp's attorney objects immediately to such a choice of words. Obligingly rephrasing his question, the prosecutor discovers that Foster had actually died five years ago. "Your honor," pleads the attorney, "would you please instruct the witness that he needn't answer any questions before consulting with his attorney?" The judge so instructs Trapp.

TRAPP—Well, I don't see what everybody's getting so excited about. I was just telling the simple facts.

PROSECUTOR—And how sad those simple facts are. Mr. Foster died five years ago. One can't help feeling sorry for the poor old gentleman.

TRAPP—He wasn't so old. Fifty-two, to be exact.

PROSECUTOR—In the prime of life! This story grows sadder and sadder. First he retires from his job, and then, before he has a chance to savor his leisure, he dies.

TRAPP—No, you've got it the wrong way round. He died while he was still working for the company. It was *after* he died that I took his place.

Smiling with satisfaction, the prosecutor now formally charges the defendant with murder. Over the objections of the defense, and to the surprise of the judge, the prosecutor justifies the charge. "One: a man has died. Two: the defendant admits that he had a motive for this man's death. Three: the defendant has revealed a distinct absence of regret for this man's death; indeed, he has revealed definite satisfaction. Four: the prosecution firmly believes in the guilt of this defendant and stakes its legal reputation on its ability to prove that guilt." Citing the great odds that the prosecutor will be fighting, and the serious damage he will do to his reputation if he fails to substantiate the charge, the judge still accepts the charge of murder in the first degree.

TRAPP—But I haven't murdered anybody. Don't you think you're carrying the joke a little too far?

JUDGE—Murder is no joke, Mr. Trapp. It is so grave a charge indeed that it clearly cannot be tried in this friendly informal atmosphere. We require a rearrangement of the physical accoutrements more suited to the nature of the proceedings. Joseph, I'll leave you to take care of that, while the prosecutor, the defense attorney, and I retire to our rooms to put on our robes of office. Pierre, please help Monsieur Pillet.

TRAPP—But why all this hocus pocus? Why do you need robes of office?

PROSECUTOR (*quietly, with significance*)—It's necessary, Mr. Trapp. (*They all exit and start up the stairs.*)

TRAPP—Mr. Pillet, won't they let you have a robe of office, too?

JOSEPH—Oh no. As soon as I rearrange the physical accoutrements, I'll be leaving.

TRAPP—You mean, you won't be here for the rest of the game? (PIERRE *exits to the kitchen with the coffee things.*)

JOSEPH—Oh no, it wouldn't be seemly. It wouldn't be in good taste. Now that we have a case of murder, a capital crime—well, for the sake of your feelings . . .

TRAPP—What've my feelings got to do with it?

JOSEPH—Didn't anybody tell you? Dear me, you should have been told. I'm not a lawyer, Mr. Trapp. For twenty-five years I served the municipality as its official hangman. (*Shocked and horrified,* TRAPP *sinks into a chair.*)

ACT II

Trapp grows increasingly disturbed as he watches Pierre and Joseph eliminate every sign of coziness by rearranging the chairs into a stiff courtroom pattern. He is worried, too, over the fate of the former defendants in this game. Inquiring of Pierre whether the mayor had been in a good mood when he left the house, he finds no solace in the mute's mischievous grin. For solace, he resorts to the brandy bottle.

Wearing his robes of office, the prosecutor hurries downstairs to have a minute with Trapp before the others arrive. He craftily offers Trapp a chance to plead guilty to murder in the second degree and thus avoid the supreme penalty. Mindful of all legalities, he offers Trapp the chance to consult his attorney before making a decision, fully aware that this would not be Trapp's way. The brandy having by now had its effect, Trapp is almost his old, cocky self. Not wanting to ruin the prosecutor's fun, Trapp says amiably that he has no intention of "copping a plea."

When the others assemble, and the attorney discovers what the prosecutor has been up to in his absence, he demands a mistrial, and that the defendant be discharged immediately. The judge asks for his arguments.

ATTORNEY—I move for a mistrial, on the grounds that the prosecution has been tampering with a witness. While your honor and I were out of the courtroom, putting on our robes of office, the prosecutor conducted a private conference with the witness, Howard Trapp. That's correct, isn't it, Mr. Trapp?

TRAPP—Sure, we had a talk—

PROSECUTOR—Your honor, this charge would be insulting if it weren't laughable. In a murder trial the defendant is always available for questioning by the authorities.

ATTORNEY—But the defendant has no legal obligations to answer questions.

PROSECUTOR—Mr. Trapp spoke to me voluntarily. Isn't that so, Mr. Trapp?

TRAPP (*following argument with amusement*)—That's a fact.

ATTORNEY—Even so, the defendant has the right to undergo such an examination in the presence of his own attorney.

PROSECUTOR—Mr. Trapp, did I or did I not inform you of that right?

TRAPP—You sure did.

PROSECUTOR—And what was your decision?

TRAPP—I decided to talk to you alone. Why not?

ATTORNEY—Mr. Trapp, was I present when you made this decision?

TRAPP—Of course not.

ATTORNEY—No arguments were advanced, then, as to why you shouldn't talk to the prosecutor alone?

TRAPP—He asked me, and I said yes. What else do you want?

ATTORNEY—Nothing whatever, Mr. Trapp. Your honor, the case is clear. Obviously the defendant was deprived of his rights—and the fact that he himself cooperated in this deprivation hardly makes it less flagrant.

PROSECUTOR—Excuse me, your honor. It must be shown that I exercised undue influence *on the defendant.* I offered him a chance to plead guilty to second-degree murder. He refused the offer—and that was that.

As the attorney and prosecutor indulge in some angry name-calling, Trapp grins, and the judge raps for order. "I cannot allow such displays of emotionalism in my court," he says. "Now as to the defense's motion—the final determination must rest with the defendant himself. Mr. Trapp, do you feel that the prosecutor used undue pressure or influence on you?" "If I say yes, that's the end of the game, isn't it?" asks Trapp. "It is," the judge tells him; "I will be obliged to dismiss the case." "Hell, I've never lost a game in my life," says Trapp, "the answer is definitely no." Smiling at the prosecutor, the attorney says: "People who won't let themselves be helped—!"

Taking the stand, Trapp carries the brandy bottle with him and is most reluctant to part with it. But at the attorney's request, the judge bids Pierre remove it.

Showing the effect of so much liquor on him, Trapp is not nearly so sharp as before and much more easily confused by the prosecutor. Vehemently denying that he murdered anybody, he refuses point-blank to accept any punishment, and, what is more, says he doesn't give a goddamn about this court. The next moment, not wanting to spoil their game, he is all apologies and promises to answer questions. And a moment later, in a surprising reversal, he confesses everything.

ATTORNEY—Mr. Trapp, for heaven's sake! Your honor, I insist that you tell the witness—

TRAPP—No, no, don't tell me anything! My conscience is bothering me too much—I *have* to talk!

JUDGE (*troubled*)—You're under no obligation, Mr. Trapp—

TRAPP—I want to, I want to!

PROSECUTOR (*with a puzzled look*)—Then tell us how you committed the murder, Mr. Trapp.

TRAPP (*dramatically*)—I went to Foster's office that morning. I knocked on the door. He said, "Come in." I went in. He said to me, "Trapp, there's an error in this report you just submitted."

PROSECUTOR (*eagerly*)—Go on, go on!

TRAPP (*in the same, low intense voice*)—I said to him, "Mr. Foster, thank you for pointing it out to me. And since you've been kind enough to do part of my work for me—I'm going to turn this week's salary check over to you." And it turned out just exactly as I planned. He dropped dead of the shock!

After Trapp has pumped this "little fun" into the game, the prosecutor gets coldly back to business, and the judge warns Trapp that no further levity will be tolerated by the court. A little subdued, Trapp answers the prosecutor. "Too bad," he says, "all kidding aside there wasn't any murder. The old gangster died of a heart attack." The prosecutor asks for more details. "It wasn't his first," answers Trapp. "He had two or three in his last few years. Pretended to be perfectly healthy, of course—kind of proud and sensitive I guess— But the fact is, every shock was dangerous." No one in the office knew this, but Trapp had found it out from the most reliable source possible—Mrs. Foster.

The prosecutor has no trouble getting Trapp to disclose that Mrs. Foster felt so close to him that she revealed her husband's secret. When the attorney objects to the prosecutor's bullying tactics, Trapp shouts: "Nobody bullies me! And I've got nothing to be ashamed of either. It wasn't anything so terrible, for God's sake! I met this Foster woman at a party one night, and she made a play for me! I was feeling pretty rotten just about then. My wife and I weren't getting along—Foster was the boy who got the free trips to Europe in those days, and he was too goddamned stingy to take his wife with him. So, she was at the party alone; I was at the party alone. All right, I gave into temptation. Hell, gentlemen, if that's a crime, half the world would be behind bars!"

The prosecutor plays on Trapp's smugness, but the judge urges him to proceed with the questioning. By now, Trapp is telling all he knows to the prosecutor as if he were his father confessor. In his own home there were no repercussions, Trapp reports, because his wife was having an affair of her own with a Greenwich Village poet. "Mrs. Trapp," says Trapp, "thinks she has a right to play around as much as she likes, but she sure raises hell when *I* do it. Not that I want to play around, you understand. She drives me to it. Take tonight. Do you think I'd be going to see this little girl in Geneva tonight if Helen hadn't been making eyes at that muscle-bound ski instructor all week?"

Now that he has Trapp talking, the prosecutor delves into his thoughts as he made love to Mrs. Foster. "I was merely wondering," says the prosecutor, "Mr. Trapp—in the course of your affair with Mrs. Foster, did the thought never occur to you that this might be a good way of hurting her husband?" "Listen, maybe you've forgotten," says Trapp, "but when you sleep with a woman, believe me, you're not thinking about her husband!" "Very true," says his attorney. In insinuating tones, the prosecutor goes on to examine how Mr. Trapp felt later, as he was lying peacefully at Mrs. Foster's side, how his eye roamed round her bedroom. Trapp remembers a picture of Mr. Foster on her dressing table, "all dressed up in his evening clothes grinning away." "Looking very pleased with himself, was he?" asks the prosecutor. "You bet he was," Trapp says.

The attorney objects to the prosecutor's putting words into Trapp's mouth. Having uncovered what he wished, the prosecutor tells the bewildered Trapp: "We know by your own testimony that your pleasure in having an affair with Mrs. Foster was considerably enhanced by your pleasure in hurting her husband." "But why should I have wanted to hurt him? What was my motive?" asks Trapp. "We'll come to that in due time perhaps," answers the prosecutor. "We agree on one thing, don't we? It would have been a terrible body blow to the late Mr. Foster if he had learned that his wife was carrying on an affair with his own assistant from the office."

TRAPP—If he had found out.

PROSECUTOR—But he *did* find out about it, didn't he?

TRAPP—I didn't say that.

PROSECUTOR—But it's the truth, isn't it? What is there in the simple truth that frightens you?

TRAPP (*angrily*)—Nothing frightens me!

PROSECUTOR—Then Mr. Foster *did* find out about the affair?

TRAPP—Even if he did, what difference does it make?

PROSECUTOR—It might make a great deal of difference. You are on trial for murdering this man, and you yourself stated a few moments ago that you had no motive. But suppose the late Foster found out several months or a year before his death that you were carrying on with his wife. What would his reaction be to that? Anger, humiliation, shame—and then the desire for revenge. That's a reasonable assumption, isn't it, Mr. Trapp?

TRAPP—It sounds reasonable.

PROSECUTOR—And how would he proceed to take his revenge? By making use of his superior position in the company, don't you agree? By persecuting you, undermining your confidence, destroying your work, making you look bad in the eyes of the top executives. Mr. Foster would use that year to force you out of your job—and you would no doubt go to great lengths to prevent him. There, Mr. Trapp, is your motive for murder!

TRAPP (*with increased bravado*)—My motive for murder? *That's* my motive for murder? Excuse me, that's funny, that makes me laugh! Man, you kill me! This whole fancy theory of yours is based on the assumption that Foster found out about his wife and me a year before he died. And the truth is, he found out about us on the day of his death!

PROSECUTOR (*smiling broadly*)—The day of his death. Thank you, Mr. Trapp.

Not having understood what he has just said, Trapp misses the next danger signals, too. Asked how Foster found out, Trapp says he doesn't know and doesn't give a damn. The prosecutor insists that, having eliminated all other possibilities, it must have been Trapp. "You've eliminated Joe Wilson, have you?" answers Trapp smugly.

His attorney stands up, desperate. "Your honor, would you instruct the defendant that he need not answer any questions which might tend to incriminate him?" "That's quite true, Mr. Trapp," says the judge. "Your last answer was almost a confession."

TRAPP (*more frightened*)—A confession of what? What did I say?

PROSECUTOR—Shall I tell you what you said, Mr. Trapp? You said you were anxious to get ahead in the world by replacing the late Mr. Foster.

TRAPP—What's wrong with that? Everybody wants to get ahead!

PROSECUTOR—You said that the late Mr. Foster had a dangerous heart condition. You said that any shock might kill him. You said that you were well aware of this.

TRAPP—Lots of people were aware of it! His family, his doctor— why aren't *they* on trial?

PROSECUTOR—Because they haven't admitted, as you did, that you deliberately carried on an affair with his wife, and when this affair reached its height you deliberately told your bitterest rival about it— knowing exactly what he would do next. Joe Wilson was your weapon, Mr. Trapp! Through him you struck the fatal blow, just as surely as if your hand had wielded a knife!

TRAPP—No, that's not true! Although I was mad at Foster that day—that damned old gangster, he couldn't talk to people as if they were human beings—so the story slipped out while Joe Wilson and I were having a couple of beers. How could I be sure he'd go straight to Foster? How could I be sure that little son of a bitch would have the guts to do a thing like that to *me?*

PROSECUTOR—When the murderer presses the trigger of his gun, Mr. Trapp, how can he be *sure* that the bullet will hit its mark? Your state of assurance is not what concerns us! Your *intention* is what concerns us!

In this court of law, which is guided by neither the Anglo-Saxon nor the Latin code, one thing seems paramount: Trapp's subconscious will determine his fate. "Think back," says the prosecutor, "even as you smiled at that woman for the first time, at that moment, wasn't there something inside of you—a voice—a feeling, an impulse —something saying, I can use this for my own purposes—I don't know when, I don't know how, but I can use this to get rid of her husband? Wasn't that the moment the idea first came into your head?" "No," answers Trapp, "it was there all the time. It was crazy—I wouldn't listen to it." He had kept pushing it out of his mind. "The impulse that told you to murder Foster," prompts the prosecutor. "I swear to God, I kept pushing it out of my mind, pushing it out of my mind," repeats Trapp. "Your honor," says the prosecutor, "the prosecution rests its case."

Having little to work with, the attorney presents his case in his summation. As Trapp listens to his defense, his confidence starts coming back, only to give way to fear when the prosecutor sums up.

PROSECUTOR—Your honor, gentlemen, I have listened with the greatest interest to the words of my distinguished colleague, and it will perhaps surprise you to hear that I agree with almost everything he said. Gentlemen, the defense comes right out and admits the essential fact—that murder was done. It merely seeks to justify this by the extraordinary statement that the defendant is like the rest of mankind, that he moves along unconsciously from passion to passion, from selfishness to selfishness.

Gentlemen, who denies this? Of all people in the world, certainly not us! What on earth is the whole point of this court, its whole reason for being, if not to deal with so-called "unconscious" criminals like Mr. Trapp? Gentlemen, the sacred duty of this court is to unearth, condemn, and punish without hesitation those crimes which the formally constituted agencies of the law are unable to reach. Have we ever allowed the plea of "unconsciousness" to sway us from this duty? We recognize the true nature of Mr. Trapp's unconsciousness, that voice, that feeling, that impulse which in his own words he kept pushing out of his mind. He rejected it in horror, but he killed the late Mr. Foster anyway. Thus his very rejection of the impulse became his most powerful rationalization: "How could I have meant to commit murder when I recoiled so violently from the idea of committing murder?" This is your unconsciousness, gentlemen, "Unconsciousness"—that most insidious of narcotics in our addled modern world, that quick complacent justification for all our sins. Naturally such a criminal as Mr. Trapp is unconscious of his actions. Naturally he feels no pangs of guilt. What is this but another way of saying that he is too thick-skinned even to have a conscience?

My distinguished colleague says that the whole world is like this, that life is a battlefield occupied by unthinking, unfeeling savages. I refuse to believe this. Men do not all behave like brutes. And then to justify it by saying, "Everybody acts the same way, it's not me . . . it's my unconscious mind—it's the pressure of life." The purpose of this court is to fight that tendency, to help in our small way to stamp it out—by stamping out those individuals who have succumbed to it too freely, who have allowed it to turn them into destroyers of their fellow men. Howard Trapp is just a destructive force, and the prosecution demands that he pay for his crime with his life!

Wildly crying out that he's quitting their game, Trapp refuses to sit through any more of this trial. "You really ought to be present while your fate is being decided," advises the attorney. Retorting that they're a bunch of lunatics, and that this court is a figment of their imagination, Trapp tries to leave but is forced back into his chair by Pierre's all too real grip. "Whatever may happen to you," says the judge, "one good thing will come out of this trial. The ends of justice will be served." And he sentences Trapp to death by hanging.

In the aftermath of the trial the old cronies, delighted with one another's performances, laugh and compliment each other. Bringing drinks to his hard-working friends, the judge considers the prosecutor's line of questioning magnificent. "Of course," he adds, "you could never have gotten away with it in any other court."

At this point, Joseph, whom they had all forgotten, pokes his head in at the door to ask if they'll be needing him tonight. "A new triumph for the prosecution, Joseph," crows the judge, "another death sentence." And since it is late, he asks that Joseph escort Mr. Trapp upstairs.

This triggers Trapp's fear. He refuses to accompany Joseph, and when Pierre approaches him, he panics.

TRAPP (*he faces them all, his control going*)—No! All right—all right, so I did it! I wanted him dead, and I made sure of it. When I was a kid I found out it's dog-eat-dog in this world, so why shouldn't I be better at it than anyone else? You're murderers too —murderers just as much as I am! Only you call it justice! What's justice? I don't believe in justice! There's no such thing as justice! There's no such thing as justice! (*He rushes out the front door into the storm.*)

JUDGE (*alarmed, rushing out to foyer*)—Mr. Trapp, come back! It's dangerous out there!

PROSECUTOR—Believe me, Mr. Trapp, I didn't mean anything personal! (PIERRE, *at the living room window, beckons the* JUDGE *as* TRAPP *rushes past. The old men crowd back into living room.*)

JUDGE—Not that way, not that way!

ATTORNEY—The precipice, Mr. Trapp! You'll kill yourself!

PROSECUTOR—Mr. Trapp, Mr. Trapp! (*They stop short, in horror, as they witness* TRAPP'S *fate.*)

Another evening, the old men are once again enjoying a game of chess, and Joseph is sitting by the fire, when the doorbell rings. Answering the ring, Pierre escorts into their presence a chic, hard, young woman. She introduces herself as Helen Trapp. "Oh yes," says the judge, "the unfortunate gentleman's wife."

Helen very much wants to hear that she wasn't the cause of the tragedy, and the judge at once reassures her that she has no reason to reproach herself. The other old gentlemen rally round with their sympathy, flattery, and attentions.

Warning Mrs. Trapp that it is unwise to drive the mountain road in the dark, they persuade her to dine and spend the night. "And," says the prosecutor, "after dinner perhaps we can think of something amusing to do—just to take your mind off your troubles. Perhaps some little parlor game." The four men laugh merrily, and, quite charmed and flattered, Helen joins in.

CALIGULA

A Play in Two Acts

By Albert Camus

Adapted by Justin O'Brien

[Albert Camus, *best known as a novelist and the winner of the Nobel Prize for Literature in 1957, has also written extensively for the theatre. Born in Mondavi, Algiers, in 1913, he was educated at the University of Algiers. During World War II, he was editor-in-chief of "Combat." In the post-World War II era he became an internationally known figure for his novels and essays, his ties with Existentialism, and for his playwriting. His fame increased during the 1950s; early in 1960 he was killed in an automobile accident.*]

[Justin O'Brien *has been a Professor of French at Columbia University since 1948. For his services in World War II, he was decorated with the Legion of Merit, the Croix de Guerre with Palm, and the Order of the British Empire, and was named Chevalier of the Legion d'Honneur. He has become widely known as a man of letters and biographer, and as a translator, in particular of Camus and André Gide.*]

BEFORE a huge column, on the steps of a state hall of the Roman Imperial Palace, a group of patricians profess anxiety at the strange disappearance of their emperor. Throwing dice, they don't seem unduly concerned however; rather they seem to take pleasure in gossiping over the cause of Caligula's running away. One old man, a master of the cliché, is sure that it was love; another remarks that grief is not eternal. It's not really possible to suffer for more than a year: having lost a wife himself over a year ago, he points out that he now suffers only an occasional pang. "Time heals all wounds," says the old patrician, "nature has a way of arranging things." Watching him scornfully from a distance, Helicon, a Roman officer, says: "Yet when I look at you, I wonder if nature is always so perfect."

Distinguished, bearded Cherea, another patrician, is more worried: "Everything was going along too smoothly," he says. "That emperor was simply too perfect."

Cassius—Yes, he was just right: conscientious and inexperienced.

Octavius—But what's the matter with you? And why all this concern? He may go right on being the emperor we have known. He loved Drusilla, to be sure. But she was his sister after all. Going to bed with her was bad enough. But to upset all Rome because she has died is going too far. I hope and trust his condition is only temporary.

Cherea—Nevertheless, I don't like it at all, and his running away looks bad to me.

Old Patrician—Yes, where there's smoke there's fire. In any event, the interests of the State can't accept an incest that takes on the proportions of a tragedy. Incest is well and good—but quietly.

Where there are so many explanations, Helicon wonders why they settle for the stupidest and most obvious. As the young poet Scipio, a friend of Caligula's and the last to see him three days ago, comes into their circle, Cherea remarks that Caligula was too fond of bad literature. "An artistic emperor is a contradiction in terms. We have had one or two of them, of course—but there are black sheep in every family. The others had the good sense to remain bureaucrats." "It was more peaceful," concedes Octavius. Another patrician says complacently that if Caligula doesn't return, they will have to choose an emperor from their own ranks; while, if Caligula comes back in a bad mood, they will merely reason with him.

It is not that easy, however. As a guard announces that the emperor has been seen in the garden, and as everyone rushes away to look, Caligula half-crawls, half-pulls himself into the empty hall, where Helicon alone awaits him. Tattered, scratched, utterly exhausted, Caligula's one order is for Helicon literally to get him the moon. He says that he is not mad: "Indeed I have never been so lucid. It's just that I suddenly felt a need for the impossible.

Things as they are do not strike me as satisfactory." The world is unbearable; Caligula needs something that is not a part of this world.

HELICON—That's logical enough. But no one could ever carry that out to its conclusion.

CALIGULA—You know nothing about it. It's because no one ever carries it out to its conclusion that nothing is ever achieved. All that is needed is to remain logical to the bitter end. (*Falling to his knees, he pushes aside* HELICON's *helping hand.*) I know what you are thinking. What a fuss over the death of a woman! No, that's not it. I think I recall, that a few days ago a woman I loved died. But what is love? Not much. That death doesn't matter, I assure you. (*Crawls on his knees.*) It is the symbol of a truth that makes the moon necessary to me. It is a quite simple and quite obvious truth, a little stupid even, but hard to discover and harder to bear.

HELICON—And what is that truth, Caius?

CALIGULA—Men die and they are not happy.

HELICON—After all, Caius, that's a truth that people live with very well. Just look around you. It doesn't keep anyone from lunching.

To Caligula, all men are living a lie and now that he has the power he will teach them to live in truth. Exhausted but unable to sleep, and sure that he will never sleep again, Caligula asks and receives Helicon's promise to help him achieve the impossible. Then hearing steps approach, Caligula hides.

Caligula's former mistress Caesonia, a faded courtesan, and the young devoted Scipio still wait for their emperor. Scipio lovingly recalls how good Caligula has been to him: "He has encouraged me and I know some of his thoughts by heart. He used to tell me that life is not easy, but there are compensations; religion, art, and the love others bear us. He would often say that making others suffer was the only human crime. He wanted to be a just man." To Caesonia, Caligula is just a child. "The only god I've ever known was my own body, and it is to that god that I should like to pray today that Caius may be brought back to me."

When Caligula appears, the patricians gather in shocked silence. The Major Domo has an unfortunate inspiration: he mentions the decisions that have to be made regarding the Treasury. Bursting into laughter, Caligula treats what has been said at face value: in other words, that money is of supreme importance. Asking the patricians to leave, he puts his plan before the Major Domo: "Now listen carefully. First phase: All patricians and all persons in the Empire having any fortune—big or little, it comes to the same thing—must disinherit their children and draw up a will immediately in favor of the State." Collapsing to his knees, the Major Domo tries to interrupt but is not allowed. "According to our needs, we shall bring about the death of those individuals following the order of a list drawn up arbitrarily. On occasion we may modify that order, still arbitrarily. And we shall inherit."

CAESONIA—What has come over you?

CALIGULA (*imperturbable*)—Since all our citizens are equally guilty, the order of the executions is not of the slightest importance. Or, rather, those executions are all of equal importance, which is equivalent to saying that they have no importance whatsoever. It is no more immoral to rob citizens directly, than to slip indirect taxes into the price of the commodities they cannot do without. Governing amounts to robbing, as everyone knows. But there are different ways of going about it. As for me, I shall rob openly. That will be a change from the penny pinchers. Carry out these orders without delay. All inhabitants of Rome must make their wills this very evening, and those in the provinces within a month at the latest. Send out your messengers.

MAJOR DOMO—Caesar, you don't seem to realize . . .

CALIGULA—Listen carefully, idiot. If the Treasury is important, then human life is not. That is obvious. All those who think as you do must accept this reasoning and cease to value their lives, since the only thing that has any value for them is money. Besides, *I* have decided to be logical and, inasmuch as I have the power, you will see what logic will cost you. I shall crush out contradictors and contradictions. If need be, I shall begin with you.

Having rid himself of the terrified Major Domo, Caligula answers Caesonia and Scipio. What he has said is not exactly a joke; it is a moral teaching. Scipio finds it impossible. "That is just it," says Caligula, "I am concerned with the impossible, or rather with making possible what is not possible." "But that's the game of a mad man," cries Scipio. With his new-found logic, Caligula explains that he has finally understood the uses of power. "It gives the impossible its chance. Today and for all time to come, my freedom knows no bounds."

When Cherea expresses his pleasure in his emperor's return, he is told to get out. Caligula says that he can't endure the lies of intellectuals.

CHEREA—If we lie, we often do so without knowing it. I plead Not Guilty.

CALIGULA—Lying is always guilty. And your lie gives importance to people and things. That is what I cannot forgive.

CHEREA—And yet one must plead in favor of this world, if we wish to live in it.

CALIGULA—No plea is necessary, the trial is over. This world has no importance and whoever recognizes that wins his freedom. And that's just it—I hate you because you are bound. I alone am free. Rejoice, for you finally have an emperor to teach you freedom. Go away, Cherea, and you, too, Scipio; friendship is a lie. Go and announce to Rome that at last it has its freedom, and that, with it, Rome will have to stand a great trial.

Left with Caesonia, Caligula weeps bitterly and confesses how bitter it is to become a man. Urging him to relax, to stop thinking and to sleep, Caesonia assures him that on awakening the world will seem the way it did and that he will use his power "for loving better what there is still to love. The possible deserves to be given its chance, too." But what Caligula now wants is beyond the power of the gods: "I want to mingle sea and sky, ugliness and beauty, and make laughter burst from the heart of suffering." Then, proclaiming wrathfully that love is nothing, that everything begins with the Treasury, Caligula invites Caesonia to an enormous celebration, to a great trial, to the greatest of spectacles. "And," he shouts, "I need people—an audience and victims and the accused." Rushing to a gong, he starts striking it. The blows rain faster and faster. "Bring in the guilty," cries Caligula. "I need the guilty. And they are all guilty. Bring in the condemned men! I want my public! Judges, witnesses, accused, all sentenced to death in advance! Ah, Caesonia, I shall show them what they have never seen—the only free man in this Empire . . ." Ordering Caesonia to obey him and to help him always, he demands that she be cruel and relentless, and that she also suffer. Over the awful din, Caesonia promises to be as Caligula wishes.

As the crowd gathers, Caligula summons Caesonia to his side before a large mirror. Ordering everyone to come closer, he swings a mallet at his reflection; the glass shatters. "All gone," he shouts. "Now you see. No more memories, and all the faces wiped away! Nothing left. And you know what remains? Come closer. Look. Come closer, all of you and look." Adopting the pose of a crazy man in front of the mirror, he shouts in a voice of triumph: "Caligula!"

Scene II

Three years later, while indulging in a blend of orgy and political meeting, the patricians talk rebellion. Insulted and pauperized, their wives put in brothels, their fathers and sons killed, the rabble urged to push them around, the patricians have reached the point of deciding to storm the palace. Putting down their drinks and casting aside their slave girls, they move to take on the palace guard when they are challenged by Cherea. "It is not as easy as you think, friends," he says. "The fear you feel cannot take the place of courage and self-control. This is all premature." He is, of course, with them—but for different reasons. They must first of all see Caligula as he is: a mad tyrant who is not mad enough. What Cherea most loathes in him is that he knows what he wants.

Octavius—He wants the death of every one of us.

Cherea—No, that is secondary. But he is using his power to further a nobler and more deadly passion; he is threatening everything we hold most sacred. To be sure, this is not the first time that a single man in our state has had unlimited power, but this is the first time that such a man has used that power in an unlimited way—to the point of negating man himself and the world itself. This is what frightens me. This is what I want to fight. Losing my life is a small matter; I shall have enough courage when the time comes. But seeing the meaning of that life undermined and our justification for living taken from us—that is what is unbearable! No one can live without justification.

Octavius—Revenge is a justification.

Cherea—Yes, and I shall share it with you. But I want you to realize that I am not defending you in your petty humiliations. I intend to fight against a great idea which, if it won out, would mean the end of my world. I am not upset by the fact that you are turned to ridicule, but I am upset at the thought that Caligula may do what he dreams of doing and all he dreams of doing. He is transforming his philosophy into corpses and, unfortunately for us, it is an irrefutable philosophy. When one cannot refute, one must strike.

Cassius—Then we must act.

They must act, agrees Cherea, but they must act with cunning against such dispassionate wickedness. The thing to do, urges Cherea, is to wait until that logic has become madness. He is even ready to encourage Caligula to continue: "We shall help organize his madness," decides Cherea, "then one day, he will stand alone, facing an Empire peopled only by the dead and relatives of the dead." Agreeing happily with this intellectual excuse for inaction, Octavius cries enthusiastically: "Then gentlemen, we stand prepared."

In the midst of this patriotic uproar, Caligula arrives with his retinue. Gazing haughtily at the conspirators who stare guiltily back, he parades in review before them, belches in their faces, and exits. He then returns. He has decided to dine at the patricians' table, and orders the patricians to set the table and to serve him. Furthermore, he orders one of their wives to join him at the table and remain at his side. He then briefly amuses himself by making Cassius, whose son he has put to death, laugh at a ghoulish story he now tells.

CALIGULA—Once upon a time, there was a poor emperor whom no one loved. He, loving Cassius, had Cassius' younger son put to death to remove that love from his heart. (*Changing his manner.*) Needless to say, that's not true. But it's funny, isn't it? You are not laughing. No one is laughing? Just listen to me, then. (*In an outburst of wrath.*) I want everyone to laugh. You, Cassius, and all the others. Stand up and laugh. (*He bangs on the table.*) I want—you hear me—I want to see you laugh. (*He pounds the table violently.* CASSIUS *rises and painfully forces laughter till it verges on weeping.* CALIGULA *then looks at each patrician in turn, while each one laughs. Then, like an orchestra leader, he conducts a series of staccato laughs from them all. He stops them with a conductor's gesture, and joins* HELICON *and* CAESONIA.) Just look at them, Caesonia. The die is cast. Decency, respectability, regard for public opinion, the wisdom of the nations, everything has ceased to have any meaning. All swept away by fear. What a noble emotion fear is, Caesonia, pure and unalloyed and disinterested, one of the few to derive its nobility from the guts. (*He passes his hand over his forehead and sits again, then says in a friendly way*)—Let us talk of something else now—

It is now Caligula's desire to have a patrician speak of his wife as —forcing the frightened woman to her knees in front of him, and all the while looking at the patrician—he unbuttons the woman's dress and with great deliberateness thrusts his hand in. The man can only say that he loves his wife. "Of course, my friend, of course," answers Caligula. "But there's nothing extraordinary about that. By the way, when I came in, you were plotting, weren't you? You were indulging in a little plot, weren't you?" "Caius, how can you?" says an old patrician. "It's not at all important, darling," Caligula replies. "Old age will have its fling. Not important at all. You are all incapable of a courageous act. It has just occurred to me that I have some matters of state to decide. But first, I must answer the overwhelming desires that nature prompts." Rising, he coolly snaps his fingers at the patrician's wife and waits at the entrance of the room, while she turns pleadingly to her husband. As the patrician averts his eyes, she strikes him in the face and rushes out with Caligula.

Having done with the girl, Caligula returns her to her husband with thanks, and moves on to more important matters. He has decided that tomorrow all the empire's granaries will be ordered shut. There will be of course a famine, a national calamity, one that only he can stop. "After all," says Caligula, "I haven't so many ways of proving I'm free. One is always free at the expense of others. It's a bore but that's the way it is." Turning to the man whose wife he has just raped, "Just try applying that thought to jealousy and you will understand. Still, how ugly jealousy is! To suffer through vanity and imagination! To picture one's wife . . ."

Being concerned with other hungers, Caligula bolts some food and announces another plan he has. He wants, with the help of the patricians, to reorganize his imperial brothel. "At your service, Caius," says Cherea. "What's the matter? Is the staff inadequate?" "No," Caligula says, "but the grosses are." Since it appears unwise to raise the prices, he has a plan to increase the volume. He lets Caesonia explain the details. "It's very simple," says Caesonia. "Caligula is creating a brand new decoration." Cherea fails to see the connection. "There is one, however," says Caesonia. "The decoration will be called the Medal of Civic Merit. It will be awarded to those citizens who have been most zealous in their patronage of Caligula's brothel." "Why it's brilliant," says Cherea. "I think so," she continues. "I forgot to tell you that the medal will be awarded each month after checking the admission tickets; any citizen who has not won a medal within twelve months is to be exiled or executed." Helicon points out for Cherea's benefit that everything is done in the most moral way. "After all, it is better to tax vice," says Helicon, "than to ransom virtue as republic societies do."

Distracted by an old patrician's drinking from a little phial, Caligula asks what he is drinking. Told that it's to help the old man's asthma, Caligula insists that it's some kind of antidote—because the man fears Caligula will poison him. "You suspect me. You don't really trust me," he says.

CALIGULA (*harshly*)—Answer me. (*In a mathematically logical tone.*) Since you are taking an antidote, you obviously think I intend to poison you.

MEREIA (OLD PATRICIAN)—Yes . . . I mean . . . No.

CALIGULA—And since you think I have decided to poison you, you are doing all you can to thwart my will. That constitutes two crimes, plus an alternative from which you can't escape. Either I had no intention of causing your death and you are unjustly suspecting me, your emperor. Or else I had such an intention and you, miserable worm, are daring to thwart my plans. Well, Mereia, what do you say of that logic?

MEREIA—It's water-tight, Caius. But it doesn't apply to the case.

CALIGULA—Ah! A third crime! You take me for an idiot. Just listen carefully. Of these three crimes, only one of them is a credit to you, the second—for the moment you attribute a decision to me and oppose it, that implies revolt. You are therefore a leader of men, a revolutionary. That is noble. (*Crosses to* HELICON *and holds hand out.* HELICON *hands him a poison phial.*) I am fond of you, Mereia. That is why you will be condemned for your second crime, the noble one, and not for the others. You will die like a man for having rebelled. Don't thank me, it's quite natural. Here. Drink this poison.

As the old man, weeping, backs away, Caligula grows impatient. With a wild leap, he catches him, throws him down, straddles his body, and jams the phial between the man's teeth. After a few convulsive movements, Mereia dies.

Getting up and automatically wiping his hands, Caligula asks: "What was it? An antidote?" "No, Caligula," says Caesonia calmly, "it was a remedy for asthma." After a pause and a glance at the body, Caligula concludes that it doesn't matter a bit. "It all comes to the same thing in the end. A little sooner, a little later . . ." And still wiping his hands, he hurries out.

In shocked tones Cassius asks what they are to do. "To begin with," suggests Caesonia, "remove the body, I should say. It's too ugly!" As that is done, Caesonia approaches Scipio. Both she and Helicon are well aware that a rebellion is brewing. She asks Scipio to understand Caligula. Scipio, turning to Helicon for help, receives very little. "Too dangerous, my little dove," says Helicon, "and poetry is a closed book to me." "You could help me," Scipio pleads, "for you know so many things." "I know," says Helicon, "that time passes and one mustn't miss a meal. I also know that you are capable of killing Caligula . . . and that he wouldn't see anything wrong in that."

Returning and handling Scipio in his own fashion, Caligula sets out to charm him. Quickly rekindling former affection, asking Scipio to recite his latest poem and listening sympathetically to it, Caligula soon wins the boy over. Embracing Scipio and caressing him, Caligula says: "If only I could know your purity! But I know only too well my own passion for life; it could never be content with nature. You can't understand that. You belong to another world. You are all good as I am all evil." "I *can* understand," Scipio assures him.

CALIGULA—No, there is something hidden in me—a pool of silence matted with rotting weeds. (*Suddenly changing his manner.*) Your poem must be very beautiful. But if you wish my opinion . . .

SCIPIO—Yes.

CALIGULA—It all lacks flesh and blood.

SCIPIO (*recoiling in horror*)—You monster! You vile monster! Again you have been leading me on. You've just been pretending, haven't you, and you're pleased with yourself?

CALIGULA (*with a touch of sadness*)—There is some truth in what you say. I have been pretending.

SCIPIO—What a vile, blood-stained heart you must have. Oh! how you must be tortured by so much evil and hatred.

CALIGULA (*gently*)—That's enough, now.

SCIPIO—How I pity and hate you!

CALIGULA (*in anger*)—That's enough, I say!

SCIPIO—And how horribly lonely you must be!

CALIGULA (*bursting into a rage, seizing* SCIPIO *by the collar, shaking him and throwing him down*)—Lonely! Do you think *you* know what loneliness is? The loneliness of poets and impotent men! There are all kinds of loneliness. You don't know that a man is never alone, that wherever he goes the same weight of future and past crushes him! Those we have killed are with us. If it were only for them, all would be easy. But those we have loved, those we didn't love though they loved us, regrets, desires, bitterness and tenderness, whores and the closed society of gods. Alone! Oh, if only—instead of this overcrowded solitude of mine—I could enjoy real silence with only the rustling of a tree! (*Seated and suddenly weary.*) Solitude! No, Scipio, it is filled with gnashing of teeth and clamorous with the din of past sounds. And lying beside any woman I caress, as night closes over us and my body is finally sated, when I hope to find myself poised between life and death, even then my solitude is filled with the stale smell of pleasure from the woman still moaning at my side. (*Young* SCIPIO *hesitantly approaches him. He stretches out his hand and lays it on* CALIGULA's *shoulder. Without turning around,* CALIGULA *covers it with his.*)

SCIPIO—All men have some secret consolation in life, toward which they turn when they are spent. It helps them to go on.

CALIGULA—That's true, Scipio.

SCIPIO—Is there nothing of the sort in your life—a sense of tears, some haven of silence? Nothing to which you can turn?

CALIGULA—Yes, there is.

SCIPIO—What is it? (*Long pause.* CALIGULA *pushes* SCIPIO'S *hand off his shoulder.*)

CALIGULA (*slowly and deliberately*)—Contempt.

ACT II

Constantly caught off guard, the patricians can never be sure of anything. If Caligula does not choose to rape or murder or betray, he may want to entertain. With Helicon's and Caesonia's ever-present help, Caligula now puts on a female impersonation act and, incidentally, a debunking of the gods.

To the clashing of cymbals and the roll of drums, Caligula—after pitchmen preliminaries by Helicon and Caesonia—rises from a huge pink shell at the top of a huge column as a naked Venus. While having Caesonia conduct ludicrous prayers to the goddess he is impersonating, Caligula also passes a collection pot among his worshippers. This done, he hastens their disorderly retreat with a reminder that he has stationed guards at some of the doors to murder them. Amid the ensuing uproar, Scipio can be heard to cry: "You blaspheme, Caius."

CALIGULA—So you believe in the gods, Scipio?

SCIPIO—No.

CALIGULA—Then, I don't understand: why are you so ready to point out blasphemy?

SCIPIO—I can deny something without feeling obliged to befoul it or deprive others of the right to believe in it.

CALIGULA—Oh, dear Scipio, how happy I am for you. And even a bit envious. You have a feeling of genuine modesty, and that's the only feeling I shall perhaps never have myself.

SCIPIO—You're not jealous of me, but rather of the gods themselves.

CALIGULA (*removes mask and sits on column base*)—With your permission, I'd like that to be the great secret of my reign. The only thing anyone can blame me for today is having taken one more step on the path of power and freedom. For a man who loves power, there is something irritating about the gods' rivalry. I have done away with that. I have proved to those capricious gods that, without previous training, a mere man, if he puts his mind to it, can practice their ridiculous profession.

Kenneth Haigh, Colleen Dewhurst and Philip Bourneuf in "Caligula"

SCIPIO—That's what I mean by blasphemy, Caius.

CALIGULA—No, Scipio, it's clarity. I have simply grasped the fact that there is only one way of equaling the gods: all that's needed is to be as cruel as they.

SCIPIO—All that's needed is to become a tyrant.

CALIGULA—What's a tyrant?

SCIPIO—A blind soul.

CALIGULA—I am not sure of that, Scipio. A tyrant is a man who sacrifices nations to his ideas or to his ambition. I have no ideas and there are no further honors or powers for me to covet. I wield this power as a compensation.

SCIPIO—For what?

CALIGULA—For the stupidity and hatred of the gods.

SCIPIO—Hatred does not make up for hatred. Power is not a solution. I know of but one way of balancing the world's hostility.

CALIGULA—What is it?

SCIPIO—Poverty.

CALIGULA (*pause*)—I must try that one too.

Caligula argues that actually because he has embarked on no wars, he is a respecter of human life. "If you knew how to count," he says, "you would realize that the least war undertaken by a reasonable tyrant would cost you a thousand times more than my whims do." "But," says Scipio, "at least it would be reasonable, and the important thing is to understand." "Fate is never understood," answers Caligula, "and that is why I have become fate. I have taken on the stupid and incomprehensible look of the gods. That's what your friends were adoring a moment ago." Scipio calls this blasphemy whereas Caligula maintains that it's art. "All those men make the mistake of not believing sufficiently in the theatre. Otherwise they would know that any man can play celestial tragedy and become a god." Doing a mock dance, he wins Helicon's and Caesonia's applause. "All that's needed," he says, "is to harden one's heart." "And you have done that, Caius," Scipio answers, "and at the same time you have hardened all hearts around you. Some day legions of human gods, just as ruthless as you, will rise up around you and bathe in blood your momentary divinity." As Caesonia remonstrates, Caligula says that he's absolutely right, though he finds it hard to picture that day. Sometimes, however, he dreams of it: "All those faces coming at me from the depths of my bitter nights, distorted by hatred and anguish. And," Caligula adds, "I welcome them. For I see in them the only god I have ever adored—crushed and rebellious humanity." Then, suddenly annoyed at Scipio for speaking out, he dismisses him.

Giving his full attention now to painting his toenails, Caligula refuses to concentrate on what Helicon is saying. As Helicon tries to tell him of the plot against his life, Caligula merely asks how his moon-catching is coming along. Vexed beyond endurance, Helicon says that whether Caligula wants to listen or not, he feels it his duty to tell Caligula that there is a plot against his life and that Cherea is the leader of it. "I came across this tablet which will tell you the essentials," says Helicon, and he places it on the stair before he leaves. "Where are you going, Helicon?" Caligula asks. "To get the moon for you," sighs Helicon.

After Helicon leaves, an old patrician arrives as an informer on his fellow-conspirators. Taunting him and daubing him with nail polish, Caligula refuses to hear him out. "I have constantly loathed cowardice so much that I could never resist having a traitor put to death," he tells the old man, "but I know your worth. And certainly, you would not intentionally either betray or die." In the end the terrified old man, taking his cue from Caligula, agrees that there is no conspiracy, that it is all a joke. Made to look a fool, he is allowed to leave. At the same time, however, Caligula bids the guard send for Cherea.

Shown into Caligula's presence Cherea, when confronted with the conspiracy, doesn't hesitate to admit his complicity or to give his reasons: "I consider you harmful. I like and need security. Most men are like me. They are incapable of living in a universe in which, within the twinkling of an eye, the strangest thoughts can become reality—where most of the time they do become reality, like a knife in one's heart. I cannot live in such a universe. I prefer to keep myself under control."

CALIGULA—Security and logic don't go together.

CHEREA—That is true. What I say isn't logical, but it is healthy.

CALIGULA—Go on.

CHEREA—I have nothing more to say. I don't want to share your logic. I have a different conception of my duties as a man. I know that most of your subjects think as I do. You stand in the way of all. It is natural that you should disappear.

CALIGULA—All that is quite clear and quite legitimate. For most men it would even be obvious. Not for you, however. You are intelligent and a man either pays dear for intelligence or else negates it. *I* am paying up. But why are *you* both unwilling to negate it and unwilling to pay up?

CHEREA—Because I want to live and be happy. I don't think a man can do either when he pushes the absurd to its extreme. I am like everybody else. In order to liberate myself from them, I have sometimes longed for the death of those I loved the most, I have coveted women that the laws of the family or of friendship forbade me. In order to be logical, I ought at such moments to kill or possess. But I consider that such vague ideas are not important. If everybody tried to realize them, we could neither live nor be happy. Let me repeat, that is what matters to me.

CALIGULA—Then you must believe in some higher ideal.

CHEREA—I believe that some acts are better than others.

CALIGULA—I believe that all are equivalent.

CHEREA—I know that, Caius, and that is why I don't hate you. But you stand in our way and you must disappear.

CALIGULA—That's quite reasonable. But why tell me and risk your life?

CHEREA—Because others will take my place and because I don't like to lie.

Patiently awaiting Caligula's judgment, Cherea, seeing the wax tablet in his hand, matter-of-factly acknowledges that he knew Caligula had it in his possession. Caligula notes in a suddenly passionate voice that this tablet is the only proof of the conspiracy. Cherea remarks indifferently that Caligula has no need of proof to put a man to death. "You are right. But for once I want to contradict myself," says Caligula. "It will harm no one, and it is so good to contradict oneself from time to time—it relaxes a man. I need relaxation, Cherea." Cherea neither understands nor cares for these subtleties; he just wishes that Caligula would get on with whatever he's going to do. Asking for patience, Caligula takes the offending tablet and dramatically melts it over a brazier's flame. "You see, conspirator," he cries. "It melts, and as this proof disappears, a new innocence dawns on your face again. What a wonderful pure face you have, Cherea. How beautiful an innocent man is, how beautiful! Marvel at my power. The gods themselves cannot renew innocence without punishing first. And your emperor needs but a flame to absolve and expiate you. Carry on, Cherea, carry out to its conclusion the wonderful reasoning you have just given me. Your emperor longs for his rest. That's his way of living and being happy."

Scene II

Rounding up his conspirators for swift action, Cherea has trouble with Scipio, who despite everything that Caligula has done to him, still balks: "I cannot choose because with all my suffering, I know what he is suffering. My misfortune is in understanding everything." "So then you have chosen to take his side," says Cherea.

Scipio—Oh no, Cherea, I beg you. I can never again take anyone's side, not anyone's!

Cherea (*with deep emotion*)—Do you know that I hate him even more for what he has done to you?

Scipio—Yes, he has taught me to accept nothing on faith.

Cherea—No, Scipio, he has taught you despair. And to drive a pure young soul to despair is a worse crime than those he had committed previously. That alone, I assure you, would justify my killing him in a burst of rage.

Suddenly Helicon and his guards herd all the conspirators together and push them onto the stairs of the palace. They are a bewildered, somewhat desperate group, standing there in the middle of the night. Knowing they should have acted sooner, they regard torture as inevitable. "I recall that Caligula gave 81,000 sesterces to a slave who, despite torture, wouldn't confess to a theft he had committed," Cherea observes coolly. "That's a great help to us at the moment," says Octavius. Cherea's calm manner doesn't desert him though there is a slight change of tone when a slave enters with a gigantic sword and war axe. "We should have acted rapidly," complains Octavius. "We waited too long." "Yes, but the lesson comes too late," says Cherea.

Finding "extreme relaxation" in all manner of ways, Caligula now makes an entrance before silken curtains in a flower-bedecked dancing skirt. With the help of a musical accompaniment, Caligula soberly executes a flowery dance and exits with the crossed weapons held high. Caesonia then comes forth and says that Caligula had just invited them all to participate with him in an artistic emotion. "He added, moreover," says Caesonia, "that anyone who had failed to participate would have his head cut off." There is a general silence. "Forgive my insistence," says Caesonia, "but I must ask you if the dance seemed beautiful to you." Econiums flow.

CHEREA (*coldly*)—It was great art.
CAESONIA (*exiting*)—Good. Now I can inform Caligula.
HELICON—Tell me, Cherea, was it really great art?
CHEREA—Yes, in a way.
HELICON—I see your meaning. You are very clever, Cherea. Deceptive as only a respectable citizen can be. But clever indeed. *I* am not clever. And yet I shall not let you touch a hair of Caius' head, even if that's what he himself wants.
CHEREA—I don't understand a word of what you're saying. But I congratulate you on your devotion to duty. I like devoted servants.
HELICON—You're really proud of yourself, aren't you? Yes, I am at the service of a mad man. But who is your master? Virtue? Let me tell you what I think of virtue. I was born a slave. Well, respectable citizen, I first heard of virtue when I used to dance to a whip. Caius never used any eloquence on me. He liberated me and took me into his palace. That is how I had a chance to watch you virtuous men. And I saw that you had a mothy look and a rotten smell, the stale smell of those who have never suffered or risked anything. I have seen the togas nobly draped when the heart was worn to a frazzle, the face screaming avarice, and the hand shifty. You, our judges? You who publicize your virtue, who dream of security as a virgin dreams of love, who will die, nevertheless, in convulsions of fright without even knowing that you have lied all your life long, you will attempt to judge a man who has suffered throughout life and who is bleeding every day from a thousand new wounds? You will flog me as you always have, but don't worry! Despise the slave. He is beyond virtue because he can still love this wretched master. And he will protect him against your noble lies and your skilful perjury.
CHEREA—Dear Helicon, you are indulging in eloquence. Frankly, your taste was better once.

HELICON—I'm very sorry, indeed. That comes from spending too much time in your company. But I'm pulling myself together, never fear, I'm pulling myself together. But just this . . . Look, do you see this face? Fine. Look at it carefully. Splendid. Now you have seen your enemy. (CHEREA *laughs and turns away.* HELICON *draws his sword and holding it flat against* CHEREA'S *face, turns his head so that he must look him in the eye, and then goes.*)

Finally made angry, Cherea is determined on action that night.

Ordered to remain at the palace, the patricians endure the calculated barbs of Caesonia and listen to her strange little news bulletins of Caligula's suddenly deteriorating health. In the excessive warmth of his good wishes for Caligula's recovery, Cassius unwisely cries: "Jupiter, take my life in exchange for his"—and Caligula, popping into view, at once takes him up on his offer, and the guards haul Cassius away.

When Cherea returns, Caesonia plays a little game on him: she announces the emperor's death. Cherea, after a brief pause, murmurs politely: "It's a great misfortune, Caesonia." Popping into the room, Caligula applauds Cherea's performance and disappears once more.

In line with his habit of alternating amusement with assassination, Caligula has decided that today will be especially devoted to the arts and has summoned a group of poets to the palace for a poetry competition. "Needless to say, there will be rewards," says Caesonia, "and the penalties won't be too severe."

As the ill-assorted group lines up, Caligula describes what they have to do: they are to write a poem on "Death" and they have one minute to write it in. He will be the judge and the timekeeper. Cherea wonders that he isn't a contestant too. Having written a poem on that theme years ago, Caligula says that he finds it unnecessary to write another. He points out for Cherea's special benefit: "It's the only poem I have ever fathered, but it's living proof that I am the only true artist Rome has ever known—the only one—I insist, Cherea—to reconcile his thoughts and his deeds." "It's only a question of power," says Cherea. "Quite right," agrees Caligula. "The others create because they lack the power. I don't need to make a work of art: I *live* it."

Converting his contest into a mad farce, Caligula with his piercing whistle stops each contestant in mid-metaphor. But when Scipio recites wearily:

> "Pursuit of happiness cleansing us,
> Sun-saturated sky,
> Oh savage rites, ecstasy without hope! . . ."

Caligula stops him gently: "You are too young to know the meaning of death so well." "I was too young to lose my father," replies
Scipio.

Ending his artistic day as suddenly as it began, Caligula, alone
with Caesonia, finds that when he is not killing he is really rather
lonely. He is comfortable only among his dead. As Caesonia, now
that he is quiet, seeks to console him in her arms, he is aware of the
clank of steel and of thousands of muffled sounds. Caesonia, sure
that no one would dare seek him out, cries vehemently: "*We* shall
defend you. There are still many of us left who love you." "There
are fewer and fewer of you," Caligula corrects her. "I have taken
care of that. Besides, let's be fair and admit that stupidity is not
my only enemy. There are also the loyalty and courage of those who
want to be happy." Wondering at Caesonia's sudden show of love
he says that certainly wasn't part of the agreement. "Hasn't it been
bad enough seeing you kill others?" she asks. "Must I now face your
being killed? Isn't it enough taking you into my bed all torn and
tearing, breathing your smell of murder when you lie on top of me?
Each day I see you slipping farther and farther away from any human likeness." Quietly taking off her wig and revealing her greying
hair, Caesonia says: "I am old and on the point of becoming ugly,
I know. But my love, my fear for you has shaped my soul so that
now I don't even care if you no longer love me. I only want to see
you get well, for you are still a child, with a whole life ahead of you!
What more do you want than a whole life? Is there more than that?"

Standing close to this witness of so many frantic and joyless nights
who alone knows so much about him, Caligula says that he "can't
resist a sort of shameful sentimental tenderness for the old woman
she will become." "Tell me that you want to keep me!" Caesonia
begs. "I don't know," says Caligula. "I am merely aware—and
this is the worst of it—that such sentimental tenderness is the only
pure emotion I've ever had." When Caesonia tries to embrace him,
he suddenly wonders: "Wouldn't it be better for the last witness
to disappear?" Aware, too, that love doesn't last, that grief doesn't
last, he knows that nothing lasts. Laughing wildly, he cries: "Think
of the value of knowing that! There are only two or three of us
in all history who have really experienced that and achieved this
insane happiness. Caesonia, you have watched out to the very end
a very strange tragedy. It is time for the curtain to fall for you."
Terrified, Caesonia throws herself at his feet: "Can this be happiness," she cries, "this terrifying freedom?" Locking his forearm
around her throat, Caligula says: "You may be sure of it, Caesonia.
Without it, I might have been a smug man. Thanks to it, I have
won the god-like lucidity of the solitary man."

His excitement increases as he gradually strangles Caesonia. "I live and kill," says Caligula for her ear alone." I wield the frenzied power of the destroyer which makes the creator's power seem laughable. That's what it is to be happy. That's what happiness is— this unbearable liberation, this universal contempt, blood and hatred all around me, this unparalleled isolation of the man who sees his whole life at once, the measureless joy of the unpunished assassin, this ruthless logic that crushes human lives, that is crushing you, Caesonia, to complete at last the eternal solitude I desire."

Hearing the distant sound of arms, realizing that he has come to the bitter end, Caligula is afraid and finds it revolting to discover other men's cowardice in himself. Dismissing fear as one more thing that does not last, Caligula finds existence still complicated by his not having the moon. "Yet everything is so simple. If I had had the moon, if love had been enough, all would be changed. But where can I quench this thirst? What heart, what god would be as deep and pure for me as a lake? Neither this world nor the other world has a place for me. Yet I know, and you know—" he stretches his hands toward the moonlight "that all I needed was for the impossible to be—"

Frantic that all this time he has taken the wrong path, that his freedom was not the right one, that in his solitude he needs Helicon, Caligula dashes wildly to the platform at the top of the column. Calling out to Helicon, he drops to knees and weeps.

Below on the palace steps an officer of the guard, a torch in one hand and an unsheathed sword in the other, starts the ascent. Helicon, answering Caligula's call for help, takes on the officer. Patrician conspirators gather as Helicon and the officer, their swords clashing, circle around. Suddenly the officer thrusts his flaming torch in Helicon's face. Blinded, Helicon staggers and cries: "Watch out, Caius! Caius!—" The slain Helicon's fall is the signal for the onslaught. Soldiers and conspirators swarm in the torchlight to the base of the column. "Live in history, Caligula! In history!" cries Caligula as he leaps. His body plummets towards the raised swords and daggers below.

TOYS IN THE ATTIC

A Play in Three Acts

BY LILLIAN HELLMAN

[LILLIAN HELLMAN *was born in New Orleans and educated in New York. She was a book reviewer and play reader before beginning her distinguished career as a playwright. Her first play, "The Children's Hour," ran for 691 performances. Other plays include "Days to Come," "The Little Foxes," "Watch on the Rhine" (which won the Critics Circle Award), "The Searching Wind," "Another Part of the Forest," "The Autumn Garden," and "The Lark." She also wrote the book for the musical "Candide."*]

THE New Orleans house of the Berniers is solidly middle-class of another generation. Its furnishings are ugly and in need of repair, but the general effect is orderly if impoverished. The furniture in the small outside garden has been painted so often as to look rickety; only the plants on the small porch seem to have received proper care.

At the end of a long afternoon, Carrie and Anna Berniers come home from work. Carrie, a once-pretty, tired woman in her late thirties, collapses into a rocker on the porch and wearily fans herself. Her older sister Anna, nice looking, calm and quiet of manner, goes about the living room tidying up. Comparing notes on their hot working day, Carrie says—through the open window—that her boss allowed her to leave the office after lunch. "You're looking a little peaked, Miss Berniers, from the heat," she mimics. "I said I've been looking a little peaked for years in the heat, in cold, in rain, when I was young, and now. You mean you're hot and want to go home, you faker, I said. Only I said it to myself." Anna reports that on a hot day like this her store had to run a coat sale that lasted so late she couldn't even go to the park.

Carrie had chosen to spend her time-off at the cemetery.

ANNA (*stops dusting, sighs*)—Everybody still there?
CARRIE—I took flowers. It's cool there. Cooler. I was the only

person there. Nobody goes to see anybody in summer. Yet those who have passed away must be just as lonely in summer as they are in winter. Sometimes I think we shouldn't have put Mama and Papa at Mount Olive Cemetery. Maybe it would have been nicer for them at Mount Great Hope with the new rich people. What would you think if we don't get buried at Mount Olive with Mama and Papa?

ANNA—Any place that's cool.

CARRIE—I bought you a small bottle of Eau d'haut Alpine. Cologne water of the high Alps, I guess. (*Holds up package.*) Your weekly present. What did you buy me, may I ask, who shouldn't?

ANNA—Jar of candied oranges.

CARRIE—Oh, how nice. We'll have them for a savory. Do you know I read in our travel book on England that *they* think a proper savory is an anchovy. Anchovy after dinner. They won't make me eat it. . . .

As Anna busies herself with cleaning, Carrie wonders if this house was always so big. "It just grew as people left," answers Anna. Carrie confesses that she never liked this house, though she knows that Anna did. Ignoring Anna's surprise at her special knowledge, Carrie says that Julian never liked it either—which was the reason for their eating supper out on the porch steps. "Did you ever know that's why I used to bring Julian out here, even when he was a baby, and we'd have our supper on the steps? I didn't want him to find out about the house. Julian and I. Nice of Mama and Papa to let us, wasn't it? Must have been a great deal of trouble carrying the dishes out here. Mama had an agreeable nature." Anna reminds Carrie that it was she who brought their dishes outside, and though she minded very much, she ate inside in that horrid dining room with their parents. Thanking Anna after so many years, Carrie finds it funny that you can live so close and not know things. Agreeing, Anna mentions that she called Mr. Shine about the house today. Not having had an inquiry in months, he suggested reducing the price on the house, but there was nothing to reduce it to. Carrie brushes this off by saying that Anna always gets mean to the house when something worries her. Anna retorts that Carrie always goes to the cemetery.

The reason for their joint worry is that for two weeks there has been no letter from Julian. "I went to the main post office today," says Carrie, "and said I was sure there'd been some confusion. Would they please call the other Berniers and see if a letter was there? And Alfie said, Carrie, there are no other Berniers in New Orleans. There are some live in Biloxi, Mississippi, with a hardware store, but the central government of the United States does not give money to Louisiana to make calls to Mississippi, although maybe you could change that if you said it was Julian who had written the letter he didn't write. I was angry, but I didn't show it. How do you know it's Julian I am talking about? I said. We're expecting letters from Paris and Rome and Strasbourg in reply to inquiries about our forthcoming tour." "Julian's busy, that's all," Anna says quietly.

As Gus, a Negro handy man, comes into the yard with ice for their icebox, Carrie frets over Julian's long silence. She confesses that she telephoned Chicago, and the hotel manager reported that Julian and Lily had moved months ago. This is no news to Anna, who had found that out when letters were returned stamped "address unknown." As Gus suggests that they ought to treat themselves to a new icebox, Carrie announces loudly that they're going to treat themselves good. They're going to sell the house, never come back, and go on a long trip.

This is the second time today that Carrie has broadcast the fact that they're going to Europe. Wondering what's got into her, she's all for going over their travel books this evening. Anna wants none of it. She doesn't want to talk or think about Europe until they're actually ready to go. Carrie says it was Anna who postponed the trip after the wedding. This Anna denies. Carrie now concedes that they had to spend their savings on a handsome wedding present for a girl as rich as Lily. Again Anna disagrees: to a girl as much in love as Lily, the wedding present wouldn't have made a speck of difference. Steering the conversation back to a European trip in the near future, Carrie asks how much is in their savings account, and has Anna made the weekly deposit? Having had no time to make the deposit, Anna reports that the balance is still $2,843. In her roundabout fashion, Carrie has found out what she wanted to know: Anna had not been to the bank. Quickly changing the subject, she suggests eating out tonight as a treat. Then going to the piano, she suggests brushing up on their French in preparation for their trip. Opening a song book, she plays and sings:

"*Une chambre pour deux dames.* Have you one room for two ladies?

"*Ah non! Trop chères!* Oh no! Too expensive!

"*Merci, M'sieur. Trop chères* . . .

"We'll stay in Paris of course, for just as long as we want. Then we'll go to Strasbourg, have the famous pâté, and put flowers on the graves of Mama's relatives." "I'll have pâté," Anna says. "You put the flowers on the graves of Mama's relatives."

Having worked herself up to the idea of the trip, Carrie now works her way out of it. She doesn't really think they should go unless they had more money to spend. They'd better save for a year more. Anna finds that at their age a year can be a long time. Exuding false excitement, Carrie says that she too wants to go now. "Come on. Let's do," she cries. "I can't tell you how much I want to go. That and a good piano. Every time there's a wishbone I say I want a good life for Julian, a piano, a trip to Europe. That's all. You know even if we can't go to Europe we could afford a little trip to Chicago. The coach fares are very cheap." "I don't think," admonishes Anna, "that we should run after Julian and Lily and intrude on their lives." It now turns out that Carrie had removed a thousand dollars from their savings account and wired it to Julian yesterday with love from Anna and herself; she felt sure that it would be properly forwarded.

ANNA (*slowly*)—I don't think you should have done that.

CARRIE—But I knew you would want to send it—

ANNA—How do you know what I would want?

CARRIE (*slowly, hurt*)—Shouldn't I know what you want for Julian? I'm sorry our trip will have to wait a little longer, but—

ANNA—I'm sorry, too. But it's not the trip. Nor the money. We are interfering, and we told ourselves we wouldn't.

Carrie would even now telephone Julian if she could, but there's nowhere to phone.

While this has been going on, Albertine Prine and Henry Simpson have entered the Berniers garden. A handsome, quietly elegant woman of about forty-five, Mrs. Prine speaks carefully as if not used to talking very much. Her companion, Henry Simpson, a colored man the same age as she is, wears a summer suit but carries a chauffeur's cap.

ALBERTINE—Is the older one Miss Caroline?

HENRY (*laughs*)—They call her Carrie. No. Miss Anna is the older one.

ALBERTINE (*smiles*)—You laugh at me. But I only met them twice before the marriage. Two long dinners. Many savage tribes have a law that people must eat alone, in silence. Sensible, isn't it? (*She moves to the porch steps and stops.*) Perhaps it would be best if you went in. I'm not good at seeing people any more, and there will be much chatter. (*He doesn't hear her. She laughs.*) Very well, but I am sure it's hot in there. Would you tell them I'm out here?

HENRY (*gently*)—*You* have come to call on *them*.

ALBERTINE—Nice to live this close to the river. I still like it down here. Soggy and steaming. The flowers aren't strong enough to cover the river smells. That's the way it should be. Very vain of flowers to compete with the Mississippi. My grandmother lived on this street when I was a little girl, and I liked it then. I used to pretend I slept under the river, and had a secret morning door up into this street. What are you holding?

HENRY—A chauffeur's cap.

ALBERTINE—You win many small battles. Never mind. Wear it if you must. Put it on now and say I am here.

HENRY—No. Just go and ring the bell.

As Anna carries out their supper of shrimp and rice, Albertine rings the bell. Carrie is very much flustered at seeing their visitor; Anna wishes her to share their supper. Albertine thanks Anna but refuses: "I eat at midnight. It's my bad habit to live at night and sleep the days away." Carrie remembers Lily having told her this. "I suppose," says Albertine, "it was hard on a child, a young girl, not to have her mother available during the day. But perhaps it was just as well. What time do you expect Lily and Julian?" Understandably confused, not having expected them at all, Carrie is all for meeting the Chicago train. "I'll get dressed right away," she cries, "are there enough shrimps and rice? Is there crayfish bisque left? We can still buy some wine. Get dressed, Anna—" Albertine points out carefully that Julian and Lily are not on the Chicago train. Lily called, and Henry took the message, and the call was from here, New Orleans. Albertine herself saw Lily two nights ago.

ALBERTINE—I didn't speak to her. She was moving back and forth in front of the house as if she wished to come in and didn't wish to come in.

CARRIE—You saw your daughter, after a whole year, walking in front of your house and you didn't speak to her? I don't understand, Mrs. Prine.

ALBERTINE—That's quite all right.

ANNA (softly)—But we need to understand.

ALBERTINE (turns her head, looks at CARRIE and then at ANNA)— Strange. Sometimes I can't tell which of you is speaking. (To CARRIE.) Your manner, Miss Carrie, is so, well, so Southern. And then, suddenly, you are saying what I had thought Miss Anna might say. It is as if you had exchanged faces, back and forth, forth and back.

CARRIE (sharply)—Did you see Julian?

ALBERTINE—There. That's what I mean. No. Julian was not

with Lily. I have simply had a message saying they would be here this evening. I have told you all I know.

CARRIE—What should we do? What are you going to do?

ALBERTINE—I will go home now and ask you to tell Lily that I will come again in the morning. Please tell them that the house is mostly closed up, but by tomorrow I can make them comfortable.

CARRIE—Oh, no. Julian will want to be here—

ALBERTINE—Oh, I'm sure they prefer to stay here, but . . .

ANNA—There must be a good reason why Julian hasn't told us he is in town. If we seem upset, Mrs. Prine, it is because we are not accustomed to—

ALBERTINE—Daughters who walk in the night and mothers who do not speak to daughters who walk in the night. I really don't know why Lily didn't come in to me, nor why I didn't ask her. Good night. Thank you. (*She moves out, followed by* ANNA, *followed by a dazed* CARRIE. HENRY *is waiting in the garden.* ALBERTINE *moves toward him, turns to the porch.*) I think you have met Henry Simpson. Miss Anna and Miss Carrie Berniers, Henry.

HENRY—Good evening. (ALBERTINE *takes his arm and they leave.*)

CARRIE (*softly*)—Is *that* the man Lily calls Henry? *That* man was there in a white coat when we went for dinner, but I didn't know that was the Henry. You mean he's a nigra? I never heard anybody introduce a nigra before. I'm sorry I didn't say something. I never think of things in time. (*Moves to join* ANNA *in the living room.*) That man Lily called Henry is a nigra. Is he a chauffeur? What is he? Last time, he was a butler. Introduces us to a nigra— (*Sits down, desperate.*) Do you believe that strange woman? Do you believe they're in town?

At first Anna suggests that Lily might be pregnant and they have come to see a doctor. Carrie disabuses her of this idea. She knows that girls like Lily want good times, not babies, the first year of marriage. Anna asks teasingly whether she found this out from those books she no longer reads. "You're saying that again. Teasing me again. No, I don't read much any more, and I don't play the piano, or put ice on my face, or walk for wild flowers—" She speaks very loudly, as if she were going to cry. "I get tired now after work and that terrible man. All I want to do is have a little something to eat and play casino, and— Don't you like to play casino with me, is that what you're saying?" "Not every night," answers Anna, "I like to read—"

It occurs to Anna that "it" has happened again, and Julian didn't want to tell them. Justifying Julian's attitude one moment, the next pretending that she doesn't understand Anna, Carrie doesn't appear particularly worried. She doesn't care to see Anna taking the news so calmly, however. She insists that Anna shouldn't be able to eat her supper, that Anna's cool behavior actually indicates nervousness. She begs her not to be cold to Julian on his arrival.

ANNA—Why do you so often make it seem as if I had always been severe and unloving? I don't think it's true.

CARRIE—I don't believe I do that. It's you who gave him everything, long before I was old enough to help.

ANNA (*takes bankbook from pocket*)—Here is the savings bankbook. Give it to him.

CARRIE (*deeply pleased*)—Oh, thank you. I'll give it to him when we're alone and Lily doesn't see.

Having attributed thoughts, motives, and emotions to Anna, Carrie now endows her with a headache. "I haven't a headache. And if I had, I wouldn't know the remedy," says Anna; "a prescription put up fresh each time Julian fails." "Oh, don't be sad," cries Carrie, "I'm not. I feel cheerful. Place and people and time make things go wrong, and then all of a sudden—" There is the noise of a car stopping.

Going to the porch, Carrie plans to greet Julian and jump into his arms as she has done since they were children. Instead there is a triumphant procession: Julian and a taxi driver laden with boxes and bags, and Lily bringing up the rear. In the excitement of Julian's arrival, Carrie pays no attention to his young wife; it takes Anna to welcome her courteously. "One year and six days," calls out Carrie; then belatedly remembering Lily, she kisses her. "Forgive me. One year and six days," she repeats. "I was so excited that I didn't see you." Ordering the driver to bring in the remaining parcels and bags, Julian shouts that he's hungry for Anna's food: "Not a good restaurant in Chicago— Would *not* know a red pepper if they saw one." "There's crayfish in the icebox," cries Carrie, "thank God, and shrimp and rice on the table." Starting at a trot for the kitchen, Carrie watches as Julian pays off the driver with a whopping tip. Anna assumes that her brother has been in another poker game. "And," she asks, "what train came in early?" Carrie tries to cover up for Julian, while Lily, making it all the harder, says that it was a long trip—when it happened.

As Julian wolfs down the shrimp on the table, Anna says: "You've given us no news. How is the shoe factory?" "What shoe factory?" asks Julian. "The shoe factory that you bought in Chicago," she answers carefully. "Oh, *that* shoe factory," says Julian. "It's gone." Anna does not care for his flipness; again Carrie tries to cover up. Noticing Carrie's gestures at Anna, Julian admits that he was being flip. "I forget that you worry about the money I lose."

ANNA—It's not the money—it's that you don't seem to care. And the money was—
JULIAN—Lily's money.
LILY—My money? Doesn't matter about my money. I don't want money.
CARRIE—You mustn't worry about it. Not worth it.
LILY—I'm not worried about money, Miss Carrie.
CARRIE—I suppose rich people always worry about money. People like us have to learn there are more important things.
LILY—I said I wasn't worried about money, Miss Carrie.
CARRIE—Well, you mustn't.

Laughing away the idea that the factory had been a crooked sell, Julian maintains that only he could have been taken in. Carrie excuses him. "Darling Carrie," says Julian, "hiding her hopes that I would come home with Chicago over my shoulder, dressed in pure gold, bringing candied oranges to hang in your hair. Well, that's just what I've done. Your hair doesn't look nice, Carrie-pie."

Anna introduces the news that Lily's mother—who had seen Lily and received her message—was here and would return in the morning. "So this is not your first night in town," she concludes. "You need not explain, but I thought we should." Julian admits that they have been in town a week, but he seems no closer to an explanation than before. Anna is sad that he thinks it all so unimportant, but Carrie won't have that kind of talk. "This is a happy, joyous night," she says stoutly.

Approaching Julian with apologies for having looked up her mother, Lily begs him not to be angry with her.

JULIAN—I am not angry with you. Have I ever been angry with you? Why do you ask me that so often?
LILY—Julian, who is the lady you talked to on the train?
JULIAN—Which lady? I talk to everybody.
LILY—The not such a young lady with the sad face.
JULIAN—Most ladies on trains are not so young and have sad faces. I often wondered why.
LILY—The one you were with yesterday and Sunday—and—
JULIAN (turns, stares at her)—Where did you see me?
LILY—I don't know. Just on the street. In front of the hotel.

Anne Revere, Jason Robards, Jr., Maureen Stapleton and Irene Worth in "Toys in the Attic"

JULIAN—No, you didn't.

LILY—No, I didn't. That's the first lie I ever told you, Julian.

JULIAN—Then it's one more than I ever told you.

LILY—I saw you in Audubon Park. On a bench. By the ducks.

JULIAN—Have you told anybody?

LILY—No.

JULIAN—Don't. The lady would be in trouble. And so would we.

LILY—And in that little restaurant. At a table—

JULIAN—Oh, Lily.

LILY—I didn't mean to walk after you, to follow you. But I was so lonely in the hotel room, locked up the way you asked me to be.

JULIAN—All right, darling, all right. Don't follow me, Lily, ever again. That's not the way to be married.

As Julian starts unpacking presents and would like the general distribution to begin, Carrie wants to give him a private surprise of her own. He calls for Anna, but Carrie shushes him. Making him sit next to her on the porch, she presents him with the bankbook that he is not to show Lily. "Anna," she declares, "doesn't want any thanks." Julian kisses her hands and, returning to the room, holds out the book for Anna to see: "God bless you. All my life it's been this way." "You are our life," Anna smiles, "it is we who should thank you." Julian takes her in his arms.

Seating Carrie in one chair, and Anna in another, Julian picks up large box after large box. But as Julian starts his gay and boisterous present-giving, the atmosphere strangely becomes less gay. His sisters become unhappily bewildered as Julian piles furs, ball gowns, cloaks, and headgear on each of them. Anna submits to being draped in this ludicrous finery, but Carrie is less passive. As Julian presents Carrie with garnets, "her birthstone," and Anna with a gold mesh bag, Anna asks quietly what all this means.

JULIAN—It is that we're rich. Just open your gold mesh bag with diamond initials—Anna, *diamond* initials—and see what's inside.

CARRIE (*loud, nervous giggle*)—The only thing could be, is a certificate to an insane asylum.

JULIAN—You're wrong. A certificate to a boat called the *Ottavia,* sailing day after tomorrow. Two rooms, one of them a parlor. Think of that, a parlor on a boat. Look at it, look at it. Of course, we had always planned to go together. But I won't be able to go with you, darling, not this time, big business here, and all that. But we'll join you in a few months.

CARRIE (*dully*)—We'll wait for you.

Anna would like to know where this comes from. "I know what you mean," Julian answers. "They were bought with my money. Mine. Yours. Ours. We're rich. How do you like that, how do you like it?" Saying she'll like it fine when it happens, Carrie starts rewrapping some of the finery. Julian tries to stop her. Lily, reappearing in a slip, while wielding a hairbrush, announces that trucking men are at the door. Julian gleefully asks her to show them in, and at the same time assures Carrie that the boat tickets she's examining are bought and stamped: "Look, it's going to be this way. The first money is for us to have things. Have fun. After that, I promise you, we'll invest. And like all people with money, we'll make more and more and more until we get sick from it.   Rich people get sick more than we do.   Maybe from worry." Beneath her anything-but-glad rags, Anna says sharply: "Poor people, too. Like me, right now.   Where did you get this money, Julian?"   Carrie doesn't care for her tone, but Julian, not minding in the least, is now superintending the trucking men.   He instructs them to wheel a large refrigerator next to Anna, and a spinet next to Carrie, and pays them off lavishly.

If anything, these grand presents fall flatter than the previous ones.   Carrie shows that she is shocked at Lily's answering the door in her underclothes, while Anna wants the answer to her question.

JULIAN—Once I liked somebody and they liked me, and she thought I was kind to her.   So years go by and she hears about a good thing, and gives me the tip on it.   And the tip works.   Boy, how it worked.   Now let it go.   I'll tell you soon, but in the meantime I gave my word because she could be in bad trouble.   Now stop worrying, and sit back—I finished the deal and collected the money at two o'clock today.   At two-eighteen, I rang the bell of Mr. Maxwell Shine.   And so here's the mortgage to the house. (*Softly*.)   Look, Anna, first time in our lives, first time in our father's life.   You have a house, without worry or asking him to wait.   Remember when I was a kid and the time you took me with you and you made me tell Mr. Shine how I wouldn't have any place to live unless—   Christ God, how I hated—   Do you remember?

ANNA—I remember.

JULIAN—Well, there'll never be such things to say again.   Not for any of us.   (*He shouts*.)   Not ever, ever.   (*Crosses to* CARRIE.)   I wrote your Mr. Barrett a letter last night.   I wrote it three times. "Your petty angers, the silk stockings at Christmas, that were always cheaper than a decent salary—   Miss Caroline Berniers will not return to work."   (CARRIE *makes a sound in her throat, stands staring at him.   He turns to* ANNA.)   For you I just wrote that Miss Anna Berniers was resigning from the coat department because she was leaving for an extended European tour.   (ANNA *lifts her head and stares at him.   There is a long silence*.)   Well.   Say something.

ANNA—I can't say something.

JULIAN—I know, I know.   All came so fast.   Well, we don't have to say things to each other, never did.   Just sit back and have fun. That's all I want.   (*To* LILY.)   And for you—give me the wedding ring.   (*Sharply she pulls back from him*.)   Give it to me.   (*He takes the ring from her finger*.)   Twenty dollars in a pawnshop, and I polished it, and prayed you wouldn't mind, or say anything.   (*He*

takes from his pocket and puts on her finger a very large diamond.)
With this, I you wed again, and forever.
LILY—Please give me my ring.

Taking an envelope from his pocket, Julian shows its contents to
each of them, assuring them that except for the money that went
for the clothes, all of the hundred and fifty thousand dollars is right
here. He's to get seventy-five and his partner the other seventy-five.
"Ain't counterfeit," he says, "twenty five-thousand-dollar bills;
fifty one-thousand-dollar bills— You'll believe it all by tomorrow.
Big successful Julian, the way you want me. The man who was
never good at anything except living on his sisters, and losing his
wife's money. I never minded failure much; you minded. But you
know what? I like things this way: making bargains, talking big—
I don't take my hat off in elevators any more. . . ." Laughing with
great pleasure, he now proceeds to the kitchen to ice some champagne.

In his wake, he leaves a furious Carrie who does not care for the
tone he uses when he speaks to her, nor for his generous gestures.
"This house, this awful house," she cries. "He's changed. He even
talks different. Didn't he know we hated this house, always, always,
always?" As for the garnets, they're not even her birthstone. "To-
paz is my birthstone," she wails. "How could he forget when he
gave me this pin with the first job he ever lost? I even wear it at
night—"

Lily is reacting oddly, too. Hearing the phone, she rushes to
answer it and to tell the woman at the other end that her husband
isn't here. Hanging up, she puts on her old ring, and flings the diamond furiously at the window.

Returning with champagne and caviar, Julian discovers that he
has not only been made to miss his important phone call, but that
nobody is wearing his presents; that Carrie won't play her piano
and that his wife doesn't know where her ring is. At this point,
having carefully retrieved the ring from the floor, Anna says tactfully that she is looking at it.

When Julian whirls Anna into a dance, Carrie stops him with a
savage comment, and when he forces her to eat caviar, she becomes
almost hysterical. "You're laughing at me. You've never laughed
at me before!" she shrills. "You're laughing at me." "No, I wasn't,
I'm just happy," says Julian, "I'm giving a party." Looking around
at the drooping figures, he asks: "What's the matter with everybody?" Drinking his champagne, he cries: "We're not having a
very nice party. What's the matter?"

ACT II

Hoping desperately that all of last night's happenings were part of a bad dream and that this morning the nightmare will be over, Carrie, cup of coffee in hand, braces herself for the day. As another strange detail in a strange night, Carrie reports to Anna that Lily was on the go all night long: "She went out. She came back. She went out. She's a very strange girl. I remember thinking that the first time I ever met her. And she doesn't know any more about this than we do. That's not natural in a good marriage. In a good marriage a man doesn't have secrets from his wife." According to Anna they aren't in any position to know anything about a good or bad marriage. "I read somewhere, that old maids are the true detectives of other people's hearts," she says, "but I don't want to be a detective of other people's hearts. I'm having enough trouble with my own." It is Carrie's opinion that nobody wants a child for a wife. In an effort to cut the conversation short, Anna starts packing her suitcase.

Determined to catch the 8:30 street car to beat her boss to the mail and prevent his reading Julian's offensive letter, Carrie advises Anna to rush to the store and take similar action. She reminds Anna that as they stand they have no jobs. Polishing shoes before packing them, Anna says calmly that Julian can take care of them now, and since he wants them to go to Europe, they should go. "Go to Europe!" cries Carrie. "What are you talking about? What's going to happen if trouble comes and we're not here to take care of it?" "Why do you think trouble will come?" asks Anna. "Because it always has," Carrie insists. "You know very well what I mean. Well, you go to Europe and I'll go to work."

Lily, wearing street dress topped by a filmy nightgown, makes a vague entrance from the bedroom. Anna asks her if Julian wants his breakfast, but Lily wouldn't know because Julian slept in another room last night. Seeing Carrie off to work, Lily says: "My! It's awfully hot to go to work." "Yes. And sometimes," snaps Carrie, "it's awfully cold."

Meeting Mrs. Prine as she leaves, Carrie gives her a curt "good morning" and hurries by Henry at the gate. Lily is in a tizzy at the sight of her mother, but after a false start she actually goes into the garden to greet her. She kisses Albertine, then demands to know what Henry had reported. She objects loudly to his coming for her last night. Albertine answers: "He said the neighborhood worried him, at two o'clock in the morning." "How did he know where I was?" asks Lily. "You told him on the phone," Albertine says quietly. Ignoring her daughter's confession of having been mean to Henry, and ignoring her apology as well, Albertine inquires how Lily is after all this time. Lily lets this pass. She acknowledges Albertine's invitation to use the garden wing of the house, and thanks her mother, but wants to know if Albertine really wants her to come home again. Albertine merely answers that Lily must want to rest after last night, and then gets up to go. Begging Albertine to stay and pleading for her help, Lily promises to talk nice and clear for her mother's benefit.

ALBERTINE—There's no need. Don't distress yourself. I've guessed your trouble and I've brought you a check. (*She takes check from her bag and places it on the table.*) Will you and Julian come and dine at eight? Then you'll decide if you wish to move in, or if, in this heat, you prefer the lake house. I've always meant to give you the lake house, Lily, and tomorrow we'll go around and have Warkins do the papers. (*When there is no answer.*) At eight?

LILY—What does Mrs. Warkins look like? Does she speak in a low voice?

ALBERTINE—I don't know. I haven't seen her in years, and then only once or twice.

LILY—You haven't seen anybody in years, except Henry, of course. How old is Mrs. Warkins?

ALBERTINE—I know little about her, Lily. It's bad enough to know Warkins. I remember her as a tall woman with a sad face. Possibly from being married to a lawyer.

LILY—Is she in love with Mr. Warkins?

ALBERTINE—That is a remarkable idea. Thank God I've never been in a position to find out. Let's waste our time saying things like each to his own taste, and shaking our heads in gossip, but let's do it another time.

LILY—Please don't smile and shrug, Mama. It always makes me nervous. You are angry because I was mean to Henry last night, and he told you.

ALBERTINE—He told me nothing.

LILY—*I was mean to Henry.* That was bad of me, wasn't it?

ALBERTINE (*wearily, softly*)—I don't know.

LILY—Well, tell him I'm sorry.

ALBERTINE—You have been saying you are sorry, in space, for many years.

Happily convinced that she has made her mother angry, Lily now repeats her need for help. Albertine indicates the check. "What is it, Mama?" asks Lily. "I told you. It's a check. A check is for money. Money. It's five thousand dollars. It's yours," says

Albertine. "Oblige me by not speaking of it again." But all Lily says is: "Don't be angry with me." "Oh, Lily," sighs Albertine, "something always happens between us."

Trying to show patience, Albertine finds herself accused of severity. "Please, Lily," she answers, "let us cease this talking about talking. Tell me or do not tell me." In clear tones, Lily announces what her trouble is: "Mama, we're rich."

Lily was so happy when Julian was penniless and they had to move into a poor little room where he stayed in bed with her all day, and she saw to it that he had her share of food as well as his own. "How often the rich like to play at being poor," says Albertine. "A rather nasty game, I've always thought. You had only to write to me." But to Lily having money simply means that she will lose Julian.

LILY—He is different. Things have changed.

ALBERTINE—Marriages change from day to day and year to year. All relations between people. Women, of course, have regrets for certain delicate early minutes, but—there is no answer to that.

LILY—Did you, Mama? Did you have those regrets?

ALBERTINE—I don't remember. I don't think so. Your father and I had very little together. And so we had little to regret.

LILY—I don't mean my father.

ALBERTINE (*after a long silence*)—I came here because you were in trouble, or so you said. Not because I am. When I come to you for that reason, feel free to say what you wish. Until then, please do not.

LILY—Julian couldn't have me last night, and when I cried he said please not to, that— And so I went out and walked and walked. I had never seen that street before. I heard noise way up, and I went in. There were people and a woman stood before them on a box. The people talked about themselves right out loud. One woman had lost a leg but said it was growing back and she proved it.

ALBERTINE—Goodness.

LILY—And the lady on the box kept saying, "Truth, truth is the way to life, and the one way, the only way. Open your hearts with this knife and throw them here." (LILY *throws up her arms.*) She had a knife in her hand—

ALBERTINE—Do sit down, Lily.

LILY—And she kissed the knife—

ALBERTINE—Strange tastes people have. Don't kiss your own hand again, please.

LILY—Everybody left and there I was. The woman said, "You want me, child?" And I said, "Could I buy your knife?" "No," she said, "the knife is not for sale." But I wanted it more than I ever wanted anything and, well—(*slyly*)—finally, we swapped something. And when it was in my hand, for the first time in my life, I just said everything, and asked. The lady said the knife of truth would dress me as in a jacket of iron flowers and though I would do battle, I would march from the battle cleansed. Then I fell asleep.

ALBERTINE—Your many religious experiences have always made me uneasy, Lily—

LILY—When I woke up I knew that I must begin my struggle up the mountain path of truth by asking you—

Lily blurts out that she wants to know if her mother had sold her to Julian. Rising and staring at her, Albertine says: "You are my child, but I will not take much more of this." She reminds Lily that Julian married her because he loved her. Worrying about the woman who is the cause of their being rich, Lily thinks only of last night when Julian wouldn't sleep with her, though always before he had liked to. Accusing her mother of not believing anyone could want her, Lily says: "I was beloved, Mama, and I flourished. Now I'm frightened. Help me." "How can I help you?" asks Albertine gently, "when I don't understand what you're talking about? Are you really saying that if Julian stayed dependent on you, all would be safe, but if he has money for himself, and need not crawl to you—" Not relishing this ugly kind of truth, Lily emphasizes her hate of money. Albertine warns her that that can be much the same as loving it.

The phone rings inside. Turning sharply to intercept the call for the second time, Lily trips on her gown, and is restrained by Henry. Thus able to pick up the phone himself, Julian reassures the lady at the other end that he has the money in his pocket at this very minute, that he has done everything she told him to do, and that she must not worry. "He just beats women," cracks Julian. Promising affectionately that he'll meet her as planned, he says goodbye.

This morning Julian is in wonderful form. Spotting Albertine, Lily, and Henry in the garden, he grabs a small box from the pile of presents and goes out to meet them. Shaking hands with Albertine and Henry, he asks Henry how's fishing up the bayou. "Anybody asked what I missed most in Chicago, I'd have said a bayou, a bowl of crayfish, a good gun for a flight of wild ducks coming over—going to buy a little place up there, first thing. You're welcome all the time."

He presents his oddly inappropriate gift to Albertine. Rising nicely to the occasion, she thanks him charmingly, causing Julian to remark on the others' scared reaction to his largesse. He suggests that perhaps after all these years it was natural for them to act that way. "No, I don't know," says Albertine carefully. "You've had good fortune and brought it home. There's something sad in not liking what you want when you get it. And something strange, maybe even mean." Almost as a warning, she adds sharply: "Nobody should have cried about your good fortune, nobody should have been anything but happy."

Enchanted with his responsive audience, Julian reports cockily on his exploits, and grandly shows off his envelope of money to Albertine. He confesses that he had been "kind of broken; I knew it, but I showed off to keep them from— It's bad to feel gone. Then like a miracle, I go in to see this bastard shaking, and I come out knowing I did fine, knowing I'm going to be all right forever. You understand it wasn't just the money?" Laughing, Albertine says that she doesn't understand very much. "All I mean," he says, "you do something right. *Just right.* You know a man's got to have what you've got—very different from trying to get a job or selling something he don't want. I just sat there calm and smiling until he got through trying to find out how I, *I,* bought two acres of swamp land before he did, and how I could know how much he needed it. . . ."

As Gus makes his daily visit with ice, Julian jubilantly points out the new refrigerator, and handing Gus several large bills, tells him that now he can have that farm. "Go find it," says Julian, "start with this." "Who the hell wants a farm?" cries Gus. "Got enough trouble. Where'd you make up that farm from?" As Gus disappears around the corner of the house, Julian exclaims: "He said since we were kids about a farm— People talk about what they want, and then— How's that?" "I guess most of us make up things we want, don't get them, and get too old, or too lazy, to make up new ones," Albertine answers. "Best not to disturb that, Julian. People don't want other people to guess they never knew what they wanted in the first place."

Coming slowly up the walk, Carrie asks Julian sharply to step inside. He doesn't care for Carrie's tone; but she, not caring for her boss's reaction to Julian's letter, nor for Julian's showing-off for Albertine's benefit, repeats her request that he come inside. He says blithely that he has no time for small matters. That sets Carrie off: "Small matters? After nineteen years. He said he didn't believe you wrote the letter. He said I wrote it, that it was like me, that he had always known about—things in me. . . ." She wants Julian to go right down and demand an apology for the terrible things said to her.

Gaily ignoring her, Julian chats with Albertine and yells out to

Lily to come show the diamond ring to her mother. Noticing that it isn't on Lily's finger, he asks where it is. All she can say is "somewhere" and ask him not to be angry. Entering the house, Julian asks Carrie if she's seen a large diamond ring. "Up to yesterday we never had such problems," Carrie answers. "How does one look for a diamond ring? Julian, he said bad things to me, Julian." She begs for his attention. "You have no time for me," she says, "we're coming apart, you and I—" Frankly puzzled, Julian wonders whether she had always used this tone when speaking to him. As Anna enters with his tray, Julian says: "Say something, so I can tell the way you talk to me." "Breakfast," announces Anna, and leaves the room to press his shirt.

Coming to the end of her visit with Lily, Albertine advises her to pretend to like the diamond ring even if she doesn't. As Lily says that she gave the woman her ring in exchange for a knife, Carrie takes up a listening post at the window.

Henry understands what Lily means. "I gave the lady the ring and she gave me the knife. I didn't want the ring," maintains Lily, "and I didn't know Julian would care. But I will go and tell him the truth now and—" Albertine stops her: "You asked my advice and here it is: you do too much. Go and do nothing for a while. Nothing. I have seen you like this before: I tell you now, do nothing." Assuring Lily that they will try to find the ring, Albertine asks her to rest herself and above all tell Julian nothing.

Smiling sweetly at Carrie, Lily heads for the kitchen as Anna returns with Julian's shirt, and at the window Carrie hears Albertine and Henry speak of the "other woman." "He's not sleeping with her," says Henry, "and he won't. But he used to."

ALBERTINE—Yes? (*When there is no answer*—)Cy Warkins is the man he's talking about, Cy Warkins who bought what he calls his two acres of swamp land. I'm not sure why Cy wanted it so much, but if it's down by the river I can make a good guess. Warkins owns fifty percent of the stock of the interstate agreement to take the railroad route along the docks. (*Laughs.*) If my guess is right, he must have been surprised that Julian knew about the best-kept secret in years. I regret not being there when Julian told him. But who told Julian? Mrs. Warkins? (HENRY *doesn't answer.*) She never liked Warkins and that was the only thing I ever knew about her. But she must be forty now. (*When there is no answer*—) But of course she wasn't always forty. (*She points inside.*) They knew each other? And she told him about the railroad? I'm not gossiping, you know that.

HENRY—I think that's what happened. She was in love with

Julian once. She hates Warkins and has wanted to leave for years.
Maybe this is the money to leave with.

ALBERTINE (*softly, in a new tone*)—How do you know about Mrs.
Warkins? Please.

HENRY—I don't know about her any more, but I used to. She's
a cousin to me.

ALBERTINE (*stares at him, then laughs*)—She's part colored?
Isn't that wonderful! Did Warkins know when he married her?

HENRY—He doesn't know now. But Julian did, and didn't care.
She's a foolish woman and grateful for such things.

ALBERTINE—That's understandable, God knows.

HENRY—Not to me. I am not grateful, nor ungrateful, nor any
word like that.

ALBERTINE—Nor should you be. You are in a bad humor with
me this morning. You are disapproving. What have I done or said?

HENRY (*softly*)—You look tired.

ALBERTINE (*rises and goes to him*)—The world has many people
who make many things too hard for too little reason, or none at all,
or the pleasure, or stupidity. We've never done that, you and I.

HENRY—Yes, we've done it. But we've tried not to. (ALBERTINE
touches his hand. HENRY *smiles and puts her hand to his face.*
ALBERTINE *turns, and as she does she sees* CARRIE *in the window.*)

ALBERTINE—Are you writing a book, Miss Carrie?

CARRIE (*softly*)—This is our house, Mrs. Prine.

ALBERTINE (*sighs*)—Indeed.

Taking Albertine's arm, Henry leaves with her, just as Lily, running into the living room, shouts: "Mama, Mama, I've cut my hand."

Carrie is upset enough over what she's managed to hear; when
Lily, holding out her cut hand to Julian, asks him to make it well
by taking her to bed, Carrie seethes. And when Julian lifts Lily
into his arms and moves with her toward the bedroom, Carrie says
loudly: "I read in a French book that there is nothing so abandoned
as a respectable young girl." "That's true," laughs Julian, kissing
Lily's hair, "otherwise nobody could stand them."

Anna observes that she saw Lily cutting herself deliberately. Not
seeing how she can stand this, Carrie says: "He comes home with
all this money nonsense. He's married to a crazy girl. I think he's
in bed with a girl—" ". . . he wanted," interrupts Anna; "it's not
our business." Carrie insists that when Julian has dealings with
the powerful, dangerous Mr. Cyrus Warkins, it is their business.
Carrie isn't quite sure what it all means, but she knows that this
money has something to do with Warkins' wife.

Anna states matter-of-factly that Julian slept with Charlotte

Warkins ten years ago, and that it has been over that long. This only excites Carrie the more. When Anna says that Julian had told her so, Carrie calls her a liar. Almost hysterical, Carrie refuses to believe this, or that Julian would have confided in Anna and not in herself. "He was closer to me— There he is, another man, not our brother, lost to us after all the years of work and care, married to a crazy little whore who cuts her hand to try to get him into bed— the daughter of a woman who keeps a nigger fancy man. I'll bet she paid Julian to take that crazy girl away from her—"

ANNA—Stop that talk. You know that's not true. Stop talking about Julian that way.

CARRIE—Let's go and ask him. Let's go and ask your darling child. Your favorite child, the child you made me work for, the child I lost my youth for— You used to tell us that when you love, truly love, you take your chances on being hated by speaking out the truth. (*Points inside.*) Go in and do it.

ANNA—All right. I'll take that chance now. Don't you know what's the matter, don't you know? You want him and always have. Years ago I used to be frightened and I would watch you and suffer for you.

CARRIE (*after a second, in a whisper*)—You never said those words. Tell me I never heard those words. Tell me, Anna. (*When there is no answer—*) You were all I ever had. I don't love you any more.

ANNA—That was the chance I took.

ACT III

Shortly after, Julian comes in singing loudly and happily that this is the best day of his entire life. As Anna hands him his shirt, he is ready to go, but Carrie stops him with a promise of a concert tonight on the new piano.

Forced to confess that they will not be here tonight, that they are leaving today, Julian nervously explains in overcheerful tones that he and Lily are going to some place like New York for a little while—a year or so—but they'll return when the ladies come back from their world travels. Concerned at Carrie's reaction, he tries a diversionary tactic by waving the bankbook and promising to deposit twenty thousand to their account. They had better get used to spending money fast, he jokes. "What was that word Mama used to use?" he asks. *"Faner,"* says Anna hastily, *"elle commence à se faner. . . ."* Promising to provide a deliciously soft resting place lined with dollar bills for their fading years, Julian is impatient to meet the lady who is the source of this money.

ANNA—Is she *fanée?*
JULIAN—Yes. A long time ago.
ANNA—Then wish her well from me.
JULIAN—I will.
CARRIE—Is the lady going to New York?
JULIAN—I don't know where she's going. I guess so. Doesn't everyone go to New York?

Catching sight of Lily, he tells her what he thinks she'll like to hear: that they are going by themselves to New York, where they will find a place to settle down. Instead of responding happily, Lily asks Julian to swear on her knife of truth to keep her with him. "Lily, what the hell's the matter with you?" he cries. "Stop talking foolish and stop playing with knives. Maybe kiddies should marry kiddies. But I'm thirty-four. Stop talking about last night and what didn't happen because it's the kind of thing you don't talk about. Can't you understand that? Now, go pack your bags and go tell your Mama we're going away."

Julian looks at his womenfolk in bewilderment. Lily clings to him; Carrie is in a state. "What's the matter? Please," he says. "It's the best day of my life. Please somebody look happy." "Go on," says Anna encouragingly. Smiling finally, Julian runs off, while Lily sits down dejectedly on the porch.

Anna knows full well that this time Julian is leaving forever. "You lusted and it showed," she tells Carrie. "He doesn't know he saw it, but he did see it, and someday he'll know what he saw. You know the way that happens? You understand something, and don't know that you do, and forget about it. But one night years ago I woke up and knew what I had seen in you, and always seen. It will happen that way with him. It has already begun." "I told you I didn't love you any more," says Carrie. "Now I tell you I hate you. We will have to find a way to live with that." "I don't think so," answers Anna, moving into the garden.

Sitting on the porch looking for trouble, Lily asks Anna if Julian will come back for her. Told to go and pack, she broods over her mother's cool tones when speaking to her in contrast to her mother's warm tones when speaking to Henry. She asks Anna point-blank if her mother had sold her to Julian to be rid of her. "What a bitter thought about the man who loves you," says Anna. "No," Lily answers, "who would want me for any other reason?" "Your modesty," says Anna, "does not excuse you."

Seeing she will get nowhere with Anna, Lily goes in to tackle Carrie and comes upon trouble. After artless questions and flattering attentions, Lily inquires of Carrie whether Julian was paid to take her off her mother's hands. Carrie says: "All he told us was that he had fallen in love and was going to be married." Allowing Lily her moment of pleasure, Carrie then applies the screw: she had always wondered why Julian chose the day before Anna's eye operation to become engaged.

CARRIE—I was happy that Julian was to be married.

LILY—You said so. (*Very loudly, as if out of control*—) I didn't believe you.

CARRIE—Oh, I could have stopped the marriage, even you must have guessed that.

LILY—Even I. But you didn't stop it because you knew my mother had paid Julian—I'm glad I helped Miss Anna, I really am—would go on paying him, and you didn't have to worry about a little girl who didn't mean anything more to anybody than a bank check.

CARRIE—I have said none of that. You have been looking for it, and you would have found it in anything I, or anybody else, could say.

LILY—I don't mind, not much. It's better to know. I will take Julian any way I can have him. *If* I can have him. I feel most bad and sad, Miss Carrie, because what he married me for, he doesn't need any more. Isn't that true?

CARRIE—I don't know. Take your questions to Mrs. Cyrus Warkins. She'll be in New York. You can have many a cozy evening.

LILY—She's coming with us?

CARRIE—No. She's going on the morning train.

LILY—I see. Is she a tall, dark lady?

CARRIE—I've never seen her. But Henry is tall and dark and she's his cousin, so perhaps. Your mother was very amused that the great lawyer Warkins had married a part nigra and didn't know it.

LILY—Does Julian love her?

CARRIE—I used to think I knew about Julian. I didn't. Ask your mother and her fancy man. They said Julian and the woman were together years ago. And my sister confirms the alliance.

LILY (*giggles too loudly*)—Alliance? Alliance in bed? What a funny way to say it. Julian told me that you talked like an old maid when you were twelve years old, and that Gus used to say you kept your vagina in the icebox, that he'd seen it there and shut the door fast.

CARRIE (*very loudly*)—Stop that filthy talk. Julian never said a thing like that—

LILY—Oh, please, I didn't mean to offend you. Julian said it in fun. Afterwards in bed, we always talked fun. That's almost the best time, when you laugh and say things you'd never say any place else, and it's all in honor bright. It's then that you ask about other girls, everybody does, Julian told me, and every man thinks it's a big bore he's got to get through for the next time, if you know what I mean. Julian said there was only one woman that ever mattered, long ago, and I wasn't to worry—(*she laughs*)—and that she was married to a bastard who beat her, and if he ever made money he'd give it to her to get away. (*She smiles.*) So now she's coming with us. What will they do with me? (*She screams.*) It pains me. I can't tell you. I'll ask her not to come. (*She turns and runs up the porch and into the room and toward the phone.*) I'll tell her I don't blame her, of course, and I'll swear on my knife of truth that if I have just one more year— (*Grabs phone book, drops it, holds it out to* CARRIE.) Please find it for me.

Noticing that Carrie doesn't seem a bit co-operative, Lily also notices that her voice is very unpleasant. But having worked Lily up to fever pitch, Carrie neatly keeps her simmering. When Lily starts to call Mr. Warkins, and wants further assurance from Carrie that what she is doing is best for Julian, Carrie doesn't know that she can give it. "The people in the bank," she says carefully, "always talk of Mr. Warkins as a low highborn man, tough and tricky, with plenty of riffraff friends to do his dirty work. Julian isn't fit to deal with such a man and God knows what could happen. Warkins is not a man to joke with."

Having primed Lily for her own dirty work, Carrie stands by as Lily calls Mr. Warkins, and when needed, prompts her that the meeting place for Mrs. Warkins and Julian is Sailor's Lane. When Lily has sufficiently inflamed Mr. Warkins with her snatches about Mrs. Warkins' connection with Julian, and about Mrs. Warkins' relation to Henry, Lily happily hangs up and goes to pack.

Anna, dressed in traveling clothes and leaving Carrie's boat ticket on the table, signifies her determination to sail alone tomorrow, and to move to a hotel today. As Carrie does her best to wound her, Anna says: "You don't love me, but you want me to stay with you." "We will find a way to live," answers Carrie. That's not good enough for Anna. She is quite prepared to face a lonely future.

Controlling herself as best she can after a nasty experience, Albertine returns with the diamond ring she was forced to buy back, only to find Lily beaming and all dressed for her trip to New York.

Lily's smiles turn to fury when her mother criticizes the knife woman and pictures her in her true colors as a morphine addict who conducts séances as a front.

Accusing her mother of wanting to deprive her of a sweet friend, Lily is deaf to Albertine's parting advice: "Now listen—I am going to give you a goodbye present. Try to make use of it: The pure and the innocent sometimes bring harm to themselves and those they love and, when they do, for some reason that I do not know, the injury is very great." Oblivious of all this, Lily turns her spleen on Henry, whom she accuses of masterminding plans to hurt her while he and her mother lie together in bed. Turning to Henry, Albertine asks pleasantly: "Is that what we do in bed? You think that's what we do in bed? You're wrong. It's where I forget the mistakes I made with you."

Henry tries to brake this outburst, but Albertine continues until what she has said has actually penetrated Lily's foggy mind. Lily asks softly if there is something the matter with her. Seeing Henry's warning hand, Albertine replies gently that there is nothing wrong.

LILY—If Julian leaves me—

ALBERTINE—Julian loves you, Lily.

LILY—I have sent a message and will keep my word. If Mrs. Warkins will give me one year—

ALBERTINE (*after a second*)—You sent a message to Mrs. Warkins? Why?

LILY—Oh, because. I spoke to Mr. Warkins and told him to ask her to wait for Julian for one more year. (ALBERTINE *turns and stares at* HENRY.) After that, if Julian doesn't want me— Where would I ever go, who would ever want me? I'm trouble, we all know that. I wouldn't have anywhere to go.

ALBERTINE (*after a long pause*)—You will come home to me. You are my child.

LILY (*warmly, sweetly*)—Thank you, Mama. Nice of you. But I couldn't go home to you—any more, as long as—

HENRY—If it ever happens, I won't be there. I won't be there.

LILY—Oh, thank you, Henry. That will be fine.

At this point Henry sees Julian. Bloody and beaten up, Julian stumbles toward the house. He will have no one help him: his one thought is of Charlotte Warkins, whom he has taken to her brother's house. Warning Henry that she'd better not stay there, he asks Henry to move her to safety.

Somehow managing to get into the house, Julian cries through his battered lips: "My poor friend. All she wanted, saved for, thought about—" he gasps, as if sick—"to get away forever. Standing there, standing in the alley, they slashed us up." Anguished that Charlotte might think he had betrayed her, he can't figure out how anyone knew. He begs Henry to assure her that he swears on his life he told no one. "No need to tell her that," says Henry. And Albertine adds: "She will not think you did. I am certain she will not think you did."

Tossing the crumpled empty money envelope to the floor, Julian says that's what's left of the money. He turns down Albertine's offer to go to the police; he's been there already. He turns down Albertine's offer to see Warkins. "What for?" asks Julian. "Is he going to tell you who told him, who he hired to beat us up— What for?" Having no answer to this, Albertine can help no more, and when Julian falls to the floor, she finds it too painful to look.

Aware of what she has done, Lily makes a frantic dash to the porch and is stopped by her mother. Cutting her daughter's confession short, Albertine orders her to go in and say nothing. "Can you have enough pity for him not to kill him with the truth? Can you love him enough to go to him, sit down *and be still?*" Nodding, Lily goes timidly to Julian's side.

Through his physical pain, and through the shock of having been beaten up, penetrates Carrie's voice. Turning, listening to her, Julian says: "Why do you start to purr at me? As if I'd done something good. You're smiling. What the hell's there to smile at? You *like* me this way? Pretty—all this. And the mortgage, and the tickets to Europe, and all the fun to come. Pretty, wasn't it?" "We didn't want them," says Carrie. "Did we?" "No," says Anna, "we didn't want them." Lily and Carrie don't care for Julian's wretched shout that he'd never been beaten before; nobody's ever going to beat him again. Lily turns away; Carrie, sighing, goes to the porch.

ALBERTINE—Mean to see a man stoke his pride. The meanest sight in the world. Don't you think?

CARRIE—Let's be glad nothing worse happened. We're together, the three of us, that's all that matters.

ALBERTINE—I counted four.

CARRIE—I mean the four of us.

ALBERTINE—Someday you will tell him about Lily? Then there will be three of you. Before you tell him, let me know. I will want to come for her.

CARRIE (*points inside*)—All that stuff has to go back, and the debts, got to find ourselves jobs. So much to do.

JULIAN (*taking cloth from* LILY *to clean his face*)—Old saying, money is a real pure lady and when the world began she swore herself an oath never to belong to a man who didn't love her. I never loved her and she guessed it. Couldn't fool her, she got good sense. (*Softly, desperately.*) Nobody ever beat me up before. Maybe once it starts—

CARRIE—There's bad luck and then there's good luck. That's all.

JULIAN—I guess so. Well, I've had the bad. Maybe I got a little luck coming to me. Other men make it easy. Plenty of room in this world for everybody. Just got to fight for it. Got to start again, start again. (*Starts to rise.*)

CARRIE—I'm going to get something nice to make soup with. You always liked a good soup when you didn't feel well. Meat and marrow, the way you like it. (*As she gets to the porch door—*) Tomorrow's another day. (*She moves past* HENRY *and* ALBERTINE *in the garden.*) Goodbye, Mrs. Prine. (*She exits. After a second* HENRY *puts his hand on* ALBERTINE'S *shoulder.*)

HENRY (*to* ALBERTINE)—Goodbye. (*He exits. In the room* JULIAN *is moving painfully toward his bedroom.* LILY, *timidly holding back, joins him. He leans on her as they move out together.* ANNA *picks up her bags, and at the same time* ALBERTINE *starts to leave.*)

THE BEST MAN

A Play in Three Acts

BY GORE VIDAL

[GORE VIDAL *was born at the United States Military Academy, West Point, N. Y., in 1925. He enlisted in the Army following his graduation from Exeter. He wrote his first novel, "Williwaw," when he was 19; some of his subsequent novels are "In a Yellow Wood," "The City and the Pillar," and "A Search for the King." He has also written many successful television and film scripts. His popular play "Visit to a Small Planet" was made into an equally popular movie.*]

IT is convention time—some July or other—in Philadelphia. The hotel housing the candidates has suites that look like all hotel suites. One unseen room of the Russell suite is an office devoted to the clatter and buzz of some campaign activity; visible are a living room for interviews, and possible deals to come, and a bedroom with twin beds. In the living room a TV set provides a view of the convention floor, and a bar provides the necessities of convention life. Various posters identifying the occupant of these rooms are propped about: "William Russell for President"— "Hustle with Russell"—"A great Governor, a great Secretary of State, and the next great President of the U. S."

As Bill and Alice Russell enter from the hall, the thrust, push, and clamor of reporters surround them. "Okay, boys, okay—give him air," yells campaign manager Dick Jensen, "one question at a time." Russell, graying, handsome and fiftyish, parries the barrage with quips that are not always appreciated or understood. A persistent newshen asks how Russell interprets this morning's Gallup poll.

RUSSELL—I don't believe in polls. Accurate or not. And if I may bore you with one of my little sermons, life is not a popularity

contest, neither is politics. The important thing for any government is educating the people about issues, not following the ups
and downs of popular opinions. . . .

BARBARA—Does that mean you don't respect popular opinion?
Do you think a president ought to ignore what the people want?

RUSSELL—If the people want the wrong thing, if the people don't
understand an issue, if they've been misled by some of the press,
then I think a president should ignore their opinion and try to
convince them that his way is the right way. . . .

TONY—Do you think the people mistrust intellectuals in politics?

RUSSELL—I'm glad you asked that question. Bertrand Russell
once wrote: "The people in a democracy tend to think they have
less to fear from a stupid man than from an intelligent one."

HOWIE—Bertrand?

RUSSELL—Bertrand Russell.

HOWIE—Oh, the same name.

RUSSELL—No relative, unfortunately.

BARBARA—Wasn't Bertrand Russell fired from City College in
New York?

RUSSELL—Yes, he was fired. But only for moral turpitude . . .
not for incompetence as a philosopher.

TOM—What image do you feel Senator Cantwell is projecting at
the moment?

RUSSELL—Image? He's behaving himself, if that's what you
mean.

TOM—But hasn't his basic image changed in the last year?

RUSSELL—I'm afraid I don't know much about images. That's
a word from advertising, where you don't sell the product, you
sell the image of the product. Sometimes the image is a fake . . .

BARBARA—But after all your own image—

RUSSELL—Is a poor thing but mine own. Paint me as I am,
warts and all. . . .

HOWIE—What?

RUSSELL—Oliver Cromwell . . .

As Jensen tries to clear the suite of reporters, the woman, lagging
behind, fires away at Alice Russell: How does she like Philadelphia?
Does she drink the tap water? Here Russell intervenes: "I have
no intention of losing Pennsylvania by admitting that I boil the
local water."

Alone at last, Russell gets hell from his campaign manager for
bringing up Bertrand Russell, of all people, in a press conference.
Promising that there will be no more jokes, and that he will
project blandness no matter what, Russell takes a look at himself

in the mirror. In this weird circus, the mirror gives Russell proof of his existence.

As Alice seizes this moment to use the bathroom, Russell yells after her: "Don't drink the *water!*" Then as Dick Jensen answers the telephone, Russell proceeds to give a hop, skip, and jump performance. Dick announces that the National Committeewoman was on the phone. "The only known link," says Russell, hopping, "between the NAACP and the Ku Klux Klan. How does she do it? How?" Dick would like to know what *he* is doing with all his hopping up and down the floor. "As we say at press conferences, I'm glad you asked that question. I am . . . oh, damn! The ancient Romans used to examine the entrails of animals in order to learn the future. I am told on very good authority that my rival Senator Cantwell goes to an astrologist in Kalorama Road, Washington, for guidance. I, lacking all superstition, study the future in multiples of threes. Put simply—and we are nothing if not experts at putting things simply, are we?—I find a carpet with a workable pattern. This one's perfect. Now if I step on a leaf . . . see? before I have completed three full steps between leaves, I will not get what I want. If, however, I can take three paces without touching that leaf, I will get what I want. I may say, I never cheat. Hell! However, on occasion I go for the best two out of three. I also make bets with myself. For instance, if the man I'm talking to does not answer me within the count of three, I get what I want. Ah, victory! I hope I've answered your question lucidly?" "Yes, you have," says Dick, "but let's keep it *our* secret . . ."

Keyed up, unable to keep still, so close is it to the final hour of nomination which—if he gets ex-President Hockstader's backing—will be his on the first ballot, Russell can still exude charm for all comers. When National Committeewoman Mrs. Gamadge arrives Russell is ready for her.

Even before Mrs. Gamadge sits down, she inquires whether Mrs. Russell is here and whether she likes the suite. Dick Jensen tries to change the subject: "Glad to meet you, Mrs. Gamadge, at last." "And I'm glad to get a chance to see you, Mr. Jensen," replies Mrs. Gamadge, "I love eggheads in politics."

DICK—Oh, well . . .

RUSSELL—What can I get you to drink?

MRS. GAMADGE—I don't drink, Mr. Secretary. A coke or a glass of soda, maybe. Anything. (*To* DICK.) Professors like you give such a tone to these conventions. No, I really mean it. Of

course a lot of the Women don't like them, but I do. . . . I like
eggheads, though of course I didn't like the New Deal.

RUSSELL—Here's your soda.

MRS. GAMADGE—A great many of the Women are suspicious of
you professors, Mr. Jensen. . . . You don't mind my speaking
like this? . . .

DICK—Certainly not, Mrs. Gamadge. Talking to you is like
. . . well, like talking to the average American housewife. (*She
reacts.*) I mean you're not average, but you speak for them. . . .

MRS. GAMADGE—Very nicely put, Mr. Jensen. (*To* RUSSELL.)
I don't know why everyone says he's conceited.

RUSSELL—Dick? Stuck up? Why, he's the spirit of humility
. . . an old shoe, in fact! As for being intellectual, he can hardly
get through the Greek Anthology without a trot.

MRS. GAMADGE—Yes. You see, the Women like a regular kind
of man, like General Eisenhower. Now he really appeals to the
Women. That nice smile. He has such a way with him . . . He
inspires confidence because he doesn't seem like anything but just
folks. You could imagine him washing up after dinner, listening
to his wife's view on important matters.

Though assuring Russell he'll get the nomination on the first
ballot, Mrs. Gamadge lays down the law: "The Women don't like
your being funny all the time." *They* would like to see more of
his wife and his two fine sons. *They* will want more of that fine
spread *Life* did on his family, but above all, his wife must be constantly at his side. "The Women must feel," says Mrs. Gamadge,
"that there is a woman behind you, as there has been a woman
behind every great man since the world began." Assuring Russell
that Alice is a tremendous asset, she says: "The Women like the
way she doesn't use make-up and looks like a lady, and seems
shy." "She is shy," manages Russell. Brooking no interruption,
Mrs. Gamadge says: "She doesn't make the Women feel jealous,
and that's good."

Calling to Alice, Russell promises she will do everything helpful
in the campaign. "You couldn't look better," Mrs. Gamadge tells
Alice. "I mean it. I like the whole thing . . . especially the
naturally gray hair, that is such an important point with the
Women. Of course Mabel Cantwell dyes her hair, but she gets
away with it because she does such a bad job the Women feel sorry
for her." Rising to her feet, she says: "I know you have a million
things to do! Anyway, I just want you to know that I'm for you,
Mr. Secretary, and I'm sure you and Mrs. Russell are a winning
team. When you're First Lady just remember this: don't do too

much . . . like Mrs. Roosevelt. The Women didn't like that. On the other hand, don't do too little . . . like Mrs. Eisenhower, the Women don't like that either. All in all Grace Coolidge was really the best, bless her heart. My husband had such a crush on her . . ."

Telling Russell to go to it, the Women are in his corner, Mrs. Gamadge starts for the door. About to leave, she mentions off-handedly that a little birdie told her that Joe Cantwell is about to smear Russell with something, but she's sure he can handle it.

Before this tidbit can be digested, Dick announces that they are about to have a visit from the distinguished ex-President. This is one visit that Alice would enjoy, but, summoned by the "Volunteer Women for Russell," she has to tidy up. The pattern of their day shapes up, as Dick now checks tonight's speech. Russell shows his dissatisfaction over other people writing his speeches. "Come off it," says Dick, "your speechwriters—" "Are the best money can buy," answers Russell. "They have written speeches for Eisenhower, Truman, Dewey, Hockstader, Roosevelt, Hoover, and Harold Stassen. Which proves they are men of overpowering conviction."

In the bedroom, watching Alice get herself together, Russell remarks that it's odd to find themselves in such close quarters after so many years of separate rooms and separate lives. "As someone sooner or later says, politics makes strange bedfellows," replies Alice. She thinks that she is probably working to make him president simply to see him occasionally. "You know," says Russell, "I do like the idea of the two of us back together again."

ALICE—Bill, I am not a Delegation from the Legion of Decency. You don't have to charm me.

RUSSELL—I wasn't trying to. I mean it. I know it's tough . . .

ALICE—Tough? Only for you. You're the one who has a problem. How to get girls into the White House. Or will you have a special place on K Street where the president, in disguise of course, can meet new . . . people?

Hearing this bitterness, Russell says that when the desire for love of someone goes, it goes, and that's what happened to them. Retorting that this holds true for him alone, that although he wanted just a friend in marriage, she wanted a husband, she continues: "I don't know why, but we never manage to say anything new when we get onto the subject of my inadequacy and your . . . what shall we call it this time? Athleticism? Since according to the ground rules of our marriage we may call it anything except plain old-fashioned promiscuity." Russell politely offers her a chance to get out of this gloomy farce. Once called by Russell's doctor after his breakdown "the link between father and sons, William Russell and the world," Alice has no intention of breaking this chain. "You are very nearly a great man," she says, "and I suppose I can endure anything because you are. So here we are." "Something past our youth," says Russell, "and friends?" Agreeing that that would be nice, Alice is off to meet the "Volunteer Women for Russell" as "a founding member of that considerable body."

"Hi, honey," says Hockstader, poking his head through the bathroom door. The ex-President explains to the startled Russells that he came through "the privy." "There's a door into the next suite. I sneaked through."

Alice tells him how well he looks after his operation, and Russell, without being asked, gets him his bourbon and branch water. When the two men are alone, Hockstader asks Russell how he likes politics.

RUSSELL—I like it so much I'm beginning to worry.

HOCKSTADER—Awful, ain't it? Worse than gambling, I sometimes think. Me, I was hooked when I was no more than this high and a certain fourflusher named William Jennings Bryan came to town. That was his last campaign, I guess. Well, they shot the works: torchlight parade and picnic and the shouting and the rantin' and then up there on this platform out in a field, as I recall . . . No, it wasn't even a platform, nothin' but the back of an old dray . . . Well, this fellow he gets up and you never heard such yellin' from a crowd. Big man he was, or so he looked to me, about nine feet tall with hair sweepin' over his collar and that square red face of his, and when he spoke I tell you it was like thunder on a summer evenin' and everything was still, listenin'. I used to know that whole speech by heart, it was the famous one . . . "You shall not press down upon the brow of labor, this crown of thorns. You shall not crucify mankind upon a cross of gold!"

RUSSELL—Hurray!

HOCKSTADER—You betcha! Anyway, it was then and there that a certain farm boy named Art Hockstader said: I am going to be a politician and get the folks riled up and eat plenty of barbecue and fried chicken at picnics and have all the pretty girls ahangin' on my every word.

RUSSELL—Your endorsement, Art, is a very important thing for anybody who wants to be nominated.

HOCKSTADER—I know it is. So, indulge an old duffer . . . Gettin' you fellows to listen to my stories and squirm a bit, waitin' to

see who I'm going to put my money on, I tell you it's the only
pleasure I have left.

Hockstader has fatherly feelings for Russell, but has doubts as
well. As his Secretary of State, Russell made a fine showing, but
no one cares about secretaries of state; as a governor, Russell was
probably good. "But Rhode Island," Hockstader points out, "is
hardly what we call a king-makin' state." But his qualifications
are not what Hockstader is speaking of; he was prejudiced against
Russell because he was a "Fancy Dan." "But I am nothing if not
a realist," adds Hockstader. "The Age of the Great Hicks to which
I belong is over. The people trust you rich boys, figurin' since
you got a lot of money of your own you won't go stealin' theirs.
I'm sure that the people who like this Rockefeller are really thinkin'
in the back of their minds if they make him president he might
decide to pay off the national debt out of his own pocket. If he
would, I'd vote for him."

Russell asks him point-blank what he thinks of Joe Cantwell.
Hockstader admits that Cantwell is nothing but plain naked ambition—he'd lie, cheat, and destroy the reputations of others. "So I
assume you are endorsing me for the nomination?" concludes Russell. "Hell, no!" says Hockstader. "Because he's a bastard don't
mean he wouldn't be a good candidate. Or even a good president . . ."

Not thinking of himself but of the country, Russell pleads with
the ex-President not to throw his support to Cantwell. Needling
Russell, Hockstader says that you'd never find Cantwell hesitat-
ing: he's sharp and he's tough. Contradicting Hockstader, Russell
says that Cantwell's toughness is pure expediency, and furthermore,
as president, Joe Cantwell could be the greatest appeaser in history.

RUSSELL—Suppose the Chinese were to threaten to occupy India
and we were faced with the possibility of a third World War, the
last World War. Now that is the kind of thing you and I understand, and I think we could handle it without going to war and
without losing India. But what would Joe do? He would look
at the Gallup poll. And what would the Gallup poll tell him?
Well, ask the average American, do you want to run the risk of
being blown up to save India, and he'll say hell, no. Joe would
do the popular thing: to hell with India and we would be the
weaker for it, and that day we're all afraid of, Art, would be
closer.

HOCKSTADER—Son, you've been reading too much of that Joe
Alsop fella. Things are never that bad! Bill, you know it gets

mighty lonely in the White House. Worse for me, I guess, than for you. I never lived in a big house with servants, the way you were brought up. But the worst part is there's nobody you can believe . . . that's the awful thing, everybody's lying to you all day long. Then my wife died. . . . The wonder is that most of us aren't worse than we are. . . . Bill, do you believe in God?

RUSSELL—Do I? . . . Well, I was confirmed in the Episcopal Church.

HOCKSTADER—Hell, that wasn't what I asked. I'm a Methodist and I'm still asking: Do you believe there's a God and a Judgment and a Hereafter?

RUSSELL—No. I believe in us. In man.

HOCKSTADER—I have often pretended I thought there was a God for political purposes.

RUSSELL—So far I haven't told a lie in this campaign and I have never used the word "God" in a speech.

HOCKSTADER—Well, the world's changed since I was politicking. In those days you had to pour God over everything like ketchup. No, I don't believe there's a Hereafter. We just pass this way once. And then . . . nothing. Bill, I am dying.

RUSSELL—What?

HOCKSTADER—The thing about the hernia was just another lie, I'm afraid. I hope you don't disapprove . . . I got the doctors to say the operation was a great success, but it wasn't. I got cancer of the innards, and they tell me I may last just long enough to attend the next inaugural.

RUSSELL—Oh, God, Art. I'm . . . Look, there isn't . . .

HOCKSTADER—There is nothin' they can do, except give me these pills to cut the pain. I can tell you, son, I am scared to death. That's a phrase for you! Scared to death is just exactly right. I don't fancy being nothin', just a pinch of dust. No, sir, I don't like that at all. . . .

RUSSELL—I know. I'd like to say something reassuring, but I can't. You wouldn't fall for it anyway.

With the Texas delegation virtually at the door, Hockstader recovers his former verve. He promises to keep Russell in suspense till the moment when he will throw his support, like a bridal bouquet, to the lucky man. In an aside, he assures Russell that those rumors of lady friends will do him no harm just so long as there's no trouble or letters. Starting out the way he came, Hockstader wishes he could hear his ever-truthful friend give the Texans the whole truth about depletion of oil-resources allowance. "Get out of here, you old bum," says Russell. And without being told, he knows that Hockstader plans to support Cantwell.

Scene II

And in the other corner of the ring, in a similar suite on another floor, Mabel Cantwell is stretched out on a couch in front of a TV set. Watching the pictures of the Russell and Cantwell arrivals in Philadelphia, she boos the Russells, cheers the Cantwells, and groans at the sight of her televised hat. In the wake of the usual crowd of reporters, Joe Cantwell strides into the room, followed closely by his campaign manager, Blades. He urges Mabel to dress for dinner which will be in exactly—he looks at his watch—thirty minutes. Mabel wants her little martini first and Blades obliges inexpertly. Mabel now gives a run-through of the "awful nice" coverage they've had on TV, though she says: "That new hat of mine is clearly a mistake, it looks like I have no chin, but even with no chin I certainly look better than Alice Russell. My God, she is a chilly-looking woman, just like an English teacher I had back at State College, the spittin' image . . . from Boston she was and always wore her hair in this bun with no make-up and of course thought she was the cat's meow."

Listening to Mabel's report that all the papers say that Hockstader is coming out for Bill Russell, Cantwell decides that he must see Hockstader right now, before that dinner. "Go up there," says Cantwell to Blades. "He's on the seventh floor. Tell him I've got to see him before dinner, which is in twenty-seven minutes." "Ay ay, my captain," says Blades, and goes.

Cantwell—Mabel, you've got to get dressed!

Mabel—I'll be ready, Joe, stop worrying . . . don't get all het-up. Why is big Poppa Bear so mean at poor little Momma Bear . . . ?

Cantwell—Baby, I'm sorry. Poppa Bear is never mean at his Momma Bear, never ever. But honey, you've got to get dressed.

Mabel—Okay, I will—I will. Joe, when are you going to spring that . . . that stuff about Bill Russell?

Cantwell—Tomorrow . . .

Mabel—The *whole* thing?

Cantwell—Pow!

Mabel—And then we are on our way to 1600 Pennsylvania Avenue . . . Oh, my, it's thrilling, isn't it? Seems just like yesterday we were skimpin' along, hardly able to pay the bills to have Gladys'

teeth straightened, and now just look at us—Poppa Bear and
Momma Bear and the baby bears, all in the White House!

"Where's my electric razor?" asks Cantwell. Going after the
razor and to put on her clothes, Joe's little helper reels off the latest
Gallup poll figures for her husband. Joe is two percent higher than
last week, with twelve percent undecided . . . Merwin gained one
percent and Russell's lost two percent. "And Red China?" asks
Cantwell, shaving furiously. "Forty-seven percent against recog-
nition," rattles off Mabel, "twenty-three percent in favor, thirty
percent don't know. I'm wearing the green organza tonight, the
one from Neiman-Marcus Allan Bates sent me. I think it looks real
summery and nice. . . ." "That's not enough in favor," says
Cantwell. "Russell's a fool making an issue out of China this
soon . . ."

Immersed in such important thoughts, Cantwell hears none of
Mabel's digs at Alice Russell, or any of her non-stop chatter. "You
never listen to poor Momma Bear any more," she says. "Joe?
Have you ever been unfaithful to me?" "No. Did you," he asks,
"see Walter Lippmann this morning? Listen to what the guy says:
'The country's affairs will be in good hands should William Russell
be our next president.' I don't know why I don't appeal to those
would-be intellectuals. My image just doesn't project to them like
his does." Seeing Mabel all dressed in her organza, he registers
momentarily and grabs her. "Oh," squeals Mabel, "what are you
doing to me? Don't mess my hair! Now come on, stop it . . .
Zip me up. . . . Joe, are you sure you haven't been unfaithful to
me? Just maybe one little time—on one of those junkets, like that
awful one to Paris you took, where the senators got drunk and
Clarence Wetlaw contracted a social disease and Helen Wetlaw was
fit to be tied?" "Mabel honey, there's nobody else, Mabel. And if
there was," says Cantwell, "how would I have the time? I operate
on a tight schedule, you know that."

Announcing that Hockstader is now on his way down, Blades
blurts out that he hadn't dropped a clue about where he was throwing his support. Snapping at Blades to get the Russell file, Cantwell
advises Mabel to go and fix her face or something. "Joe," she en-
courages, "play it cool, like the kids say now."

Looking at the Russell file, finding all its information "very cute,"
Cantwell is sure it will do the trick. Reminding Blades to flatter
Hockstader, Cantwell stands at the door ready to greet him.

Leaving the swarm of reporters outside, Hockstader seems in fine
fettle. When no drink is immediately forthcoming, he asks for one.
"I know Joe doesn't have the habit," he says. "People who don't

drink never realize how thirsty we old bucks get along sundown.
. . . No, sir, you don't drink, you don't smoke, you don't philander,
fact you are about the purest young man I have ever known in
public life." "I try to be," says Cantwell.

The compliments become somewhat qualified. Hockstader finds
Joe has done a good job in the Senate *most* of the time, other times
he has questioned his methods. Cantwell says quickly that he believes the end to justify the means. Hockstader has news for him.
In life and politics, there are no ends, only means.

Donning his crusading TV technique, Cantwell says: "Then am I
to assume, Mr. President, from the statement you have just made,
that you are against planning anything?"

HOCKSTADER—Oh, here it comes! I know that voice . . . Senator Cantwell, boy crusader, up there on the TV with these small-
time hoodlums cringing before his righteousness.

BLADES—Now, Mr. President, Joe was assigned that subcommit-
tee. He didn't ask for it . . . and that's a fact.

HOCKSTADER—Sure. Sure. And he just fell into that big issue;
how the United States is secretly governed by the Mafia . . .

CANTWELL—It happened to be true. Any time you want to look
at my files, Mr. President.

HOCKSTADER—Last time somebody asked me to look at his files,
it was Senator McCarthy.

CANTWELL—I hope, sir, you're not comparing me to him.

HOCKSTADER—No . . . no, Joe. You're a much smoother article.
After all, you've got an end to which you can justify your means,
getting to be president. Poor old McCarthy was just wallowing in
headlines . . . sufficient to the day were the headlines thereof.
You're much brighter, much more ruthless.

CANTWELL—I realize some of my methods upset a lot of people.

BLADES—But, Mr. President, if we hadn't been tough we would
never have cracked the Mafia the way we did.

CANTWELL—What's so funny about that, sir?

HOCKSTADER—Nothing, except you know and I know and everybody knows—except, I'm afraid, the TV audience—that there wasn't
a Mafia like you said. There was no such thing. You just cooked
it up.

CANTWELL—We're going to get that number, are we? Well, my
figures prove . . .

HOCKSTADER—You went after a bunch of poor Sicilian bandits
on the Lower East Side of New York and pretended they were running all the crime in America. Well, they're not. Of course we
have a pretty fair idea who is . . . but you didn't go after any of

them, did you? No sir, because the big rascals are heavy contribu-
tors to political campaigns.

BLADES—Maybe Joe didn't go after all of them, sir.

HOCKSTADER—Just barely scratched the surface. . . .

CANTWELL—But *you* should talk. J. Edgar Hoover considered
you the most morally lax president in his entire career . . .

HOCKSTADER—I reserve my opinion of J. Edgar Hoover for a
posthumous memoir or maybe a time capsule to be dug up when
he has finally cleansed the republic of undesirables . . .

CANTWELL—Hoover is a great American.

HOCKSTADER—We're all great Americans, Joe. No, I don't object
to your headline-grabbing and crying "Wolf" all the time, that's
standard stuff in politics, but it disturbs me that you take it so seriously. It's par for the course trying to fool the people, but it's
downright dangerous when you start fooling yourself.

CANTWELL—Mr. President, I take myself seriously. Because I
am serious this is important to me—to all of us. Which is why I
don't want any little lectures from you on how to be a statesman.
And if you really want to know, I think the record of your ad-
ministration is one of the heaviest loads our party has to carry.

Mabel dashes in to pour oil on the waters with a bit of flattery;
and, having stopped her angry husband, she returns to eavesdrop
in the bedroom. File in hand, Joe now gets down to the reason
for Hockstader's visit. He knows Hockstader doesn't like him.
Hockstader agrees; nor does Cantwell like Hockstader, or expect
him to come out for him tonight. Hockstader warns him that he
has often endorsed men whom he disliked or mistrusted because he
thought they would do the job. All tied up with his plans for Russell, Joe neglects to listen to Hockstader. He briefly notes Hockstader's apparent physical distress as he gulps down a pill with his
drink. As Hockstader repeats the questions he had posed earlier
to Russell, Cantwell answers automatically that he is a very religious guy, but he doesn't even hear Hockstader tell him that he
is dying.

"Now, it's all here," says Cantwell, displaying the Russell files.
"Psychiatrist reports, everything. And don't ask *how* I got it. My
means might've been ruthless, but for once I think you'll agree the
end was worth it." "What's all this . . . crap?" asks Hockstader.
Cantwell said his candidate William Russell had what was called a
nervous breakdown several years ago; he was raving mad for almost
a year. "He was not raving mad," says Hockstader, "it was exhaustion from overwork." Cantwell says that he has the real story
right here, political dynamite, that he deserted his wife and at-

tempted suicide. "He never attempted suicide," says Hockstader. "I'm sorry. It says right here that he did," replies Cantwell. "There: suicidal tendencies."

HOCKSTADER—We've all got suicidal *tendencies*. But he never tried to kill himself.

CANTWELL—Yes, but the point is he *could*.

HOCKSTADER—I thought you said he did try.

CANTWELL—I didn't say he did. I said he could. And all that combined with playing around with women . . .

HOCKSTADER—So what?

CANTWELL—I suppose you find promiscuity admirable?

HOCKSTADER—I couldn't care less. I was brought up on a farm and the lesson of the rooster was not entirely lost on me. Lots of men need a lot of women and there are worse faults, let me tell you.

CANTWELL—What do you mean by that?

HOCKSTADER—Just that there are rumors about every public man. Why, when I was in the White House they used to say I had paresis, and how I was supposed to be keeping this colored girl over in Alexandria, silliest damn stories you ever heard but it gave a lot of people a lot of pleasure talking about it. You know, when that Kinsey fellow wrote that book about how many men were doing this and how many men were doing that, I couldn't help but think how right along with all this peculiar activity there was a hell of a lot of *nothin'* going on!

Cantwell will demand that Russell be examined before Wednesday by a non-partisan group of psychiatrists to determine if he's sane. "Wow," exclaims Hockstader, "you sure play rough, don't you?" Pointing out that this leaves Cantwell open to similar treatment, Hockstader asks if he's sure he hasn't anything to hide.

CANTWELL—Just try anything.

HOCKSTADER—Well, I see we're going to have an ugly fight on our hands. Yes sir, a real ugly fight. Son, now I am going to let you have it. . . . When I finish with you, my boy, you will know what it is like to get in the ring with an old-time killer. I am going to have your political scalp and hang it on my belt, along with a lot of others.

CANTWELL—Don't mix with me, Hockstader.

HOCKSTADER—You can't touch me. I can send you back to the insurance business. And just think: I was going to endorse *you* for president.

CANTWELL—I don't believe you.

HOCKSTADER—It's not that I mind your being a bastard, don't get me wrong there. . . . It's your being such a *stupid* bastard, I object to.

ACT II

Instead of worrying over what Cantwell is about to toss in his direction, Russell, a problem to the party hacks, tells Senator Carlin that he's worried about the labor plank in the platform. "Christ, Bill," cries Carlin, "lay off labor, will you? You got their vote now, so don't go stirring up a lot of snakes. After all, *you're* the Liberal Candidate . . ." "What's a liberal, Senator?" asks Russell. Carlin groans: "And I thought Adlai Stevenson was a pain in the neck . . ." Carlin does, however, get a direct, curt "no" to his question whether Russell would give Cantwell second spot on the ticket.

Thinking ahead to an open convention, Carlin says: "I suppose we better try for a Catholic—that seems to be the big thing this year —for *second* place, that is. Bill, don't make things tough for yourself! You got the nomination, now leave the controversial things alone . . ."

RUSSELL—I can't help it. I am driven by a mad demon, by the imp of the perverse . . . That is, I am *compelled* to say what I think.

CARLIN—Okay, but lay off stuff like Red China, especially when Henry Luce is an absolute nut on China and you don't want to lose *Time* and *Life* at this point, when they're already behind you in the interests of good government and all that crap. . . . So keep Henry Luce happy, will you? Once you're president, you can eat with chopsticks for all anybody cares.

RUSSELL—I will be diplomatic.

CARLIN—You know, Cantwell's releasing a statement today. To all the delegates. He says it'll knock you off.

RUSSELL—We're ready for him. He may be the master of the half truth and the insinuation, but we've got the facts . . .

CARLIN—And the *whole* truth?

RUSSELL—No man has the whole truth . . .

CARLIN—Oh, brother! Good luck, Bill. Let me know if there's anything I can do for you. I'm with you one hundred percent in spite of your damned dictionary.

Carlin is not the only one who finds Russell's vocabulary disconcerting. Alone with Russell, Dick says: "You could've cut the air with a knife when you made that crack about being 'driven by a mad demon. . . .' " "Well, they've re-elected Eisenhower after a heart attack and an ileitis operation," says Russell. "Didn't seem to hurt him." "But there was never any question about his mind or his judgement being affected . . ." answers Dick; and, watching Russell do his hopping trick, says: "Well, what's the score?"

RUSSELL—I still get it on the first ballot, but it was a near miss . . . I nearly stepped on that square, the one by the table . . . it's a bitch. What about your daily horoscope?

DICK—"A.M. Fine for getting apparel in order. P.M. Don't quarrel with loved one." Bill, you may have to pull a "Nixon."

RUSSELL—And what does "pull a Nixon" mean?

DICK—Go on television. And cry on the nation's shoulder. With *two* cocker spaniels.

Regarding any such action as impossible and even idiotic, Russell refuses point-blank.

Alice, on joining the men and realizing that Russell's situation is getting more precarious, staunchly advises him not to quit under fire. Then remembering her own unpleasant duty to meet the press with Mabel Cantwell, she says: "We're meeting in her suite. She made the point very tactfully over the phone that according to protocol the wife of a reigning senator outranks the wife of a former secretary of state."

Hockstader pops in, as usual by his secret passageway. All keyed up for a knockdown fight, he intends Cantwell to be finished off. But when Dr. Artinian, Russell's former psychiatrist, arrives, Hockstader gives him hell for letting his files be pinched. "Apparently somebody from Cantwell's office bribed one of our nurses," apologizes Artinian. "They got the whole file."

RUSSELL—Robert, in one hour Cantwell's releasing that file on me. I know this sounds silly. When he does, I want you to meet the press and tell them I am *not* mentally unstable.

ARTINIAN—Of course I will. You don't know how guilty I feel about this.

HOCKSTADER—He *is* all right, isn't he?

ARTINIAN—Mr. Russell is one of the sanest men I ever have known.

The file's technical phrases and jargon might sound sinister to a layman, says Artinian: "Anyone's psychological profile could be made to sound damaging." Ushering him out, Dick says: "We'll find a room for you here, Doctor. And I'll get somebody to help you with your statement." Thanking him, Artinian says: "I also brought the Institute's lawyer with me. By way of making amends, Bill, we're filing suit against Cantwell for theft." "That's the ticket," says Hockstader, "go to it, Doc."

Disgusted that Russell refuses to fight this thing on TV, Hockstader says that Artinian will be of little use when Cantwell insists on having half the medical profession examine Russell between now and tomorrow. "Up all night—on the go all morning seeing delegates . . . I tell you," says Hockstader, "there is nothing like a dirty low-down political fight to put the roses in your cheeks."

RUSSELL—How *do* you feel?

HOCKSTADER—Immortal! Now a lot of the delegates know that something's up. They don't know what . . .

RUSSELL—Art, why didn't you endorse me last night?

HOCKSTADER—Look, Bill, this isn't easy to say, you might as well know: I came to Philadelphia to nominate Cantwell.

RUSSELL—I knew that.

HOCKSTADER—You did. How?

RUSSELL—Prince Hamlet has second sight. He sees motives as well as ghosts upon the battlement.

HOCKSTADER—Guess I ain't as sly as I figured I was.

RUSSELL—Art, did you decide to help me because of what Joe's doing? . . . bringing up that breakdown business?

HOCKSTADER—No. No. Matter of fact . . . speaking as a professional politician, I kinda admire what he's doing. It's clever as all hell. No, Joe Cantwell lost me because he wasn't smart. He made a mistake. He figured I was going to back you when I wasn't. You get my message. Joe didn't. Now that's a serious error. Shows he don't understand character, and a president, if he don't understand anything else, has got to understand people. Then he got flustered when I needled him. A president don't get flustered when a man gives him the needle. He keeps a straight face, like poker. Like you're doing right now. What does Joe do? He don't run scared. He runs terrified. He fires off a cannon to kill a bug. And that is just plain dumb, and I mean to knock him off. . . . So I guess that means you are going to be the next president.

RUSSELL—President by default. Because you still have your doubts about me, don't you?

HOCKSTADER—Yes, I still have my doubts. Bill, I want a strong president. . . .

Dick now produces Sheldon Marcus, who served with Cantwell in the Aleutians. Hesitant, palpitant, sweating, this sad sack has in-

Frank Lovejoy, Melvyn Douglas and Lee Tracy in "The Best Man"

formation on Cantwell but has trouble conveying it before the ex-president. Russell asks Dick what he's trying to pull. "I had a lead on this months ago," says Dick, "and I finally tracked it down. Tell them, Mr. Marcus."

MARCUS—Well, Joe Cantwell was a captain and I was a captain and Joe Cantwell was . . . was . . . well, he was . . . you know how it is sometimes when there's all those men together and . . . and . . .

DICK—And no female companionship.

MARCUS—That's right, though we had some nurses later on, but not enough to make much difference—I mean there were all those men . . .

Telling them not to get ahead of themselves, Hockstader finally addresses Marcus: "Major Marcus, am I to understand by the way you are beating slowly around the bush that Joe Cantwell is what, when I was a boy, we called a "de-genrate"?

MARCUS—Yes, sir, Mr. President, sir, that's just what I mean . . .

RUSSELL—I don't believe it! Nobody with that awful wife and those ugly children could be anything but normal!

HOCKSTADER—Bill! Patience. Whether *you* believe it or not is beside the point.

DICK—It's dynamite!

RUSSELL—Even if it's true, I'll be damned if I'll smear him with something like that . . .

HOCKSTADER—Bill, I, like you, am a tolerant man. I *personally* do not care if Joe Cantwell enjoys deflowering sheep by the light of a full moon, but I am interested in finding a way to stop him cold.

RUSSELL—Now damn it, Art, this is exactly the kind of thing I went into politics to stop! This business of gossip instead of issues, personalities instead of policies . . . We've got enough on Cantwell's public life to defeat him without going into his private life, which is nobody's business . . .

Retorting that Cantwell is using Russell's personal life, Hockstader gets nowhere. He begins to wonder if he's backing the wrong team. He persuades Russell, as a favor to "an old man in his sunset years," to sit down, relax, and let events take their course. Then turning his charm on Marcus, Hockstader bids him tell his story, omitting no details, however sordid.

SCENE II

Down in Mabel's room, Alice is having a rough time. Surrounded by reporters and photographers, and flanked by Mabel and Mrs. Gamadge, she finds it difficult to answer questions because of Mabel's constant interference. When the press leaves—after Mabel has hogged attention, chattered professionally, and interrupted deliberately—Alice would coolly withdraw. Mabel insists, however, that she stay on for a drink.

Performing for Mrs. Gamadge, and using a feminine version of her husband's technique, Mabel flatters Alice: "You are wonderful and courageous. I always say Alice Russell is the most courageous woman in public life, don't I, Sue-Ellen?" She refers to that committee Alice was on: "You know—in New York City, the one where you did all that work for birth control . . ." Mrs. Gamadge is plainly startled. "Well," answers Alice, "it was twenty years ago. And of course I'm not supposed to mention it now . . . as *you* know." "I should hope not," Mrs. Gamadge breathes. "You'll have the Catholics down on you like a ton of bricks. The rhythm cycle, yes, but anything else . . . is out." Parading her virtue, Mabel proceeds to get in more of her venomous digs until, seeing no need to listen further, Alice gets up and goes to the door. "Oh, by the way," says Mabel, "how *is* Mr. Russell's health? I mean *really?* I thought he looked so tired last night at the dinner and someone did say—" "The reporters are gone, Mrs. Cantwell," replies Alice, "you know as well as I do he's perfectly all right. Goodbye." And she leaves.

MABEL—Well . . . listen to her! "The reporters are gone, Mrs. Cantwell!" If she wasn't so high-and-mighty she'd take the hint and start saying right now he isn't feeling good, so that when he has to pull out there'll be some preparation . . .

MRS. GAMADGE—Mabel, I don't like anything about what Joe's doing. It's plain dirty and I should warn you—I'm a loyal party worker and I'll see that the Women are behind him.

MABEL—Under him is more their usual position—it's just sex, sex, sex, morning, noon and night with Bill Russell.

MRS. GAMADGE—Now, Mabel, unless you were in the room how do you know?

MABEL—I read that report—Bill Russell is a neurotic who has had a breakdown and his sex life is certainly not normal. Sleeping with all those women is just plain immature—and we don't want an immature president—do we?

MRS. GAMADGE—We had some very good presidents who have slept around a lot more than Bill Russell ever did—and in the White House, too.

As Cantwell and Blades make an assured entrance, Mrs. Gamadge is surprised to see Senator Carlin in tow. Before leaving, she warns the men that anything having to do with private lives is out: by throwing dirt, one only gains sympathy for the victim of the smear, and makes the aggressor vulnerable.

The minute she has left, Cantwell mans the battle stations. Ready to go into action at three-thirty with photostats and six hundred releases for the delegates, Cantwell gets a telephone call from Dick Jensen. Halfway through the call, Cantwell's cockiness turns to close-mouthed alarm. Freezing, Cantwell says: "Do I know *who?* Shel-don Mar-cus? No? I don't think so. Where? Oh. Yes— Will you try and fix it? Okay. I'll be right here."

Asking Blades to hold up the release, and Carlin to excuse him, Cantwell waits until Carlin has left the room, then orders a halt on the release. "Joe, what did Russell say to you?" gasps Mabel. "What's he doing to you? It's not . . . it's not . . . Oh, God!"

SCENE III

Dick is elated over the change in Cantwell, who now is anxious to see Russell. Ushering out Marcus, who hopes he won't have to face Cantwell, Dick sympathizes with his nervousness and his fear of Cantwell's temper.

Dick crows that they've stopped Cantwell. "I'm not going to use this," says Russell. Alice provides a brief diversion on her return from the press conference with Mabel and Mrs. Gamadge. "My cheeks are tired from smiling for the camera," she says, "but I must say I'm beginning to like politics, Mr. President, especially when Mrs. Gamadge tells me that I'm an inspiration to American Woman, in my way." "You're an inspiration to me, Miss Alice," says Hockstader. "Excuse me for not getting up, but would you fetch me some plain branch water?" Listening to her report, Hockstader says: "Worst damn thing ever happened to this country, giving the women the vote. Trouble, trouble, trouble. They got no more sense than a bunch of geese. Give 'em a big smile and a pinch on the . . . anatomy and you got ten votes."

Told of the new developments on Cantwell, Alice backs up Hockstader and tells Russell: "If you took a gun and shot him I'd help you if I thought that was the only way of keeping our lives private." Full of moral compunctions, Russell still balks.

When Blades and Jensen report that the coast is clear for Russell's trip to the Cantwell suite, Hockstader says: "Here is your chance. Your last chance. Take it. Go down there because I want a strong president to keep us alive a while longer." Directing Jensen and Blades to wait for him outside, Russell says: "And so one by one these compromises, these small corruptions, destroy character. . . ."

HOCKSTADER—To want power is corruption already. Dear God, you hate yourself for being human.

RUSSELL—No. I only want to *be* human . . . and it is not easy. Once this sort of thing starts there is no end to it, which is why it should never begin. And if I start . . . Well, Art, how does it end, this sort of thing, where does it end?

HOCKSTADER—In the grave, son, where the dust is neither good nor bad, but just nothing. (RUSSELL *leaves*.)

ALICE—You are a very good man, Mr. President.

HOCKSTADER—I reckon I am, when all's said and done.

ALICE—But I don't know if this is the right thing for Bill to do.

HOCKSTADER—At least I put a fire under the candidate. I just hope it don't go out. Now don't you get alarmed, but I want you to go over and pick up that phone and ask for Dr. Latham. He's in the hotel. Tell him I'm in here . . . tell him to come quick and bring a stretcher through the back way, because I can't move. I'm afraid the old man is just about dead.

ACT III

Mabel is learning fast to hate politics as Cantwell tries desperately to reach a General Conyers by long distance phone. "Are you sure General Conyers will back you up?" she asks. "He better," answers Cantwell. His man is out playing golf, however, and cannot be reached. Cantwell leaves his number for the General to call him. "But you've got to talk to him before they come down here!" cries Mabel. "It's too late now," says Cantwell, and decides that maybe it's just as well. "Joe, I'm scared to death," she says. "Well, don't be. Come here, poor Momma Bear, and don't worry. Poppa Bear isn't going to get shot down this close to the honey tree." The telephone rings, but it's Alice with news of Hockstader's collapse. "Oh, that's awful!" says Cantwell. "And you say he's . . . Yes, of course. Of course I'll tell Bill. The second he gets here. Yes . . . He's a great guy. Yes, thank you. Goodbye, Mrs. Russell. . . . Art Hockstader just collapsed. They've taken him to the hospital. He's dying." Mabel only wants to know what this is going to do to them. Instead Cantwell warns her: "Not a word about Hockstader. I don't want anything to upset this meeting."

When Russell and Dick Jensen arrive, Cantwell first demands to see Sheldon Marcus, and then without further ado, launches an attack of "multiple lie" proportions. "Mr. Chairman! Mr. Chairman!" says Russell. "Point of order! Oh, how're you going to keep them down in the Senate once they've been on TV?" "Very funny. Very cute," snaps Cantwell. "I like that—you should have had your own TV show."

RUSSELL—Thank you, and I'm sure you meant that as a compliment, Joe. I came down here to convince you that there are some things a man cannot do even in politics.

CANTWELL—Now I have given you every hint, every opportunity in the past two days to pull out of the race. Considering your medical history, it could be done so easily . . . so logically. All you'd have to do is claim exhaustion, fatigue, and everybody would understand and this ugly business would never get out. And then the party could unite behind its candidate . . .

RUSSELL—You?

CANTWELL—And we take the election in November.

Listening to this demagogue's performance, Russell finds it amazing: "I came down here with enough political nitroglycerine not only to knock you out of the race but out of politics altogether, and there you sit and blandly tell me I'm the one to withdraw." Never listening, Cantwell now has the gall to offer Russell any cabinet post, or even the ambassadorship to Red China, *when he* recognizes it. It apparently doesn't bother him in the least that he's offering these plums to a man he is calling unstable. Wanting to get this whole dirty business over with, Russell asks that they both declare a moratorium on mudslinging. Instead, Cantwell has Sheldon Marcus brought before him.

After an unscrupulous, shifty, intimidating interview, Cantwell promises Marcus that if he says a word of this to anyone he will involve Marcus personally in the whole Aleutian mess, and that by the time he's finished with him, Marcus will wish he'd never been born. Then as he practically throws him out—into the arms of reporters—Cantwell places an arm about Marcus' shoulder, gives him a fond, folksy farewell.

CANTWELL—I'm sorry to disappoint you, Bill, this won't work. I'm covered on every side. You won't be able to make this thing stick for two minutes. And I should also warn you: this is the kind of desperate last-minute smear that always backfires on the guy who makes it. Ask Art Hockstader. He'll tell you. Well, go on. If you don't believe me, you got General Conyers' number in your hand. Call him.

RUSSELL—True? False? We've both gone beyond the "truth" now. We're in dangerous country . . .

CANTWELL—Every word I said was true . . .

RUSSELL—You are worse than a liar. You have no sense of right or wrong. Only what will work. Well, *this* is going to work.

CANTWELL—But you're not going to use that now?

RUSSELL—Yes. Yes, I'll use *anything* against you. I can't let you be president.

Russell having left, Cantwell calls for his man Blades. Mulling over what Russell has said of his not understanding character, Cantwell is about to show him: "I am a very good judge of character. You can release that stuff on Russell now. One copy to every delegation. Bill, we're home free. And I'll make you a bet: Russell quits before the first ballot."

Scene II

By the sixth ballot, Dick Jensen is still doing his frantic best to make Russell sling his mud. The voting stands at: Cantwell—474, Russell—386, and Merwin—214; and nobody's budging. Waiting for the best deal in the way of throwing his votes, Merwin, according to Russell, is showing unexpected character. Russell merely answers Dick's wails with "Wait." In spite of Joe's having done his worst, they're still in business, but they have lost three hundred votes. Russell says: "But not all to Cantwell. Merwin picked up over a hundred of my votes. And that is a sign of something." "Disgust," says Dick. "Decency," thinks Russell. "Decency? At a *convention?*" cries Dick.

Coming in from her packing, Alice inquires after Hockstader. "They wouldn't let me see him," replies Russell, "he's still unconscious." As Dick brings him back to the ever-present subject, Cantwell calls for another interview. He obviously wants a deal. "What else does Joe Cantwell ever want?" says Russell. "Oh, have you seen his latest statement? 'The rumors about William Russell's health have been maliciously exaggerated.' He's wonderful." Once more Dick begs Russell to let him call Senator Joseph with their release about Cantwell. Once more Russell refuses. "Leave him alone, Dick," says Alice.

Watching the TV view of the convention, Russell says: "There is a certain relief to knowing that the worst has happened to you and you're still alive and kicking. Ah (*peering at the screen*) . . . there's my old friend, Senator Carlin—true to the end.

CARLIN'S VOICE—*This sovereign state casts forty-four votes for the next preznighstays Joe Cantwell!*

"Senator Carlin," observes Russell, "has every characteristic of a dog—except loyalty."

On Cantwell's arrival, Russell has the delightful opportunity of preventing Joe from getting a word in edgewise by employing Cantwellian methods. Then, having had his fun, he lets Joe talk. This time Cantwell is ready to ask him to be on his ticket. "Well, that's very generous, Joe," he says, "but tell me, how could I possibly run for vice-president when I am at this very moment suffering from one of my frequent nervous breakdowns?" "How could I keep a report like that secret?" cries Cantwell. "Anyway, you've got to admit we handled the whole thing darned well, I mean look at the papers, practically no mention . . ." "Just as there was no mention of the fact that Art Hockstader is dying," says Russell. "Art didn't want anybody to know how sick he was," says Cantwell. "He was a great old guy. You know he's dead, don't you? Now, Bill, as I see the picture delegate-wise . . ." "I didn't know . . . Art was dead," Russell manages.

Listening to Cantwell's calculated, cold-blooded talk, and to Blade's cheap, unfeeling remarks, Russell is revolted. He orders Cantwell and his man Blades to get out. Instead of leaving, Cantwell proposes that Russell should show him some gratitude. With Blades backing him up, Cantwell promises Russell anything that he wants.

As Russell's second in this duel, Dick points out that Cantwell and Blades are now scared, sweating ice; and he loudly asks Russell to watch them squirm: "Bill, we got 'em. We really got 'em. Shall I call Senator Joseph?" This time Russell gives him the go-ahead signal. But when Russell comes to the phone he announces to Senator Joseph that he's withdrawn from the race. "Bill!" cries Dick. "Mr. Secretary," says Blades, "I swear you won't regret . . ." "And," continues Russell, "I am releasing my 384 delegates with instructions to support Governor John Merwin."

The main thing for Russell is that Joe Cantwell, whom he had said he would never let be president, is through in politics. Cantwell reacts numbly: "I don't understand you." "I know you don't," says Russell, "because you have no sense of responsibility toward anybody or anything, and that is a tragedy in a man and it is a disaster in a president! You said you were religious. Well, I'm not. I profoundly believe in *this* and what we do to one another and how this monstrous 'I,' the self, must become 'we' and draw the line at murder in the games we play with one another, whether it's politics or marriage or the ordinary living of a day and try to be good even when there is no one to force us to be good."

As usual, Cantwell has absorbed nothing. To the bitter end he is sure that it is the other fellow who doesn't understand politics, the country or its people. "You are a fool," he tells Russell as he leaves. Dick says: "I'm afraid, Bill, your conscience is my enemy."

As the break in the deadlock is marked on television, and Russell's votes start to flow to Merwin, Alice and William Russell make plans to stay together in private life. Russell invites her to share these autunm years even though she'll never have a chance to be another Grace Coolidge. Leaving the suite for the convention floor in Alice's company, Russell tells clamoring reporters: "You may say that I think Governor Merwin will make a fine candidate. I shall do everything I can to help him and the party. And I am of course happy the best man won!"

DUEL OF ANGELS

A Play in Three Acts

By Jean Giraudoux

Translated and Adapted by Christopher Fry

[Jean Giraudoux *was born in 1882 and died in 1944, before the production of "The Madwoman of Chaillot," which he refused production while his country was in the hands of the enemy. One of the most admired of French novelists and dramatists, he has enjoyed success in America as well. Among plays of his done on Broadway are "Amphitryon 38," "Siegfried," "The Enchanted," "Ondine," "The Madwoman of Chaillot," and "Tiger at the Gates."*]

[Christopher Fry *was born in Bristol, England, in 1908, the son of an architect, Charles Harris, who wanted him to become a clergyman. After his father's death he took his mother's maiden name. While a young man he acted and taught. Success came to him after World War II with "The Lady's Not for Burning," a verse-play taken from an old German short story. Since then he has written "Venus Observed," "A Sleep of Prisoners," "The Dark Is Light Enough," as well as several adaptions, including "Tiger at the Gates."*]

IT is 1868, and at a teashop in Aix-en-Provence people are sitting on the terrace under the lime trees. Dashing Count Marcellus, seated at a central table, asks the waiter to bring him not a drink but something that goes well with "vice": "Mr. Justice Blanchard has just proclaimed in open court that I am Vice, Joseph." Excusing himself, Joseph goes to refer this matter to the manager. A flower-seller approaches Marcellus. "Mr. Justice Blanchard," says Marcellus, "has insisted that from now on my buttonhole should carry an orchid streaked with blood, stinking of corruption." The girl thinks that antirrhinums might do, but she is not allowed to bring them to Count Marcellus's house. "Justice Blanchard," she reminds him, "has forbidden any girls under sixteen, especially flower-girls and laundry-maids, to go to the houses of unmarried gentlemen alone, sir." "Bring your mother," counters Marcellus, "we can install her in the kitchen." "My mother's in prison," answers the girl. "Mr. Justice Blanchard sent her there for taking some letters from the city treasurer to the prefect's wife."

Beautiful Paola, accompanied by her husband Armand, approaches Marcellus and greets him: "Good afternoon, Vice. Shall we sit next to Vice, Armand?" They seat themselves and report on Justice Blanchard's performance in court. "He thinks," says Paola, "our dear city of Aix is as bad as Sodom and Gomorrah." Marcellus wants to hear all that was said about him.

ARMAND—He said they can't imprison you for debt, because you're rich. They can't run you out of the district for being a nuisance, because you're too wily. No family is going to complain about you, because you would threaten them with blackmail. But he took it upon himself to execrate your name at the bar of justice, and—to point out your face for anyone to spit at who cares to.

MARCELLUS—A very detailed report.

ARMAND—I've a very good memory.

MARCELLUS—To spit at, he said?

ARMAND—That's what he said. He also mentioned debauchery. He also mentioned vice.

MARCELLUS—Precisely in that tone of voice?

ARMAND—I've been an actor in my time. I know how to copy an inflection. He said he had a mission to perform: to see that this town didn't run downhill to perdition, and since you stand for—a kind of symbol of the town, he would start his attack with you.

As Paola asks her husband not to side with those hypocrites, Joseph, having done his homework, reappears. He recites: "Vice is the natural propensity to evil, sir. We have a dictionary in the office. And the manager advises sherry with a drop of grenadine. That was the strongest thing he remembers them serving at the Café Anglais. But he would like you to be so very good as to choose another table. This one is reserved, sir." In another moment, Marcellus finds out that his table is reserved for Madame Lionel Blanchard, the wife of the justice. Leaping to his feet, seizing the opportunity offered, Marcellus announces that the duel can begin. "Have you a drum, Joseph?"

Joseph, with an Egyptian gong provided by a relative of de Lesseps, bangs away agreeably and the patrons hastily leave because of the racket.

Today everyone in Aix seems to have a mission. Marcellus now proclaims his: Vice will introduce Virtue to all those present. "You will see her in the flesh, sitting enthroned in this chair. Give her your careful attention. She can revive your drooping senses far more effectively than Vice can. You will see her, Monsieur Oscar, tasting an ice with a tongue which has never ventured beyond the kiss of a dutiful wife. You will hear her, Monsieur Julius, speaking with a mouth which has never told an untruth. You will watch her picking up a biscuit with fingers which have never strayed away in the dark, my dear Armand."

ARMAND—Kindly leave me out of this.

MARCELLUS—But above all, virtuous wives and excellent husbands of Aix, her coming here will throw light on your own marriages. Wherever this lady goes, life takes on the agreeable charm of the Last Judgment. I don't know how it is, considering she never listens to gossip, but one touch of human frailty and she knows it, and, as far as she's concerned, that's the end of you. Watch her closely. I can tell you, she is absolutely unmerciful. If she refuses to acknowledge an acquaintance, you can be quite sure that acquaintance has found a lover. . . .

ARMAND—Here she is, I think, Marcellus. You'd better shut up.

MARCELLUS—If she suddenly refuses to speak to some poor husband, his wife has betrayed him; and any husband so betrayed she holds personally responsible.

Marcellus gallantly relinquishes his table to beautiful, cool Lucile, entirely clothed in white. She graciously thanks him. Marcellus even receives a smile. He goes to a distant table, and Paola and Armand also move to another.

Seated with her friend and confidante Eugénie, Lucile sends Joseph into ecstasy with her kind regards to his wife.

EUGÉNIE—There's beginning to be a lot of talk in the town about your likes and dislikes. They're so extraordinary. . . . For instance, you don't seem to have any particular aversion to thieves. Or drunkards: I've seen you being most pleasant to them. You let liars compliment you, and compliment them back. Even that murderer we saw being arrested: you looked as though you pitied him.

LUCILE—He was much to be pitied. And my husband is the judge. One judge in the family is enough.

EUGÉNIE—You can face any of these faults and crimes quite

cheerfully, be talkative, and gracious, and in the best of spirits.
Then you suddenly freeze and clench your teeth and refuse to speak,
as though your flesh had been turned to stone.

LUCILE—But you know why.

EUGÉNIE—Yes, I do. Someone in love had just happened to go
past.

Warming to her subject, Eugénie says that before the Blanchards'
arrival, Aix was like a town of love. "Aix bred love like a fever,"
she says, "and nobody minded. We left typhoid and cholera to
Marseilles; here we had love." That is, until the day Lucile and
Lionel Blanchard arrived from Limousin, "the country which has
bred more Popes and fewer lovers than any other in the world."
With the Blanchards arrived calamity. "I brought calamity?" says
Lucile. "Your ices, Madame," announces Joseph, and, noticing that
Lucile now has no smile for him, he retires a wreck.

Eugénie recalls that the first month Lucile was here, every man
in Aix fell in love with her. By turning her back on people, she
killed love, and unloosed embarrassment and mischief in the town.
"The town has something serious against you," Eugénie says; "they
believe you're guilty of reintroducing original sin." She needn't
think that she's another Lucrece; she's simply the angel of evil.
It's all much simpler for Lucile: "I realize perfectly well that if I
were a saint I shouldn't despise them for it. But I can't help it.
On every incontinent person I see a creature." Correcting herself,
Eugénie says that Lucile hasn't come from Limousin, she's come
right out of the Middle Ages.

LUCILE—Our bodies are what God has given into our keeping,
Eugénie. He takes care of our souls Himself.

EUGÉNIE—I'm surprised that you've noticed your body. Have
you really been daring enough to look at it in the mirror? Don't
you tie yourself up in a sack when you sleep with the judge?

LUCILE—I have a great respect for my body. It is healthy, loyal,
and sensible. I keep well away from that common burial ground
which promiscuity leads to. Who are you smiling at?

EUGÉNIE—At Paola. Acknowledge her. She's waving to you.

LUCILE—Never.

Nor will Lucile acknowledge Paola's beauty. Beauty which takes
a lover isn't there for her to see. All that she is able to see are
thousands of praying mantises that cover Paola.

Having been icily ignored, Armand seeks out Lucile and finds a
statue. Asking why she hasn't acknowledged Paola's wave, he won-

ders how at a mere twenty feet, in a red dress, Paola could have become invisible. "I'm only saying"—and he says this at some length—"the town is deeply disturbed by Madame Blanchard's attacks of blindness and deafness." Eugénie apologizes but can suggest no cure. Armand, however, is sure that if every couple in town were perfect, Madame Blanchard would be a true chatterbox.

Declaiming his love for his wife, Armand wants no charity or lies. At long last, finding an opening wedge, Eugénie musters sufficient tact to send Armand back to Paola's table. "You can now congratulate yourself," she berates Lucile, "that you kept the word 'love' safe in your mouth like an acid drop."

But back again comes Armand. Maintaining that he is a huntsman who can see, and a visionary who can foresee, he declares that he has never had any apprehensions about Paola. And besides, he adds, if Paola were unfaithful, he should have known it since he comes home unexpectedly each day and always comes upon complete innocence.

Eugénie invites him to sit and have an ice with her, but to refrain from trying to make Lucile speak. While agreeing to these terms, Armand wishes one favor: "If Madame Blanchard agrees to tell me without words that I'm right, let her simply raise her glass to her lips. May I tell her that it's a very hot day, and she may enjoy it." Lucile does not drink, but as Armand goes away, she unconsciously raises her glass to her lips—to his delight. "How silly of me!" she cries. "I drank without thinking." She breaks the glass. "You know what you're doing, don't you?" cries Eugénie. "You're stirring up a scandal and a tragic drama. Armand was a magnificent peacock with a hundred blind eyes in his tail. And now you're making those eyes able to see."

Eugénie feels most sympathetically towards a woman like Paola, who would like to be a virgin for each new lover: "But what can she do? She has twenty loves and only one body." Furthermore, it maddens Eugénie listening to Lucile proclaim her virtue in a teashop: "like a martyr professing his faith in the arena. It's in bad taste, and with a tigress like Paola, it's dangerous."

Another warning is now added to Eugénie's. A stranger, on the pretext of looking for a coin, advises Lucile that Paola is not to be trifled with: "Madame Paola had an enemy once before, someone as beautiful as you are, who tried to take away her husband." He warns Lucile that there was little left of that other woman when Paola finished with her. When the man disappears, Eugénie urges Lucile to speak to Armand, or to leave. Paola may be inexorable, but Lucile is stubborn, and insists on staying.

As Eugénie had predicted, Armand returns and shows that already he is aware of Paola's imperfections, just as he is very much aware of Madame Blanchard's own fine points. Finding this all intolerable, Eugénie says she will not stay.

ARMAND—And yet Paola was so very dear to me until this morning. Madame Blanchard can have no idea what her tenderness used to be. I can remember so many things, which are very revealing. How she used to come back late for lunch, when the food had already gone cold, and put her hands over my eyes and say, "Guess who it is." And I always guessed right. The care she took not to wake me; how she would slip into my arms without disturbing me when she came back from those solitary midnight visits she so loved making, to a church where the incense had the smell of tobacco; I noticed how the smell of it clung to her. And how, when it rained, her shoes would still be miraculously dry, because one of the saints had carried her home. It was a church where they gave red roses to the faithful, and she always chose the two most perfect roses to put in a vase by my side. I could smell the scent of them all through the night. And how brave she was, how she would hide from me the scratches and bruises she was so often giving herself, on her neck or her mouth, by knocking up against something, she said, or accidentally biting herself. Kiss me, and I shall be cured, she would say. She would bruise her shoulders, and her breasts . . . Just like a child . . . Sometimes even her belly. Oh God, I don't know!

EUGÉNIE—You're both going mad, both of you, you who can't stop talking, and my friend who refuses to speak at all; you're both losing your senses.

Listening to this confession of sudden clear-sightedness on Armand's part, Eugénie asks whether Lucile is now satisfied, and departs. Lucile turns a teary gaze full on Armand, and tells him the reason for her silence: "Someone told me you had spoken ill of my husband. That is why I've been reserved with you. I wasn't for a moment thinking of Paola." Under his worshipful look, she is quite ready to swear that Paola has been faithful to him, if he repeats what he had said about her husband. "I said that virtue was the weakness of strong generals, and the strength of weak magistrates," recites Armand. Paola, interrupting this, sends Armand back to the house for her shawl, and at last has Lucile to herself.

Undeterred that Lucile can't bear women of her kind, Paola tells Lucile exactly what *she* is: a woman who loves men. "That may be," replies Lucile, "when they've earned the right to be called man." "Like Charlemagne for instance? Or Alexander?" asks Paola. "Or that saint who took such care of the children? I've forgotten his name." "You haven't forgotten his name," says Lucile, "it's avoiding you."

PAOLA—You're a fairly rare type, but not unheard of. You're one of the women who never get used to living among millions of male bodies and souls. Day and night, you're astonished at being a woman. Your reserve, and apparent modesty, come from this inability to take your sex for granted. You're curious about the woman you are, and at the same time rather frightened. You look at her in the mirror without ever getting to know her. When you're alone it's as though you'd made a shy arrangement to meet her; you move anxiously towards her when you're in bed.—But that's not how you feel about men; men to you are clear, complete, and male, in body and spirit; and this game of virtue you play is nothing but affectation, to cover up the alarm you feel when you compare your own elusive womanhood with the definite, unaltering statues of flesh which the gentlemen surround you with.

LUCILE—You describe yourself well.

PAOLA—It's no description of me. I'm the complete opposite: I can never see or love more than one man. Not always the same one, I admit; I change him, but I love no one else. Not another man exists in the world. When he is with me, the rest are invisible, gone clean out of existence. When I love, every ship sails the sea without sailors, carriages travel without coachmen, the cakes in this shop make their own way up from the kitchen, the baritone solo at the opera forms itself from the air, the deep chest notes come out of the lungs of infinite space. In the confessional I'm given absolution by an echo. I watch other women dancing in a void, taking emptiness by the hand, laughing and chattering with what has no existence; because the only man who has any substance, flesh, or blood, is in my arms.

LUCILE—Does your husband also go clean out of existence?

PAOLA—My husband? No. He is still there, a vague center of my consciousness, the agreeable obsession who is my husband. Like a memory which we don't turn to because we're so occupied with the present time. A companion, more shadow than flesh, who has my everyday life in his keeping. My interests, and habits, and likes, and dislikes are all safely in his care; my conversation on his lips, with everything I shall urgently need on the day I give up my latest lover: there he will be waiting, as it were, with my gloves and spectacles, that's to say the way I handle and look at the world between love affairs. So when that awful day comes, the first man to emerge will be my husband. He will immediately become substantial, and encourage all other men to come gradually out of the void where I had banished them. That's why I hold on to my husband. He doesn't only carry my belongings and common sense, but my fancies and inclinations, too, so that I'm able to fall in love again. And now you know why I don't intend to let you separate us. Where should we find our next lover, without a husband to put men back into the world again?

Paola adds that Lucile's husband, the justice, means less to Lucile than that: while Lucile reads to him from her metaphysical poets, her mind is listening like Eve in the garden.

Paola has come to warn Lucile that the freemasonry of women will not stand for her betraying them to the men: "The one inviolable pact since the creation of the world has been this agreement between women. And the woman who breaks it is bound for disaster." "I suppose," says Paola, "it's your unconscious appetite for men which makes you think they're sensitive, and passionate, and worthy of the truth. But believe me, if you enlighten them it won't do you any good. A man is only good and beautiful and strong when he's left in control of his make-believe life, which gives him mastery of the world, so he thinks, but in fact delivers him blind and feeble over to us. Adam knows, without any doubt, he has been driven out of the earthly paradise. Eve isn't so sure, and anyway behaves as though she were still there. So lay that to your heart. And remember there are some of us who are not going to tolerate the way you're behaving."

Paola now wishes to prescribe for Lucile: "When you see a friend going off to visit her lover, you will give her your hand, in spite of what you see her intention is; and when she's returning, you'll smile at her; you'll talk and laugh with the deceived, indulgent husband; you will make quite sure that what you do won't lead a man into making believe to see things as they are, and perhaps committing a crime."

On Armand's arrival, Lucile disregards all this advice. Without flourishes she tells this man whom she considers good and long-suffering that Paola has been unfaithful to him twenty times over, so that he must leave her. "Leave her," she commands, "it's better to have twenty-four hours of truth a day than twenty-four hours of lies. Twenty-four hours of honor instead of twenty-four hours of shame. Leave her; it will give you the chance to rediscover all the things you've been missing for some time, the good opinion of the world, of the natural world, of animals and trees; and, more important still, you will have your own good opinion, and you will have mine."

Overjoyed at this simplification of his life, Armand is sure that happiness will follow him all the rest of his days. "Armand!" cries

Paola. "It's so simple, and nobody thinks of it," answers Armand. "Here's your wrap, Paola. Put it on. You're stark naked." He leaves.

Having said so much, Lucile is thirsty. She drinks from a glass into which Paola surreptitiously drops a drug. Lucile starts to leave, but Paola takes her firmly by the arm. "A peculiarity of mine," remarks Paola, "is to measure both the people I love and the people I hate by the same yardstick. They all rouse the same desire in me, to touch them, or better still hold them. So I hold you. I will let you go when I think fit. A woman with something in her grasp has fingers more tenacious than the jaws of a bulldog." "Whether you let me go or not, I don't belong to your regiment of women," says Lucile. "You don't belong!" answers Paola. "You will see what happens to a woman who leaves it."

As Lucile faints, Paola lowers her gently into her chair at the table, and dismissing the onlookers with a casual explanation, she asks Joseph to run for Madame Barbette, the blood-letter.

Looking down on the more than ever silent Lucile, Paola wonders what she is going to do with her. Cause scandal? Disaster? "I have here the golden key of Pandora's box. And it's just as you wanted it, Lucile; you wanted to unlock hatred and let it out."

On her arrival, the unsavory Madame Barbette is ready to do any dark deed for Paola and is rather disappointed that no violence is required. Rejecting any plan that might mar Lucile's beauty, Paola proposes merely taking her to Barbette's house: "We will take her in my carriage. Lay her down on your sheets, and be sure you soil them. Then you can undo her bodice, loosen her stockings, and let down her hair. Lying disheveled is a splendor she never knew with her law-giving husband, her God the judge. So give it to her. Put your big mirror in a position where she will catch sight of herself as soon as she opens her eyes, and see herself as she has never seen or imagined herself before, so that she'll know at once that ruin and disaster have come to her." And ruin should be given the name of handsome, well-bred, and most corrupt Count Marcellus. Giving the count's handkerchief to Barbette to put in Lucile's hand, Paola concludes: "It is Ariadne's handkerchief, which leads irrevocably to disaster."

ACT II

Early the following morning, Paola arrives unexpectedly at the count's house. This early-morning visiting is an old failing of hers, but this time her purpose is different. She has come to announce to Marcellus that this is his wedding morning. There is to be a true marriage of Vice with Virtue. "Vice!" cries Marcellus, "you're talking like the Justice Blanchard and he talks like an old maid, and she talks like God. You can't expect a man to be Vice at eight o'clock in the morning. At that hour of the day Vice is essentially feminine." Paola had often observed this as Marcellus slept on and on at her side; she had found in him a childlike "kind of open candor which really had no purpose except to throw the blame on her!" She points out: "You sleep without your desire, Marcellus, without your needs, and without your strength, like Lionel Blanchard sleeping without his decorations."

MARCELLUS—Without his decorations? I doubt that. But at any rate he sleeps with Madame Blanchard, which is what I find it hard to forgive him; and I mean to make him pay for it.

PAOLA—But it wouldn't be hard to forgive, would it, if he wasn't the only one who slept with her?

MARCELLUS—I've noticed for some time, Paola, your cynicism is losing quality. Cynicism, like modesty, should come straight from the heart.

PAOLA—Do you think I am jealous of Madame Blanchard?

MARCELLUS—I think you're jealous of innocent women in general. If you didn't know that, I'm telling you now. And I suggest you should be on guard against it. You become very provincial whenever you're with them. You follow them about, and study them, as though purity were a secret which could be learnt. You look as though you were trying to catch up with the latest fashion: like someone anxious to copy a hat, or remember the details of a dress: to find the secret you will never know: how to caress a man without seeing him, how to see him without defining him: the secret of Lucrece, and of Madame Blanchard.

Paola is delighted to break the news that since last night Madame Blanchard does not at all fit his description: Madame Blanchard has fallen prey to a seducer—at Barbette's house. As indignant as a betrayed husband, Marcellus accuses Paola of lying. All last night he had joyfully planned his own trap for Madame Blanchard, a conquest which for the first time in his life would have also given him revenge. "Are you sure it was only for revenge?" asks Paola. "From what I saw yesterday, it looked as if revenge was handing the affair over to something softer-hearted. And I noticed that though she pretends to see some unpleasant crawling creature on anyone not strictly chaste, she could see no such thing on you. But I can." Marcellus demands to know the name of this brute who will have to answer to him. Paola is happy to answer: "It's you, it's yourself." And she's not joking with him—she explains what, in her female way, she had planned as revenge. "How can she be-lieve it?" says Marcellus. "Barbette has faked up a hundred women to seem like virgins in her time," says Paola; "for once, she had to do the opposite, and you can be sure she did it splendidly. And anyway, the victim was clutching your handkerchief. That's the tradition. I know my classics. And now," she demands, "thank me." "What for?" he asks. "For giving away to my shadow what I was going to get for myself?"

Asking Marcellus not to exaggerate, that his charms are on the decline, Paola says that Madame Blanchard, purity herself, is his with the power that she, Paola, has handed him. And adding that the husband will not be back today, Paola hands him Madame Blanchard's key and tells him to get to work. Not thinking much of his chances, Marcellus is still willing to try. "Your chances couldn't be better," she admonishes him, "understand that. She doesn't belong to her husband any more. She may refuse. But these women who don't hold with love, are all the more likely to believe in possession, and she belongs to you. All you have to do is to take her back. You don't have to compete with the judge any more: only with your own ghost. So as long as you're not inferior to that, all is well."

Before Marcellus can surprise the lady in her house, she calmly arrives at his. As the manservant announces the visitor, Paola de-cides that since she has had an exhausting night, she will step into Marcellus's bedroom, and for the first time, use it for sleeping.

Beautiful, unruffled, and as virtuous as ever, Lucile confronts Marcellus with *his* shame. Instead he merely confesses his love for her. "Did you make these protestations to me when I couldn't hear them?" she asks. "Yes," says Marcellus, "but you did hear them, and answered me with your body, clear promises without the shadow of a doubt."

Lucile seems to think that Marcellus has no idea of what she has come to ask of him. Staring at her, he isn't really thinking much about it. She asks him to listen closely: "If I touched you I should have to cry out. But I can't see how it is possible to ignore the truth as it is in the sight of God: because it was God you compelled to be my witness last night. You, a man I hate, have taken me, and poisoned everything, even the things I love. Neither despair nor reason can help me. And I'm not one who can find any comfort in resignation. Your crime has left me nothing to do except give up the only respect I still have any right to, my own self-respect. There's no other way to make myself clean again, so I have to accept it. I am bound to you; any other tie is broken. My happiness has gone, my beloved husband has been taken away; nothing is left to

me except misery and a loathsome husband." Before Marcellus can
get much satisfaction out of the word "husband," Lucile elaborates.
She wishes to be Marcellus's widow before the judge returns the following morning. Knowing that she has done nothing to deserve
death, she matter-of-factly prescribes death for him in order to speak
of him without disgust. Marcellus finds that his death would follow
very soon upon his marriage, but for Lucile, it would not be soon
enough. Clinging to the idea of his death, "like a child to its
mother," Lucile thinks it the one means of returning her to life.

Marcellus goes into action. He takes her, struggling, into his arms.
He promises to die afterwards, if she will be his wife one more time.
"Your marriage promises call you," he says. "Lie down!"

Bursting into the room, Armand comes to Lucile's rescue. Ordered
to leave the house, he refuses: "No. I'm not suggesting the house
is mine. But they tell me that my wife used to come here every
morning last year. So I have the right to come here one morning
this year. One single morning. And I've come at the time she used
to come. You won't see me here again."

MARCELLUS—You're late, as a matter of fact.

ARMAND—I was late to start with, I agree. I had come here because of my wife. I was as late as trusting husbands always are
when they've been deceived. A year late, or a month, it's all the
same. But I've been here some few minutes—the door was on the
latch, and I made my way up—I've heard all that you've been saying; and I get the impression that I'm right on time.

Armand felt today to be a day of reckoning the minute he opened
the shutters. Come to challenge Marcellus because of Paola, he had
forgotten her before he reached his door. "And then," says he,
"I overheard your conversation with Madame Blanchard. So now
if you don't mind, it will be because of Madame Blanchard." "Just
as you like, you ass," says Marcellus. "I'm entirely at your service.
It can be because of every woman who ever came into this house, if
that's what you want."

Armand entreats Madame Blanchard for permission to defend her
honor. Lucile gives a lovely, composed "Yes."

MARCELLUS—Downstairs we go, then, you gallant defender! One
thing I'll tell you to put you in good form: the favors of Paola at
her most lively are nothing compared with Madame Blanchard's
when she's unconscious!

ARMAND—You're taking leave of her now. Is that all you have
to say to her?

MARCELLUS—That's all. If she hadn't accepted you, I should probably have told her something else, something which might have been worth at least another kiss to me, and the most grateful kiss of them all. But she'll never hear it now, whether I live or die. Neither will you.

Before Lucile can leave, Paola glides in, and one sight of her is enough to convince Lucile that the terrible nightmare is all her doing. It is not enough that Paola had drugged her, Paola is also aware of her secret shame. Very much amused, Paola informs Lucile that another thing she has to learn is that a woman in love is not hidden by her secret, but fully exposed: "It is the same for you as it has been for all other women since the creation of the world; even though you were unconscious, you were stretched out there in front of us all, in the full public gaze." "Oh God," moans Lucile. Paola includes God, too, in the audience but excludes all men. The men would never suspect unless Lucile told them, and unfortunately she has this foolish habit. "I'm not talking about Armand, and your treacherous behavior yesterday. But Marcellus would never have known, if you hadn't come here to confront him this morning, that he had held in his arms Virtue, Honesty, and Honor, which are really the adolescent forms of passion, audacity, and pleasure. He didn't deserve that. Left to himself, he would never have guessed it. You made him a present there, which we should never give to any man; we should always try to be nameless. Don't fail us again, that's my last word of advice."

Hearing a bell, Lucile is sure that they are back, but Paola dissuades her. Enveloping herself in dignified virtue, Lucile denounces Paola to Paola, sure that Paola must feel small and ashamed in the face of Lucile's suffering. At her own level of unhappiness, Lucile knows that she "can count on all the resources of God, from miracles to death." Not at all unhappy, Paola finds it rather presumptuous of Lucile to call on the help of saints and martyrs over so slight and venial an accident. Lucile explains very grandly that one calls on whoever will reply: "When *you* call, Barbette comes to you, and all your other companions in this town. Slander comes, and jealousy, and lechery. When I called, all those women answered, you know that what has been done can be redeemed; whose lives have proved that there are days when all misdeeds are avenged, not by punishment, but because they have vanished, and not left a trace. If their presence makes you uncomfortable, so much the worse for you, but there they are. Those who were stripped naked in front of the crowd, and yet made a cloak out of their nakedness and crossed the town by the main streets. . . ." She knows that she will lie on her bed tonight as untouched as she was before. And hearing someone coming, Lucile is sure that it is God's answer. It turns out, however, to be a manservant announcing that Justice Blanchard is downstairs. "I am lost," cries Lucile. "A pause in the high drama," says Paola, "while we indulge in a scene of domestic comedy."

Afraid to see her husband before Armand's return, Lucile receives unexpected help. Paola will see Blanchard for her. "God hasn't given you the day," she says, "but the women will at least give you an hour: the hour that will give you time to get ready, not to be seen—there's no risk of that—but to see." And Paola shows her a little stairway that leads into the street.

PAOLA—Off you go. I'll bring you the news of the duel myself and at the same time see the transformation in your household.

LUCILE—I wish I could tear you to pieces!

PAOLA—But you can, Lucile; my sister Lucile.

LUCILE—I can't. I can never be one of your kind. Your devilish tricks are no use. Hissing like a snake isn't going to do you any good. (*Exits.*)

PAOLA (*slowly, taking pleasure in hissing the words*)—Oh, yes, Lucile, it is, yes, it is!

~~ACT III~~

Justice Blanchard is trying to work in his study with his clerk on the Thomass poison case, but his thoughts wander to Lucile, who has avoided him since his return. She is now locked in their bedroom.

Sending his clerk off on an errand, Blanchard persuades Lucile to appear, and greets her as tenderly as ever. Keenly disappointed in such blindness, Lucile proceeds to correct it, in a somewhat roundabout way. She asks Lionel to suppose that early in her life she had had another husband and was now a widow. "Would you take me back again?" she asks. "Would you marry me again?" This is just so much chatter to Lionel, but as she persists with this odd line of talk, he finally calls a halt: "Stop all this childish nonsense. If another man had touched my wife, whether the calendar went forwards or backwards, I wouldn't see her again as long as I lived."

LUCILE—Remembering she had been unconscious, Lionel, lifeless and unconscious?

LIONEL—The flesh is never unconscious.

LUCILE—The flesh! How can you apply that terrible word to me?—to say I have flesh!

LIONEL—You force me to. There are a thousand different ways

of talking of the spirit, but the flesh is the flesh, even when it's yours. If a man had touched my wife, whether it was in the moon or in limbo, I should never touch her or speak to her again for the rest of my life.

LUCILE—Goodbye, then . . .

LIONEL—But what has happened? What are you trying to tell me?

LUCILE—What has happened is that you'll never touch me again. You'll never speak another word to me.

LIONEL—A man has dared to lay hands on you?

LUCILE—He has dared to marry me.

LIONEL—Stop using that ridiculous word! A man has touched you!

LUCILE—My word is the right word. This other marriage took place yesterday, and I'm not that other husband's widow yet. And if I'm not his widow soon, it will be your fault. Why did you come back so soon, Lionel? I had to have time to put it right. And death had to have time to get here. But you haven't given either of us time enough.

LIONEL—A lover. You have a lover!

LUCILE—Everything good and innocent was rallying to help me. By coming home so soon, you've spoilt it all.

LIONEL—It's Marcellus! That's why you went to his house.

LUCILE—He drugged me last night, and carried me to one of his houses. I woke up, and Marcellus had gone.

LIONEL—Swear to me, swear that's true.

LUCILE—I didn't ever see him. The reason I went to his house this morning—

LIONEL—Was to give this crime a face and a voice, to give him eyes to see you with!

LUCILE—Was to ask him to kill himself. And almost at the same moment, Armand came to challenge him because of Paola. And now I'm waiting.

LIONEL—And you've even left it to someone other than me to avenge your honor.

LUCILE—I still kept my honor, it's the only thing that's not destroyed in me.

LIONEL—And you dare to call this degrading incident your second marriage!

LUCILE—It's the only way I could purify it. You, too! You, too!

Lucile assures him that there may be only a minute or two to wait. Taking a pistol from a drawer and dashing out, Lionel cries: "It won't be many more, whatever happens."

Having fatally wounded Marcellus, who obviously knew he was

doomed from the start, Armand rushes back to Lucile. He presents his news, and provides the understanding and sympathy that she found so singularly lacking in Lionel.

Lucile is horrified that Lionel understood nothing: "Oh, Armand, there must be a reason why God so often lets the criminal have the glory while the victim is left in the shadow; but it's dreadful to think that if you take a man's wife away from him, he is changed from someone just, and good, and generous, into an egotistical bully. But that's what I've seen with my own eyes. His wonderful cloak of virtue, which he was so proud of, as I was, too, has fallen suddenly into rags. Everything he says sounds like hypocrisy and wrong-thinking, even though he is using words like honor and justice and the family. He quoted Latin as if he had lifted up a gravestone and woodlice had swarmed out from underneath it. Even the scent of the lotion on his chin, which I chose for him, and the cloth of his suit which I also chose, were as alien and hostile to me as he was." Armand asks why she tells him all this. "So that you can reassure me," says Lucile. "This isn't what life is going to offer me from now on, is it? It can't be that the erring wife is going to sit in moral judgment on this poor innocent man! Marcellus's crime isn't going to glorify me and dishonor Lionel?—Ever since he went out of the room, every minute seems to have made him look worse to me. And now I'm waiting in such terror for him to come back. What monster will he have become?"

Comforting her, Armand explains that this morning all men will look ugly to her, each will carry the mark of the beast. "No," says Lucile, "you do not." Through Armand alone Lucile feels renewed. "For all your indignation and pity," she explains, "you kept yourself so far away from me that I could feel innocent, and almost happy. You can be there, and move towards me, and take my hands, there is still this marvelous distance between us. Oh, Armand, tell me what a man is, drive away this nightmare, and I'll believe you."

ARMAND—What a man is? From what I know of myself, all I can say is that he's neither complicated nor unique.

LUCILE—But generous and strong, isn't that so?

ARMAND—Gullible and unreal. He believes, first of all, if he's modest, that the world belongs to him completely. Then if he's intelligent, he believes that woman belongs to him, and love belongs to him. Then, when his hope in life has given place to the pleasures of living, he groans away the night in silence, and weeps with a dry eye.

LUCILE—Is that everything?

ARMAND—Everything up to yesterday.

LUCILE—Go on. What is he today?

ARMAND—Today he is dead. Not the harmless one: he is going to prison for murder. He has destroyed his life. He has seen you. He is happy.

LUCILE—Thank you. Lionel can come back. Goodbye. (PAOLA *enters, followed by* BARBETTE.)

PAOLA—What's more, a man is pretentious, if he's one of the simple sort. Weak and feeble, if he's one of the passionate sort. And if he's timid, he gambles with destiny like a madman. And by that, I mean you.

Paola is delighted to listen to these two together. She is sure that "martyrs have never mutually crowned each other with such laurels before." Actually she finds them screaming love at each other like a pair of cats. For herself, she has come to avenge Marcellus, which won't be difficult. "Leave Marcellus to his death, where you put him," snaps Armand. "Don't quibble," Paola answers, "you're the murderers. She killed him. You killed him. You, out of vanity. She by thinking she was virtuous. You, by the honor of a gentleman, both of you by chasing after tragedy when you're up to the neck in farce. But you won't be able to look at each other when I've said what I have to say to her." Fixing the blame for Lucile's predicament directly on Lucile, Paola says: "It was true there was a rape last night in the Brignoles Road, but it wasn't Marcellus who was responsible." Over Lucile's cries, Paola bids Barbette tell her the truth, which will undoubtedly horrify her and turn her against herself. At the same time, Armand will be delighted with the news. "But Madame Blanchard will be less relieved. She has a suspicion already that her dignity and respectability are escaping her: that she isn't Marcellus's widow after all; that this soft, guilty, pulsating body is hers by nature. Because Marcellus hasn't held her in his arms. Barbette is witness to that. There was no assault last night: though you would hardly believe that, to look at her. Her eyes are more languid than Elvira's were after her episode with Don Juan! But this morning she is just as she was yesterday, when she sat eating her strawberry ice, a narrow-minded woman, quite intact, who has never been touched by the hands or lips of anyone except the honorable husband. Barbette was in charge of the whole production. No other actors, and no director. Nothing else was necessary."

As predicted, Armand is overjoyed, but Lucile is mortally wounded. Watching her, Paola observes her hands shaking. And she knows it isn't just the shame of looking ridiculous. "What a disaster it is," she sympathizes, "to lie down a martyr and rise a virgin!" Everything has been the work of Madame Blanchard herself—"a case, you might say," Paola points out, "of purity destroying itself. It needed no more than this little fairy tale, an idea for a melodrama, to bring her in one day to the point we other foolish women take years to arrive at."

Barbette corroborates all that Paola has said. Thus, her mission nearly finished, Paola repeats now what she had told Lucile yesterday: "When you see a friend going off to visit her love, you will give her your hand. . . ." Then hearing Lionel's carriage, Paola starts making her farewells: "A dead man is waiting for me, and a policeman is waiting for Armand, and neither of them, as we know, care to be kept waiting."

Rushing into the room, Lionel is met by Lucile's plea to save her, and by Armand's demand that he hear the true story. Instead, Lionel orders Lucile from his house. "What a fool I've been, these five years," says Lionel, "meekly going on respecting her virtue and innocence, respecting this body if you please, when it refused every invitation from her husband, only to go and accept a lover. Oh, heavens, instead of all this, all this solemn high-thinking and timidity, what Marcellus-like nights I could have given myself!" "There it is," says Lucile, "it's over."

Armand demands that Lionel question Barbette for the truth. With Lucile's grateful approval, Barbette reverses her story: Unconscious as Lucile was, she thanked Marcellus and smiled—but unconsciously. "When he was leaving, what did she do?" asks Lionel. "With her arms around his waist and his neck," reports Barbette, "she tried to hold him back, but unconsciously." His case thus concluded, Justice Blanchard leaves.

Armand can't understand why Barbette lied, or why Paola smiles. "One can smile," answers Paola, "there stands Lucile, the woman." Paola can see but two futures for such a woman: one, resuming her act of degraded vestal virgin; the other, starting a career much like Paola's, with Armand thrown in for good measure.

Suddenly ordering Paola to get on her knees, Lucile bids her ask pardon of everyone alive or dead for having said that life is without worth or purity.

PAOLA—Well, isn't it? What worth can you see in today, for instance?

LUCILE—Today is horrible. It has mocked at everything, made everything vile. The world is infested with a pitiful vermin which hugs itself and devours itself. Human life.

PAOLA—And is he pure, this man here? Another woman's husband. And don't you love him?

LUCILE—Yes, I love him. And I know I hate my husband. And this man is another woman's husband, and I know I love him.

PAOLA—Then we're in complete agreement, Lucile. It's a defeat for you, my poor friend, and there's no way out of it.

LUCILE—No way out of it? How wrong you are! The way out is here, in my hand. I went for help to a little girl, of my own age and my own name, who swore, when she was ten years old, never to accept evil, swore to prove, even by death if it had to be, that the world was a noble place, and that human beings were pure in heart. Now this world has become empty and terrible to her, and life nothing but corruption; but it doesn't matter, it isn't even true, because she is still going to keep the vow she swore.

BARBETTE—What are you doing? Why do you say this? O Lord God, she has taken poison.

And Lucile makes a last request.

LUCILE—My last wish, Armand! That my husband never knows the truth. Let him believe Barbette. If Marcellus preferred to die without betraying his innocence, I'm not going to die betraying my crime, my crime without end, my condemnation of life. It's as though I can see my husband now, clear to the bone in a bright flash of judgment. He will live from now on scorning an innocent woman, as she has been scorning him: and admiring the guilty woman who hated life. He will live in a false legend, but what legends are true? Truth is always the poor lamb being sacrificed. What else could I have done, Armand? What else except play the heroine? Heroes are men who glorify a life which they can't bear any longer. And so it has come about with me. Is Paola kneeling?

PAOLA—Yes.

LUCILE—She is still standing, but she said Yes. I have won. The world has purity, Paola, beauty and light. Tell me so yourself. I want to hear you say so. Tell me quickly.

ARMAND—Tell her; say it to her.

PAOLA—It is true . . . for this moment.

LUCILE—I'm content with that. A moment will do. Thank you. Don't let Paola come near me. Barbette will dress me for burial. Let her do it well, and not disguise me as though I were still alive. In heaven they're not so easily fooled. (*She slips to the ground.*) She was called Lucrece . . . wasn't that so?

A THURBER CARNIVAL

A Revue in Two Acts

By James Thurber

[James Thurber *was born in Columbus, Ohio, in 1894. He begin to write at the age of 10 and to draw at the age of 14. He worked in the State Department as a reporter for various newspapers, was on the staff of the New York "Post" and in 1927 joined the staff of "The New Yorker." He has written more than 20 successful books, including "Fables of Our Time," "My Life and Hard Times," and, more recently, "The Years with Ross." His stories have been made into movies, radio and television scripts. "The Male Animal," a play which he wrote with Elliott Nugent, had a long run on Broadway and a successful revival.*]

[Don Elliott *is one of the most versatile jazz men of our time. For the seventh consecutive year he won the Downbeat poll. Professionally he first appeared as a vocalist with "Hi-Lo, Jack and the Dame" accompanying Lena Horne at the Copacabana. He has been with George Shearing and Benny Goodman, and had his own group headlining such spots as Basin Street, Birdland, and the Newport Jazz Festival.*]

THE cool jazz of Don Elliott's quartet, serving as an overture to the show, creates a carnival spirit; it provides the Thurberesque pace, while the author's own line-drawings used on curtains and backdrops add the final, *echt* touch.

For the opening number—it's called "Word Dance"—eight mis-mated Thurber people are dancing—as they might in Ohio or Connecticut. At a break in the music, they all suddenly freeze, and one woman, turning front, can be heard saying out of the blue: "You may call it sleepwalking, but I say she's promiscuous." The dancing resumes. Two bars later, the freeze sets in and a man says: "So she said to me, why did we have to purchase Louisiana when we got the other states for nothing?" Turning back to the dance, he continues till the music stops, and a woman now asks: "Well, if I called the wrong number, why did you answer the phone?" Next, a dapper man, stopping short, admits: "I didn't mind her buying the pistol, but it makes me nervous when she holds it on her lap at breakfast."

As the dance turns into a rumba, a man says for no presumable reason: "Her husband went up to bed one night and was never seen again." A few pauses later, one overhears: "She says he proposed something on their wedding night her own brother wouldn't have suggested." "Do you realize," a woman next asks of no one in particular, "it took Paul Revere two and a half hours to rouse the Widow Mathews that night?" When the music stops, all eight dancers, sitting on the edge of the platform, bombard the audience with such irrelevancies as: "Then I had an affair with this twelve-year-old girl. Think of it, Mrs. Bixby, I was only ten at the time . . ."

The music and dancing resume. The music shifts from dirge to square dance. The first woman says: "My husband wanted to live in sin, even after we were married." They all do-ci-do and then make a London Bridge pattern. "I wanted to be a *femme fatale*," the third woman tells the third man, "but I don't want to get mixed up with men." "Well, good luck," the third man says for the only reply of the evening.

Dancing patterns change while maintaining the same two-bar rhythm of music and movement. The third man now lets it be known: "No matter who is nominated, my mother is going to vote for Lindbergh . . ." And on the final two bars of music, the eight dancers break and exit on beat—the women going their way and the men their's.

After "Word Dance (Part I)," there follows a series of Thurber sketches, monologues and "Fables for Our Times." Among them are the following, which are given here in full: "The Unicorn in the Garden," "If Grant Had Been Drinking at Appomattox," "Mr. Preble Gets Rid of His Wife," "File and Forget" and "The Secret Life of Walter Mitty."

THE UNICORN IN THE GARDEN

(*The music begins. It is shimmering and delicate, like crystal. A spot light picks up the* NARRATOR, *seated against the left portal. The traveller opens revealing* MAN, *seated on a sidechair.* SHE *is seated but asleep back of a bed cutout. He is in shirt-sleeves, and* SHE *wears a lace bed-jacket.*)

NARRATOR—Once upon a sunny morning, a man who sat in a breakfast nook looked up from his scrambled eggs to see a white unicorn with a golden horn quietly cropping the roses in the garden. (*The* MAN *looks up, rises and crosses down right, looking at the unicorn. Apparently he sees it clearly. All we see is a small light flashing on the roses.*) The man went up to the bedroom where his wife was still asleep and woke her.

MAN—There's a unicorn in the garden, eating roses.

NARRATOR—She opened one unfriendly eye and looked at him.

SHE (*awakes, sits up*)—The unicorn is a mythical beast.

NARRATOR—She turned her back on him. The man walked slowly downstairs and out into the garden. The unicorn was still there; he was now browsing among the tulips.

MAN—Here, unicorn.

NARRATOR—And he pulled up a lily and gave it to him. (*The* MAN *pantomimes "pulling up a lily" and feeds it to the unicorn. He runs his fingers lightly up the imaginary unicorn's horn and gently pats the top.*) The unicorn ate it gravely. With a high heart, because there was a unicorn in his garden, the man went upstairs and roused his wife again.

MAN—The unicorn ate a lily.

NARRATOR—His wife sat up in bed and looked at him, coldly.

SHE—You are a booby and I am going to have you put in the booby hatch.

NARRATOR—The man, who had never liked the words "booby" and "booby hatch," and who liked them even less on a shining morning when there was a unicorn in the garden, thought for a moment.

MAN—We'll see about that.

NARRATOR—He walked over to the door.

MAN (*turning back to her*)—He has a golden horn in the middle of his forehead.

NARRATOR—Then he went back to the garden to watch the unicorn; but the unicorn had gone away. The man sat down among the roses and went to sleep. (MAN *looks for the unicorn, and, not seeing it, wistfully sits on the edge of the platform and nods off to sleep.*)

as the husband had gone out of the house, the wife got up
sed as fast as she could. She was very excited and there
gloat in her eye. (SHE *dials an imaginary telephone*.) She
ned the police and she telephoned a psychiatrist; she told
to hurry to her house and bring a strait-jacket. When the
and the psychiatrist arrived they sat down in chairs and
d at her, with great interest.

SHE—My husband saw a unicorn this morning.

NARRATOR—The police looked at the psychiatrist and the psychiatrist looked at the police.

SHE—He told me it ate a lily.

NARRATOR—The psychiatrist looked at the police and the police looked at the psychiatrist.

SHE—He told me it had a golden horn in the middle of its forehead.

NARRATOR—At a solemn signal from the psychiatrist (*the* PSYCHIATRIST *signals "thumbs down"*), the police leaped from the chair and seized the wife. (*The* POLICEMAN *rises and grabs the wife by one shoulder and places one hand over her mouth, struggling wildly. The* PSYCHIATRIST *binds her feet with imaginary rope*.) They had a hard time subduing her, for she put up a terrific struggle, but they finally subdued her. Just as they got her into the strait-jacket the husband came back into the house.

POLICEMAN (*still holding the woman*)—Did you tell your wife you saw a unicorn?

MAN—Of course not. The unicorn is a mythical beast. (SHE *beats her feet against the floor*.)

PSYCHIATRIST—That's all I wanted to know. I'm sorry, sir, but your wife is as crazy as a jay bird. (*The* POLICEMAN *and the* PSYCHIATRIST *pick up the chair on which the wife is sitting and carry her off*. SHE *looks back cursing and screaming without making a sound. The music supplies it very effectively*.)

NARRATOR—So they took her away, cursing and screaming, and shut her up in an institution. (*The* MAN *waves farewell to his wife, sits in the chair, and folds his hands behind his head*.) The husband lived happily ever after. Moral:

MAN—Don't count your boobies until they are hatched.

IF GRANT HAD BEEN DRINKING AT APPOMATTOX

(*The music is a crisp military theme. Three book cutouts appear, entitled in order: "If Booth Had Missed Lincoln" by Tom Haddock; "If Washington Had Drowned in the Delaware: A Speculative History" by Oliver Finney; "If Grant Had Been Drinking at Appo-*

mattox" by James Thurber. As the spot light hits the third book, the NARRATOR *rises.*)

NARRATOR—The morning of the ninth of April, 1865, dawned beautifully. General George Meade was up with the first streaks of crimson in the eastern sky. General Hooker and General Burnside were up, and had breakfasted by a quarter after eight. The day continued beautiful. It drew on toward eleven o'clock. General Ulysses S. Grant was still not up. He was asleep in his famous old navy hammock swung high above the floor of his headquarters bedroom. (*The traveller opens to reveal the headquarters of* GENERAL GRANT, *who lies asleep in a cutout hammock. The scene depicts a Thurber version of the almost demolished interior of the Appomattox Courthouse. Windows are broken, curtains flying, and boots and bottles are in unlikely places. On a table are several glasses and a wine bottle. Also there is a low black stool with a scotch bottle on it, and a military map covering the General's sock, on the floor. A corporal, wearing a Confederate army hat, jacket and puttees, enters and goes to the foot of* GRANT'S *bed.*)

SHULTZ (*saluting*)—Pardon, sir, but this is the day of surrender. You ought to be up, sir. (*Swings hammock a little.*)

GRANT (*uncovers his head*)—Don't swing me! I feel terrible. (*Covers his head.*)

SHULTZ—General Lee will be here any minute now. (*Swings the hammock again.*)

GRANT (*uncovers his head*)—Will you cut that out? Do you want to make me sick or what? (SHULTZ *salutes.*) What's he coming here for?

SHULTZ—This is the day of surrender, sir.

GRANT—Three hundred and fifty generals in the Northern armies, and he has to come to *me* about this. What time is it?

SHULTZ—You're the Commander-in-Chief, that's why. It's eleven twenty-five, sir.

GRANT—Don't be crazy. Lincoln is the Commander-in-Chief. Nobody in the history of the world ever surrendered before lunch. Doesn't he know that an army surrenders on its stomach? (*Pulls the blanket over his head and settles himself again.*)

SHULTZ—The generals of the Confederacy will be here any minute now. You really ought to be up, sir.

GRANT—All right, all right . . . (*He gets slowly to a sitting position and looks around the room.*) This place looks awful. Are you sure I'm here? What place is this, Sargeant?

SHULTZ—Appomattox Courthouse, Virginia.

Tom Ewell and Paul Ford in "A Thurber Carnival"

GRANT—Don't call me Virginia!   My name is—Telemachus, or something like that.

SHULTZ—Ulysses, sir.

GRANT—That's close enough.

SHULTZ—You must have had quite a time of it last night, sir.

GRANT—Yeh.   I was wrassling some general.   Some general with a beard.   (*He gets off the bed.   He wears his trousers, suspenders hanging down, a woolen undershirt, and one sock.*)   Where's my other sock?   (*He and* SHULTZ *start looking around for the sock.* GRANT *spots a map on the floor next to the table.*)   Hmmmm. (*Crosses to the map, lifts it.*)   Secret military maps and my other sock. (GRANT *picks up a glass from the table and a bottle of scotch standing on the low stool and pours himself a drink.*)

SHULTZ—I don't think it's wise to drink, sir.

GRANT (*drinks*)—Never mind about me. (*Helps himself to a second.*) I can take it or leave it alone. Didn't ya ever hear the story about the fella went to Lincoln to complain about me drinking too much? "So-and-so says Grant drinks too much," this fella said. "So-and-so is a fool," said Lincoln. So this fella went to "What's-his-name and told him what Lincoln said and he came roaring to Lincoln about it. "Did you tell So-and-so I was a fool?" he said. "No," said Lincoln, "I thought you knew it." (*Smiles reminiscently.*) That's how I stand with Lincoln. (*Soft thudding of horses' hooves is heard.*) Hoof steps.

SHULTZ—It's General Lee and his staff.

GRANT (*rises and grabs up scotch bottle*)—Show him in. (SHULTZ *waves the group on.*) And see what the boys in the back room will have. (GRANT *takes a hefty belt from the bottle as* LEE *and two staff members enter to the accompaniment of a drum roll and fanfare.* GRANT, *staring at them, pulls the bottle from his mouth.*) I know who you are. You're Robert Browning, the poet.

LEE STAFF MAN—This is General Robert E. Lee.

GRANT—Oh. I thought he was Robert Browning. He certainly looks like Robert Browning. (*A step toward* LEE.) There is a poet for you, Lee: Browning. Di ja ever read "How They Brought the Good News from Ghent to Aix?" "Up Derek, to saddle, up Derek, away; up Dunder, up Blitzen, up Prancer, up Dancer, up Bouncer, up Vixen, up . . ."

LEE (*with great dignity, and an impeccable southern accent*)—Shall we proceed at once to the matter in hand?

GRANT—Some of the boys was wrassling here last night. I threw Burnside or some general a whole lot like Burnside. It was pretty dark. (*Looks at* LEE.) Get a glass, somebody. (*Crosses to the aide standing down right of* LEE.) I've seen you someplace before.

LEE—May I present General John Longstreet, General Grant? And General Pendleton? (*There is a crash of glass offstage.*)

GRANT—Spies. You've got the noisiest spies in the history of warfare, General. They sound like Mosby gettin' there fustest with the mostest.

LEE—I had the pleasure just now of meeting my old friend and West Point classmate, General George Meade. I said to him, "General, I did not remember you as having so many gray hairs," to which he was gallant enough to reply: "You put them there, General."

GRANT—Good man, Meade. Gray as a badger, though.

LEE—I should like to have this over with as soon as possible, General. (GRANT *looks inquiringly at* SHULTZ.)

SHULTZ—The surrender, sir, the surrender.

GRANT—Oh, sure, sure. (*Takes a drink from the bottle.*) Here we go. (*He gets his sword and belt, hanging on the bedpost. As he crosses back to* LEE, *he starts to put the sword on. Then he presents it to* LEE.) There you are, General. We dam' near licked you. If I'd been feeling better, we *would* have licked you.

MR. PREBLE GETS RID OF HIS WIFE

(*The music begins the Preble Theme, and after a few seconds the traveller opens and the lights come up on an office scene.* MR. PREBLE *is dictating letters to his secretary,* MISS DALEY.)

MR. PREBLE (*rises from desk*)—To the American Badge and Novelty Company, 430 South Main Street. (*He is close to* MISS DALEY.) That's a sweet fragrance you're wearing, Miss Daley. What is it?

MISS DALEY—I'm glad you like it, Mr. Preble. It's called "Flight."

MR. PREBLE—Flight. Let's run away together.

MISS DALEY—All righty.

MR. PREBLE (*moves away from her*)—Gentlemen . . . My wife would be glad to get rid of me and vica versa. (*Noticing that* MISS DALEY *has taken this down, he crosses back to her.*) No, no, I don't want the American Badge and Novelty Company to know about us.

MISS DALEY (*scratching out the words*)—Oh, I see.

MR. PREBLE—Let's run away together.

MISS DALEY—All righty. Would your wife give you a divorce?

MR. PREBLE—I don't suppose so.

MISS DALEY—You'd have to get rid of your wife. (*The stage lights dim rapidly to black, but* PREBLE *is left, thinking, for a moment in the lingering follow spot. A slight smile lights up his face. The lights come up to reveal the* PREBLE *living room and* MRS. PREBLE.)

MR. PREBLE—Let's go down in the cellar.

MRS. PREBLE (*not looking up from her reading*)—What for?

MR. PREBLE—Oh, I don't know. We never go down in the cellar any more.

MRS. PREBLE—We never did go down in the cellar that I remember. I could rest easy the balance of my life if I never went down in the cellar.

MR. PREBLE—Supposing I said it meant a whole lot to me.

MRS. PREBLE—What's come over you? It's cold down there and there is absolutely nothing to do.

MR. PREBLE (*rises and crosses to her*)—I could show you how to regulate the new furnace.

MRS. PREBLE—I don't have to know about that. The thermostat regulates the furnace. Anyway, I'm reading.

MR. PREBLE (*looking off at cellar*)—Listen, I wish you'd come down in the cellar with me. You can read down there, as far as that goes.

MRS. PREBLE—There isn't a good enough light down there, and anyway, I'm not going to go down in the cellar. You may as well make up your mind to that.

MR. PREBLE (*kicks the carpet, like a small boy*)—Gee whiz! Other people's wives go down in the cellar. Why is it you never want to do anything together? I come home worn out from the office, and you won't even go down in the cellar with me. God knows it isn't very far—it isn't as if I was asking to go to the movies or some place.

MRS. PREBLE—I don't want to go.

MR. PREBLE—All right, all *right*. (*He sits on the sofa.*)

MRS. PREBLE (*a long pause*)—You probably want to get me down there to bury me. (*Laughs.*)

MR. PREBLE—All right. I might as well tell you the truth. I want to get rid of you so I can marry my stenographer. Is there anything especially wrong about that? People do it every day. Love is something you can't control.

MRS. PREBLE (*patting his head absentmindedly*)—We've been all over that. I'm not going to go all over that again. I suppose this filing person put you up to it.

MR. PREBLE—You needn't get sarcastic. Miss Daley's my secretary. I have plenty of people to file without having her file. She doesn't know anything about this. She isn't in on it. I was going to tell her you had gone to visit some friends and fell over a cliff. She wants me to get a divorce.

MRS. PREBLE—*That's* a laugh. You may bury me, but you'll never get a divorce.

MR. PREBLE—I told her that. I mean—I told her I'd never get a divorce.

MRS. PREBLE—Oh, you probably told her about burying me too.

Mr. Preble—That's not true. That's between you and me. I was never going to tell a soul.

Mrs. Preble—You'd blab it to the whole world; don't tell me. I know you.

Mr. Preble—I wish you were buried now and it was all over with.

Mrs. Preble—Don't you suppose you would get caught, you crazy thing? They always get caught. Why don't you go to bed? (*She tweaks his nose, pats his cheek and pinches his chin in rhythm with her words. Her tone is cajoling; as though she were talking to a recalcitrant four-year-old.*) You're just getting yourself all worked up over nothing.

Mr. Preble (*looks at her, then jumps up*)—I'm not going to bed. I'm going to bury you in the cellar. I've got my mind made up to it. I don't know how I could make it any plainer.

Mrs. Preble (*putting down her book*)—Listen, will you be satisfied and shut up if I go down in the cellar? Can I have a little peace if I go down in the cellar? Will you let me alone then?

Mr. Preble—Yes, but you spoil it by taking that attitude.

Mrs. Preble—Sure, sure, I always spoil everything. Have you got an envelope?

Mr. Preble—What do you want an envelope for?

Mrs. Preble—I want to mark my place in this book.

Mr. Preble—Why? You're not going to have a chance to finish it. (*She puts the book on the couch and rises.*) You go first.

Mrs. Preble—All right, you lead the way. (*They exit as the lights go to black. Their voices are heard off left, and then* Mrs. Preble *enters, in the black. The three panels are black with white drawings of ominous-looking cellar fixtures. A furnace and its pipes and a naked light bulb seem to leap out of the dark.*) You *would* think of this, at this time of year! Any other husband would have buried his wife in the summer.

Mr. Preble (*following, but staying behind*)—You can't arrange these things just whenever you want to. I didn't fall in love with this girl till late fall.

Mrs. Preble—Mercy, but it's cold down here, and I can never find the light. (*She reaches up for the light cord, and the lights come on. On top of a crate is a strange wrench.* Mr. Preble *stands in the entrance with a shovel concealed behind his back.*) What have you got there?

Mr. Preble (*showing her*)—I was going to hit you over the head with this shovel.

Mrs. Preble—You were, huh? Well, get that out of your mind. Do you want to leave a great big clue right here in the middle of everything where the first detective that comes snooping around will find it? Go out in the street and find some piece of iron or something.

Mr. Preble—Like what, for instance? It's just like you to think there's always a piece of iron lying around in the streets.

Mrs. Preble (*looking around and spotting the wrench*)—Well, let me see now. (*Picks up the wrench, hefts it.*) Oh, here's the perfect thing. It's what they call a heavy blunt instrument.

Mr. Preble—That isn't ours. We don't have a monkey wrench like that in this house.

Mrs. Preble—No. That's what I'm trying to tell you. The plumber left this last week after he fixed the sink in the kitchen. And it doesn't belong to either one of us.

Mr. Preble—What's it doing down here? Why didn't you give it back to him? Didn't he find out he had left it here?

Mrs. Preble—Well, you see it was this way. He *did* call up about it, but I told him he hadn't left it here. So then I brought it down to the cellar. (*She reaches into her bodice and pulls out a long white glove which she pulls onto her right hand.*)

Mr. Preble—Where did you get that glove?

Mrs. Preble—Oh, I had stuck it in my bodice, absentmindedly. I guess I was thinking about something else. (*With her gloved hand she polishes the tip of the wrench, presumably removing fingerprints.*)

Mr. Preble—Are you going to give it to me? (*She smiles.*) That's why you were so willing to come down here. (*He is backing away from her toward the steps; glancing back of him he sees a hole in the corner.*) Hey! Who's been digging here in this corner?

Mrs. Preble—Well, if I were a cop, I'd want to know whose fingerprints were on that shovel. (Preble *looks at her, then at the shovel. He casts it from him, then runs up onto the steps.*)

Mr. Preble—Don't you come near me! (*She takes a quick step toward him.*)

Mrs. Preble—Where are you going, dear?

Mr. Preble—First I'm going up and call the plumber and tell him you've got his wrench. And then—let's go to bed.

Mrs. Preble (*starts removing her glove; smiles*)—All righty!

FILE AND FORGET

(*As the lights come up,* Mr. Thurber *enters followed by* Miss Bagley. *He sits in the armchair and he carries a sheaf of papers.*)

Thurber (*crisply*)—Take a letter, Miss Bagley.

Bagley—Are you all right, Mr. Thurber?

THURBER—No. (BAGLEY *sits in chair, and gets out her book and pencil*.) To Miss Alma Winege, The Charters Publishing Company, New York.

Dear Miss Winege:

Your letter of October 25th, which you sent me in care of The Homestead, Hot Springs, Arkansas, has been forwarded to my home in West Cornwall, Connecticut, by the Homestead, Hot Springs, Virginia. As you know, Mrs. Thurber and I sometimes visit this Virginia resort, but we haven't been there for more than a year. Your company, in the great tradition of publishers, has sent so many letters to me at Hot Springs, Arkansas, that the postmaster there has simply taken to sending them on to the right address, or what would be the right address, if I were there. I explained to your Mr. Cluffman, and also to your Miss Lexy, that all mail was to be sent to me at West Cornwall. I suggest that you remove from your files all addresses of mine except the West Cornwall one. Another publishing firm recently sent a letter to me at 65 West 11th Street, an address I vacated in the summer of 1930. I was thirteen years old when we lived there, back in 1908.

As for the contents of your letter of the 25th, I did not order thirty-six copies of Peggy Peckham's book, "Grandma Was a Nudist." I trust that you have not shipped these books to me in care of The Homestead, Hot Springs, Arkansas, or anywhere else.

Sincerely yours,
J. Thurber

(MISS WINEGE *enters and sits in the chair back of the desk. She is followed by her secretary*, MISS WYNNE, *who sits on the sidechair left of desk. A follow spot lights the area; otherwise the stage is in darkness*.)

WINEGE—Take a letter, Miss Wynne, to Mr. James Thurber, West Cornwall, Connecticut.

WYNNE—All right, Miss Winege.

WINEGE—

Dear Mr. Thurber:

I am dreadfully sorry about the mixup over Miss Peckham's book. We have been pretty much upset around here since the advent of Mr. Clint Jordan and his installation of a new system. I still cannot understand from what file our shipping department got your address as 165 West 11th Street. I have removed the Hot Springs, Arkansas address from the files, and have so notified our Mr. Cluffman, who has charge of such matters, I believe. I trust that we will not disturb your tranquility further up there in Cornwall.

Sincerely yours,
Alma Winege

P.S. It must be lovely this time of year in Virginia, and I envy you and Mrs. Thurber. Have a lovely time at The Homestead.

(*Lights go down left, and* WINEGE *and* WYNNE *exit. Lights come up on* MR. THURBER, *who is momentarily fairly pleasant.* BAGLEY *enters right.*)

BAGLEY—Good morning, Mr. Thurber.

THURBER—Good morning. The mail is late this morning.

BAGLEY—It just came. There's a letter from Mrs. J. C. Edwards, of 568 Oak Street, Columbus, Ohio.

THURBER—Read it. I haven't got the strength.

BAGLEY (*sits, takes out letter, and reads*)—

Dear Mr. Thurber:

I have decided to come right out with the little problem that was accidentally dumped in my lap yesterday. I hope you will forgive me for what happened, and perhaps you can suggest what I should do with the books. There are three dozen of them and, unfortunately, they arrived when my little son Donald was alone downstairs. By the time I found out about the books, he had torn off the wrappings and built a cute little house out of them. I have placed them all on a shelf out of his reach while awaiting word as to where to send them. As soon as that word comes, I will ship them to you C.O.D. I heard from old Mrs. Winston next door that you and your family once lived here at 568 Oak Street. She thinks it was also the year of Halley's Comet.

Sincerely yours,
Mrs. J. C. Edwards

THURBER (*rises and crosses behind the big chair*)—Take a letter, Miss Bagley. To Leon Charters, The Charters Publishing Company, New York City.

Dear Mr. Charters:

BAGLEY—But you always call him Leon.

THURBER (*firmly*)—

Dear Mr. Charters:

I am enclosing a letter from a Mrs. J. C. Edwards of Columbus, Ohio, in the fervent hope that you will do something to stop this insane flux of books. I never ordered these books. I have not read "Grandma Was a Nudist." I do not intend to read "Grandma Was a Nudist." I want something done to get these volumes off my trail and out of my consciousness. I have written Miss Winege about the situation, but I'm afraid to take it up with her again, because she might send them to me in care of the Department of Journalism at Ohio State University, where I was a student nearly forty years ago.

Sincerely yours,
J. Thurber

P.S. Maybe Miss Jeanette Gaines in your Stock Order Department could straighten out this mess. Once, when I met her, she came very close to making sense.

(*Spot light travels left and settles on the chair behind the desk.* MISS GAINES *and* MISS WYNNE *enter and* WYNNE *sits on the sidechair.* GAINES *crosses around the table and leans against its right side. She smokes a cigarette. She is ultra and wears her smart jacket reversed.*)

WYNNE—Good morning, Miss Gaines.

GAINES—I'm sorry my own secretary is sick, Miss Wynne, and I hate to burden you, but will you take a letter to Mr. James Thurber?

WYNNE—West Cornwall, Connecticut, Miss Gaines?

GAINES—Yes.

Dear Mr. Thurber:

Mr. Charters has turned your letter of the 19th over to me. I have asked Mr. Cluffman to write to Mrs. J. C. Edwards in Columbus and arrange for the reshipment of the thirty-six copies of "Grandma Was a Nudist."

I find that you have, in the past, three times ordered copies of your own book, "Thurber's Ark," to be shipped to you at West Cornwall. I take it that what you really want is thirty-six copies of your own book, and they are being sent out to you today with our regrets for the discomfort we have caused you.

(*Exiting left.*)

Cordially yours,
Jeanette Gaines
Stock Order Dept.

(*Spot light travels right and settles on* MR. THURBER. *He is grim.* GAINES *and* WYNNE *exit left.*)

THURBER—Take another letter, Miss Bagley. To Henry Johnson, The Charters Publishing Company?

BAGLEY—Dear Harry?

THURBER—Yes.

I have the forlorn and depressing feeling that I no longer know anybody down there who understands English except you. I turn to you as a last resort. What I want, or rather, what I don't want, is simple enough, Harry. God knows it's simple.

I don't want any more copies of my book. I don't want any more copies of my book. I don't want any more copies of my book.

As ever,
Jim

(*The lights go down, and spot light travels left again settling on chair. As the lights go up,* WYNNE *enters and sits behind table.* JORDAN *enters after her and stands at the sidechair.*)

WYNNE—Good morning, Mr. Jordan.

JORDAN—Good morning. What's happened to all the other secretaries, Miss Wynne?

WYNNE—I guess they're sick, or getting married, Mr. Jordan. Things like that.

JORDAN (*sits*)—Take a letter—keep your seat—to Mr. James Thurber, The Homestead, Hot Springs, Virginia.

WYNNE—He's in West Cornwall, Mr. Jordan.

JORDAN—Okay. Okay. Don't expect me to keep minor details in mind.

Dear Jim Thurber:

Your letter to Harry Johnson has just come to my attention and I regret to say that Harry is no longer with us. He went to Simon and Schuster last summer. All of us feel very deeply about your having turned against your book, "Thurber's Ark." I note that in your present mood you have the feeling that you never want to see it again. Well, Jim, let me assure you that this is just a passing fancy, derived from a moment of depression. When you put in your last order for thirty-six copies, you must surely have had some definite use in mind for them, and I am banking on tweny years' experience in the book-publishing game when I take the liberty of sending these thirty-six books off to you today.

Cordially,
Clint Jordan

(*As the lights go down left,* JORDAN *exits.* *When the lights come back up,* WYNNE *moves to the sidechair and* CLUFFMAN *enters.*)

CLUFFMAN (*moves behind table and pushes chair under*)—My secretary has left us to work for Chock Full O' Nuts. Will you take a letter, Miss Wynne?

WYNNE—Yes, Mr. Cluffman.

CLUFFMAN—

Dear Mr. Thurber:

I hope you will forgive me for having inexcusably mislaid the address of the lady to whom the thirty-six copies of "Grandma Was a Nudist" were sent by mistake. I understand that we have already dispatched to you at your home another thirty-six copies of that book to replace those that have gone astray. My apologies again.

Sincerely yours,

H. F. Cluffman

(*The lights go down left, and* CLUFFMAN *and* WYNNE *exit.* *Spot light travels right and settles on* MR. THURBER, *who is grimly dictating to* MISS BAGLEY.)

THURBER—

Dear Mr. Cluffman:

The lady's name is Mrs. J. C. Edwards, and she lives at 568 Oak Street, Columbus, Ohio.

I have explained as clearly as I could in previous letters that I did not order thirty-six copies of "Grandma Was a Nudist." If you have actually shipped to me another thirty-six copies of this book, it will make a total of seventy-two copies, none of which I will pay for. The thirty-six copies of "Thurber's Ark" that Mr. Jordan has written me he intends to send to West Cornwall would bring up to one hundred and eight the total number of books that your firm, by a conspiracy of confusion unique even in the case of publishers, has mistakenly charged to my account. If your entire staff of employees went back to "Leslie's Weekly," where they belong, it would set my mind at rest.

Sincerely yours,

J. Thurber

Now read me that letter to Clint Jordan that I want you to sign.

BAGLEY (*takes out letter and reads*)—

Dear Mr. Jordan:

I am sure that you will be sorry to learn that Mr. Thurber has had one of his mild spells as a result of the multiplication of books and misunderstanding that began with Miss Alma Winege's letter of October 25th. Those of us around Mr. Thurber are greatly disturbed by the unfortunate circumstances that have caused him to give up writing, at least temporarily, after a long, fallow period. Thirty-six copies of Mr. Thurber's book and thirty-six copies of "Grandma Was a Nudist" have arrived at his home here, and he has asked me to advise you that he intends to burn all seventy-two. West Cornwall is scarcely the community for such a demonstration . . . he proposes to burn them in the middle of U. S. Highway Number 7.

Mr. Thurber wishes me to tell you that he does not want to hear from any of you again.

Sincerely yours,
Ellen Bagley
Secretary to Mr. Thurber

(*The lights go down right and* BAGLEY *exits. As the lights come up right,* CLUFFMAN *and* WYNNE *enter,* WYNNE *sitting in the side-chair and* CLUFFMAN *going around to the right of the table.*)

CLUFFMAN—

Dear Mr. Thurber:

In reference to your letter of recent date, "Leslie's Weekly" ceased publication many years ago. I could obtain the exact date if you so desire.

Sincerely yours,
H. F. Cluffman

(*The lights go down left, and* CLUFFMAN *and* WYNNE *exit. As the lights come up right,* MISS BAGLEY *enters.* MR. THURBER *seems weary.*)

BAGLEY—Captain Kelly just phoned, Mr. Thurber.

THURBER—Who is *he?*

BAGLEY—You know. The State Police barracks about the bonfire.

THURBER—Oh, yes. I've told them everything I'm going to tell them. Just say that I have lapsed into a coma.

BAGLEY—I've told them that you weren't here. Here's a letter from your mother, Mr. Thurber. (*She hands him a letter and sits.*)

THURBER—I've just about enough strength for that. (*Reads.*)

Dear Jamie:

I don't understand the clipping from the Cornwall Journal Helen's mother sent me, about someone burning all those books of yours in the street. I never heard of such a thing in all my born days, and don't understand how they could have taken the books without your knowing it, or what you were doing with so many copies of the novel about the naked grandmother. The very idea, at her age! She couldn't carry on like that in Columbus, let me tell you. Why, when I was a girl, you didn't dare walk with a man after sunset, unless he was your husband, and even then there was talk. It's a good thing that state policeman came along in time to save most of the books from being completely ruined, and you must be thankful for the note Mr. Jordan put in one of the books, for the policeman would never have known who they belonged to if he hadn't found it.

A woman here in Columbus, Mrs. J. C. Edwards, phoned this morning and said that her son Donald collects your books and wants to send them to you—to be autographed, I suppose. I told her you simply wouldn't have time to sign all of them, and she said she didn't care what you did with them. And then she said they weren't your books at all, and so I just hung up on her.

With love,
Mother

P.S. This Mrs. Edwards just called again and said she lives at 568 Oak Street. I told her we used to live there and she said God knows she was aware of that. I don't know what she meant. I was afraid this little boy would send you all those books to sign at West Cornwall and I know you hate to autograph books when you're working. So I told her to send them to you at The Homestead in Hot Springs.

Be sure to bundle up when you go out.

The Secret Life of Walter Mitty

(*The music begins the Mitty Theme, which sends* WALTER MITTY *off into dreams of perilous adventure, noble sacrifice or great drama. We hear the* NARRATOR *over the loud speakers, and, during his speech, the traveller opens revealing the Thurber interpretation of Main Street, Waterbury, Connecticut. It is busy and cluttered. None of the buildings seem to belong together, but are huddled there as if for protection. On the center stage, seated behind a cutout of a well-worn but trusty-looking automobile, are* WALTER MITTY *and* MRS. MITTY. WALTER MITTY *wears a brown sack suit and brown felt hat. He is a timid man except during his daydreams. As the characters in his dreams are very real to him, they always appear in the proper setting and wearing the proper clothes. Since we enter the dreams through* MITTY's *mind, we see the various characters as he sees them, but we see him as he is, in his brown sack suit and felt hat. However, a tilt of his hat brim, or the turning up of his coat collar illustrate more clearly than a change of costume, the transformation taking place in his mind.*

MRS. MITTY *sits beside him. She is a practical earth-bound woman, who complains bitterly about her impractical husband, but would resent him if he weren't. She wears a well-cut tweed coat and velvet beret. She carries a large bag.* MR. MITTY *is driving the car, and she is watching him, about ready to explode.*)

NARRATOR—Walter Mitty lives in every town and city in our land. You have met him many times. Middle-aged, married, in love with long ago and far away, he is the lonely wanderer in the crowd, the silent daydreamer, the fellow that stares out at sea long after the ship has sailed. Right now he is driving his wife to the hairdresser's in Waterbury, Connecticut—or part of him is, anyway. (*The sound of an airplane is heard.*)

MRS. MITTY—That plane is flying too low. They always fly too low. Why do they have to fly so low?

MITTY (*glancing up*)—Navy plane. (*He stares steadily ahead, slowly becoming invincible. The lights of reality start to fade down, and the panels behind them suddenly take on a purple, dreamlike quality.*) Eight engine bomber. (MITTY *rises slowly, leaves the car, and steps down center. He stands there, full of purpose and strength. He pulls his hat brim down over one eye.* YOUNG MAN *and* LIEUT. BERG *appear wearing Naval Officer's caps. The panels behind them show formless dream shapes.*)

YOUNG MAN—We'll never make it.

BERG—This is the worst storm in twenty years of Navy flying. (*They sway back and forth with the storm.* MITTY *stands almost rock steady.*)

YOUNG MAN—We'll never reach our target in this weather.

MITTY—We're going through. Our mission is to obliterate the enemy's North Atlantic fleet. We will not turn back.

NARRATOR—Commander Mitty's voice was like thin ice breaking. He wore his full dress uniform with the heavily braided white cap pulled down rakishly over one cold gray eye.

BERG—We can't make it, sir. It's spoiling for a hurricane, if you ask me.

MITTY—I'm not asking you, Lieutenant Berg. Throw on the

power lights! Rev her up to eighty-five hundred! We're going through!

NARRATOR—The Commander stared at the ice forming on the pilot window. He walked over and twisted a row of complicated dials. (MITTY *crosses to behind the car cutout and spins the steering wheel.*)

MITTY—Switch on number eight auxiliary!

BERG—Switch on number eight auxiliary!

YOUNG MAN (*almost with* BERG)—Switch on number eight auxiliary!

MITTY (*pantomiming microphone*)—Naval operations. Clear all signals. Priority A one. Navy bomber SN 202, Mitty commanding. Ceiling thirty point two below, glass falling, winds one hundred and thirty-five m.p.h. Approaching target. (*To his men.*) Full strength in number three turret!

BERG—Full strength in number three turret.

YOUNG MAN (*echoing* BERG)—Full strength in number three turret.

BERG—The emergency wind barriers are crevulating, sir.

MITTY—Let them crevulate!

YOUNG MAN—The Old Man will get us through!

BERG—The Old Man ain't afraid of hell!

YOUNG MAN—The Old Man could straight-arm the Death Angel!

BERG—Target sighted!

MITTY—Douse all lights. (*A blackout, except for the follow spot on* MITTY *and the turning colored lights.*) Count down!

YOUNG MAN—. . . four . . . three . . . two . . . one!

MITTY—Bombs away! (*The sound of an enormous bomb exploding.*) Mission accomplished. (*The two officers exit echoing "Mission accomplished, mission accomplished, mission accomplished . . ."* MITTY *sits in the car seat again, and resumes driving but in his mind he is still in the plane and in command.*) Now rev her up to ninety-five hundred! (*Lights come up on the city again.*)

MRS. MITTY—Not so fast! You're driving too fast! What are you driving so fast for?

MITTY (*vaguely—jolted a bit*)—Hmm? What did you say?

MRS. MITTY—You were up to fifty-five. You know I don't like to go more than forty. You were up to fifty-five. (*MITTY turns front and seems to shrink.*)

NARRATOR—Ex-Commander Walter Mitty drove on toward Waterbury in silence, the roaring of the SN 202 through the worst storm in twenty years of Navy flying fading in the remote, intimate airways of his mind. (*MITTY continues to drive tensely.*)

MRS. MITTY—You're tensed up again. (*MITTY mutters some-*

thing.) You're talking to yourself again. It's one of your days. I wish you'd let Dr. Renshaw look at you. Stop! Stop here! This is the hairdresser's. You *know* I'm going to the hairdresser's. And put on your gloves. It's cold. (MITTY *puts on his gloves.*) And don't you dare forget to buy those overshoes. Do you want to catch your death? And, oh yes. Remember to get a box of puppy biscuit. And here's the shopping list with the rest of the things I want you to buy. Don't lose it. I *do* wish you'd let Dr. Renshaw look at you. (*Rises and crosses off down left.*) Maybe Dr. Renshaw is in his office now. (*She exits.* MITTY *rises and we see him leaving reality, as the reality lights dim to out. The dream panels appear, and at* MITTY's *wave, a nurse wheels on an operating table with a patient on it.*)

NURSE—Oh, we're all so glad you got here in time, Dr. Mitty. (*The lights of the operating room come up. The* NURSE *has placed the operating table directly in front of the car.*) It's the millionaire banker, Wellington McMillan.

MITTY (*supremely polished and confident—the perfect surgeon—crosses to the* NURSE)—The great friend of the President's? That explains why I was reached through the White House and flown here in the President's private plane. (*The* NURSE *helps* MITTY *into an imaginary doctor's gown.*)

NURSE—You were performing a post-partem on Admiral Kerrington, weren't you?

MITTY—Yes. Pre-frontal. Took a bit of doing.

NURSE—Here is Dr. Renshaw.

RENSHAW (*shaking* MITTY's *hand*)—Hello, Dr. Mitty. Thank God you could get here! We're having the devil's own time. Complications.

MITTY—Fractional deviation?

RENSHAW—Yes, but how in the world could you know that? (MITTY *shrugs it off as three more doctors enter and move up left to form a line.*) Dr. Benbow is assisting me, but we also have Dr. Remington here from New York and Mr. Pritchard-Mitford from London. We would all appreciate your counsel, Dr. Mitty.

MITTY—Glad to be of service. Shall we proceed? (*They all move around the table to form a line behind it.*)

PRITCHARD-MITFORD—I've read your paper on streptothricosis. A brilliant performance, sir.

MITTY—Thank you.

REMINGTON—Didn't know you were in the States, Mitty. Coals to Newcastle, bringing Mitford and me up here for a tertiary.

MITTY—You are very kind. (*Turns to the* NURSE, *at the right end of the group.*) The anesthetic is cyclopropane 202, I presume.

(*The* NURSE *swings out a complicated cutout of an anesthetizing machine, which is hinged to the right end of the operating table.* RENSHAW *assists by locking it in place.*)

REMINGTON—Precisely. But I'm afraid of that new and complicated anesthetizing machine. (*They all turn upstage and begin to* "*scrub up.*" *A light begins to flash on the machine, and a sound not unlike plucked guitar strings issues forth. A puff of smoke emerges from the machine.* RENSHAW *turns just in time to see the smoke waft away.*)

RENSHAW—Good God, the machine is crevulating! (*They all turn to look at it.*)

NURSE—There is no one this side of San Francisco who can fix it!

BENBOW—We're lost.

MITTY—Steady, men. (*He reaches his hand into the back of the machine and there is a loud squeak.*) Give me a fountain pen, somebody. (*They all fumble but come up with nothing.*) Never mind, I'll use my own. (*He reaches into his pocket and takes out a pen which he places between his teeth. Then he reaches into the back of the machine and pulls out a piece of pipe—presumably the defective part—which he hands to* RENSHAW. *Then* MITTY *inserts the pen in its place. He steps back, brushing off his gloves.*) That will hold for ten minutes.

RENSHAW—This man's not only a distinguished surgeon, he's a mechanical genius as well.

PRITCHARD-MITFORD—We shall have to work fast. (*As the others turn to finish their scrub-up, he unzips a zipper in the sheet covering the body and looks in.*) Good Lord! Will you come here a moment, Dr. Remington? (REMINGTON *looks.*)

REMINGTON—Heaven help us. Coreopsis has set in.

MITTY (*to* NURSE)—What did Dr. Remington say, Nurse?

NURSE—Coreopsis has set in.

RENSHAW—Will you take over, Mitty?

BENBOW—It's our only hope.

PRITCHARD-MITFORD—The patient's life is in your hands, Dr. Mitty.

REMINGTON—You must take over, Doctor.

MITTY (*modestly*)—If you wish. (*He stands behind the body, and the* NURSE *hands him surgical instruments as he calls for them. These are all real except as noted.*) Scalpel! (*He takes each instrument as he gets it, works within the opening of the sheet, then drops the instrument inside.*) Forceps! Hemostat! Suture! (*This one looks a lot like a steel knitting needle with a piece of white yarn attached.*) Bifurcated invertebrator! (RENSHAW *and the* NURSE *lean over and reach under the table for it.*)

PRITCHARD-MITFORD—Good God, that complicated instrument hasn't been used since the Duke of Warrington was operated on for obstreosis of the ducal track. (NURSE *hands* MITTY *the bifurcated invertebrator which resembles a meat grinder with a gas-mask hose attached to its snout.* MITTY *raises it into position and grinds away.*)

MITTY—We're going through. (*Lights dim.*)

NURSE (*looking up, as do the others*)—The lights are going out.

RENSHAW—It's a short circuit in the power transformer.

MITTY—Steady, gentlemen. I shall operate in the dark. (*The lights are out except for the spot on* MITTY.) By the sense of touch.

REMINGTON—Magnificent!

BENBOW—Wonderful!

PRITCHARD-MITFORD—A smashing performance, sir.

MITTY—Thank you. He will sail his yacht again. (*As the others begin a slow exit,* MITTY *starts taking off his gloves.*) If you will take my gloves, nurse. (*The follow spot goes out on* MITTY. *A loud truck horn is heard. As the city street appears once again, the lights come up and the follow spot hits* MITTY. *The horn has jolted him back to reality, and he throws his gloves on the car seat, regretfully. He steps away from his car, and then remembers his shopping list and begins feeling through his pockets for it. Instead he pulls out his fountain pen, which he looks at, and returns to his pocket. He tries to remember the list.*) Kleenex? Toothpaste? Razor blades? No. Toothbrush, bicarbonate, carborundum, initiative and referendum? No.

MRS. MITTY (*rushes on and meets him*)—I have been looking all over for you. Dolores wasn't there. Dolores is the only hairdresser in the world who understands my hair. I just *knew* you wouldn't get a thing done. Haven't you bought the puppy biscuit yet?

MITTY—Things close in.

MRS. MITTY—What? Did you get the overshoes?

MITTY (*with a slight show of spirit*)—I've been thinking. Does it ever occur to you that I am sometimes thinking?

MRS. MITTY (*alarmed*)—I'm going to take your temperature when I get you home. (*Kindly.*) I'll get the puppy biscuit. You'd be sure to get the wrong kind. You just wait for me here. I *wish* you'd get your overshoes. I think it's going to rain. If you don't take care of yourself, you're sure to catch your death. (MITTY *raises the collar of his jacket and tilts his hat brim.*) And for heaven's sake, relax. You look as if you were going to be shot, standing there like that. (*She exits. He's off again, and a panel suggesting a war scene appears at center. The* LEADER, *wearing a military cap with a German insignia, comes on.*)

LEADER (*with a distinct German accent*)—Walter Mitty, do you wish to be blindfolded?

MITTY—To hell with the blindfold. (*He takes out a cigarette.*)

LEADER—May I have the honor?

MITTY—Honor?

LEADER (*taking out lighter*)—It is an honor to light the last cigarette of the bravest and cleverest spy of them all. (*There is the sound of approaching marching men, and he turns toward the sound.*) Squad halt!

MITTY—Captain, will you extend me the traditional courtesy of giving the last commands to the firing squad?

LEADER—Jawohl! (*He calls to the men.*) You will take your orders from Lieutenant Commander Mitty. (*He crosses to MITTY, embraces him, and crosses down to the right portal, facing off and hiding his eyes. MITTY stiffens.*)

MITTY—Present arms! Port arms! Right shoulder arms! About face! (*He looks at the LEADER, and then front.*) Forward march! (*The footsteps off left start up and fade away.*)

LEADER (*turning, and running off after the fading sound*)—Halt, Idioten! Come backen Sie here! (*MITTY smiles and jauntily walks down center, puffing his cigarette.*)

Concluding the Carnival, the horn player plays on stage and a "Word Dance" concludes, as it opened, the evening. "So I said to the bank teller," says the second woman, "how could I be overdrawn when I have all those checks left?" The music continues between each speech: "He's having all his books translated into French. They lose something in the original," remarks the third man. Actors and musicians, coming on singly and in pairs, are now performing in unison on stage. "How could I tell him what happened when I didn't know the French for 'I have flushed my passport'?" The Drummer beats time with his foot—the actors move to the center of the stage and stop. The second woman crossing downstage allows: "I never *dreamed* their union had been blessed with issue till their little daughter stabbed the Superintendent of Schools . . ."

The first man has the final word. He asks the audience: "Let us ponder this fact about the human—ahead of every man, not behind him, is a woman." And walking to the edge of the stage, he says confidentially: "The women will now please keep their seats while the men leave the auditorium. They need, God knows, a head start." He steps back, the music swells and the curtain—with its Thurber dogs—falls.

FIORELLO!

A Musical in Two Acts

BOOK BY JEROME WEIDMAN AND GEORGE ABBOTT

MUSIC BY JERRY BOCK

LYRICS BY SHELDON HARNICK

[JEROME WEIDMAN *was born in New York City in 1913, and attended the College of the City of New York, Washington Square College, and New York University Law School. His successful first novel, "I Can Get It for You Wholesale," was followed by a number of other books of fiction and travel, among them "The Horse That Could Whistle Dixie," "Letter of Credit," "The Lights Around the Shore," "Traveler's Cheque" and the recent bestseller, "The Enemy Camp." An established writer, Mr. Weidman also has had publishing experience and worked during World War II for the O.W.I. "Fiorello!" is his first Broadway production.*]

[GEORGE ABBOTT *was born in Forestville, N. Y., in 1889, and, after attending the University of Rochester and Harvard, turned actor. It was, however, as co-author and as director that he was to establish himself, in a long series of comedies, farces and musicals characterized by his sense of pace and vitality. Among the hits he directed are "Three Men on a Horse," "Room Service," "On Your Toes," "Boy Meets Girl," "Pal Joey," "On the Town," "Call Me Madam," "The Pajama Game" and "Damn Yankees."*]

[JERRY BOCK *was born in New Haven, majored in music at the University of Wisconsin, and gained great practical experience writing, for three years, as many as ten revue scores a season at Camp*

*Tamiment in the Poconos. He began his Broadway career compos-
ing some of the songs for "Catch a Star," which led to his writing
the full score for "Mr. Wonderful," starring Sammy Davis, Jr.*]

[SHELDON HARNICK *was born in Chicago in 1924 and was a student and a soldier before coming to Broadway. His first Broadway
song, "The Boston Beguine," was a high point of "New Faces of
1952," and since then he has written songs for such shows as "John
Murray Anderson's Almanac," the first and second "Shoestring Re-
vues," and "The Body Beautiful," in which he and Jerry Bock first
joined forces.*]

ACT I

Prologue: After a few bars of "The Marine Hymn," a radio announcer introduces His Honor Fiorello H. LaGuardia, Mayor of New
York. At first we only hear the voice—that memorable mélange of
notes from a soprano saxe, of sounds that only a bird dog could hear,
and the occasional bleat of a sheep. Then we see His Honor in front
of the WNYC mike, reading the comics section of the papers to New
York's children. Releasing box by box the trials and tribulations of
one little Shirley in the corrupt world, Fiorello suddenly recalls that
there were a lot of corrupt men running the city way back before
the First World War—when he had his office in Greenwich Village.

SCENE I

In 1914, LaGuardia's law office is doing a land-office business with
insolvent Greenwich Villagers. Crowding into his waiting room, they
voice their appeals in accents that originated on Mediterranean
shores all the way from Spain to Palestine. LaGuardia's hard-
pressed assistants, Neil and Morris, try to quiet the polyglot clamor.
Promising LaGuardia's help, Neil sings of his trust in his boss:

> "My life will be selfless and pure
> Like Upton Sinclair,
> Working with this man
> On the side of the Angels.

(Concluding.)

> So give me your tired, your poor,
> And scoundrels beware:
> Here we stand in chorus,
> He and I and Morris—

> Standing firm, side by side
> On the side of the Angels!"

At the phone, Morris tries to quiet his own domestic confusion: "Shirley, how can I tell you when to put the roast in? . . . No, Shirley, only God and Mr. LaGuardia know when I'll be there, and neither one tells me till the last minute. . . . I would ask him, but he hasn't come in yet. . . . What a man is right." Turning from the phone, Morris sings his version of "On the Side of the Angels":

> "What a job—
> What a man—
> What an office—
> That line of poor and friendless . . .
> Endless!

(He concludes.)

> That bench stays crowded,
> It's a regular wailing wall.
> Penniless and helpless,
> Ignorant and scared—
> He collects 'em all!
>
> There's never a moment's relief;
> But this much I know—
> Each poor soul I see there
> Could be me there . . .
> So I stay with this man
> On the side of the Angels!"

A cute little thing named Dora comes in to find her friend Marie Fischer, LaGuardia's secretary. She, too, is looking for help. Dora explains that the leader of their shirtwaist-company strike has been arrested. "For picketing? They can't do that," says Marie. "Marie, . . . not for picketing," answers Dora, "for soliciting. That crooked cop—he claims she was trying to pick up somebody." Actually their leader, Thea, had merely been carrying a banner. "She wasn't—oh—flirting with anybody—or wiggling or anything?" asks Marie. Stoutly maintaining that their leader isn't that kind of girl at all, Dora insists that LaGuardia must get her out of jail. Marie promises her boss's help and tells Dora to wait outside—with the other petitioners—just as LaGuardia strides in.

Marching through the waiting room to his office, an enormous outsize sombrero on his head, Fiorello abruptly sits down at his desk, then just as quickly jumps up, goes to the office door and points a commanding finger at Marie to summon her to his presence.

As Marie tries to tell him about Dora's friend who was arrested in the strike, Fiorello interrupts. He wants Marie to introduce him to Ben Marino, the Republican leader of the Fourteenth District who is having trouble finding a Congressional candidate. What's more, Fiorello himself wants the nomination. Marie is incredulous: "In the Fourteenth? Mr. LaGuardia, Tammany has that district sewed up. No Republican has ever gone to Congress from the Fourteenth. I can't believe you're serious." Not only is he serious, but he thinks he has found the right opening to win.

When Dora is ushered in, Fiorello knows all about the shirtwaist strike, and the first women ever to be on a picket line, and the terrible treatment they have endured.

FIORELLO—My dear girl, I understand Mr. Schimer and people like him. They'll stop at nothing. They murdered my father. (*He turns to* MARIE.) Marie! Telephone Ben Marino and tell him we're on the way over.

DORA—They murdered your father?

FIORELLO—They did. (*Turns to* MARIE.) Marie! Never mind. It's better just to walk in and surprise him. (*To* DORA.) They poisoned him.

DORA (*aghast*)—The Nifty Shirtwaist Corporation?

FIORELLO—No, the exploiters. That's the trouble with this younger generation. You don't grasp issues. You see the little things —and miss the big ones. They sold rotten food to the Army in the Spanish-American war—and my father died.

Then, ordering Marie to get Morris, Morris to get a bail bond for Dora's friend, and Dora to get back to strike headquarters where he promises to meet her, Fiorello opens the door to the waiting room and calls out to the crowd: "All right, my friends. Who's first?" The petitioners, along with Marie, Morris, and Neil sing in counterpoint "On the Side of the Angels."

Scene II

In the main room of the Ben Marino Association, Marino's cronies are sitting around a green baize-covered table at a game of five-card stud, while Ben, with too much on his mind to take a hand, tries to dream up that "damn candidate."

When a seedy-looking character shambles in for a hand-out, one of the players cracks: "That's your man, Ben, run him." "May come to that yet," says Ben. Having half-heartedly tried to rope in one of the players and been rebuffed and told to get a brand-new sucker, Ben and cronies sing "Politics and Poker":

BEN—
    Gentlemen, here we are, and one thing is clear:
    We gotta pick a candidate for Congress this year.
DEALER—
    Big Ace.
SECOND PLAYER—
    Ace bets.
THIRD PLAYER—
    You'll pay—through the nose.
FOURTH PLAYER—
    I'm in.
FIFTH PLAYER—
    So am I.
DEALER—
    Likewise.
SECOND PLAYER—
    Here goes.
DEALER (*examining the hands*)—
    Possible straight,
    Possible flush,
    Nothing.
BEN—
    Gentlemen, how about some names we can use?
    Some qualified Republican who's willing to lose?
SECOND PLAYER—
    How's about we should make Jack Riley the guy?
THIRD PLAYER—
    Which Riley are you thinking of?   Jack B. or Jack Y.?
BEN—
    I say neither one,
    I never even met 'em.
FOURTH PLAYER—
    I say:
    When you got a pair of Jacks,
    Bet 'em!
ALL—
    Politics and poker,
    Politics and poker—
    Shuffle up the cards
    And find the joker.

Neither game's for children,
Either game is rough.
Decisions, decisions, like:
Who to pick,
How to play,
What to bet,
When to call a bluff.

BEN (*spoken*)—All right, now, Fellas, politics or poker? Which
is more important? (*They sing.*)

DEALER—
Pair of treys. . . .

Over the plays of the players, Ben sings in counterpoint of the
political possibles; but for a variety of reasons, such as they've just
died or they're in jail, they're no good. At this point Marie arrives
to break the ice for her boss, Mr. LaGuardia. "Who?" asks Ben.
"That little wop with the big hat," says one of the players. "There
are no little wops, just big ones," announces Fiorello as he strides
into the room. "As I'm ready and willing to demonstrate." "A modest guy, huh?" says a player. "No," answers Fiorello, "just a guy
who happens to believe the way to beat Tammany is not"—he
reaches over, takes a player's cards and tosses them to the center
of the table—"by throwing in your cards. I came over to get the
nomination."

Presently, having got the nomination, Fiorello leaves. In his wake
his bored, unenthusiastic backers continue their poker and their song.
Joining the game, Ben sings:

". . . Some guys
Always gotta try to fill an inside straight. . . ."

SCENE III

In the street outside strike headquarters, a listless group of girl
pickets go parading around in a circle, ineffectually singing out:
"Unfair." From the sidelines, male hecklers badger them and an
unsympathetic cop keeps moving them along. When one girl stops
to adjust the cardboard in her shoe, Floyd, the cop, calls out: "Keep
moving. No loitering allowed." When he gets tough with Dora,
she gets tough right back and makes a fool of him. Flustered, he
threatens to haul them all to the station house on a charge of soliciting. "I saw you wigglin'," he says. "I saw you trying to get those
men over there. They'll testify." "All right, then, arrest me," snaps
Dora. "Look, I'm wigglin'." And she does, to the hecklers' cheers.
"Go ahead," she urges, "why don't you! And I'll get over there and

we'll have a doctor's examination, and I guess that'll prove who's a liar. That'll prove whether I'm one of those women or not." "Oh, you're a pure thing, eh?" says Floyd. "You're goddamn right, I am" answers Dora.

Arriving with Marie to take charge, Fiorello orders the girls back to headquarters and draws Floyd aside. "The name is Fiorello H. LaGuardia," he says, "and you better get it firmly in your mind because you're going to hear a good deal about me in the next few months."

FLOYD—I am, eh?

FIORELLO—If there is any further interference with these girls in the exercise of their constitutional rights, I'll slap a writ of inter-dictum on each and every perpetrator of such interference—beginning with you.

FLOYD (suddenly uneasy)—I'm just doing my duty, Counselor.

FIORELLO—I suggest you do it the way you promised under oath when you joined the force. I know what goes on behind the scenes, my friend. I know that this sweatshop and others like it have bought protection, and I intend to fight every one of them. I wouldn't like to see a nice, intelligent fellow like you get caught in the middle.

FIRST HECKLER—Listen to him—

THIRD HECKLER—You gonna stand for that—

FLOYD (blustering at them to save face)—Keep moving! Don't loiter! None of your lip! (HECKLERS having left, FLOYD turns to LaGuardia.) I'll go back to the station house and report what you —what you just said about—about—you know.

FIORELLO—And if the lieutenant has any difficulty understanding, I'll be glad to explain it to him, too. (Hands FLOYD a card.) That's my office number. I answer calls from anybody.

An admiring witness to this performance, Marie is about to return to the office to raise bail in case the girls are arrested, when Fiorello invites her to dinner. Saying he had always wanted to know her better, he arranges to pick her up at the office in an hour.

No sooner has Marie left than Thea, surrounded by her admiring strikers, presents herself to Fiorello: he promptly forgets Marie. "She's out on Ike Feeney's $500.00 and her own recognizance," explains Morris, "but I promised the judge that you'd be personally responsible. I'd have had her here sooner, but she insisted on washing her face." "I can see that," says Fiorello. And with so impressive an example before him, he has a suggestion for all the girls: "I don't want to see only one clean face. I want a lot of clean faces. In short, when you come back, I want you to look like girls again."

Alone with Thea, Fiorello says that not only has she a just cause
but it is *his* issue, for two reasons: he believes in it, and it will help
send him to Congress.   Thea offers her help and is immediately
enlisted in LaGuardia's campaign.   "Maybe you can help in more
ways than one.   You're an Italian girl; you're beautiful; you're
smart.   You can help me.   One of the things I'm going to do is organize the Italian-Americans into political clubs."   Fiorello wants
people, when they think of Italians, to think of artists and patriots,
not of crooks and the Mafia.   But when Thea thinks of her native
city, Trieste, she wonders if a just cause can win: "Trieste, ground
under the heel of the Imperialistic Austrian invader . . . didn't
win."   Asking her to be patient and believe in him, Fiorello assures
her they will win this strike.   "But do you know all about this situation?" asks Thea.   Knowing nothing about it, Fiorello counts on
her to explain it to him, and arranges to take her out to dinner so
they can go to work on it immediately.

As the strikers enter, singing "Management's unfair, Management's unfair . . . ," Fiorello advises putting more fight into their
strike technique.   Rehearsing a chorus of clean-faced pickets, he
soon has them hollering and howling "Unfair!" at the top of their
voices.

Scene IV

Back at the office, Marie has successfully raised bail for the girls,
but finds she is less successful with her own affairs.   When La-
Guardia calls to cancel their dinner date, she cries to Morris that
she's just a fool.   "There's no law against that," sympathizes Morris.
Not only should there be a law, Marie feels, but she's ready to make
it.   Dictating to Morris "Marie's Law," she sings:

MARIE—
  My law shall state,
  "To whom it may concern—"
MORRIS—
  Your law shall state
  "To whom it may concern—"
MARIE—
  "When a lady loves a gentleman,
  He must love her in return."
MORRIS—
  "Loves a gentleman he must love her in re . . ."
MARIE—
  In re, my law
  Ad hoc, to wit, to woo—

Morris—
> *In re,* your law
> *Ad hoc,* to wit, to woo—

Marie—
> When a lady feels affectionate
> Then the man must follow through. . . .

Scene V

With LaGuardia's campaign under way, Neil and Thea, Fiorello's vanguard, whip up the enthusiasm of street-corner crowds. At the ripe moment, Fiorello turns up and finishes the job.

Fiorello—Friends, I want each and every one of you to take a long deep breath! Like this! You know what that smell is? Tammany! They've been stinking up this district long enough. It's time to get the garbage off the doorsteps, and I've got the shovel to do it with—your vote! Put that pencil cross next to the name of Fiorello H. LaGuardia! L-A-G-U-A-R-D-I-A! (*He sings "The Name's LaGuardia."*)

> Now here's another name
> T-A-M-M-A-N-Y, what's that?

Voice (*spoken*)—Tammany?
Fiorello (*spoken*)—Wrong! (*Sings.*)

> The answer's Tyranny.
> Tammany spells Tyranny.
> Like R-A-T spells rat.
>
> Now there's a double "M" in Tammany
> And a double "L" in call—
> Just like the double-dealing,
> Double-crossing,
> Double-talking,
> Double-dyed duplicity,
> Of Tammany Hall!
>
> But you can change it all.
> Go use the ballot box—
> And cast your spell come next Election Day.
> The name's LaGuardia—
> L-A-G-U-A-R-D-I-A! . . .

At another corner, another crowd—this time an Italian audience—listens to Thea. "And who is against tyranny of every type," she asks, "and who believes that Trieste should go back to the Italian people—" cheers interrupt her—"and here he is, Fiorello LaGuardia!" Above the cheers, LaGuardia addresses the crowd and sings his Tammany tirade, "The Name's LaGuardia," in Italian. Retiring to a chorus of: "Bravo, LaGuardia, bravo!" he appears the next moment in front of a largely Jewish audience whom Morris has been warming up.

FIORELLO—Friends—I've just come from Mulberry Street.

HECKLER—Little Italy, huh? You're always talking about your Italian background. I hear you're half-Jewish. How come you never brag about your Jewish background?

FIORELLO—I figure if a man is only half-Jewish it isn't enough to brag about.

Fiorello sings the Yiddish version of the song, *"Ich bin LaGuardia,"* and the meeting ends in a stomping, dancing crowd.

SCENE VI

In contrast to the enthusiasm on the street after the election, Ben Marino's clubhouse is a morgue. Ben and his poker-playing cronies sing "The Bum Won":

> ". . . I'd like to know just how the hell it happened,
> What we did right.
> Fellas, the whole thing is cockeyed.
>
> We got a winner at last,
> We got a star which is in the ascendant.
>
> If he feels that we sloughed him off,
> He could become, God forbid, Independent. . . ."

SCENE VII

On the roof of a Greenwich Village tenement, life has changed a great deal since the shirtwaist-strike days. Floyd McDuff, the Tammany cop, has courted Dora so successfully that she not only likes his embraces, but listens to his opinions. At the moment he is explaining that her idol LaGuardia is up to his ears in trouble. Trying to get us into war, he has made his district hate him, and has lost all possibilities of re-election.

FLOYD—They was talkin' about it over to the Wigwam. How come they let that little squirt walk off with the Fourteenth District right from under their noses? And I give my opinion: overconfidence, I says. And one of the very important guys there—he says to me—Floyd McDuff—you're only walking a beat now, but mark my words, he says, one of these days I expect you to be a sergeant, he says. And maybe even higher, he says.

DORA—I bet you will, too. I believe in you, Floyd.

FLOYD—And you know what he says: he says—with a kind of a wink, you know—he says—you may not be the smartest guy on the force, but you're loyal.

DORA—And what did you say to him?

FLOYD—I says, Judge, thank you.

DORA—That was real smart.

When Floyd leaves to go on duty, Marie drops by to borrow a hat to wear to Washington. Ignored by LaGuardia, Marie finds life difficult. But Dora, courted by Floyd, finds life more difficult still, because—as she sings—"I Love a Cop." This, in her circle, is enough to make people think she's gone berserk. All the same, she can't help feeling it's wonderful for two people to be in love. "Yes, even for one people," says Marie, confessing that her only reason for going to Washington is that Ben Marino is sending her on business: "He thinks I can tell Mr. LaGuardia what to say in Congress— which is utterly ridiculous. . . ."

SCENE VIII

In Washington, despite party pleas and the tradition that Representatives do not speak on the floor of Congress during their first term, LaGuardia is ready to come out in favor of the Draft Act. Marie, brought to Washington by Ben Marino, tries to warn Fiorello that this will be a piece of folly, that in the Fourteenth people don't care about the issue: they just want to keep their boys at home.

FIORELLO (*very quiet*)—When the people of the Fourteenth voted for me, and sent me down here, they changed me a little. They may not have known they were doing it—they may not even be aware they've done it—but they made me a little different from themselves. I can no longer think the way they think, as a single individual, a father or a mother thinking about a son. I have to think about the whole country, all the people in it, what's best for all of them. I'm not a guy hanging around a political club any more, Ben. I'm a Congressman now.

BEN (*sore*)—I wonder how your thinking would go if this Draft Act applied not only to people but also to Congressmen?

FIORELLO (*quietly*)—You can stop wondering about that. I enlisted this morning.

SCENE IX

On the way to a farewell party for Fiorello, a group of soldiers passes Floyd and Dora. Suddenly cowed by the sight of so many uniforms, and feeling self-conscious in mufti, Floyd balks at going to the party. Buttering him up, Dora says consolingly that he can't help his flat feet, and after all, he did try to enlist. "I'm so proud of you," she coos, "you're so handsome, and you're going up in the world." And, since Floyd *is* bribable, Dora promises that if he goes to the party she will be very nice to him afterwards. "I Love a Cop," she sings; and the soldiers who are on their way to the party join in the refrain, and carry Floyd off.

SCENE X

As the farewell dance progresses at Ben Marino's clubhouse, Marie tries to hide her sadness while Morris tries to buck her up. Arriving in uniform as Thea's escort, Captain LaGuardia wants to settle one thing before he goes off: he wants Thea to marry him on his return.

Although she would like to change the subject, she admits that the possibility of marriage has been enough on her mind for her to go to the Church for advice.

THEA—I asked a friend of mine, Father O'Rourke. I asked him did he think it a good idea for an Italian Catholic girl to marry an Italian Jewish Episcopalian?

FIORELLO—You chose the right person to ask all right.

THEA—You know what he said?

FIORELLO—Of course, I know. What could he say—but I noticed something else.

THEA—What?

FIORELLO—I notice you're thinking about marrying me or you wouldn't have asked him.

Wanting no further arguments, Fiorello says that when he has captured Trieste just for Thea, he's going to come back and marry her. But with last-minute business to take care of, and with the dancing and general excitement, the matter is left at that.

In the clubhouse yard, the servicemen and their girls stop dancing to listen to Ben Marino's farewell to "his boy." When the music resumes and darkness falls, Thea leads them all in singing "Till To-morrow."

SCENE XI

A vintage Pathé newsreel shows Flying Congressman F. H. La-Guardia leaving his Washington desk for Air Force training and action abroad. After a shot of an aerial dogfight, LaGuardia is shown downing his first German plane. The camera then switches to Italy and King Victor Emmanuel reclaiming Trieste, whose favorite son, F. H. LaGuardia, is shown next. Pictures of Armistice crowds are followed by pictures of troopships entering New York harbor. As soldiers stream down the gangplanks, Fiorello walks down a real gangplank, past Marie, to Thea. "Thea," he says, "I brought you a present—a key to the city—Trieste." Fiorello receives his proper reward as crowds throw confetti and sing: "Home Again."

ACT II

Starting his campaign for Mayor, LaGuardia is so keyed up that nothing exists for him beyond his notes and speeches and his carefully wrinkled suit for platform appearances. A wan and frail Thea —whose health is obviously failing—tactfully helps out where needed.

When Ben phones Fiorello to warn him against his constant re-hashing of his ten-year-old war record, Fiorello abruptly hangs up on him. "Thinks I talked too much about my war record in that interview," he reports. "These nickle-and-dime ward heelers!"

When Dora visits Thea, Fiorello shows no enthusiasm for Floyd's rise in the world from sewers to garbage. As he dashes about look-ing for this and that set of figures to prove the amount of city funds Jimmy Walker spent for his own private needs, Thea listens pa-tiently and sympathetically to Dora's excited confidences. Dora finds it wonderful that Jimmy Hines stopped at their table to say "hello," and that she and Floyd now have a penthouse.

During all this, Ben tries to reach LaGuardia, who wants Thea to tell Ben to stick to his poker-playing and let Fiorello run his own campaign. Naturally, Thea says nothing of the kind: "I'm sorry, Ben. I can't get him now. But I'll give him your message." Then turning to Dora, who is leaving, she asks sweetly to be remembered to Floyd. When Dora pops back in a minute later, it is because she had forgotten to ask about Thea's health. Not wanting Fiorello to hear, Thea asks Dora to forget she had ever mentioned not being well: "I'm a little tired, the doctor says, and maybe a little run-down, and all I need is rest." Begging her to follow the doctor's orders, Dora finally leaves.

In bounces Fiorello—this time looking for his figures on Alexander Marconi's bank deposits.

THEA—Is he in trouble?

FIORELLO—Now, honeybunch, I know he heads the charity for Trieste and all the Italians are soft on him, but a crook is a crook. If Morris or Marie call, tell them I'm on my way.

THEA—I haven't seen Marie in weeks. Why don't you ask her to dinner some night?

FIORELLO—All right, honeybunch, when you're feeling a little stronger.

THEA—Is she going steady with anyone now?

FIORELLO—How do I know? Oh, you women!

THEA—Well, she should get married.

FIORELLO—Then what'll I do?

THEA (*giving him a reproving glance*)—Darling!

FIORELLO—No, I didn't mean it. If she finds the right man, I'll scream to high heaven, but I'll be happy for her.—Now don't send any more suits out to be pressed until this campaign is over. I don't know when I'll be home. This rally starts at eleven. But if you're still awake, and you keep your window open, around midnight you should hear a long loud scream. (*He gives* THEA *a quick kiss and snatches up his ten-gallon hat.*) That will be Jimmy Walker yelling uncle!

As he bounces out, Thea stares after him a second, then sings "When Did I Fall in Love?"

SCENE II

At Floyd and Dora's penthouse, there is grandiose planning to entertain Tammany bigwigs without wives but not without girls. Mitzi Travers, the Broadway musical star and good friend of Jimmy Walker's, heads the entertainment, with a dozen or so chorines to back her up and to keep such Tammanyites as Judge Carter, the Commissioner, and gangster Frankie Scarpini amused.

Dora, who has not been consulted, isn't in the least amused by the guest list, and she tangles with Floyd over having chorines and a gangster in her home. "The Commissioner wants to see him," says Floyd; "now mind your own business or I'll give you a clout." When she fights back, as always, Floyd collapses. "Listen, Dora," he pleads, "I asked him here because I wanted to show off the pent-house and oil paintings and everything. Dora, please, I don't care about those girls. I ain't never looked at no other dame but you since we first met up." Mollified, Dora perches on his lap and accepts his apology.

With the arrival of the first guest, Dora discreetly retires, leaving the men to their business, which consists of how to rid themselves of the gadfly LaGuardia.

The Commissioner doesn't care at all for the statements Fiorello has been making about him, and neither, he might add, does Hines or Marconi. Judge Carter thinks that a truck might hit LaGuardia on purpose. "I don't know if it's practical," says Floyd, "he's awful fast on his feet."

Dora provides a diversion by bringing in Mitzi Travers and the girls. "All right, folks," says Floyd, "now pay attention. Maybe we'll put this song right in front of Jimmy Walker's big speech."

All the flavor of the twenties and its musical-comedy politics appears in "Gentleman Jimmy," Mitzi Travers' *pièce de resistance*. As she finishes belting out this song, and everyone congratulates her on what is bound to be the hit of the rally, Frankie Scarpini's arrival with his bodyguard adds the final 1920's touch.

With the girls momentarily out of the way, the men return to their business. Slipping back onto the terrace, Dora loudly disapproves of Scarpini. Floyd at first says he's not so bad when you get to know him, and *he is loyal*. Dora merely finds him mean-looking. "For God's sake," says Floyd, "keep quiet. You want me bumped off?"

Tammany's dignified Commissioner has it all figured out with Scarpini's help. When LaGuardia speaks at 106th Street, they'll get him. "We'll brain him," says Scarpini, "don't worry." Then wanting to mix pleasure with business, he asks them to bring on the "tomatoes."

Next given the tap-dance treatment, "Gentleman Jimmy" with its line-up of cuties is headed for the rally, to be tacked right on to Mitzi's song.

Scene III

In his single-minded pursuit of Tammany, Fiorello has estranged the Italian vote. Listening to LaGuardia being interviewed, Ben is disgusted. "I've got a delicate stomach," he says, "some kinds of things upset me." The way LaGuardia is running his campaign, for instance. Fiorello lashes back at him, and reminds him of the way he used to run his lousy district before Fiorello took over. He would like Ben to remember that he's been right and Ben's been wrong.

BEN—Yes, Major, you've been right, and you've done a hell of a lot of things that nobody thought you could, but once in a while you used to listen to some of us dumb bastards make a suggestion. You're going to lose, Major. Why? Because you can't play ball—not for one minute. We all know about your war record. We all know how incorruptible you are. You don't have to prove it so many times a day. You had to throw the Italian vote out of the window to prove you're a fearless leader. You're not trying to win an election. You're just hoping that some day they'll put your statue up in Central Park.

FIORELLO—That's quite a speech, Ben.

BEN—That's the short version.

FIORELLO—Well, take it home and work on it—and don't come back.

He angrily orders Ben out of his office and then, still angry, picks up the phone to speak to Dr. Marsini, who is calling about Thea.

Outside, in the waiting room, Dora has come to warn Marie about the ambush at 106th Street. As Fiorello now relays the doctor's orders to Thea, Marie sees Dora out. "Now, honeybunch," he says to Thea, "what's the use of paying the doctor good money if you don't do what he tells you to do? You've heard me make speeches before, and you'll hear me make plenty more. So you can forget about this one tonight and take care of yourself. I want you to go to bed and stay there. The doctor says you need rest."

Although life is becoming increasingly worrisome for LaGuardia, Marie's revelation of the plot to kill him seems just the thing to cheer him up. "First they're going to turn in a fire alarm at Madison and 105th," reports Marie. "Then some other thugs are going to be up on a roof and they're going to have a baby carriage full of paving blocks. And then in all the excitement, they're going to push it off the roof on top of your head!" Immediately deploying Morris and Neil to guard the firebox and to place sentries on the offending roof, Fiorello is prepared for action.

NEIL—I was just thinking, Major, suppose it's a policeman.

FIORELLO—Tell him if the law won't protect us—we'll have to protect ourselves. Get tough with him. And if you have to—hit him. Don't hesitate.

NEIL—Sock a cop?

FIORELLO—Yes. Punch him in the eye. Come on, get moving.
MORRIS (*to switchboard girl*)—Call Shirley and tell her I'm in jail.

SCENE IV

At Madison Avenue and 105th Street, coping as best he can with the various toughs assigned to put in a fire alarm, Neil is tired of keeping them at bay. But he sticks to his post until, of a sudden, Morris arrives. "Neil, she died," says Morris. "Mrs. LaGuardia— They called up—I didn't know what to do." Fiorello's two devoted helpers are so upset that they forget about leaving the firebox unguarded and rush off to find LaGuardia. The minute they're out of sight, there is a dash for the box; the alarm is sounded, and soon the air is filled with the noise of screaming sirens.

SCENE V

Unable to reach Fiorello before the paving blocks are dumped, Neil and Morris return dejectedly to the office where Marie has been holding the fort.

Coming in upon this melancholy group, an enraged Fiorello lashes out at the two men, who stand there helplessly. Finally, Morris manages to tell LaGuardia of Thea's death. Turning from them without saying a word, LaGuardia leaves the office, and, in it, three very worried people. Neil bolts out the door after him; Morris follows; Marie, left to turn out the lights, continues to sit and look straight ahead.

SCENE VI

That Election Night there is a record landslide for Walker. Never left alone for a minute by his devoted trio, Fiorello finally thanks them for being such good friends, but asks that they go. Suddenly his manner changes. "There's work to do," says Fiorello. "Everyone gets hit in the head with a baseball bat once in a while, sometimes twice in succession. I don't want to feel sorry for myself and I don't want you to feel sorry for me. . . . They're out there and we'll fight them. If we can't fight them in City Hall, we'll fight them in the courts. I'll see you in the office tomorrow morning at nine o'clock." "Yes, Major," answers Morris. "Good night."

"The Name's LaGuardia," sings Fiorello, "L-A-G-U-A-R-D-I-A!"

SCENE VII

In Ben Marino's smoke-filled clubroom his poker-playing chums are having a field day with the Seabury investigation.

SECOND PLAYER—Listen. Then after he gets this joker on the stand and he's sworn in, Judge Seabury says: "From 1929 when Mayor Walker appointed you till today in 1933 your official salary totalled $40,000."

BEN—"Will you please tell the investigating committee how you were able to maintain a Wall Street brokerage account?"

FIFTH PLAYER—No, that was the Commissioner of Hospitals yesterday.

SECOND PLAYER—With this boy it's a $75,000 mansion in Teaneck, New Jersey.

FIFTH PLAYER—And you know where he got it?

BEN—Out of a little tin box his wife keeps on the kitchen shelf. (*Gets up and goes to look at the newspaper.*)

SECOND PLAYER—That's right.

BEN—Give 'em hell, Judge. Give 'em hell.

SECOND PLAYER—Your witness.

ED—
   Mr. "X," may we ask you a question?
   It's amusing, is it not,
   That the city pays you slightly less
   Than fifty bucks a week,
   Yet you purchased a private yacht?
BEN—
   I'm positive your honor must be joking.
   Any working man can do what I have done.
   For a month or two I simply give up smoking
   And I put my extra pennies one by one—

   Into a little tin box,
   A little tin box
   That a little tin key unlocks.
   There is nothing unorthodox
   About a little tin box.
MEN—
   About a little tin box
   About a little tin box
   In a little tin box
   A little tin box
   That a little tin key unlocks . . .
BEN—
   There is honor and purity . . .
ALL—
   Lots of security
   In a little tin box.

FIFTH PLAYER (*spoken*)—Next witness.
THIRD PLAYER—
    Mr. "Y," we've been told you don't feel well,
    And we know you've lost your voice;
    But we wonder how you manage on the salary you make
    To acquire a new Rolls-Royce.
BEN—
    You're implying I'm a crook and I say, no sir!
    There is nothing in my past I care to hide.
    I've been taking empty bottles to the grocer,
    And each nickel that I got was put aside . . .

All kidding aside, the old problem still arises: Who are they to run in the Fourteenth? "We gonna run just exactly whoever Judge Seabury picks to run," says Ben, hoping against hope that it won't be that reformer. Since it's a Fusion ticket, he'd even take a Democrat in preference to LaGuardia.

Wanting to heal this breach of over three lean years, Marie arrives to speak to Ben. Naturally, LaGuardia has no idea that she's taken this step. "We all know what he is," she says. "A megalomaniac, that's what he is—" says Ben—"and I've had it." Soft-soaping him, Marie says: "You're too big for that—honestly, don't you want to beat Tammany?" "I do," says Ben, "with a candidate who appreciates me. Good God, Marie. I should think you'd have had it too. You going to wait around for him all your life?" "No," she answers, "I'm not. After this campaign, I'm quitting, but that doesn't mean I won't always be loyal to him."

As Ben goes to take a call from a potential Fusion candidate, Morris, who has also arrived, asks Marie what she means by "quitting." Wanting to get married, Marie feels that the way to go about it is by dating, and LaGuardia gets angry every time she's off for the evening. Morris is convinced that she'll never be able to quit. "Won't I?" says Marie; and she sings "The Very Next Man":

    "I shall marry the very next man who asks me,
        You'll see.
    Next time I feel
    That a man's about to kneel—
    He won't have to plead or implore,
    I'll say Yes before his knee hits the floor . . ."

"Well, boys and girls," says Ben returning to the room, "I just had a very cooperative talk with a certain candidate for Mayor. Honest but grateful."

Morris reveals that Seabury's candidate is to be LaGuardia and that the Judge will offer him the nomination tomorrow morning. "You don't say," answers Ben. Morris admits that he isn't sure that LaGuardia will accept. "He always accepts," snarls Ben. "He's in a very strange mood, Ben," says Marie. "But if you came to him, if you were in his office tomorrow at ten, I think he would." "Tell him to call me," says Ben, "tell him to get in touch."

When Marie leaves, she is somehow sure that Ben and the boys will be there. As one of his cronies reads the newspaper and asks gleefully: "Guess who Seabury has got on the rack now?" "I'll tell you who," answers Ben. "Me!" And the refrain of "Politics and Poker" has a special poignancy.

Scene VIII

There are few peaceful moments at Fiorello's office. Finding that almost every case that they have prepared for the last three years has been removed from the court docket by Judge Carter—that if any crook has a friend at Tammany he can avoid a trial—Fiorello is boiling with frustration. He claims he is too weary to wage this endlessly futile battle. Trying to put some fight into him, Marie won't accept his excuse of being tired. "You're scared," she says. Fiorello reacts sharply, as she knew he would. Marie continues: "You're afraid they'll turn their backs on you again. That's what's wrong. You're scared you'll lose a second time."

In the outside office, the poker players start straggling in, and finally Ben appears. His warm welcome can be heard inside. Fiorello, going to his office door and looking in astonishment at the gathering outside, says: "Well, this is a great honor. What the hell are you doing in this office?" Told that they've come to help him in his next campaign, Fiorello says he has no campaign. Prodded by Morris's reminder of Judge Carter, Fiorello's temperature rises and, as Judge Seabury's phone call comes through, he hesitates only long enough to say: "And if I should decide to run again, I want all you politicians to know that my chief qualification for Mayor of this great city is my monumental ingratitude."

Returning after the call without saying a word to anyone, Fiorello points a commanding finger at Marie and retires to his office. "That guy kills me. He just plain kills me," says Ben.

Giving Marie hell for going to Ben for help, Fiorello says sarcastically: "It's nice to know you've taken over running my life. You're getting very independent lately." As Marie beats a retreat, he calls her back—to fire her. "I can't court a girl who's working for me," says LaGuardia. He knows, he says, that his proposal is kind of sudden. "Sudden!" cries Marie; "yes, it is." He thinks she can learn to love him. She thinks she can: she's been practicing for fifteen years. As Fiorello tells of his plans for the two of them, Marie sings "I'll Marry the Very Next Man"—while outside, in the waiting room, the politicians brush up on: "The Name's LaGuardia."

A GRAPHIC GLANCE

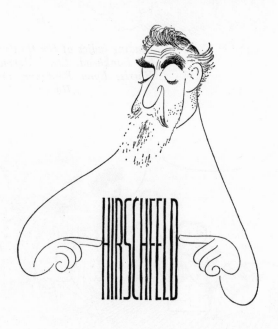

*Leading ladies of the theatre: Tallu-
lah Bankhead, Ethel Merman, Julie
Harris, Lynn Fontanne and Helen
Hayes*

*Katharine Cornell, Judy Holliday,
Judith Anderson, Ruth Gordon
and Shirley Booth*

Players who play performers: Sandra Church ("Gypsy"), Geraldine Page ("Sweet Bird of Youth"), Gwen Verdon and Richard Kiley ("Redhead"), Christopher Plummer ("J.B."), Dolores Gray ("Destry") and Pat Suzuki ("Flower Drum Song")

*Claude Allister, Nancy Kelly and
Polly Rowles in "A Mighty Man
Is He"*

Lauren Bacall and Sydney Chaplin in "Goodbye Charlie"

Among the villains on Broadway: Herbert Berghof ("Andersonville Trial"), Stefan Gierasch ("The Sound of Music"), Marc Breaux, George Reeder, Swen Swenson and Art Lund ("Destry"), Leonard Stone ("Redhead") and Jane White ("Once Upon a Mattress")

Brooks Atkinson, retiring drama critic of The New York Times,
making his farewell speech

Edith King, Horst Buchholz, Lucy Landau, Kim Stanley and Lilli Darvas in "Chéri"

Maureen O'Hara in "Christine"

Shelley Berman, Bert Lahr, Nancy Walker and Dick Van Dyke in
"The Girls Against the Boys"

The bell-ringing scene from "La Plume de Ma Tante"

Bruce McKay, Ellen McCown, William Chapman, John Megna,
Cecil Kellaway, Anthony Perkins, Lee Cass and Pert Kelton in
"Greenwillow"

Barbara Cook and Farley Granger in a revival of "The King and I"

Broadway first-nighters

PLAYS PRODUCED IN NEW YORK

PLAYS PRODUCED IN NEW YORK

June 1, 1959—May 31, 1960

(Plays marked "Continued" were still running on June 1, 1960)

BILLY BARNES REVUE

(87 performances)

Musical revue in two acts, with music and lyrics by Billy Barnes; sketches and dialogue by Bob Rodgers. Produced by George Eckstein, in association with Bob Reese, at the John Golden Theatre, August 4, 1959.

Principals—

Joyce Jameson	Jackie Joseph
Bert Convy	Patti Regan
Ken Berry	Bob Rodgers
Ann Guilbert	Len Weinrib

Staged by Bob Rodgers; production designed by Glenn Holse; lighting by Peggy Clark; costume supervision by Peggy Morrison and Berman Costume Company; musical director, Billy Barnes; associate musical director, Armin Hoffman; stage manager, Howard Ostroff; press representative, Samuel J. Friedman.

Sketches and musical numbers—

ACT I

"Do a Revue" ....The Company
"Where Are Your Children?" .....Ken Berry, Bert Convy, Jackie Joseph, Ann Guilbert, Patti Regan and Len Weinrib
"Las Vegas"
   Herman ....Bob Rodgers
   Girl with Hat ....Ann Guilbert
   Tanya ....Joyce Jameson
   Her Fellas ....Bert Convy and Ken Berry
"Medic"
   Surgeon ....Len Weinrib
   Staff ....Ann Guilbert and Patti Regan
"Foolin' Ourselves" ....Bert Convy and Ken Berry
"Safari à la Marilyn"
   Papa ....Len Weinrib
   Arthur ....Bob Rodgers
   Marilyn ....Joyce Jameson
"The Pembrooke Story"
   Arthur ....Ken Berry
   Edythe ....Ann Guilbert
   Miss O'Brien ....Jackie Joseph
   John ....Bert Convy
   Peter ....Len Weinrib
"Whatever" ....Patti Regan
"City of the Angels"
   Lily ....Joyce Jameson
   Lolly ....Ann Guilbert
   Dolly ....Jackie Joseph

"Listen to the Beat!"
```
Host ...................................................Len Weinrib
Jack ...................................................Ken Berry
Mary Lou .............................................Ann Guilbert
Dean ..................................................Bert Convy
Sarah .................................................Joyce Jameson
The Prophet ..........................................Len Weinrib
Beatniks ............Bob Rodgers, Patti Regan and Jackie Joseph
```
"Home in Mississippi"
```
Maggie ...............................................Patti Regan
Big Daddy ............................................Len Weinrib
Big Mama .............................................Ann Guilbert
Brick .................................................Bob Rodgers
No-neck Monsters .....................................Themselves
```
"Tyler My Boy" ....Bert Convy
"Whatever Happened" ....Patti Regan
"The Thirties"
```
Narrator .............................................Bob Rodgers
Peddler ..............................................Patti Regan
Fred ..................................................Ken Berry
Ginger ...............................................Joyce Jameson
Forgotten Woman ......................................Ann Guilbert
Forgotten Man ........................................Len Weinrib
Shirley ...............................................Joyce Jameson
Daddy .................................................Bert Convy
Step-Mommy ...........................................Patti Regan
Gold Digger ..........................................Jackie Joseph
J.N. ..................................................Len Weinrib
Sam ...................................................Ken Berry
Ruby ..................................................Ann Guilbert
Dick ..................................................Bert Convy
Jeanette ..............................................Joyce Jameson
Nelson ................................................Bob Rodgers
```

ACT II

"A Dissertation on Transportation; or, It All Started
with the Wheel"
```
Principal ............................................Bob Rodgers
P.T.A. Principal .....................................Joyce Jameson
Teacher ..............................................Patti Regan
Sweet Little Girl ....................................Jackie Joseph
Sour Little Girl .....................................Ann Guilbert
Teacher's Pet ........................................Ken Berry
Bully .................................................Len Weinrib
Bert Convy ...........................................Bert Convy
```
"The Fights" (Introduced by Ann Guilbert)
```
Shirley ...............................................Joyce Jameson
Harry .................................................Bob Rodgers
```
"The Vamp and Friends"
```
Vamp ..................................................Ann Guilbert
Champ .................................................Ken Berry
Tramp .................................................Patti Regan
Camp ..................................................Len Weinrib
```
"Blocks"
```
Husband ..............................................Bob Rodgers
Wife ..................................................Jackie Joseph
```
"Hellahahana"
```
Natives ................Bert Convy, Ken Berry, Joyce Jameson,
                              Len Weinrib and Jackie Joseph
Turista ...............................................Ann Guilbert
```
"Whatever Happened To" ....Patti Regan
"World at Large"
```
Moderator ............................................Bert Convy
```
World at Large No. 1
```
Rosabelle Haley ......................................Joyce Jameson
Warden ................................................Len Weinrib
Matron ................................................Ann Guilbert
```
Station Break
```
Fire Prevention Queen ................................Patti Regan
```
World at Large No. 2
```
Mr. Lernstein ........................................Bob Rodgers
Choral Group .........................................Choral Group
```

World at Large Preview

```
Oed .............................................Ken Berry
Jo ..............................................Patti Regan
"Too Long at the Fair" .........................Joyce Jameson
"One of Those Days"
  Poor Soul .....................................Len Weinrib
  Ads .................Bert Convy, Jackie Joseph and Ken Berry
Finale .........................................The Company
```

(Closed October 17, 1959)

MUCH ADO ABOUT NOTHING

(58 performances)

Comedy in three acts by William Shakespeare. Produced by arrangement with the Producers Theatre and the Cambridge Drama Festival at the Lunt-Fontanne Theatre, September 17, 1959.

Cast of characters—

```
Don Pedro, Prince of Arragon ..............Micheal MacLiammoir
Don John, his bastard brother .....................Hurd Hatfield
Claudio, a young lord of Florence .................Barrie Ingham
Benedick, a young lord of Padua ...................John Gielgud
Leonato, Governor of Messina ....................Malcolm Keen
Antonio, an old man, his brother .................Herbert Ranson
Balthasar, attendant on Don Pedro .............Jonathan Anderson
Followers of Don John { Borachio .....................Paul Sparer
                      { Conrade ....................Mark Lenard
Friar Francis ...............................David King-Wood
Dogberry, a constable ...........................George Rose
Verges, a headborough ...........................Donald Moffat
A Sexton .......................................Barry Macollum
A Boy ...........................................Willie Wade
1st Watch ......................................Howard Fischer
2nd Watch ......................................Graham Jarvis
A Messenger ....................................Donald Moffat
Hero, daughter to Leonato ........................Jean Marsh
Beatrice, niece to Leonato .....................Margaret Leighton
Waiting Gentlewomen { Margaret ............Betsy von Furstenberg
  Attending on Hero { Ursula ...................Nancy Marchand
Watch ...........................Theodore Tenley, Joe Ponazecki
Pages .............. Edward Moor, Ralph Williams, Louis Negin,
                    John Valva, Arthur Teno Pollick, D. F. Gilliam
Ladies ............Virginia Robinson, Juliete Hunt, Joan Hackett,
                    Fay Tracey, Elizabeth Winship
Lords ..................Neil Vipond, Allessandro Giannini, David
                    Thurman, Martin Herschberg
Captains ............Donald Barton, Richard Buck, Joseph Hoover
An Acolyte .....................................Peter deVise
```
The action of the play takes place in Messina, Sicily, during a period of four days.

Staged by John Gielgud; settings and costumes after designs by Mariano Andreu; costumes executed by Ray Diffen; supervision and lighting by Paul Morrison; music by Leslie Bridgewater; dances by Pauline Grant; production stage manager, Keene Curtis; stage manager, Howard Fischer; press representative, Barry Hyams.

(Closed November 7, 1959)

THE GANG'S ALL HERE

(132 performances)

Play in three acts by Jerome Lawrence and Robert E. Lee. Produced by Kermit Bloomgarden Productions, Inc., in association with Sylvia Drulie, at the Ambassador Theatre, October 1, 1959.

Cast of characters—

Walter Rafferty	E. G. Marshall
Joshua Loomis	Bernard Lenrow
Charles Webster	Paul McGrath
Tad	Bill Zuckert
Higgy	Howard Smith
Judge Corriglione	Victor Kilian
Doc Kirkaby	Fred Stewart
Frances Greeley Hastings	Jean Dixon
Griffith P. Hastings	Melvyn Douglas
Cobb	Edwin Cooper
Maid	Anne Shropshire
Bruce Bellingham	Arthur Hill
Arthur Anderson	Bram Nossen
Alex Maley	Bert Wheeler
Laverne	Yvette Vickers
Renee	Alberta MacDonald
Piano Player	John Harkins
John Boyd	Clay Hall

Time: Quite a while ago. Act I.—Scene 1—A hotel room in Chicago; past midnight during a political convention. Scene 2—The executive suite, 1600 Pennsylvania Avenue, Washington. Act II.—Scene 1—A basement-room on L Street in Washington. Scene 2—The executive suite. Act III.—The presidential suite of a hotel in San Francisco.

Staged by George Roy Hill; settings and lighting by Jo Mielziner; costumes by Patricia Zipprodt; production stage manager, Kermit Kegley; stage manager, Clifford Cothren; press representative, Arthur Cantor.

(Closed January 23, 1960)

THE GREAT GOD BROWN

(32 performances)

Play in three acts by Eugene O'Neill. Produced by Theatre Incorporated (T. Edward Hambleton and Norris Houghton) at the Coronet Theatre, October 6, 1959.

Cast of characters—

Mrs. Brown	Sasha Von Scherler
William A. Brown	Robert Lansing
Mr. Brown	Patrick Hines
Mrs. Anthony	Patricia Ripley
Mr. Anthony	J. D. Cannon
Dion Anthony	Fritz Weaver
Margaret	Nan Martin
Cybel	Gerry Jedd
Eldest Son	John Hillerman
Second Son	Murray Levy
Youngest Son	Corydon Erickson

Older Draftsman ....Elliott Sullivan
Younger Draftsman ....John Heffernan
A Client ....Eric Berry
Committeemen ....Ray Reinhardt, Albert Quinton, Eric Berry
Police Captain ....Albert Quinton
Policemen ....Ray Reinhardt, Tom Bellin
    Act I.—Prologue—The pier of the Casino; moonlight in middle June.
Scene 1—Sitting room of Margaret Anthony's apartment; afternoon,
seven years later. Scene 2—Billy Brown's office; the same afternoon.
Scene 3—Cybel's parlor; that night. Act II.—Scene 1—Cybel's parlor;
dusk, seven years later. Scene 2—Drafting room, William A. Brown's
office; that evening. Scene 3—Library, William A. Brown's home; that
night. Act III.—Scene 1—Brown's office; morning, a month later.
Scene 2—Library, Brown's home; that evening. Scene 3—Sitting room
of Margaret's home; that night. Scene 4—Brown's office; late afternoon, weeks later. Scene 5—Library, Brown's home; hours later.
Epilogue—the pier of the Casino; four years later.
    Staged by Stuart Vaughan; settings and costumes by Will Steven
Armstrong; lighting by Tharon Musser; music composed by David
Amram; production stage manager, Richard Blofson; stage manager,
Gordon Davidson; press representatives, Ben Kornzweig and Karl Bern-
stein.

(Closed November 1, 1959)

HAPPY TOWN

(5 performances)

Musical comedy in two acts, with book adapted by Max Hampton; music by Gordon Duffy; lyrics by Harry M. Haldane; additi-
tional music and lyrics by Paul Nassau. Produced by B & M Productions at the Fifty-fourth Street Theatre, October 7, 1959.

Cast of characters—

Lint Richards ....George Blackwell
Bub Richards ....Bruce MacKay
Sib Richards ....George Ives
Glenn Richards ....Michael Kermoyan
Janice Dawson ....Cindy Robbins
Craig Richards ....Biff McGuire
Clint Yoder......................................Tom Williams
Bobbie Jo Hartman ....Alice Clift
Molly Bixby ....Lee Venora
Judge Ed Bixby ....Dick Elliott
Jim Joe Jamieson ....Frederic Tozere
A Reporter ....Rico Froehlich
Pert Hawkins ....Ralph Dunn
Claney ....Charles May
Doc Spooner ....Will Wright
Mrs. Hawkins ....Liz Pritckett
Reverend Hornblow ....Edwin Steffe
Mult ....Roy Wilson
Luke Granger ....Chester Watson
    Townswomen of Back-A-Heap: Diana Baron, Lillian Bozinoff, Alice
Clift, Colleen Corkrey, Dori Davis, Isabelle Farrell, Laurie Franks,
Rita Golden, Connie Greco, Marian Haraldson, Marilyn Harris, Judy
Keirn, Maxine Kent, Patricia Mount, Robbi Palmer.
    Townsmen of Back-A-Heap: John Buwen, Bob Daley, Rico Froehlich,
James Gannon, George Jack, Danny Joel, Charles May, Jim McAnany,
Nixon Miller, Howard Parker, Tom Pocoroba, Stewart Rose, Roy
Wilson.
    Act I.—Scene 1—A private office in the T.B.A. Exchange. Scene
2—Back-A-Heap, Texas; the main street, a few hours later. Scene 3—
Bixby's Super Market; a little later. Scene 4—The main street; im-

mediately following. Scene 5—Bixby's Super Market; immediately
following. Scene 6—The T.B.A. office; a little later. Scene 7—The
main street; that evening. Scene 8—Back-A-Heap Town Hall; immediately following. Scene 9—The main street; immediately following.
Scene 10—Fairgrounds; next morning. Scene 11—The T.B.A. office.
Scene 12—The prairie. Act II.—Scene 1—The main street; late the
next day. Scene 2—E Street; immediately following. Scene 3—The
T.B.A. office; at about the same time. Scene 4—Fairgrounds; two
weeks later. Scene 5—A street; immediately following. Scene 6—The
main street. Scene 7—T.B.A.'s office. Scene 8—The main street;
later. Seene 9—Bixby's Super Market. Scene 10—A street; immediately following. Scene 11—Town Hall; later.

Staged by Allan A. Buckhantz; choreography by Lee Scott; settings
by Curt Nations; costumes by J. Michael Travis; lighting by Paul
Morrison; musical direction and vocal arrangements by Samuel Krach-
malnick; orchestrations by Nicholas Carras; production stage manager,
Lawrence N. Kasha; stage manager, Jim Cavanaugh; press representative, Shirley E. Herz.

Musical numbers—

ACT I

"It Isn't Easy" ....Janice, Glenn, Bub, Lint and Sib
"Celebration!" ....Townspeople
"Something Special" ....Craig
"The Legend of Black-Eyed Susan Grey" ....Susan Grey and
                                                    Townspeople
  (Susan Grey danced by Leigh Evans)
"Opportunity!" ....Craig, Reverend Hornblow,
                                     Mrs. Hawkins and Townspeople
"As Busy as Anyone Can Be" ....Clint and Girls
"Heaven Protect Me!" ....Janice and Girls
"I Feel Like a Brother to You!" ....Craig and Molly
"Hoedown!" ....Townspeople
"I Am What I Am!" ....Craig and Molly
"The Beat of a Heart" ....Molly
"Mean" ....Janice
"It Isn't Easy" (Reprise) ....Glenn, Bub, Lint and Sib
"When the Time Is Right" ....Reverend Hornblow

ACT II

"Pick-Me-Up!" ....Townspeople
"I'm Stuck with Love" ....Molly
"It Isn't Easy" (Reprise) ....Glenn, Bub, Lint and Sib
"Nothing in Common" ....Janice and Molly
"Talkin' 'Bout You" ....Janice, Clint and Townspeople
"Something Special" (Reprise) ....Craig and Molly
"Y' Can't Win" ....Janice
"Opportunity!" (Reprise) ....Entire Company

(Closed October 10, 1959)

AT THE DROP OF A HAT

(215 performances)

An intimate revue in two acts, written and performed by Michael
Flanders and Donald Swan. Produced by Alexander H. Cohen, in
association with Joseph I. Levine, at the John Golden Theatre, October 8, 1959.

Musical numbers—

A Transport of Delight   The Youth of the Heart
Song of Reproduction   (lyrics by Sydney Carter)
The Hog Beneath the Skin   Greensleeves

The Wompom	In the Bath
Sea Fever	Design for Living
A Gnu	Tried by the Centre Court
Judgement of Paris	Misalliance
Songs for Our Time	Kokoraki
A Song of the Weather	Madeira, M' Dear?
The Reluctant Cannibal	The Hippopotamus

Lighting by Ralph Alswang; frontcloth by Al Hirschfeld; stage manager, Irving Vincent; press representatives, Richard Maney, Martin Schwartz and Tom Trenkle.

(Closed May 14, 1960)

MOONBIRDS

(3 performances)

Comedy in two acts by Marcel Ayme, adapted by John Pauker. Produced by Leo Kerz, George Justin and Harry Belafonte at the Cort Theatre, October 9, 1959.

Cast of characters—

Alexander Chabert	Michael Hordern
Sylvie	Phyllis Newman
Elisa	Anne Meacham
Mrs. Martinon	Marjorie Nichols
Raoul Martinon	Mark Rydell
Duperrier	Carl Reindel
Valentine	Wally Cox
Mrs. Armandine Chabert	Helen Waren
Mrs. Bobignot	Dorothy Sands
Ariane	Dran Seitz
Arbelin	Dino Narizzano
Detective Inspector Petrov	Joseph Buloff
Detective Grindet	William H. Bassett
Mr. Perisson	Rex Everhart
Etienne Perisson	William Hickey
Martine	Peggy Pope
Inspector-General Davin	Arthur Malet
Seligmann	Peter Trytler
Escandier	Anthony Ray
Hermelin	Nick Hyams
Marchandeau	Bill Shawn

The action of the play takes place at Professor Chabert's Tutoring School in a small French town not far from Paris. Act I.—Scene 1— Professor Chabert's office; ten A.M. Scene 2—The same; a few hours later. Act II.—Scene 1—The roof of the school; the next day. Scene 2—The anteroom of the school; one week later.

Entire production staged and designed by Leo Kerz; costumes by Frank Thompson; production stage manager, Joseph Olney; stage manager, Sam Locante; press representative, Barry Hymas.

(Closed October 10, 1959)

CHÉRI

(56 performances)

Play in three acts by Anita Loos, based on the novels "Chéri" and "The Last of Chéri" by Colette. Produced by the Playwrights'

Company and Robert Lewis at the Morosco Theatre, October 12, 1959.

Cast of characters—

Charlotte Peloux .... Edith King
Madame Valerie Aldonza .... Frieda Altman
Baroness de Berche .... Lucy Landau
Count Anthime Berthellmy .... Jerome Collamore
Madame Lili .... Jane Moultrie
Prince Guido Ceste .... Angelo del Rossi
Butler .... Byron Russell
Léa de Lonval .... Kim Stanley
Patron .... John Granger
Frédérick Peloux (Chéri) .... Horst Buchholz
Rose .... Margot Lassner
Edmée .... Joan Gray
Coco .... Lili Darvas
Fanchette .... Ginger

Act I.—Scene 1—Charlotte's villa at Neuilly; spring, 1911. Scene 2
—Garden of Léa's villa in Normandy; autumn, 1911. Scene 3—Léa's
boudoir in Paris; spring, 1914. Act II.—Scene 1—Charlotte's villa;
spring, 1919. Scene 2—Coco's apartment; evening, same day. Scene
3—Léa's boudoir; later that night. Act III.—Scene 1—Charlotte's
villa; ten years later. Scene 2—Léa's boudoir; immediately following.
Scene 3—Coco's apartment; immediately following.

Staged by Robert Lewis; settings by Oliver Smith; costumes by Miles
White; lighting by Peggy Clark; production stage manager, Robert
Downing; stage manager, Charles Forsythe; press representative, Wil-
liam Fields.

(Closed November 28, 1959)

GOLDEN FLEECING

(84 performances)

Comedy in three acts by Lorenzo Semple, Jr. Produced by Courtney Burr and Gilbert Miller at Henry Miller's Theatre, October 15,
1959.

Cast of characters—

A Porter .... Buck Kartalian
Ensign Beauregard Gilliam .... Robert Carraway
Jackson Eldridge .... Robert Elston
Lt. Ferguson Howard .... Tom Poston
A Waiter .... Alfred Hesse
Pete di Lucca .... Ralph Stanley
Julie .... Suzanne Pleshette
Ann Knutsen .... Constance Ford
Benjamin Dane .... John Myhers
Admiral Fitch .... Richard Kendrick
Signalman Taylor .... Mickey Deems
Shore Patrolman .... Red Granger
Shore Patrolman .... John Thomas

The entire action of the play takes place in a suite of the Gritti Palace
Hotel in Venice. Act I.—Twilight. Act II.—Scene 1—Later that
evening. Scene 2—Still later. Act III.—Near midnight.

Staged by Abe Burrows; setting and lighting by Frederick Fox; in-
cidental music by Dana Suesse; stage managers, Charles Durand and
Richard Bender; press representatives, Richard Maney, Martin
Schwartz and Tom Trenkle.

(Closed December 26, 1959)

HEARTBREAK HOUSE

(112 performances)

Comedy in three acts by Bernard Shaw. Produced by Maurice Evans and Robert L. Joseph at the Billy Rose Theatre, October 18, 1959.

Cast of characters—

Ellie	Diane Cilento
Nurse Guiness	Jane Rose
Captain Shotover	Maurice Evans
Lady Utterword	Pamela Brown
Mrs. Hushabye	Diana Wynyard
Mazzini Dunn	Alan Webb
Hector Hushabye	Dennis Price
Boss Mangan	Sam Levene
Randall	Patrick Horgan
Burglar	Sorrell Booke

The action of the play takes place in England some time ago. Act I.—Late afternoon. Act II.—After dinner. Act III.—Later.

Staged by Harold Clurman; production designed and lighted by Ben Edwards; costumes by Freddy Wittop; stage manager, Harry Young; press representative, Harvey B. Sabinson.

(Closed January 23, 1960)

THE MIRACLE WORKER

(258 performances)
(Continued)

Play in three acts by William Gibson. Produced by Fred Coe at the Playhouse, October 19, 1959.

Cast of characters—

Doctor	Roger De Koven
Kate Keller	Patricia Neal
Captain Keller	Torin Thatcher
Martha	Miriam Butler
Percy	Caswell Fairweather
Viney	Beah Richards
Helen Keller	Patty Duke
James Keller	James Congdon
Aunt Ev	Kathleen Comegys
Anagnos	Michael Constantine
Annie Sullivan	Anne Bancroft
Children	Lori Heineman, Dale Ellen Bethea, Rita Levy, Lynn Schoenfeld, Eileen Musumeci, Donna Pastore
John	John Marriott
Mary	Juanita Bethea

Act I.—Time: 1882; 1886; 1887. The Keller homestead, Tuscumbia, Alabama; the Perkins Institution for the Blind, Boston, Mass.; the Tuscumbia depot. Act II.—Time: March, 1887. The Keller homestead; the garden house. Act III.—Time: April 5, 1887. The garden house; the homestead.

Staged by Arthur Penn; scenery and lighting by George Jenkins; costumes by Ruth Morley; production stage manager, Porter Van Zandt; stage manager, Dick Via; press representative, Arthur Cantor.

THE WARM PENINSULA

(86 performances)

Play in two acts by Joe Masteroff. Produced by Manning Gurian at the Helen Hayes Theatre, October 20, 1959.

Cast of characters—

Ruth Arnold .... Julie Harris
Joanne de Lynn .... June Havoc
Steve Crawford .... Larry Hagman
Jack Williams .... Farley Granger
Iris Floria .... Ruth White
Howard Shore .... Laurence Haddon
Tony Francis .... Thomas Ruisinger
    The action of the play takes place in Miami, Florida. The time is the present.
    Staged by Warren Enters; scenery and lighting by Frederick Fox; costumes by Kenn Barr; production stage manager, Perry Bruskin; stage manager, George Petrarca; press representatives, Sol Jacobson, Lewis Harmon and Mary Ward.

(Closed January 2, 1960)

FLOWERING CHERRY

(5 performances)

Play in two acts by Robert Bolt. Produced by the Playwrights' Company and Don Herbert, in association with Don Sharpe Enterprises, and by arrangement with H. M. Tennent, Ltd. and Frith Banbury, Ltd., at the Lyceum Theatre, October 21, 1959.

Cast of characters—

Isobel Cherry .... Wendy Hiller
Tom .... Andrew Ray
Cherry .... Eric Portman
Gilbert Grass .... George Turner
Judy .... Phyllis Love
David Bowman .... Roy Poole
Carol .... Susan Burnet
    The action of the play takes place in the kitchen and garden of Mr. Cherry's house in the suburbs of an English city. The time is the present. Act I.—An afternoon in April. Act II.—Scene 1—One month later; afternoon. Scene 2—The same day; two hours later.
    Staged by Frith Banbury; setting by Boris Aronson; costumes by Theoni V. Aldredge; lighting by Paul Morrison; production stage manager, James Gelb; press representative, William Fields.

(Closed October 24, 1959)

TAKE ME ALONG

(254 performances)
(Continued)

Musical in two acts, based on the play "Ah, Wilderness" by Eugene O'Neill; book by Joseph Stein and Robert Russell; music and lyrics by Robert Merrill. Produced by David Merrick at the Sam S. Shubert Theatre, October 22, 1959.

Cast of characters—

Nat Miller	Walter Pidgeon
Mildred Miller	Zeme North
Art Miller	James Cresson
Tommy Miller	Luke Halpin
Essie Miller	Una Merkel
Lily	Eileen Herlie
Richard Miller	Robert Morse
Muriel Macomber	Susan Luckey
Dave Macomber	Fred Miller
Sid	Jackie Gleason
Wint	Peter Conlow
Lady Entertainers	Valerie Harper, Diana Hunter, Rae McLean
Bartender	Jack Collins
Belle	Arlene Golonka
The Drunk	Gene Varrone
Patrons of the Bar	Elna Laun, Paula Lloyd, Janice Painchaud, Jack Konzal, Pat Tolson, Lee Howard
Salesman	Bill McDonald
The Beardsley Dwarf	Charles Bolender
Salome	Rae McLean

Townswomen: Nicole Barth, Renee Byrns, Lyn Connorty, Barbara Doherty, Katia Geleznova, Valerie Harper, Diana Hunter, Elna Laun, Paula Lloyd, Nancy Lynch, Rae McLean, Janice Painchaud.

Townsmen: Alvin Beam, Frank Borgman, John Carter, Lee Howard, Jack Konzal, Bill McDonald, Henry Michel, Jack Murray, John Nola, Bill Richards, Harry Lee Rogers, Walter Strauss, Jimmy Tarbutton, Gene Varrone, Marc West, Pat Tolson, Rusty Parker, Chad Block, Bill Starr.

The action takes place in Centerville, Connecticut, 1910. Act I.—Scene 1—The Miller home; early morning of July 4th. Scene 2—The Macomber home; the same morning. Scene 3—The Car Barn; later that morning. Scene 4—The Miller home; a little later. Scene 5—A street. Scene 6—The picnic grounds; that afternoon. Scene 7—The Miller home; that evening. Act II.—Scene 1—Bar room of the Pleasant Beach House; the same night. Scene 2—The Miller home; later that night. Scene 3—Richard's bedroom; afternoon of the following day. Scene 4—The beach; that evening. Scene 5—The Miller home; a little later. Scene 6—The Car Barn; later that evening.

Staged by Peter Glenville; dances and musical numbers by Onna White; production designed by Oliver Smith; lighting by Jean Rosenthal; costumes by Miles White; musical direction and vocal arrangements by Lehman Engel; ballet and incidental music by Laurence Rosenthal; orchestrations by Philip J. Lang; production stage manager, Lucia Victor; stage manager, Charles Blackwell; press representatives, Harvey B. Sabinson, David Powers and Ted Goldsmith.

Musical numbers—

ACT I

"The Parade"	Nat and Townspeople
"Oh, Please"	Nat, Essie, Lily and Family
"I Would Die"	Muriel and Richard
"Sid, Ol' Kid"	Sid and Townspeople
"Staying Young"	Nat

"I Get Embarrassed" ....Sid and Lily
"We're Home" ....Lily
"Take Me Along" ....Sid and Nat
"For Sweet Charity" ....Sid, Nat, Lady Entertainers and
                                                    Townspeople
"Pleasant Beach House" ....Wint
"That's How It Starts." ....Richard

ACT II

"The Beardsley Ballet" ....Richard, Muriel, the Dwarf, Salome
                                                    and Ensemble
"Oh, Please" (Reprise) ....Nat and Essie
"Promise Me a Rose" ....Lily and Sid
"Staying Young" (Reprise) ....Nat
"Little Green Snake" ....Sid
"Nine O'Clock" ....Richard
"But Yours" ....Sid and Lily
"Take Me Along" (Reprise) ....Lily, Sid and Townspeople

THE GIRLS AGAINST THE BOYS

(16 performances)

Musical revue in two acts, with sketches and lyrics by Arnold B. Horwitt; music by Richard Lewine; additional music by Albert Hague. Produced by Albert Selden at the Alvin Theatre, November 2, 1959.

Principals—

Bert Lahr	Imelda De Martin
Nancy Walker	Richard France
Shelley Berman	June L. Walker
Dick Van Dyke	Maureen Bailey
Joy Nichols	Buzz Halliday

Mace Barrett

Staged by Aaron Ruben; dances and musical numbers staged by Boris Runanin; scenery and lighting by Ralph Alswang; dance music arranged by John Morris; costumes by Sal Anthony; musical director, Irving Actman; orchestrations by Sid Ramin and Robert Ginzler; production stage manager, Paul Leaf; stage manager, Sterling Mace; press representative, Arthur Cantor.

Sketches and musical numbers—

ACT I

"The Girls Against the Boys" ....Dick Van Dyke, Mace Barrett,
                                        Buzz Halliday and Ensemble
"Rich Butterfly"
  Husband ....Shelley Berman
  Wife ....Nancy Walker
"Can We Save Our Marriage?"
  Counselor ....Dick Van Dyke
  Stella ....June L. Walker
  Harry ....Bert Lahr
"I Gotta Have You" ....Imelda De Martin, Richard France,
                                        Caroljane Abney, Sandra Devlin, Ray
                                        Pointer and Noel Schwartz
"Home Late"
  Husband ....Shelley Berman
  Wife ....Nancy Walker
"I Remember" ....Bert Lahr
  Butler ....Mace Barrett
"Assignation"
  Jock ....Dick Van Dyke
  Cynthia ....Joy Nichols

Essie ....Nancy Walker
Waiter ....Martin Charnin
Counterman ....Ray Pointer
Man at Center Table ....Bob Roman
Max ....Noel Schwartz
Other Patrons ....Cy Young, Jo Ann Tenney, Roger LePage,
    Mal Throne, Mona Pivar and Al Fiorella
Shelley Berman ....Written by Mr. Berman
"Where Did We Go? Out" ....Mace Barrett, Maureen Bailey,
    Richard France and Imelda De Martin
"Too Young to Live" ....Bert Lahr and Nancy Walker
"Overspend" ....Shelley Berman, Joy Nichols and Ensemble

ACT II

"Girls and Boys"
Observer ....Mace Barrett
Mother ....Joy Nichols
Groom ....Dick Van Dyke
Bride ....Imelda De Martin
Best Man ....Richard France
Father ....Bob Roman
Maid of Honor ....Maureen Bailey
Bridesmaids ....Mona Pivar, Margaret Gathright,
    Sandra Devlin and Buzz Halliday
Guests ....The Ensemble
"Nightflight" ....By Arnold Horwitt and Aaron Ruben
Passenger ....Bert Lahr
Girl ....Joy Nichols
Man ....Mal Throne
Hostess ....June L. Walker
Mother ....Buzz Halliday
Four People ....Mace Barrett, Cy Young, Bob
    Roman and Nina Popova
"Light Travelin' Man" ....Shelley Berman and Richard France
Girls ....Sandra Devlin, Caroljane Abney
    and Margaret Gathright

"He and She"
Introduction ....Shelley Berman
He ....Dick Van Dyke
Goat ....Noel Schwartz
Skunks ....Caroljane Abney and Roger LePage
Rabbits ....Mitchell Nutick and Beatrice Salten
Ducks ....Ray Pointer and Mona Pivar
Wolf ....Al Fiorella
Lamb ....Jo Ann Tenney
She ....Nancy Walker
Snake ....Sandra Devlin
It ....Jim Sisco
"Old-Fashioned Girl"
Doorman ....Mal Throne
Monroe Fuller ....Bert Lahr
Tawny ....June L. Walker
Usher ....Beatrice Salten
Treasurer ....Sandra Devlin
Male Dancer ....Roger LePage
Show Girls ....Buzz Halliday, Margaret Gathright, Caroljane
    Abney, Jo Ann Tenney, Ellen Graff and Mona Pivar
Shelley Berman ....Written by Mr. Berman
"Hostility" ....By Arnold Horwitt and Aaron Ruben
Husband ....Bert Lahr
Wife ....Nancy Walker
"Nobody Else But You" ....Bert Lahr and Nancy Walker
Finale ....Entire Company

(Closed November 14, 1959)

THE HIGHEST TREE

(21 performances)

Play in three acts by Dore Schary. Produced by the Theatre Guild and Dore Schary at the Longacre Theatre, November 4, 1959.

Cast of characters—

Aaron Cornish	Kenneth MacKenna
Isabel	Miriam Goldina
Dr. Robert Leigh	William Prince
Susan Ashe	Natalie Schafer
Frederick Ashe	Howard St. John
Frederick Ashe, Jr. (Buzz)	Robert Redford
Steven Cornish	Frank Milan
Caleb Cornish	Richard Anderson
Amy Cornish	Gloria Hoye
Mary Macready	Diana Douglas
Bronislau Partos	Joe De Santis
Jane Ashe	Elizabeth Cole
Arkady Clark	Robert Ritterbusch
John Devereaux	Larry Gates
Gloria Cornish	Shirley Smith

The action of the play takes place in the home of Dr. Aaron Cornish in the East Sixties, New York City. Act I.—Two days before Thanksgiving; early evening. Act II.—Scene 1—Late afternoon; the next day. Scene 2—An hour later. Act III.—Scene 1—Later that night. Scene 2—The next morning; Thanksgiving Day.

Staged by Dore Schary; setting and lighting by Donald Oenslager; costumes by Marvin Reiss; associate producer, Walter Reilly; production manager, Jean Barrere; stage manager, Arthur Marlowe; press representative, Nat Dorfman.

(Closed November 21, 1959)

THE TENTH MAN

(238 performances)
(Continued)

Play in three acts by Paddy Chayefsky. Produced by Saint Subber and Arthur Cantor at the Booth Theatre, November 5, 1959.

Cast of characters—

Hirschman	Arnold Marle
Sexton	David Vardi
Schlissel	Lou Jacobi
Zitorsky	Jack Gilford
Alper	George Voskovec
Foreman	Jacob Ben-Ami
Evelyn Foreman	Risa Schwartz
Arthur Brooks	Donald Harron
Harris	Martin Garner
Rabbi	Gene Saks
Kessler Boys	Alan Manson, Paul Marin
Policeman	Tim Callaghan

The action of the play takes place in an orthodox synagogue. Act I.—Before the morning prayers. Act II.—Scene 1—The morning prayers. Scene 2—Before the afternoon prayers. Act III.—The exorcism.

Staged by Tyrone Guthrie; settings and lighting by David Hays; costumes by Frank Thompson; associate, Caroline Swann; production stage manager, David Kanter; press representatives, Harvey B. Sabinson, David Powers and Ted Goldsmith.

THE SOUND OF MUSIC

(226 performances)
(Continued)

Musical in two acts, suggested by "The Trapp Family Singers" by Maria Augusta Trapp; book by Howard Lindsay and Russel Crouse; lyrics by Oscar Hammerstein II; music by Richard Rodgers. Produced by Leland Hayward, Richard Halliday, Richard Rodgers and Oscar Hammerstein II at the Lunt-Fontanne Theatre, November 16, 1959.

Cast of characters—

Maria Rainer, a postulant at Nonnberg Abbey	Mary Martin
Sister Berthe, Mistress of Novices	Elizabeth Howell
Sister Margaretta, Mistress of Postulants	Muriel O'Malley
The Mother Abbess	Patricia Neway
Sister Sophia	Karen Shepard
Captain Georg Von Trapp	Theodore Bikel
Franz, the butler	John Randolph
Frau Schmidt, the housekeeper	Nan McFarland

Children of Captain Von Trapp:
Liesl	Lauri Peters
Friedrich	William Snowden
Louisa	Kathy Dunn
Kurt	Joseph Stewart
Brigitta	Marilyn Rogers
Marta	Mary Susan Locke
Gretl	Evanna Lien

Rolf Gruber	Brian Davies
Elsa Schraeder	Marion Marlowe
Ursula	Luce Ennis
Max Detweiler	Kurt Kasznar
Herr Zeller	Stefan Gierasch
Baron Elberfeld	Kirby Smith
A Postulant	Sue Yaeger
Admiral Von Schreiber	Michael Gorrin

Neighbors of Captain Von Trapp, nuns, novices, postulants, contestants in the Festival Concert: Joanne Birks, Patricia Brooks, June Card, Dorothy Dallas, Ceil Delly, Luce Ennis, Cleo Fry, Barbara George, Joey Heatherton, Lucas Hoving, Patricia Kelly, Maria Kova, Shirley Mendonca, Kathy Miller, Lorna Nash, Keith Prentice, Nancy Reeves, Bernice Saunders, Connie Sharman, Gloria Stevens, Tatiana Troyanos, Mimi Vondra.

The story is laid in Austria early in 1938. Act I.—Scene 1—Nonnberg Abbey. Scene 2—Mountainside near the Abbey. Scene 3—The office of the Mother Abbess; the next morning. Scene 4—A corridor in the Abbey. Scene 5—The living room of the Trapp Villa; that afternoon. Scene 6—Outside the Trapp Villa; that evening. Scene 7—Maria's bedroom; later that evening. Scene 8—The terrace of the Trapp Villa; six weeks later. Scene 9—A hallway in the Trapp Villa; one week later. Scene 10—The living room; the same evening. Scene 11—A corridor in the Abbey. Scene 12—The office of the Mother Abbess; three days later. Act II.—Scene 1—The terrace; the same day. Scene 2—A corridor in the Abbey; two weeks later. Scene 3—The office of the Mother Abbess; immediately following. Scene 4—A cloister overlooking the chapel. Scene 5—The living room; one month later. Scene 6—The concert hall; three days later. Scene 7—The garden of Nonnberg Abbey; that night.

Staged by Vincent J. Donehue; settings by Oliver Smith; musical numbers staged by Joe Layton; costumes by Lucinda Ballard; Mary Martin's clothes by Mainbocher; lighting by Jean Rosenthal; musical director, Frederick Dvonch; orchestrations by Robert Russell Bennett; choral arrangements by Trude Rittman; production stage manager, Peter Zeisler; stage manager, Randall Brooks; press representatives, Frank Goodman and Ben Washer.

Musical numbers—

ACT I

Preludium
"The Sound of Music" .... Maria
"Maria" ...... Mother Abbess, Sisters Margaretta, Berthe and Sophia
"My Favorite Things" .... Maria, Mother Abbess
"Do Re Mi" .... Maria and Children
"You Are Sixteen" .... Liesl and Rolf
"The Lonely Goatherd" .... Maria and Children
"How Can Love Survive?" .... Elsa, Max and Captain
"The Sound of Music" (Reprise) ...... Maria, Captain and Children
"So Long, Farewell" .... Children
"Climb Every Mountain" .... Mother Abbess

ACT II

"No Way to Stop It" .... Captain, Max and Elsa
"Ordinary Couple" .... Maria and Captain
"Processional" .... Ensemble
"You Are Sixteen" (Reprise) .... Maria and Liesl
"Do Re Mi" (Reprise) .... Maria, Captain and Children
"Edelweiss" .... Captain, Maria and Children
"So Long, Farewell" (Reprise) .... Maria, Captain and Children
"Climb Every Mountain" (Reprise) .... Company

ONLY IN AMERICA

(28 performances)

Play in three acts by Jerome Lawrence and Robert E. Lee, based on the book by Harry Golden. Produced by Herman Shumlin at the Cort Theatre, November 19, 1959.

Cast of characters—

Helen Cheney .... Lynn Hamilton
Herbert Loomis .... Martin Huston
Mrs. Archer-Loomis .... Enid Markey
Harry Golden .... Nehemiah Persoff
Fred .... Daniel Keyes
Wes .... Howard Wierum
Ray .... Wayne Tippit
Telephone Man .... Alan Alda
I. Birnbaum .... Ludwig Donath
Jed .... Josh White, Jr.
Velma .... Dinnie Smith
Lucius Whitmore .... Shepperd Strudwick
Balthasar .... Jerry Wimberly
Calvin .... David Baker
Ruth-Ella .... Charlotte Whaley
Kate Golden .... Shannon Bolin
Hershey M. Stoddard .... Edwin Whitner
Chairman .... Vincent Gardenia
State Senator Claypool .... Harry Holcombe
Dr. Leota Patterson .... Flora Cambell
Legislator .... Laurens Moore
Stenotypist .... Edmund Williams
Bill Drake .... Don Fellows
Young Man .... Norris Borden

The time is the recent past; the place, Charlotte, North Carolina, and the state capitol at Raleigh. Act II takes place five years after Act I.

Staged by Mr. Shumlin; settings by Peter Larkin; costumes by Ruth Morley; lighting by Tharon Musser; production stage manager, Michael Thoma; stage manager, Edmund Williams; press representative, Reuben Rabinovitch.

(Closed December 12, 1959)

FIORELLO!

(218 performances)
(Continued)

Musical comedy in two acts, with book by Jerome Weidman and George Abbott; music by Jerry Bock; lyrics by Sheldon Harnick. Produced by Robert E. Griffith and Harold S. Prince at the Broadhurst Theatre, November 23, 1959.

Cast of characters—

Announcer	Del Horstmann
Fiorello	Tom Bosley
Neil	Bob Holiday
Morris	Nathaniel Frey
Mrs. Pomerantz	Helen Verbit
Mr. Lopez	H. F. Green
Mr. Zappatella	David Collyer
Dora	Pat Stanley
Marie	Patricia Wilson
Ben	Howard Da Silva
Ed Peterson	Del Horstmann
2nd Player	Stanley Simmonds
3rd Player	Michael Quinn
4th Player	Ron Husman
5th Player	David London
6th Player	Julian Patrick
Seedy Man	Joseph Toner
1st Heckler	Bob Bernard
2nd Heckler	Michael Scrittorale
3rd Heckler	Jim Maher
4th Heckler	Joseph Toner
Nina	Pat Turner
Floyd	Mark Dawson
Sophie	Lynn Ross
Thea	Ellen Hanley
Secretary	Mara Landi
Senator	Frederic Downs
Commissioner	Michael Quinn
Frankie Scarpini	Michael Scrittorale
Mitzi	Eileen Rodgers
Florence	Deedy Irwin
Reporter	Julian Patrick
1st Man	Scott Hunter
2nd Man	Michael Scrittorale
Tough Man	David London
Derby	Bob Bernard
Frantic	Stanley Simmonds
Judge Carter	Joseph Toner

Singers: David Collyer, Barbara Gilbert, Del Horstmann, Deedy Irwin, Mara Landi, David London, Julian Patrick, Ginny Perlowin, Patsy Peterson, Silver Saundors, Ron Husmann.

Dancers: Charlene Carter, Bob Bernard, Elaine Cancilla, Ellen Harris, Patricia Harty, Scott Hunter, Bob La Crosse, Lynda Lynch, James Maher, Gregg Owen, Lowell Purvis, Dellas Rennie, Lynn Ross, Dan Siretta, Michael Scrittorale, Pat Turner.

Act I.—New York City, shortly before World War One. Act II.—Ten years later.

Staged by George Abbott; choreography by Peter Gennaro; scenery and lighting by William and Jean Eckart; musical direction by Hal Hastings; orchestrations by Irwin Kostal; dance music arranged by Jack Elliott; production stage manager, Ruth Mitchell; stage manager, Bert Wood; press representatives, Sol Jacobson, Lewis Harmon and Jack Toohey.

Musical numbers—

ACT I

"On the Side of the Angels" .... Bob Holiday, Nathaniel Frey, Patricia Wilson
"Politics and Poker" .... Howard Da Silva and Politicians
"Unfair" .... Tom Bosley, Pat Stanley and Girls
"Marie's Law" .... Patricia Wilson and Nathaniel Frey
"The Name's LaGuardia" .... Tom Bosley and Company
"The Bum Won" .... Howard Da Silva and Politicians
"I Love a Cop" .... Pat Stanley
"I Love a Cop" (Reprise) .... Pat Stanley and Mark Dawson
"Till Tomorrow" .... Ellen Hanley and Company
"Home Again" .... Company

ACT II

"When Did I Fall in Love?" .... Ellen Hanley
"Gentleman Jimmy" .... Eileen Rodgers and Dancing Girls
"Gentleman Jimmy" (Reprise) .... Company
"Little Tin Box" .... Howard Da Silva and Politicians
"The Very Next Man" .... Patricia Wilson
"The Very Next Man" (Reprise) .... Patricia Wilson
Finale .... Company

LYSISTRATA

(24 performances)

Play in two acts by Aristophanes, adapted by Dudley Fitts. Produced by Theatre Incorporated (T. Edward Hambleton and Norris Houghton) at the Phoenix Theatre, November 24, 1959.

Cast of characters—

Lysistrata .... Nan Martin
Kalonike .... Gerry Jedd
Myrrhine .... Sasha Von Scherler
Suburbans .... Alice Drummond, Marcie Hubert
Lampito .... Patricia Falkenhain
Boiotian .... Juliet Randall
Korinthian .... Joanne Ellsperman
Leader of Chorus .... Elliott Sullivan

Men's Chorus
{ Phaidrias .... J. D. Cannon
{ Drunk .... Rex Everhart
{ Lykon .... John Heffernan
{ Strymodoros .... Ray Reinhardt
{ Philourgos .... Edwin Sherin

Leader of Chorus .... Patricia Ripley

Women's Chorus
{ Kratylla .... Alice Drummond
{ Megra .... Joanne Ellsperman
{ Stratyllis .... Betty Hellman
{ Nikodike .... Bette Henritze
{ Kalyke .... Marcie Hubert

Magistrate .... Patrick Hines
Constables .... Thomas Bellin, Harald Horn, John Waller
1st Woman .... Juliet Randall

```
2nd Woman .....................................Marcie Hubert
3rd Woman ....................................Alice Drummond
Kinesias .......................................Donald Madden
Manes ...........................................John Waller
Spartan Herald .................................Thomas Bellin
Spartan Ambassador ..........................Albert Quinton
Spartan Commissioners ..............Thomas Bellin, J. D. Cannon,
                                                  Edwin Sherin
Athenian Commissioners ............John Heffernan, Harald Horn,
                                                  John Waller
Goddess of Peace ............................Martha Cutrufello
Sentry ........................................Ray Reinhardt
Drunk ........................................Rex Everhart
```

The action of the play takes place in Athens: first, a public square; later, beneath the walls of the Akropolis. The time is early in 411 B.C.

Staged by Jean Gascon; settings and costumes by Will Steven Armstrong; lighting by Paul Morrison; music composed by David Amram; choreography by John Waller; stage manager, Richard Blofson; press representatives, Ben Kornzweig, Karl Bernstein and Robert Ganshaw.

(Closed December 13, 1959)

A LOSS OF ROSES

(25 performances)

Play in two acts by William Inge. Produced by Saint Subber and Lester Osterman at the Eugene O'Neill Theatre, November 28, 1959.

Cast of characters—

```
Mrs. Helen Baird .................................Betty Field
Kenny (her son) ...............................Warren Beatty
Geoffrey Beamis (Jelly) .....................Michael J. Pollard
Lila Green .......................................Carol Haney
Ronny Cavendish ...............................James O'Rear
Mme. Olga St. Valentine ...................Margaret Braidwood
Ricky Powers ..................................Robert Webber
Mrs. Mulvaney .................................Joan Morgan
```

The action of the play takes place in the modest bungalow of Mrs. Helen Baird in a small town outside of Kansas City. The year is 1933. Act I.—Scene 1—Late summer. Scene 2—Two hours later. Scene 3—Late the next morning. Act II.—Scene 1—One month later. Scene 2—Early the next morning.

Staged by Daniel Mann; setting by Boris Aronson; costumes by Lucinda Ballard; lighting by Abe Feder; music edited by Robert Emmett Dolan; production stage manager, Burry Fredrik; stage manager, Frank Callender; press representatives, Harvey B. Sabinson, David Powers, Ted Goldsmith and Bud Westman.

(Closed December 19, 1959)

FIVE FINGER EXERCISE

(207 performances)
(Continued)

Play in two acts by Peter Shaffer. Produced by Frederick Brisson and the Playwrights' Company, by arrangement with H. M. Tennent, Ltd., at the Music Box Theatre, December 2, 1959.

Cast of characters—

Louise Harrington .... Jessica Tandy
Stanley Harrington .... Roland Culver
Clive Harrington .... Brian Bedford
Pamela Harrington .... Juliet Mills
Walter Langer .... Michael Bryant
    The action of the play takes place in the Stanley Harringtons' week-end country house in Suffolk, England. Act I.—Scene 1—A Saturday morning in early September; breakfast time. Scene 2—Late October; after dinner Saturday night. Act II.—Scene 1—The following (Sunday) morning; breakfast. Scene 2—Sunday night; after dinner.
    Staged by John Gielgud; production designed by Oliver Smith; lighting by Tharon Musser; production stage manager, Fred Herbert; stage manager, William Dodds; press representative, William Fields.

SILENT NIGHT, LONELY NIGHT

(124 performances)

Play in two acts by Robert Anderson. Produced by the Playwrights' Company at the Morosco Theatre, December 3, 1959.

Cast of characters—

Katherine .... Barbara Bel Geddes
Mae .... Eda Heinemann
John .... Henry Fonda
Janet .... Lois Nettleton
Philip .... Bill Berger
Jerry .... Peter de Vise
    The action of the play takes place in a room in a Colonial Inn in a New England town. Act I.—Scene 1—Christmas Eve. Scene 2—Later that evening. Act II.—Scene 1—Later that night. Scene 2—Christmas morning.
    Staged by Peter Glenville; production designed and lighted by Jo Mielziner; costumes by Theoni V. Aldredge; production stage manager, Keene Curtis; stage manager, Fred Baker; press representative, William Fields.

(Closed March 19, 1960)

JOLLY'S PROGRESS

(9 performances)

Play in three acts by Lonnie Coleman. Produced by the Theatre Guild and Arthur Loew at the Longacre Theatre, December 5, 1959.

Cast of characters—

Robie Sellers .... Charles McClelland
Warren Holly .... James Knight
Buford Williams .... Peter Gumeny
Charlie .... Joseph Boland
Lon Keiler .... Drummond Erskine
Mr. Scarborough .... Laurie Main
Mr. Mendelsohn .... Nat Burns
Reverend Furze .... Ellis Rabb
Emma Ford .... Anne Revere
David Adams .... Wendell Corey
Jolly Rivers .... Eartha Kitt

Portia Bates ....Joanne Barry
Dora ....Vinnette Carroll
Thompson Bates ....Humphrey Davis
Thelma ....Eulabelle Moore
    Act I.—Scene 1—A train station in Pluma, Alabama; early spring.
Scene 2—The David Adams house; the following morning. Scene 3—
Two weeks later. Act II.—Scene 1—Two weeks later. Scene 2—
Sunday night. Act III.—Scene 1—Two weeks later. Scene 2—The
station; a day in September.
    Staged by Alex Segal; settings by George Jenkins; costumes by Gene
Coffin; stage manager, Karl Nielsen; press representatives, Nat Dorf-
man and Dick Weaver.

(Closed December 12, 1959)

SARATOGA

(80 performances)

Musical in two acts, based on "Saratoga Trunk" by Edna Ferber;
with book by Morton DaCosta; music by Harold Arlen; lyrics by
Johnny Mercer. Produced by Robert Fryer at the Winter Garden,
December 7, 1959.

Cast of characters—

Cupide ....Tun Tun
Clio Dulaine ....Carol Lawrence
Kakou ....Carol Brice
Belle Piquery ....Odette Myrtil
The Drapery Man ....Mark Zeller
The Carpenter ....Albert Popwell
Shorty ....Augie Rios
Maudey ....Brenda Long
The Charwoman ....Virginia Capers
Mrs. LeClerc ....Martha King
M. Augustin Haussy ....Richard Graham
Clint Maroon ....Howard Keel
M. Begué ....Truman Gaige
Grandmother Dulaine ....Natalie Core
Madame Dulaine ....Beatrice Bushkin
Charlotte Thérèse ....Jeannine Masterson
Léon, a waiter ....Mark Zeller
Editor ....Truman Gaige
Haberdashery Clerk ....Frank Green
Fabric Salesman ....Barney Johnston
M. LaFosse ....Lanier Davis
Mrs. Sophie Bellop ....Edith King
Mrs. Porcelain ....Natalie Core
Mr. Gould ....Truman Gaige
Bart Van Steed ....Warde Donovan
Mr. Bean ....James Millhollin
Daisy Porcelain ....Gerrianne Raphael
Clarissa Van Steed ....Isabella Hoopes
Miss Diggs ....Janyce Wagner
    Market vendors, townspeople, waiters, busboys, gamblers, croupiers,
hotel guests and others: Betsy Bridge, Beatrice Bushkin, Virginia
Capers, Martha King, Ina Kurland, Jeannine Masterson, Carol Taylor,
Gerrianne Raphael, Lois Van Pelt, Janyce Wagner, Beverley Jane
Welch, Socrates Birsky, John Blanchard, Joseph Crawford, Lanier
Davis, Paul Dixon, Vito Durante, José Falcion, Julius Fields, John
Ford, Jerry Fries, Gene Gavin, Frank Green, Nathaniel Horne, Barney
Johnston, Louis Kosman, Jack Matthew, Oran Osburn, John Pero,
Herold Pierson, Albert Popwell, Charles Queenan, Mark Zeller, Mer-
ritt Thompson.

Children: Brenda Long, Linda Wright, Augie Rios, Wayne Robertson.

Act I.—Scene 1—The Rampart Street house, New Orleans, 1880. Scene 2—Exterior of the Rampart Street house. Scene 3—The waterfront market. Scene 4—The museum. Scene 5—Begué's Restaurant. Scene 6—The garden of the Rampart Street house. Scene 7—The Casino. Scene 8—The United States Hotel, Saratoga. Scene 9—Clint's and Clio's rooms in the United States Hotel. Act II.—Scene 1—The Springs, Saratoga. Scene 2—Corridor of the United States Hotel. Scene 3—Clint's and Clio's rooms. Scene 4—The verandah. Scene 5—The corridor. Scene 6—On a flatcar and at the railroad station, Binghamton, New York. Scene 7—The corridor. Scene 8—The ballroom of the United States Hotel.

Staged by Morton DaCosta; settings and costumes by Cecil Beaton; choreography by Ralph Beaumont; lighting by Jean Rosenthal; musical direction by Jerry Arlen; vocal arrangements by Herbert Greene; orchestrations by Philip J. Lang; dance music by Genevieve Pitot; production stage manager, Edward Padula; stage manager, Duane Camp; press representative, Arthur Cantor.

Musical numbers—

ACT I

"I'll Be Respectable" ....Clio
"One Step—Two Step" ....Clio, Shorty, Maudey and Ensemble
"Gettin' a Man" ....Belle and Kakou
"Petticoat High" ......Charwoman, Clio, Belle, Cupide and Ensemble
"Why Fight This?" ....Clio and Clint
"Game of Poker" ....Clint and Clio
"Love Held Lightly" ....Belle
"Game of Poker" (Reprise) ....Clio, Clint and Belle
"The Gamblers" ....Clio and the Gamblers and the Croupiers
"Saratoga" ....Clint and Clio
"Saratoga" (Reprise) ....Ensemble
"The Gossip Song" ....Mrs. Bellop and Ensemble
"Countin' Our Chickens" ....Clio and Clint
"You or No One" ....Clint

ACT II

"The Cure" ....Ensemble
"The Men Who Run the Country" ....The Robber Barons
"The Man in My Life" ....Clio and Clint
"The Polka" ....Clio, Bart and Ensemble
"Love Held Lightly" (Reprise) ....Clio
"Goose Never Be a Peacock" ....Kakou
"Dog Eat Dog" ....Clint and His Men
"The Railroad Fight" ....Clint, Cupide and the Men
"Petticoat High" (Reprise) ....Clio and Ensemble

(Closed February 13, 1960)

THE FIGHTING COCK

(87 performances)

Play in two acts by Jean Anouilh, adapted by Lucienne Hill. Produced by Kermit Bloomgarden Productions, Inc., at the ANTA Theatre, December 8, 1959.

Cast of characters—

The General ....Rex Harrison
The Doctor ....Geoffrey Lumb
Toto, the General's son ....Claude Gersene
Marie-Christine, the General's daughter ....Judy Sanford

The Milkman's Son ....Rhoden Streeter
The Milkman ....Roger De Koven
Father Gregory ....Michael Gough
Sophie, the General's daughter ....Margo Anders
Tarquin Edward Mendigales ....Roddy McDowall
Bise, the General's sister ....Jane Lillig
Aglae, the General's wife ....Natasha Parry
Lebelluc ....Arthur Treacher
Michepain ....Gerald Hiken
Baron Henri Belazor ....Alan MacNaughtan
    Time: The present. Place: a country house in France. Act I.—Scene
1—The General's study; late afternoon. Scene 2—The same; the same
evening. Act II.—The garden; an afternoon a few days later.
    Staged by Peter Brook; settings and costumes by Rolf Gerard; light-
ing by Howard Bay; production stage manager, Kermit Kegley; stage
manager, Walter Neal; press representative, Arthur Cantor.

(Closed February 20, 1960)

GOODBYE, CHARLIE

(109 performances)

Comedy in two acts by George Axelrod. Produced by Leland
Hayward at the Lyceum Theatre, December 16, 1959.

Cast of characters—

Greg Morris ....Frank Roberts
George Tracy ....Sydney Chaplin
Franny Saltzmann ....Michelle Reiner
Irving ....Clinton Anderson
Mr. Shriber ....Dan Frazer
Rusty Mayerling ....Sarah Marshall
Charlie ....Lauren Bacall
    The setting of the play is the beach house of the late Charlie Sorel,
a few miles north of Malibu, California. The time is the present.
Act I.—Scene 1—About eight o'clock Sunday evening. Scene 2—A
half hour later. Scene 3—A few minutes later. Act II.—Scene 1—
Late the following afternoon. Scene 2—That night.
    Staged by George Axelrod; setting by Oliver Smith; lighting by
Peggy Clark; production stage manager, David Grey, Jr.; stage manager, Frank Roberts; press representative, Abner D. Klipstein.

(Closed March 19, 1960)

PICTURES IN THE HALLWAY

(11 performances)

Revival of the stage reading, adapted by Paul Shyre from the second of six autobiographical volumes written by Sean O'Casey. Produced by Theatre Incorporated (T. Edward Hambleton and Norris
Houghton) at the Phoenix Theatre, December 26, 1959.

Principals—

Mildred Dunnock	J. D. Cannon
Donald Madden	Rex Everhart
Gerry Jedd	Eric Berry
As the Dubliners—	
Johnny Casside	Old Biddy
Mrs. Casside	Mr. Greenberg
Archie Casside	Mr. Dyke
Young Kelly	Alice Boyd, the Presbyterian
Uncle Tom	Reverend Harry Fletcher
The Warder	Ayamonn O'Farrell
Mrs. Middleton	Mrs. Nearus
The Dung-Dodgers	The Doctor
Ella	Daisy Battles
	Mrs. Anthony Dovergull

Staged by Stuart Vaughan; flutist, John Perras; stage manager, Richard Blofson; press representatives, Ben Kornzweig, Karl Bernstein and Robert Ganshaw.

(Closed January 3, 1960)

THE ANDERSONVILLE TRIAL

(177 performances)
(Continued)

Play in two acts by Saul Levitt. Produced by William Darrid, Eleanore Saidenberg and Daniel Hollywood at Henry Miller's Theatre, December 29, 1959.

Cast of characters—

General Lew Wallace, President of the Court ....Russell Hardie
Lieutenant, Clerk of the Court ....Robert Burr
Lt. Col. N. P. Chipman, the Judge Advocate ....George C. Scott
Otis H. Baker, the Defense Counsel ....Albert Dekker
Captain Williams ....Al Henderson
Henry Wirz, the Defendant ....Herbert Berghof
Louis Schade, Assistant Defense Counsel ....James Arenton
Lt. Col. Chandler ....Robert Carroll
Dr. John C. Bates ....Ian Keith
Ambrose Spencer ....Moultrie Patten
Dr. C. M. Ford, Prison Surgeon ....Douglas Herrick
Major D. Hosmer, Assistant Judge Advocate ....Howard Wierum
James H. Davidson ....James Greene
Jasper Culver ....Robert Gerringer
George W. Gray ....Frank Sutton
Newspapermen ....Robert Mayer, Richard Poston, William Scharf
Union Soldiers ....Robert Downey, Martin West, Lou Frizzell

	General Mott ....Clifford Carpenter
	General Thomas ....Taylor Graves
	General Geary ....John Leslie
Assisting Judges	General Fessenden ....Owen Pavitt
	General Ballier ....William Hussung
	Colonel Allcock ....Archie Smith
	Colonel Stibbs ....Freeman Meskimen

The action of the play takes place in the United States Court of Claims, Washington, D. C.   Act I.—Scene 1—A day in August, 1865. Scene 2—Some time later.   Act II.—Scene 1—The following morning. Scene 2—The next day.

Staged by Jose Ferrer; production designed and lighted by Will Steven Armstrong; production stage manager, Morty Halpern; stage manager, Julian Barry; press representatives, Frank Goodman and Ben Washer.

A MIGHTY MAN IS HE

(5 performances)

Comedy in three acts by Arthur Kober and George Oppenheimer. Produced by Edward Joy and Diana Green at the Cort Theatre, January 6, 1960.

Cast of characters—

Edwards	Claud Allister
Rachel Krupp	Nancy Cushman
Jason Smith	Doug Lambert
Frederick McMahon	Gene Blakely
Barbara Smith	Nancy Kelly
Elizabeth Talbot	Kimetha Laurie
Doctor Holden	John Cecil Holm
Phyllis Clyde	Polly Rowles
Jennifer Grant	Diana Van Der Vlis

The action of the play takes place in the living room of Alexander Smith's home in New York City. The time is the present. Act I.—Early afternoon. Act II.—An hour or so later. Act III.—A few minutes later.

Staged by Reginald Denham; scenery and lighting by Frederick Fox; costumes by Virginia Volland; production stage manager, William Weaver; stage manager, Alan Bandler; press representative, Harvey Sabinson.

(Closed January 9, 1960)

PEER GYNT

(32 performances)

Play in three acts by Henrik Ibsen; English version by Norman Ginsbury. Produced by Theatre Incorporated (T. Edward Hambleton and Norris Houghton) at the Phoenix Theatre, January 12, 1960.

Cast of characters—

Peer Gynt	Fritz Weaver
Aase, his mother	Joanna Roos
Old Woman	Gerry Jedd
Kari	Patricia Ripley
A Man	Albert Quinton
A Woman	Patricia Falkenhain
Aslak, the smith	Rex Everhart
Ingrid's Father	Patrick Hines
Mads Moen, the bridegroom	Nicholas Kepros
His Father	Elliott Sullivan
His Mother	Joanne Ellsperman
Solveig	Inga Swenson
Her Father	John Heffernan
Helga, her sister	Jan Jarrett
Ingrid, the bride	Alice Drummond
1st Cowherd Girl	Jenifer Heyward
2nd Cowherd Girl	Juliet Randall
3rd Cowherd Girl	Marcie Hubert
The Woman in Green	Patricia Falkenhain
The Troll King	Eric Berry
His Chamberlain	Albert Quinton

The Boyg ....Albert Quinton
The Ugly Brat ....Nicholas Kepros
Mister Cotton ....Patrick Hines
M. Ballon ....Eric Berry
Herr Von Eberkopf ....Rex Everhart
Eunuch ....John Heffernan
Thief ....Nicholas Kepros
Receiver ....Elliott Sullivan
Anitra ....Gerry Jedd
Begriffenfeldt ....Patrick Hines
Keepers { Schlingelberg ....Ray Reinhardt
         { Schaffman ....Thomas Bellin
         { Schmidt ....John Heffernan
Fellah ....Albert Quinton
Hussein ....Edwin Sherin
Sea Captain ....Elliott Sullivan
Strange Passenger ....J. D. Cannon
Sailors ....John Heffernan, Nicholas Kepros,
                                  Albert Quinton, Ray Reinhardt
Button Moulder ....J. D. Cannon
    Wedding guests, trolls, sailors, Anitra's attendants, madwomen and
churchgoers: Alice Drummond, Joanne Ellsperman, Betty Hellman,
Bette Henritze, Jenifer Heyward, Marcie Hubert, Juliet Randall,
Patricia Ripley, Thomas Bellin, John Heffernan, Nicholas Kepros, Ray
Reinhardt, Edwin Sherin, John Waller.
    The action of the play takes place during the 19th Century in Nor-
way and North Africa.
    Staged by Stuart Vaughan; settings and costumes by Will Steven
Armstrong; lighting by Tharon Musser; choreography by John Waller;
music and songs composed by David Amram; stage manager, Richard
Blofson; press representatives, Ben Kornzweig, Karl Bernstein and
Robert Ganshaw.

(Closed February 7, 1960)

A DISTANT BELL

(5 performances)

Play in three acts by Katherine Morrill. Produced by Norman
Twain at the Eugene O'Neill Theatre, January 13, 1960.

Cast of characters—

Keene Stanfield ....Frieda Altman
Dora Greer ....Nydia Westman
Burton Greer ....Richard Nicholls
Mrs. Brighton ....Mabel Cochran
Lucy Greer ....Martha Scott
Barrett Greer ....Patricia Roe
Waverly Greer ....Phyllis Love
Flagg Greer ....Evans Evans
Mr. Wilbur ....Louis Girard
John Creighton ....Andrew Prine
Clara Hurd ....Lynda Carr
Jackson Dunne ....Mark Fleischman
Arthur Wilson ....Dale Helward
Newsboy ....Michael Gleason
    The action of the play takes place in the Greer home in a small New
England town in the mid-thirties. Act I.—Scene 1—Early morning in
late April. Scene 2—Early evening the following Saturday. Scene 3—
Late afternoon three weeks later. Act II.—Scene 1—Eleven P.M. that
night. Scene 2—Three A.M. a week later. Scene 3—The following
afternoon. Act III.—Scene 1—Nine P.M. that evening. Scene 2—
Early the next morning.
    Staged by Norman Twain; settings by Mordecai Gorelik; lighting by

Peggy Clark; costumes by Theoni V. Aldredge; production stage manager, Frederic deWilde; stage manager, Howard Fischer; press representatives, Ben Kornzweig and Karl Bernstein.

(Closed January 16, 1960)

CUT OF THE AXE

(2 performances)

Play in two acts by Sheppard Kerman, based on the novel by Delmar Jackson. Produced by Rita Allen and Milton Cassel at the Ambassador Theatre, February 1, 1960.

Cast of characters—

Roy Slater	Charles Carlson
John Brown	Paul Sparer
Morales	Cal Bellini
Homer Fry	James Westerfield
Paul Carr	Robert Lansing
Harry Nichols	Milo Boulton
Rollie Evans	Thomas Mitchell
Martha Evans	Susan Brown
Doc	John Gibson
Charlie	Raymond Van Sickle
Johnson	William Severs
John Nichols	John Stark
Pete	John Thomas

Townspeople: Ernesto Gonzales, Joe Hardy, James Carville, Michael Egan and Herbert Voss.

The action takes place in a sparsely populated town in a midwestern state. The time is from dawn to dusk of the fifth of July in the present. Act I.—Scene 1—The jail and office of Marshal Homer Fry. Scene 2—Home of Rollie Evans. Scene 3—Same as Scene 1. Act II.—Scene 1—The jail and office of Marshal Homer Fry. Scene 2—Home of Rollie Evans; the jail; the office.

Staged by John O'Shaughnessy; settings and lighting by Howard Bay; costumes by Audré; production stage manager, Phil Friedman; stage manager, Robert Crawley; press representative, Reuben Rabinovitch.

(Closed February 2, 1960)

THE DEADLY GAME

(39 performances)

Play in two acts by James Yaffe, based on a novel by Friedrich Duerrenmatt. Produced by Alton Wilkes and Joe Manchester, in association with Emil Coleman, at the Longacre Theatre, February 2, 1960.

Cast of characters—

Emile Carpeau	Ludwig Donath
Bernard Laroque	Claude Dauphin
Joseph Pillet	Pat Malone
Pierre	Frank Campanella
Howard Trapp	Pat Hingle

Gustave Kummer ....Max Adrian
A Visitor ....Frances Helm
The action of the play takes place in the house of Emile Carpeau in the Swiss Alps. Act I.—A winter evening. Act II.—Scene 1—The same evening. Scene 2—Several days later.
Staged by William Gaskill; production designed and lighted by Wolfgang Roth; associate producers, Morton Segal and Barbara Griner; production stage manager, George Mully; press representative, Harvey B. Sabinson.

(Closed March 5, 1960)

ROMAN CANDLE

(5 performances)

Comedy in three acts by Sidney Sheldon. Produced by Ethel Linder Reiner at the Cort Theatre, February 3, 1960.

Cast of characters—

Sgt. Eddie Remick ....Eddie Firestone
Eleanor Winston ....Julia Meade
Mrs. Otis ....Mildred Chandler
Sgt. Smitty ....Stan Watt
Mark Baxter ....Robert Sterling
Senator John Winston ....Lauren Gilbert
Lieut. General Dayton ....Walter Greaza
Admiral Trenton ....Stephen Elliott
Colonel Grey ....Lon Clark
Elizabeth Brown ....Inger Stevens
Fire Control Officer ....John Lasell
Range Officer ....Chester Doherty
Secretary of Defense ....Stan Watt
Sgt. Seidel ....Tony Kraber
Dr. Alden ....Lloyd Gough
Act I.—The adjoining apartments of Mark Baxter and Eleanor Winston on the fifth floor of the Washington Apartments in Washington, D. C. The time is the present—a day in spring. Act II.—Scene 1—A secret missile launching site in Alaska; dawn the following day. Scene 2—The Washington Apartments; that afternoon. Scene 3—The missile site; immediately following. Scene 4—Washington Apartments; the next morning. Act III.—A short time later.
Staged by David Pressman; settings and lighting by David Hays; costumes by Ruth Morley; production stage manager, Bernard Gersten; stage manager, Leon Gersten; press representatives, Frank Goodman, Ben Washer and Ruth Cage.

(Closed February 6, 1960)

A LOVELY LIGHT

(17 performances)

A dramatization of the poems and letters of Edna St. Vincent Millay, arranged and presented by Dorothy Stickney. Produced by Sol Hurok at the Hudson Theatre, February 8, 1960.

ACT I

"The world stands out on either side
No wider than the heart is wide."

ACT II

"I know not how such things can be!
I breathed my soul back into me."

ACT III

"The soul can split the sky in two
And let the face of God shine through."

Staged by Howard Lindsay; setting and lighting by Lee Watson; Miss Stickney's gowns by Helene Pons; stage manager, John Christopher; press representative, Walter Alford.

(Closed February 20, 1960)

BEG, BORROW OR STEAL

(5 performances)

Musical in two acts, from a story by Marvin Seiger and Bud Freeman; with book and lyrics by Bud Freeman; music by Leon Prober. Produced by Eddie Bracken with Carroll and Harris Masterson at the Martin Beck Theatre, February 10, 1960.

Cast of characters—

Mrs. Plonsky	Jean Bruno
Junior	Biff McGuire
Ollie	Estelle Parsons
Phil	Betty Rhodes
Judy	Karen Sargent
Clara	Betty Garrett
Pistol	Eddie Bracken
Rafe	Larry Parks
Jason	Roy Stuart
Ethel	Bernice Massi
Lovers	Mary Sullivan and Del Hanley
Modern Dance Leader	Sally Lee
Dance Class	Carmen Morales, Garold Gardner, Ellen Halpin and Willard Nagel
Rug Hooker	Michael Davis
Pottery Girl	Colleen Corkrey
Bar Girl	Esther Horrocks
Knitters	Fran Leone and Keith Willis
Painter	Tom Hester
Chess Players	Michael Stuart and Arthur Whitfield
Flamenco Dancers	Adriana Keathley and Harold Da Silva
Guitarist	Fred Kimbrough
Kibitzer	Mara Wirt
Poet	John Tormey
Poetry Lovers	Shelia Dee, Georgia Kennedy and Virginia Barnes
Sculptor	Chuck Arnett
Model	Beti Seay
Mobile Artist	Lucinda Stevens
Frieda	Claiborne Cary
Patriot	Jack Drummond
Sam Lee Howard	Richard Armbruster
Muscle	Bill Linton
Koppisch	Richard Woods
Blanding	David Doyle

The action takes place in a run-down section of a monster American city. Time: the 1950s. Act I.—Scene 1—The street. Scene 2—The store. Scene 3—The street. Scene 4—The pit. Scene 5—The park.

Scene 6—The street. Scene 7—The pit. Scene 8—Rafe's attic. Scene 9—The store. Scene 10—The street. Scene 11—The pad. Scene 12—The pit. Act II.—Scene 1—The office. Scene 2—The street. Scene 3—Chez pit. Scene 4—The office. Scene 5—The street. Scene 6—The pad. Scene 7—Chez pit. Scene 8—The street. Scene 9—The store.

Staged by Billy Matthews; dances and musical numbers by Peter Hamilton; directed by David Doyle; scenery, lighting and costumes by Carter Morningstar; musical direction by Hal Hidey; orchestrations by Peter Matz and Hal Hidey; stage managers, Bob Paschall, Joseph Dooley, Bruce Blaine; press representatives, Harry Davies and Irvin Dorfman.

Musical numbers—

ACT I

"Some Little People" ....The Ensemble
"Rootless" ....Biff McGuire
"What Are We Gonna Do Tonight?" ...Estelle Parsons, Betty Rhodes
  and Karen Sargent
"Poetry and All That Jazz" ....Claiborne Cary and Ensemble
"Don't Stand Too Close to the Picture" ....Larry Parks, Betty Garrett
  and Ensemble
"Beg, Borrow or Steal" (Recitative) ....Larry Parks
"Beg, Borrow or Steal" ....Larry Parks
"No One Knows Me" ....Betty Garrett
"Zen Is When" ....Eddie Bracken, Biff McGuire, Bernice Massi
  and Roy Stuart
(Ballet danced by the Ensemble)
  Soloist ....Colleen Corkrey
  The Lovers ....Carmen Morales and Arthur Whitfield
"Clara" ....Biff McGuire
"You've Got Something to Say" ......Larry Parks and Betty Garrett
"You've Got Something to Say" (Reprise) ....Larry Parks, Betty
  Garrett, Eddie Bracken, Biff
  McGuire and Company

ACT II

"Presenting Clara Spencer" ....Betty Garrett. Assisted by Keith
  Willis, Michael Stuart, Chuck Arnett,
  Harold Da Silva, Willard Nagel, Garold
  Gardner and Arthur Whitfield
"I Can't Stop Talking" ....Betty Garrett and Biff McGuire
"It's All in Your Mind" ....Larry Parks and Betty Garrett
"In Time" ....Biff McGuire
"Think" ....Betty Garrett
"Little People" ....Eddie Bracken and Company
  Danced by Keith Willis, Sally Lee and Michael Stuart
"Rafesville, U.S.A." ....Bernice Massi and Roy Stuart
"Beg, Borrow or Steal" (Reprise) ....Larry Parks and Ensemble
"Let's Be Strangers Again" ....Betty Garrett and Biff McGuire
"Little People" (Reprise) ....The Entire Company

(Closed February 13, 1960)

THE LONG DREAM

(5 performances)

Play in three acts by Ketti Frings, based on the novel by Richard Wright. Produced by Cheryl Crawford and Joel Schenker, in association with October Productions, Inc., at the Ambassador Theatre, February 17, 1960.

Cast of characters—

Rex (Fishbelly) Tucker ....Al Freeman, Jr.
Tyree Tucker ....Lawrence Winters
Emma Tucker ....Gertrude Jeannette
Tony ....Josh White, Jr.
Chris ....Clarence Williams, III
Zeke ....Edward Phifer
Chief of Police Gerald Canley ....R. G. Armstrong
Clem ....Clifton James
Phil ....Jim Jeter
Doc Bruce ....Stanley Greene
Lt. Harvey ....Charles A. McDaniel
Gladys ....Isabelle Cooley
Maude Carter ....Helen Martin
Vera Mason ....Joya Sherrill
Jim Bowers ....Walter Mason
Mr. McWilliams ....Arthur Storch
Rev. Ragland ....John Garth, III
White Girl ....Barbara Loden
   Other citizens of Clintonville: Jeannette DuBois, Marshall Hill,
Peggy Pope, Leonard Parker, Mary Louise and Sylvia Ray.
   The action of the play takes place during three weeks in summer in
Clintonville, Mississippi.   Act I.—Scene 1—The Black Belt; Tyree's
home. Scene 2—The police station. Scene 3—The grove. Scene 4—
The Tucker Funeral Parlor. Act II.—Scene 1—The Tucker Funeral
Parlor. Scene 2—Same; that evening. Scene 3—The high school gym.
Act III.—Scene 1—The Tucker Funeral Parlor. Scene 2—The Black
Belt. Scene 3—Vera's house.
   Staged by Lloyd Richards; scenery by Zvi Geyra; lighting by Tharon
Musser; costumes by Ruth Morley; original music by Pembroke Daven-
port; production stage manager, Robert Downing; stage manager, James
E. Wall; press representative, Arthur Cantor.

(Closed February 20, 1960)

CALIGULA

(38 performances)

Play in two acts by Albert Camus, adapted by Justin O'Brien.
Produced by Chandler Cowles, Charles Bowden and Ridgely Bullock
at the Fifty-fourth Street Theatre, February 16, 1960.

Cast of characters—

Octavius ....Frederic Tozere
Darling ....Sorrell Booke
Lucius ....Edgar Daniels
Cassius ....James O'Rear
Helicon ....Edward Binns
Cherae ....Philip Bourneuf
Scipio ....Clifford David
Guard ....Gene Pellegrini
Caligula ....Kenneth Haigh
Caesonia ....Colleen Dewhurst
Major Domo ....Frederic Warriner
Mucius ....Victor Thorley
Mereia ....Harrison Dowd
Mucius' Wife ....Sandra Kazan
Metullus ....John Ramondetta
1st Poet ....Paul Cambeilh
2nd Poet ....Ralph Lee
3rd Poet ....Roger C. Carmel
4th Poet ....John Wynne-Evans
5th Poet ....Dal Jenkins

6th Poet ....Gene Gregory
Wives ....Marion Baker, Francesca Fontaine, Barbara Hall
Patricians ....Wyley Hancock, Al Kavanagh,
Al Leberfeld, Nick Savian
Slaves ....Henri Leon Baker, Michael Baseleon,
Ralph Newman, Garth Pillsbury
Soldiers ....Matt Bennett, Gordon Blackmon, Cliff Carnell,
Bill Fletcher, Frank Koomen, Grant Michaels,
T. J. Murphy, John Tyrános

Act I.—Scene 1—The Imperial Palace. Scene 2—A room in Cherea's house. Act II.—Scenes 1 and 2—The Imperial Palace.

Staged by Sidney Lumet; scenery and costumes by Will Steven Armstrong; lighting by Jean Rosenthal; music by David Amram; production stage manager, Richard Evans; stage manager, Richard Casey; press representatives, Frank Goodman, Ben Washer and Ruth Cage.

(Closed March 19, 1960)

THE COOL WORLD

(2 performances)

Play in two acts by Warren Miller and Robert Rossen, based on the novel by Mr. Miller. Produced by Lester Osterman at the Eugene O'Neill Theatre, February 22, 1960.

Cast of characters—

Duke Custis ....Billy Dee Williams
Hurst ....P. Jay Sidney
Priest ....Raymond Saint-Jacques
Gramma Custis ....Eulabelle Moore
Mrs. Custis ....Lynn Hamilton
Mrs. Thurston ....Alice Childress
Foxy ....Clebert Ford
Mau Mau ....Philip Hepburn
Cowboy ....George Gatlin
Rod ....Martin Golar
Cherokee ....Cheyenne Sorocki
Saint ....Herb Coleman
Savage ....Donald Blakely
Little Man ....Lamont Washington
Blood ....Calvin Lockhart
Lu Ann ....Alease Whittington
Royal Baron ....Roscoe Lee Browne
Miss Dewpont ....Hilda Simms
Father Christmas ....Wardell Saunders
Hermit ....Melvin Stewart
Girl ....Cicely Tyson
Boy ....David Downing
Pusher ....Maxwell Glanville
Harrison Thurston ....James Earl Jones
Chester ....Harold Scott
Bebop ....Marvin Camillo
Lucky ....Art Aveilhe
Old Man ....Jim Oyster
Woman at the Beach ....Ethel Ayler
First Policeman ....Jim Oyster
Second Policeman ....Duke Williams

Prologue—The street. Act I.—Scene 1—The street; morning. Scene 2—The Custis apartment; immediately following. Scene 3—The clubhouse of the Royal Crocodiles; that evening. Scene 4—Royal Baron's apartment; thirty minutes later. Scene 5—Lu Ann's bedroom; late that night. Scene 6—Hermit's Luncheonette; several days later. Act II.—Scene 1—The clubhouse; later. Scene 2—Chester's apartment; that evening. Scene 3—The clubhouse; evening of the next day. Scene 4—Coney Island; the next day. Scene 5—The street; later the same night. Scene 6—Hurst's apartment; an hour later.

Staged by Robert Rossen; settings and lighting by Howard Bay; costumes by Ann Roth; production stage manager, Charles Durand; stage manager, Louis Criss; press representative, Harvey B. Sabinson.

(Closed February 23, 1960)

PICCOLO TEATRO DI MILANO

(16 performances)

"The Servant of Two Masters" ("Arlecchino, Servitore di due Padroni"), a play in three acts by Carlo Goldoni. Produced by Jerry Hoffman, in association with the New York City Center, at the New York City Center, February 23, 1960.

Cast of characters—

Pantalone de'Bisognosi	Gianrico Tedeschi
Clarice, his daughter	Giulia Lazzarini
Doctor Lombardi	Bruno Lanzarini
Silvio, his son	Giancarlo Dettori
Beatrice, from Turin (in man's clothes, impersonating Federigo Rasponi)	Relda Ridoni
Florindo Aretusi, from Turin, her lover	Warner Bentivegna
Brighella, innkeeper	Gianfranco Mauri
Smeraldina, Clarice's maid	Narcisa Bonati
Arlecchino, servant to Beatrice and then to Florindo	Marcello Moretti
A Servant of the Inn	Vincenzo de Toma
A Porter	Angelo Corti
A Servant	Ferruccio Soleri
Other Servants	Augusto Salvi, Giuliano Mariana, Fernando Mazzola

The action of the play takes place in Venice.

Staged by Giorgio Strehler; sets and costumes by Ezio Frigerio; music by Fiorenzo Carpi; masks by Amleto Sartori; stage manager, Corrado Nardi; press representative, Arthur M. Brilant.

(Closed March 6, 1960)

THE TUMBLER

(5 performances)

Play in three acts by Benn W. Levy. Produced by Alfred de Liagre, Jr. and Roger L. Stevens, in association with Laurence Olivier, at the Helen Hayes Theatre, February 24, 1960.

Cast of characters—

Lennie	Rosemary Harris
Kell	Charlton Heston
Nina	Martha Scott
The Doctor	William Mervyn
George	Donald Moffat

Act I.—Scene 1—A barn; on a mid-summer's eve. Scene 2—The same; a few hours later. Act II.—Scene 1—The farmhouse kitchen;

a little later. Scene 2—The same; the following morning. Act III.—
The barn; an hour or two later.

Staged by Laurence Olivier; settings by Roger Furse; lighting by
Tharon Musser; associate producer, Don Herbert; production stage
manager, William Chambers; stage manager, Arthur Marlowe; press
representatives, Frank Goodman and Ben Washer.

(Closed February 27, 1960)

TOYS IN THE ATTIC

(110 performances)
(Continued)

Play in three acts by Lillian Hellman. Produced by Kermit
Bloomgarden at the Hudson Theatre, February 25, 1960.

Cast of characters—

Carrie Berniers ....Maureen Stapleton
Anna Berniers ....Anne Revere
Gus ....Charles McRae
Albertine Prine ....Irene Worth
Henry Simpson ....Percy Rodriguez
Julian Berniers ....Jason Robards, Jr.
Lily Berniers ....Rochelle Oliver
Taxi Driver ....William Hawley
Moving Men ....Clifford Cothren, Tom Manley and Maurice Ellis

The action of the play takes place in the Berniers' house in New
Orleans. Act I.—Six P.M. on a summer Tuesday. Act II.—Eight A.M.
the following morning. Act III.—Shortly after.

Staged by Arthur Penn; setting and lighting by Howard Bay; costumes by Ruth Morley; production stage manager, Kermit Kegley;
stage manager, Clifford Cothren; press representative, Arthur Cantor.

A THURBER CARNIVAL

(109 performances)
(Continued)

A revue in two acts by James Thurber. Produced by Michael
Davis, Helen Bonfils and Haila Stoddard at the ANTA Theatre,
February 26, 1960.

Program—

ACT I

"Word Dance (Part I)" .....Peggy Cass, Paul Ford, John McGiver,
Alice Ghostley, Peter Turgeon, Wynne Miller,
Margo Lungreen, Charles Braswell
"The Night the Bed Fell" ....Tom Ewell
"Fables (Part I)"

The Wolf at the Door

Narrator ....Alice Ghostley
Daughter ....Wynne Miller
Mother ....Peggy Cass
Father ....Paul Ford
Wolf ....Charles Braswell

The Unicorn in the Garden

Narrator ....Peter Turgeon
Man ....Paul Ford
She ....Alice Ghostley
Psychiatrist ....John McGiver
Policeman ....Charles Braswell

The Little Girl and the Wolf

Narrator ....Peggy Cass
Wolf ....Paul Ford
Little Girl ....Wynne Miller

"If Grant Had Been Drinking at Appomattox"

Narrator ....Peter Turgeon
Schultz ....Charles Braswell
Grant ....Tom Ewell
Lee ....Paul Ford
Lee's Staff Man ....John McGiver
Officer ....Peter Turgeon

"Casuals of the Keys"

Visitor ....John McGiver
Darrel Darke ....Paul Ford

"The Macbeth Murder Mystery"

He ....Tom Ewell
She ....Peggy Cass

"Gentlemen Shoppers"

Salesgirl ....Alice Ghostley
Westwater ....John McGiver
Bargirl ....Wynne Miller
Anderson ....Tom Ewell
Bailey ....Paul Ford

"The Last Flower" ....Tom Ewell

ACT II

"Pet Department"

The Pet Counsellor ....Tom Ewell
Miss Whittaker ....Alice Ghostley
A Girl ....Wynne Miller

"Mr. Preble Gets Rid of His Wife"

Preble ....Paul Ford
Miss Daley ....Wynne Miller
Mrs. Preble ....Peggy Cass

"File and Forget"

James Thurber ....Tom Ewell
Miss Bagley ....Margo Lungreen
Miss Alma Winege ....Peggy Cass
Miss Wynne ....Wynne Miller
Jeannette Gaines ....Alice Ghostley
Clint Jordan ....Paul Ford
H. F. Cluffman ....John McGiver

"Take Her Up Tenderly"

John ....Paul Ford
Nellie ....Alice Ghostley
Lou ....Peggy Cass

"Fables (Part II)"

The Owl Who Was God

Narrator ....Alice Ghostley
Owl ....John McGiver
Moles ....Peter Turgeon, Charles Braswell
Secretary Bird ....Paul Ford
Red Fox ....Margo Lungreen

The Clothes Moth and the Luna Moth

Narrator ....Tom Ewell
Luna Moth ....Wynne Miller
Clothes Moth ....Charles Braswell

"The Secret Life of Walter Mitty"

Narrator ....Peter Turgeon
Walter Mitty ....Tom Ewell
Mrs. Mitty ....Peggy Cass
First Voice ....Charles Braswell
Lt. Berg ....Peter Turgeon
Nurse ....Wynne Miller
Dr. Renshaw ....John McGiver

Dr. Benbow ....Charles Braswell
Dr. Remington ....Peter Turgeon
Mr. Pritchard-Mitford ....Paul Ford
The Leader ....Paul Ford
"Word Dance (Part II)" ....Entire Company
Staged by Burgess Meredith; scenery by Marvin Reiss; lighting by Paul Morrison; associate director, James Starbuck; men's costumes by Ramsé Stevens; music composed and performed by the Don Elliott Quartet (Jack Six, Jim Raney, Don Elliott and Ronnie Bedford); production stage manager, Daniel S. Broun; stage manager, Malcolm Marmorstein; press representative, George Ross.

THERE WAS A LITTLE GIRL

(16 performances)

Play in two acts by Daniel Taradash, from a novel by Christopher Davis. Produced by Robert Fryer and Lawrence Carr at the Cort Theatre, February 29, 1960.

Cast of characters—

Toni Newton ....Jane Fonda
Stan Walters ....Dean Jones
Waiter ....Val Ruffino
Nicky Walters ....Peter Helm
Harry Adams ....Michael Vandever
Mr. Newton ....Whitfield Connor
Mrs. Newton ....Ruth Matteson
Lucille Newton ....Joey Heatherton
Neill Johns ....Sean Garrison
Ralph ....Gary Lockwood
Lt. Goldman ....William Adler
Policeman ....Mark Slade
Bartender ....Phillip Pruneau
Tom Fraser ....Tom Gilleran
Dancers ....Val Ruffino, Sharon Forsmoe,
Mark Slade, Barbara Davis
The action of the play takes place in and around Philadelphia, during a summer.
Staged by Joshua Logan; settings and lighting by Jo Mielziner; costumes by Patton Cambell; original music by Lehman Engel; production stage manager, Robert Linden; stage manager, Howard Whitfield; press representative, Betty Lee Hunt.

(Closed March 12, 1960)

HENRY IV, PART I

(65 performances)

Play in two acts by William Shakespeare. Produced by Theatre Incorporated (T. Edward Hambleton and Norris Houghton) at the Phoenix Theatre, March 1, 1960.

Cast of characters—

King Henry the Fourth ....Fritz Weaver
The King's sons { Henry, Prince of Wales ....Edwin Sherin
{ Prince John of Lancaster ......Nicholas Kepros
Earl of Westmoreland ....Robert Blackburn

Sir Walter Blunt ....Franklin Cover
Thomas Percy, Earl of Worcester ....Patrick Hines
Henry Percy, Earl of Northumberland ....Elliott Sullivan
Henry Percy ("Hotspur"), his son ....Donald Madden
Edmund Mortimer, Earl of March ....Thomas Bellin
Archibald, Earl of Douglas ....Ray Reinhardt
Owen Glendower ....Albert Quinton
Sir Richard Vernon ....John Heffernan
Sir John Falstaff ....Eric Berry
Poins ....J. D. Cannon
Peto ....Jerry Hardin
Bardolph ....Rex Everhart
Vintner of the Boar's Head Tavern ....Ray Reinhardt
Francis, a waiter ....John Heffernan
Travellers ....Nicholas Kepros, John Heffernan
Sheriff ....Franklin Cover
Hotspur's Servant ....Pirie MacDonald
Messenger ....Jerry Hardin
Lady Percy, Hotspur's wife ....Nan Martin
Lady Mortimer, Glendower's daughter ....Juliet Randall
Mistress Quickly, hostess of the Boar's Head Tavern   Gerry Jedd
    Soldiers, tapsters: Bill Alexander, James Corpora, William Hind-
man, George O'Halloran, Joel Parsons, Rex Robbins, Edmund Shaff,
Stephen Strimpell.
    The action of the play takes place in England and Wales.
    Staged by Stuart Vaughan; settings and costumes by Will Steven
Armstrong; lighting by Jean Rosenthal; music and songs composed
by David Amram; stage manager, Richard Blofson; press representatives, Ben Kornzweig, Karl Bernstein and Robert Ganshaw.

(Closed May 29, 1960)

THE GOOD SOUP

(21 performances)

Play in two acts by Felicien Marceau, adapted by Garson Kanin.
Produced by David Merrick at the Plymouth Theatre, March 2,
1960.

Cast of characters—

The Croupier ....Jules Munshin
The Barman ....Pat Harrington
Marie-Paule I ....Ruth Gordon
Monsieur Gaston ....Ernest Truex
Marie-Paule II ....Diane Cilento
Marie-Paule's Mother ....Mildred Natwick
Roger ....Morgan Sterne
The Customer ....Bill Becker
Madame Roger ....Dorothy Whitney
The Doorman ....George S. Irving
The Shady One ....Lou Antonio
The Skater ....Barbara Lou Mattes
Odilon ....Sam Levene
The First Patron ....John Myhers
Irma ....Sasha von Scherler
The Second Patron ....Morgan Sterne
Mauricette ....Hilda Brawner
The Third Patron ....Lou Antonio
Monsieur Alphonse ....George S. Irving
The Chambermaid ....Barbara Lou Mattes
The Fourth Patron ....Bill Becker
Lecasse ....Lou Antonio
Joseph ....Ernest Truex
Angele ....Mildred Natwick

Raymond ....George S. Irving
The House Painter ....Bill Becker
Jacquot ....Charles Robinson
Minouche ....Hilda Brawner
The Tough ....George S. Irving
The Second Tough ....Pat Harrington
Armand ....John Myhers
The Other Man ....George S. Irving
Armand's Mother ....Mildred Natwick
Ernest ....Bill Becker
Berthe ....Hilda Brawner
Madame Desvaux ....Sasha von Scherler
Madame Thonnard ....Dorothy Whitney
Jeannine ....Nicola Lubitsch
Mollard ....Morgan Sterne
    The action of the play takes place in Monte Carlo, Paris, and its
environs. The time is the present and the past.
    Staged by Garson Kanin; sets and costumes by Jacques Noel; sets
and costumes supervised by William Pitkin; lighting by Albert Alloy;
production stage manager, Neil Hartley; stage manager, Ben Janney;
press representatives, James D. Proctor and Merle Debuskey.

(Closed March 19, 1960)

THE VISIT

(16 performances)

Play in three acts by Friedrich Duerrenmatt, adapted by Maurice
Valency. Revived by the City Center of Music and Drama, by
arrangement with the American Theatre Society (under the auspices
of the Council of the Living Theatre), and the Producers' Theatre
at the New York City Center, March 8, 1960.

Cast of characters—

Hofbauer ....William Callan
Helmsberger ....David Clarke
Wechsler ....Geoffrey Bryant
Vogel ....Lance Cunard
The Painter ....Burford Hampden
Station Master ....Joseph Leberman
Burgomaster ....Thomas Gomez
Professor Muller ....Glenn Anders
Pastor ....William Hansen
Anton Schill ....Alfred Lunt
Claire Zachnassian ....Lynn Fontanne
Conductor ....Frank Hamilton
Pedro Cabral ....Myles Eason
Bobby ....John Wyse
Police Chief Schultz ....Michael Lewis
First Grandchild ....Donna Francis
Second Grandchild ....Katharine Dunfee
Mike ....Lucky Kargo
Max ....James MacAaron
First Blind Man ....James Dukas
Second Blind Man ....Roy Johnson
Frau Burgomaster ....Nora Dunfee
Frau Block ....Edna Preston
Frau Schill ....Edith Gresham
Ottilie Schill ....Aina Niemela
Karl Schill ....John Vickers
Doctor Nusslin ....Ronald Bishop
Athlete ....Larry Casey

Truck Driver .... John Kane
Reporter .... Jack DeMave
    Original production staged by Peter Brook; designed by Teo Otto;
supervision and lighting by Paul Morrison; Miss Fontanne's clothes
by Castillo; production stage manager, Joseph Brownstone; stage
manager, Frank Hamilton; press representative, Reginald Denenholz.

The Visit was first produced by the Producers' Theatre at the
Lunt-Fontanne Theatre, May 5, 1958, for 189 performances.

(Closed March 20, 1960)

GREENWILLOW

(97 performances)

Musical in two acts, based on the novel by B. J. Chute; with
book by Lesser Samuels and Frank Loesser; music and lyrics
by Frank Loesser. Produced by Robert A. Willey, in association
with Frank Productions, Inc., at the Alvin Theatre, March 8, 1960.

Cast of characters—

Jabez Briggs .... John Megna
Clara Clegg .... Dortha Duckworth
Mrs. Hasty .... Maggie Task
Mr. Preebs .... Jordon Howard
Mrs. Lunny .... Marie Foster
Reverend Lapp .... William Chapman
Gramma Briggs .... Pert Kelton
Maidy .... Elaine Swann
Emma .... Saralou Cooper
Gideon Briggs .... Anthony Perkins
Dorrie Whitbred .... Ellen McCown
Amos Briggs .... Bruce MacKay
Micah Briggs .... Ian Tucker
Martha Briggs .... Lynn Brinker
Sheby Briggs .... Brenda Harris
Thomas Clegg .... Lee Cass
Reverend Birdsong .... Cecil Kellaway
Young Churchgoer .... Thomas Norden
Will .... David Gold
Nell .... Margery Gray
Andrew .... Grover Dale
    Singers: Kenny Adams, Betsy Bridge, Marie Foster, Rico Froeh-
lich, Russell Goodwin, Jordon Howard, Marion Mercer, Carl Nicho-
las, Virginia Oswald, Bob Roman, Shelia Swenson, Maggie Task,
Karen Thorsell.
    Dancers: Jere Admire, Don Atkinson, Estelle Aza, Joan Codding-
ton, Ethelyne Dunfee, Richard Englund, David Gold, Margery Gray,
Mickey Gunnerson, Patsi King, Jack Leigh, Nancy Van Rhein,
Jimmy White.
    The action of the play takes place in and about Greenwillow dur-
ing four seasons. Act I.—Scene 1—The square. Scene 2—Briggs
farm. Scene 3—The mill. Scene 4—The willow. Scene 5—The
square. Scene 6—Cleggs farm. Scene 7—The mill. Scene 8—
Briggs farm. Scene 9—The church. Scene 10—The square. Act
II.—Scene 1—The square. Scene 2—Briggs farm. Scene 3—
Cleggs house. Scene 4—The square. Scene 5—Briggs farm.
    Staged by George Roy Hill; settings by Peter Larkin; choreography
by Joe Layton; costumes by Alvin Colt; lighting by Feder; orchestrations by Don Walker; musical direction by Abba Bogin; production stage manager, Terence Little; stage manager, Arthur Rubin;
press representatives, Phillip Bloom and David Lipsky.

Musical numbers—

ACT I

"A Day Borrowed from Heaven" ....The Villagers
"A Day Borrowed from Heaven" ....Gideon
Dorrie's Wish ....Dorrie
"The Music of Home" ....Amos, Gideon and the Villagers
"Gideon Briggs, I Love You" ....Gideon and Dorrie
"The Autumn Courting" ....All the Villagers
"The Call to Wander" ....Amos
"Summertime Love" ....Gideon and the Villagers
"Walking Away Whistling" ....Dorrie
"The Sermon" ....Reverend Lapp and Reverend Birdsong
"Could've Been a Ring" ....Clegg and Gramma
"Gideon Briggs, I Love You" (Reprise) ....Dorrie
"Halloweve" ....The Young Villagers
"Never Will I Marry" ....Gideon
"Greenwillow Christmas" (Carol) ....Martha and the Villagers

ACT II

"The Music of Home" (Reprise) ....The Villagers
"Faraway Boy" ....Dorrie
"Clang Dang the Bell" ....Gideon, Gramma, Martha, Micah,
                                                    Sheby and Jabez
"What a Blessing" ....Reverend Birdsong
"He Died Good" ....The Villagers
"The Spring Courting" ....Andrew, Dorrie and the Young Villagers
"Summertime Love" (Reprise) ....Gideon
"What a Blessing" (Reprise) ....Reverend Birdsong
"The Call" ....Gideon
"The Music of Home" (Reprise) ....All of Greenwillow

(Closed May 28, 1960)

SEMI-DETACHED

(4 performances)

Play in three acts by Patricia Joudry. Produced by Philip Rose at the Martin Beck Theatre, March 10, 1960.

Cast of characters—

Joy Friar ....Rosalyn Newport
Papa ....Edgar Stehli
Paper Boy ....Paul Mace
Emile Duschene ....Frank Silvera
Frank Friar ....Ed Begley
Winnie Friar ....Jean Muir
Chris Friar ....Ronnie Tourso
Marie Duschene ....Vivian Nathan
Jean-Michel Duschene ....Brad Herrman
Milkman ....Frank Chase
Pierre Boudreau ....James Dimitri
Simone ....Doris Belack
Father Gagnon ....Dana Elcar
Workman ....Robert Alvin
    Act I.—Spring. Act II.—Early summer and late summer. Act III.—End of summer.
    Staged by Charles S. Dubin; setting by Boris Aronson; lighting by Klaus Holm; costumes by Helene Pons; production stage manager, Leonard Auerbach; stage manager, Norman Shelly; press representatives, James D. Proctor and Merle Debuskey.

(Closed March 12, 1960)

DEAR LIAR

(52 performances)

A "Comedy of Letters" in two parts, adapted for the stage by Jerome Kilty from the correspondence of Mrs. Patrick Campbell and Bernard Shaw. Produced by Guthrie McClintic, in association with Sol Hurok, at the Billy Rose Theatre, March 17, 1960.

Cast of characters—

Mrs. Patrick Campbell ....Katharine Cornell
George Bernard Shaw ....Brian Aherne
Part I.—1899-1914.   Part II.—1914-1939.

Staged by Jerome Kilty; set by Donald Oenslager; lighting by Jean Rosenthal; costumes by Cecil Beaton; incidental music by Sol Kaplan; stage manager, Edmund Baylies; press representative, Martin Feinstein.

(Closed April 30, 1960)

ONE MORE RIVER

(3 performances)

Play in three acts by Beverley Cross. Produced by Mary K. Frank, by arrangement with Laurence Olivier, at the Ambassador Theatre, March 18, 1960.

Cast of characters—

Louis, cook ....Louis Guss
Ross, a cadet ....Thomas Hawley
Danny, deck boy ....David Winters
Jacko, ordinary seaman ....Robert Drivas
Johnny Condell, bo's'n ....Lloyd Nolan
Smitty, able seaman ....Don Gantry
Colombus, able seaman ....Al Lewis
Pompey, able seaman, ex-Navy ....Harry Guardino
Kelly, "Chips," carpenter ....John McLiam
Trim, wiper ....Lance Taylor
Mick, wiper ....Buck Kartalian
Sewell, mate ....Alfred Ryder

The action of the play takes place on the after-deck of a tramp freighter, flying a flag of convenience, lying in the Bonny River, West Africa. The time is New Year's Eve during the four hours of a single watch, from eight in the evening till midnight. Act I.—Eight o'clock. Act II.—Immediately following. Act III.—Immediately following.

Staged by Windsor Lewis; setting and lighting by George Jenkins, costumes by Anna Hill Johnstone; production stage manager, Karl Nielson; stage manager, Paul Leaf; press representatives, Frank Goodman, Ben Washer and Bernard Simon.

(Closed March 19, 1960)

THE BEST MAN

(70 performances)
(Continued)

Play in three acts by Gore Vidal. Produced by the Playwrights'
Company at the Morosco Theatre, March 31, 1960.

Cast of characters—

Dick Jensen	Karl Weber
First Reporter	Howard Fischer
William Russell	Melvyn Douglas
Mike	Martin Fried
Second Reporter	Tony Bickley
Third Reporter	Barbara Berjer
Fourth Reporter	Tom McDermott
Alice Russell	Leora Dana
Assistant to Dick Jensen	Ruth Maynard
Mrs. Gamadge	Ruth McDevitt
Arthur Hockstader	Lee Tracy
Mabel Cantwell	Kathleen Maguire
Bill Blades	Joseph Sullivan
Joseph Cantwell	Frank Lovejoy
Senator Carlin	Gordon B. Clarke
Dr. Artinian	Hugh Franklin
Sheldon Marcus	Graham Jarvis
Reporters, Delegates, etc.	John Dorrin, Mitchell Erickson, Ruth Tobin

Place: A Presidential Convention in Philadelphia. Time: Summer,
1960. Act I.—Scene 1—A Sheraton Hotel Suite. Scene 2—Senator
Joseph Cantwell's suite; the same evening. Act II.—Scene 1—William Russell's suite; the following morning. Scene 2—Cantwell
suite; a few minutes later. Scene 3—Russell suite; a few minutes
later. Act III.—Scene 1—Cantwell suite; a few minutes later.
Scene 2—Russell suite; the next morning.

Staged by Joseph Anthony; settings and lighting by Jo Mielziner;
costumes by Theoni V. Aldredge; production stage manager, Bill
Ross; stage manager, Howard Fischer; press representative, Abner
D. Klipstein.

VIVA MADISON AVENUE!

(2 performances)

Comedy in three acts by George Panetta. Produced by Selma
Tamber and Martin H. Poll at the Longacre Theatre, April 6, 1960.

Cast of characters—

Joe Caputo	Buddy Hackett
Copy Chief	Carl Low
George Caruso	Lee Krieger
Jim Leary	William Windom
Sandy Neal	Robert Dowdell
Dee Jones	Frances Sternhagen
The Stag	Jed Allan
Toro	Paul E. Richards
Peggy	Jan Miner
Head of Research	Burt Berger
Research Assistant	Richard Poston
Frank O'Boyle	Earl Rowe

Ed Noone ....Fred Clark
Jane, receptionist ....Mary Alice Bayh
Girl in the Hotel ....Peggy Pope
Engineer ....Edward Earle
    Act I.—Scene 1—Joe Caputo's office at Lowell & Lynch Advertis-
ing; a Friday afternoon. Scene 2—Conference room at Lowell &
Lynch Advertising; later that night. Act II.—Scene 1—Joe's office; the following Monday morning. Scene 2—Conference room; a
Friday night, two weeks later. Act III.—Scene 1—Room in a hotel;
later that night. Scene 2—Joe's office; the following Monday morning.
    Staged by Aaron Frankel; scenery and lighting by William and
Jean Eckart; costumes by Frank Thompson; production stage manager, Burry Fredrik; stage manager, Richard Merrell; press representative, Dorothy Ross.

(Closed April 7, 1960)

A SECOND STRING

(29 performances)

Play in three acts by Lucienne Hill, adapted from a novel by
Colette. Produced by Leonard Sillman and Carroll and Harris Masterson at the Eugene O'Neill Theatre, April 13, 1960.

Cast of characters—

Paul ....Ben Piazza
Jane ....Nina Foch
Fanny ....Shirley Booth
Clara ....Cathleen Nesbit
Inez ....Carrie Nye
Farou ....Jean Pierre Aumont
    The action of the play takes place in Southern France and Paris.
Time: August; the present day. Act I.—Farou's holiday residence in
Southern France. Act II.—Scene 1—Farou's Paris apartment; four
weeks later. Scene 2—A week later; early evening. Act III.—
Farou's apartment; two weeks later.
    Staged by Raymond Gerome; settings and lighting by Ben Ed-
wards; costumes by Robert Mackintosh; production associate, Jacque-
line Adams; production stage manager, Peter Pell; stage manager,
Bruce Laffey; press representative, Betty Lee Hunt.

(Closed May 7, 1960)

BYE BYE BIRDIE

(54 performances)
(Continued)

Musical comedy in two acts, with book by Michael Stewart;
music by Charles Strouse; lyrics by Lee Adams. Produced by
Edward Padula at the Martin Beck Theatre, April 14, 1960.

Cast of characters—

Albert Peterson ....Dick Van Dyke
Rose Grant ....Chita Rivera

Teen Agers:
    Helen ....Karin Wolfe
    Nancy ....Marissa Mason
    Alice ....Sharon Lerit
    Margie Ann ....Louise Quick
    Penelope Ann ....Lada Edmund
    Deborah Sue ....Jessica Albright
    Suzie ....Lynn Bowin
    Linda ....Judy Keirn
    Carol ....Penny Ann Green
    Martha Louise ....Vicki Belmonte
    Harold ....Michael Vita
    Karl ....Jerry Dodge
    Harvey ....Dean Stolber
    Henry ....Ed Kresley
    Arthur ....Bob Spencer
    Freddie ....Tracy Everitt
    Peyton ....Gary Howe
Ursula Merkle ....Barbara Doherty
Kim MacAfee ....Susan Watson
Mrs. MacAfee ....Marijane Maricle
Mr. MacAfee ....Paul Lynde
Teen Trio ....Louise Quick, Jessica Albright, Vicki Belmonte
Sad Girl ....Sharon Lerit
Another Sad Girl ....Karin Wolfe
Mae Peterson ....Kay Medford
Reporters ....Lee Howard, Jim Sisco, Don
                                    Farnworth, John Coyle
Conrad Birdie ....Dick Gautier
Guitar Man ....Kenny Burrell
Conductor ....Kasimir Kokich
Cheerleaders ....Judy Keirn, Lynn Bowin
Mayor ....Allen Knowles
Mayor's Wife ....Amelia Haas
Hugo Peabody ....Michael J. Pollard
Randolph MacAfee ....Johnny Borden
Mrs. Merkle ....Pat McEnnis
Old Woman ....Dori Davis
Neighbors ....Amelia Haas, Jeannine Masterson, Ed Becker,
                Oran Osburn, George Blackwell, Lee Howard
Mr. Henkel ....Charles Nelson Reilly
Gloria Rasputin ....Norma Richardson
Ed. Sullivan's Voice ....Will Jordan
TV Stage Manager ....Tony Mordente
Charles F. Maude ....George Blackwell
Shriners ....Allen Knowles, John Coyle, Dick Crowley, Don
                Farnworth, Bud Fleming, Kasimir Kokich, Jim Sisco
    Act I.—Prologue. Scene 1—Office of Almaelou Music, New York.
Scene 2—Sweet Apple, Ohio. Scene 3—MacAfee home, Sweet Ap-
ple. Scene 4—Pennsylvania Station, New York. Scene 5—Railroad
station, Sweet Apple. Scene 6—Courthouse Steps, Sweet Apple.
Scene 7—MacAfee home, Sweet Apple. Scene 8—Stage, Central
Movie Theatre, Sweet Apple. Scene 9—Backstage office, Central
Movie Theatre, Sweet Apple. Scene 10—Stage, Central Movie The-
atre, Sweet Apple. Act II.—Prologue—The world at large. Scene
1—MacAfee home, Sweet Apple. Scene 2—Street outside MacAfee
home. Scene 3—MacAfee's back door. Scene 4—Maude's Roadside
Retreat. Scene 5—Private dining room, Maude's Roadside Retreat.
Scene 6—Back door, Maude's Roadside Retreat. Scene 7—The Ice
House. Scene 8—Railroad station, Sweet Apple.
    Staged and choreographed by Gower Champion; scenery by Robert
Randolph; costumes by Miles White; lighting by Peggy Clark; musical director, Elliot Lawrence; orchestrations by Robert Ginzler;
dance arrangements by John Morris; hair styles by Ernest Adler;
production stage manager, Michael Thoma; stage manager, Edward
Nayor; press representative, Reuben Rabinovitch.

Musical numbers—

ACT I

"An English Teacher" .... Rose and Albert
"The Telephone Hour" ....Sweet Apple Kids

"How Lovely to Be a Woman" ....Kim
"We Love You, Conrad!" ....Teen Trio
"Put on a Happy Face" ....Albert and Two Sad Girls
"Normal American Boy" ....Rose, Albert and Chorus
"One Boy" ....Kim, Deborah, Sue and Alice
"One Boy" (Reprise) ....Rose
"Honestly Sincere" ....Conrad and Townspeople
"Hymn for a Sunday Evening"......Mr. MacAfee, Mrs. MacAfee,
                                    Kim, Randolph and Neighbors
"Ballet: How to Kill a Man" ....Rose, Albert and Company
"One Last Kiss" ....Conrad and Company

ACT II

"What Did I Ever See in Him?" ....Rose and Kim
"A Lot of Livin' to Do" ....Conrad, Kim and Teenagers
"Kids" ....Mr. MacAfee and Mrs. MacAfee
"Baby, Talk to Me" ....Albert and Quartet
"Shriners' Ballet" ....Rose and Shriners
"Kids" (Reprise) ....Mr. MacAfee, Mrs. MacAfee, Randolph
                                    and Townspeople
"Spanish Rose" ....Rose
"Rosie" ....Albert and Rose

HENRY IV, PART II

(31 performances)

Play in two acts by William Shakespeare. Produced by Theatre Incorporated (T. Edward Hambleton and Norris Houghton) at the Phoenix Theatre, April 18, 1960.

Cast of characters—

Rumor (the Presenter and Epilogue) ....Jerry Hardin
King Henry IV ....Fritz Weaver
Prince Henry, afterwards King Henry V ....Edwin Sherin

Sons to Henry IV and Brothers to Prince Henry
  Prince John of Lancaster ....Nicholas Kepros
  Humphrey of Gloucester ....Rex Robbins
  Thomas of Clarence ..John Hillerman

Earl of Northumberland ....Elliott Sullivan
Richard Scroop, Archbishop of York ....John Frid
Sir John Falstaff ....Eric Berry
Lord Mowbray ....Thomas Bellin
Lord Hastings ....William Hindman
Travers ....Franklin Cover
Morton ....Pirie MacDonald
Earl of Westmoreland ....Robert Blackburn
Lord Chief Justice ....Albert Quinton
Gower ....Rex Robbins
Harcourt ....Tom Gruenewald
Country Justices Robert Shallow ....John Heffernan
                  Silence ....Franklin Cover
Poins ....J. D. Cannon
Bardolph ....Rex Everhart
Pistol ....Ray Reinhardt
Peto ....Jerry Hardin
Falstaff's Page ....Michael Crosby
Davy, servant to Shallow ....George O'Halloran
Two Sergeants Fang ....James Corpora
               Snare ....Nicholas Kepros
Country Soldiers
  Ralph Mouldy ....James Corpora
  Simon Shadow ....Jerry Hardin
  Thomas Wart ....Joel Parsons
  Francis Feeble ....Tom Gruenewald
  Peter Bullcalf ....Pirie MacDonald

Drawers { Francis ....John Heffernan
Ralph ....George O'Halloran
Will ....Joel Parsons
Porter ....John Hillerman
Lady Northumberland ....Alice Drummond
Lady Percy ....Juliet Randall
Mistress Quickly ....Gerry Jedd
Doll Tearsheet ....Patricia Falkenhain
    Lords, tapsters, grooms, soldiers, attendants, priests: Bill Alex-
ander, Michael Baseleon, Frederick Combs, Daniel Durning, Joseph
Hamer, John O'Leary, Tom Sawyer.
    The action of the play takes place in England in the 15th Century.
    Staged by Stuart Vaughan; settings and costumes by Will Steven
Armstrong; lighting by Jean Rosenthal; music and songs composed
by David Amram; stage manager, Richard Blofson; press representatives, Ben Kornzweig, Karl Bernstein and Robert Ganshaw.

(Closed May 29, 1960)

DUEL OF ANGELS

(49 performances)
(Continued)

Play in three acts by Jean Giraudoux, translated and adapted
by Christopher Fry. Produced by Roger L. Stevens and Sol
Hurok at the Helen Hayes Theatre, April 19, 1960.

Cast of characters—

Joseph ....James Valentine
Count Marcellus ....Peter Wyngarde
Gilly ....Aina Niemela
Paola ....Vivien Leigh
Armand ....John Merivale
Lucile ....Mary Ure
Eugénie ....Ludi Claire
Mace-Bearer ....Felix Deebank
Barbette ....Margaret Braidwood
Servant ....Ken Edward Ruta
Mr. Justice Blanchard ....Alan MacNaughtan
Clerk of the Court ....Donald Moffat
Servant ....Theodore Tenley
Customers at the Café ....Key Meersman, Byron Mitchell, Donald
                Moffat, Virginia Robinson, Ken Edward
                Ruta, Alicia Townsend
    The action of the play takes place in Aix-en-Provence. The
time: about 1868. Act I.—The terrace of a café under the lime
trees; a summer's day. Act II.—A room in Count Marcellus'
house; early the next morning. Act III.—Mr. Justice Blanchard's
study; immediately following.
    Staged by Robert Helpmann; settings by Roger Furse; lighting
by Paul Morrison; women's costumes designed by Christian Dior;
production stage manager, John Maxtone-Graham; stage manager,
Jonathan Anderson; press representative, William Fields.

FROM A TO Z

Musical revue in two acts, produced by Carroll and Harris
Masterson at the Plymouth Theatre, April 20, 1960.

Principals—

Hermione Gingold
Elliott Reid
Alvin Epstein
Louise Hoff
Nora Kovach
Kelly Brown
Paula Stewart

Stuart Damon
Bob Dishy
Isabelle Farrell
Michael Fesco
Larry Hovis
Doug Spingler
Beryl Towbin

Virginia Vestoff

Staged by Christopher Hewett; choreography by Ray Harrison; settings, lighting and costumes by Fred Voelpel; musical direction and vocal arrangements by Milton Greene; dance arrangements by Jack Holmes; orchestrations by Jay Brower and Jonathan Tunick; production stage manager, Fred Hearn; stage manager, Joseph Olney; press representative, Irvin Dorfman.

Sketches and musical numbers—

ACT I

"Best Gold" (Music and lyrics by Jerry Herman) Hermione Gingold, Nora Kovach, Kelly Brown, Michael Fesco, Doug Spingler, Beryl Towbin, Virginia Vestoff, Stuart Damon, Paula Stewart

Bardolatry ....Louise Hoff, Elliott Reid
"Pill Parade" (Music and lyrics by Jay Thompson)
    Narrator ....Alvin Epstein
    Average Man ....Kelly Brown
    Vitamins ....Michael Fesco, Doug Spingler
    Benzabang ....Beryl Towbin
    Pilltown ....Virginia Vestoff
    Sexaphine ....Nora Kovach
    One more Pill ....Isabelle Farrell
"Togetherness" (Music and lyrics by Dickson Hughes and Everett Sloane)
    Grandmother ....Hermione Gingold
    Father ....Elliott Reid
    Mother ....Louise Hoff
    Daughter ....Paula Stewart
    Son ....Stuart Damon
Psychological Warfare (By Woody Allen)
    Sergeant ....Alvin Epstein
    Privates ....Larry Hovis, Doug Spingler
    Enemy ....Bob Dishy
    Medics ....Stuart Damon, Michael Fesco
"Balloons" (Music and lyrics by Jack Holmes) Nora Kovach, Kelly Brown, Michael Fesco, Doug Spingler, Beryl Towbin, Virginia Vestoff

Music Talk ....Hermione Gingold
"Hire a Guy" (Music by Mary Rodgers, lyrics by Marshall Barer)
    The Star ....Louise Hoff
    The Director ....Elliott Reid
    The Writer ....Stuart Damon
    Patsy ....Bob Dishy
"Interlude" (Music by Jack Holmes)
    Ladies ....Beryl Towbin, Virginia Vestoff, Isabelle Farrell
    Gentlemen ....Kelly Brown, Michael Fesco, Doug Spingler
    A Stranger ....Nora Kovach
    A Man ....Stuart Damon
Hit Parade (By Woody Allen)
    Girl ....Hermione Gingold
    Boy ....Alvin Epstein
Conventional Behavior ....Elliott Reid
"I Said to Love" ....Louise Hoff
    (Music by Paul Klein, lyrics by Fred Ebb)
Winter in Palm Springs (By Herbert Farjeon)
    Colonel Spicer ....Alvin Epstein
    Mrs. Twiceover ....Hermione Gingold
    Alice ....Beryl Towbin
"Charlie" ....Paula Stewart
    (Music and lyrics by Fred Ebb and Norman Martin)

"The Sound of Schmaltz" (Music by William Dyer, lyrics by Don
    Parks)
                        Cast of characters
Head Nanny ....Louise Hoff
Nannies ..Nora Kovach, Beryl Towbin, Virginia Vestoff, Isabelle
                                                        Farrell
Alice Cadwallader-Smith ....Hermione Gingold
Baron von Klaptrap ....Elliott Reid
Children .... Kelly Brown, Alvin Epstein, Michael Fesco, Doug
        Spingler, Stuart Damon, Bob Dishy, Paula Stewart
                    Synopsis of scenes
        1. The offices of "International Nannies, Ltd."
            (with an interlude in Central Park)
        2. The von Klaptrap nursery
        3. Baron von Klaptrap's apartment
        4. The von Klaptrap living room
                        ACT II
"Grand Jury Jump" (Music by Paul Klein, lyrics by Fred Ebb)
    Nora Kovach, Paula Stewart, Beryl Towbin, Virginia Vestoff,
    Isabelle Farrell, Kelly Brown, Stuart Damon, Michael Fesco,
                        Doug Spingler, Larry Hovis
"South American Way" ....Alvin Epstein, Bob Dishy
    (Music by Norman Martin, lyrics by Norman Martin and Fred
    Ebb)
Snapshots (By Herbert Farjeon)
    She ....Hermione Gingold
    He ....Elliott Reid
"Time Step" ....Kelly Brown
    (Music by Paul Klein, lyrics by Fred Ebb)
Bobo ....Elliott Reid
Queen of Song ....Hermione Gingold
Surprise Party (By Woody Allen)
    Fred .... Bob Dishy
    Harry ....Kelly Brown
    Myrna ....Louise Hoff
    Linda ....Beryl Towbin
    Ruthie ....Nora Kovach
    Rita ....Isabelle Farrell
    Virginia ....Virginia Vestoff
    Blonde ....Paula Stewart
On the Beach ....Alvin Epstein
    (Devised by Mark Epstein and Christopher Hewett)
Park Meeting (By Nina Warner Hook)
    Governess ....Hermione Gingold
    Woman ....Louise Hoff
"Red Shoes" (Music by Jack Holmes)
    Introduced by .... Bob Dishy
    Danced by .....Kelly Brown, Isabelle Farrell, Michael Fesco,
            Larry Hovis, Doug Spingler, Beryl Towbin,
                                        Virginia Vestoff
"Four for the Road" ....Hermione Gingold
    (Music by Paul Klein, lyrics by Lee Goldsmith and Fred Ebb)
"What Next?" (Music by Charles Zwar, lyrics by Alan Melville)
                                            The Company

                    (Closed May 7, 1960)

                    WEST SIDE STORY

                    (39 performances)
                    (Continued)

    Musical in two acts, based on a conception of Jerome Robbins;
book by Arthur Laurents; music by Leonard Bernstein; lyrics by
Stephen Sondheim. Revived by Robert E. Griffith and Harold S.

Prince (by arrangement with Roger L. Stevens) at the Winter Garden, April 27, 1960.

Cast of characters—

The Jets:

Riff, the leader .... Thomas Hasson
Tony, his friend .... Larry Kert
Action .... George Liker
A-Rab .... Alan Johnson
Baby John .... Barry Burns
Big Deal .... Martin Charnin
Diesel .... Donald Corby
Snowboy .... Eddie Gasper
Mouth Piece .... Eddie Miller
Tiger .... Richard Corrigan
Gee-Tar .... Glenn Gibson

Their Girls:

Graziella .... Sandy Leeds
Velma .... Audrey Hays
Clarice .... Lee Lewis
Pauline .... Judy Aldene
Anybodys .... Pat Birch
Minnie .... Barbara Monte

The Sharks:

Bernardo, the leader .... George Marcy
Maria, his sister .... Carol Lawrence
Anita, his girl .... Allyn Ann McLerie
Chino, his friend .... Miguel De Vega
Pepe .... Ben Vargas
Indio .... Robert Avian
Luis .... Sterling Clark
Estella .... Danii Prior
Burro .... Vince Baggetta
Nibbles .... Ed Dutton
Toro .... Kent Thomas
Moose .... Marc Scott

Their Girls:

Rosalia .... Gloria Lambert
Teresita .... Hope Clarke
Francisca .... Anna Marie Moylan
Marguerita .... Poligena Rogers
Consuelo .... Genii Prior

The Adults:

Doc .... Albert M. Ottenheimer
Schrank .... Ted Gunther
Krupke .... Roger Franklin
Gladhand .... Ross Hertz

Staged and choreographed by Jerome Robbins; co-choreographer, Peter Gennaro; production associate, Sylvia Drulie; settings by Oliver Smith; costumes by Irene Sharaff; lighting by Jean Rosenthal; musical director, Joseph Lewis; orchestrations by Leonard Bernstein, with Sid Ramin and Irwin Kostal; production stage manager, Joe Calvan; stage manager, Ross Hertz; press representatives, Sol Jacobson and Lewis Harmon.

West Side Story was first produced by Robert E. Griffith and Harold S. Prince (by arrangement with Roger L. Stevens) at the Winter Garden Theatre, September 26, 1957, for 732 performances.

FINIAN'S RAINBOW

(25 performances)
(Continued)

Musical comedy in two acts, with book by E. Y. Harburg and Fred Saidy; lyrics by E. Y. Harburg; music by Burton Lane. Revived by the New York City Center Light Opera Company (Jean Dalrymple, Director) at the New York City Center, April 27, 1960.

Cast of characters—

Buzz Collins	Eddie Bruce
Sheriff	Tom McElhany
First Sharecropper	John McCurry
Second Sharecropper	Knute Sullivan
Susan Mahoney	Anita Alvarez
Henry	Michael Darden
Maude	Carol Brice
Finian McLonergan	Bobby Howes
Sharon McLonergan	Jeannie Carson
Sam	Arthur Garrison
Woody Mahoney	Biff McGuire
Og (a Leprechaun)	Howard Morris
Senator Billboard Rawkins	Sorrell Booke
First Geologist	Barney Johnston
Second Geologist	Robert Guillaume
Howard	Jim McMillan
Diane	Patty Austin
Mr. Robust	Edgar Daniels
Mr. Shears	Joe Ross
First Passion Pilgrim Gospeleer	Jerry Laws
Second Passion Pilgrim Gospeleer	Bill Glover
Third Passion Pilgrim Gospeleer	Tiger Haynes
First Deputy	Don Grey
Second Deputy	Larry Mitchell

Singers: Issa Arnal, Nan Courtney, Marnell Higley, Mary Louise, Lispet Nelson, Stephanie Reynolds, Alice Elizabeth Webb, Beverly Jane Welch, John Boni, Hugh Dilworth, Bill Glover, Don Grey, Robert Guillaume, Tiger Haynes, Barney Johnston, Jerry Laws, John McCurry, Larry Mitchell, Knute Sullivan.

Dancers: Marilynn Allwyn, Ellen Halpin, Sally Lee, Diane McDaniel, Carmen Morales, Mavis Ray, Sandra Roveta, Jacqueline Walcott, Myrna White, Julius C. Fields, Jerry Fries, Gene Gavin, Loren Hightower, Nat Horne, Ronald Lee, Paul Olsen, Wakefield Poole, Jaime Juan Rogers, Ron Schwinn.

Staged and choreographed by Herbert Ross; scenery and lighting by Howard Bay; costumes by Stanley Simmons; orchestrations by Robert Russell Bennett and Don Walker; musical director, Max Meth; co-choreographer, Peter Conlow; production stage manager, Herman Shapiro; stage manager, Chet O'Brien; press representative, Tom Trenkle.

Finian's Rainbow was first produced by Lee Sabinson and William R. Katzall at the Forty-sixth Street Theatre, January 10, 1947, for 725 performances.

CHRISTINE

(12 performances)

Musical in two acts, adapted from "My Indian Family" by Hilda Wernher; book by Pearl S. Buck and Charles K. Peck, Jr.; music by Sammy Fain; lyrics by Paul Francis Webster. Produced by Oscar S. Lerman and Martin B. Cohen, in association with Walter Cohen, at the Forty-sixth Street Theatre, April 28, 1960.

Cast of characters—

```
Beggar ........................................Joseph Crawford
Servants to Dr. Singh ..Arthur Tookoyan, Tony Gardell, John Anania
Auntie ........................................Nancy Andrews
Uncle .........................................Phil Leeds
Rainath .......................................Bhaskar
Jaya ..........................................Leslye Hunter
Rajendra ......................................Augie Rios
Krishna .......................................Steve Curry
Mohan Roy .....................................Jonathan Morris
Servant to Mohan Roy ..........................Nicholas Bianchi
Station Master ................................Louis Polacek
Sita Roy ......................................Janet Pavek
Lady Christine FitzSimons .....................Maureen O'Hara
Dr. Rashil Singh ..............................Morley Meredith
Dr. MacGowan ..................................Daniel Keyes
The Matchmaker ................................Barbara Webb
```

```
                        ⎧ Tara .......................Mai-Lan
                        ⎪ Lakshmi ....................Jinja
The Prospective Brides  ⎨ Amora ......................Laurie Archer
                        ⎩ The Twins ..........Anjali Devi, Sasha
```

```
Children of the Town ....Donna Lyn, Jan Rhodes, Luis Hernandez
The Priest ....................................John Anania
```
Townspeople, Hindus, Muslims, vendors, beggars.

Dancers: Laurie Archer, Sandra Bowman, Anjali Devi, Jinja, Mai-Lan, Jonalee Sanford, Sasha, Vito Durante, Dino Laudicino, Joseph Nelson, Alan Peterson, Joe Rocco, Gil Schwartz.

Singers: Bea Barrett, Diana Corto, Marceline Decker, Josephine Lang, Jen Nelson, Barbara Webb, John Anania, Nicholas Bianchi, Joseph Crawford, Tony Gardell, Louis Polacek, Arthur Tookoyan.

The story is laid in the little town of Akbarabad, India. The time is the present. Act I.—Scene 1—The railroad station in Akbarabad. Scene 2—The study in Dr. Rashil Singh's home. Scene 3—Outside the clinic. Scene 4—The living room; six days later. Scene 5—The veranda; two months later. Scene 6—The living room. Scene 7—The veranda. Scene 8—The drawing room. Scene 9—The clinic. Scene 10—The city square. Act II.—Scene 1—The veranda at Rashil's house. Scene 2—An open plain. Scene 3—A shrine. Scene 4—The living room. Scene 5—The veranda. Scene 6—The drawing room. Scene 7—The veranda. Scene 8—Mohan Roy's home.

Choreography and musical numbers by Hanya Holm; settings and lighting by Joe Mielziner; costumes by Alvin Colt; vocal and dance arrangements by Trude Rittman; orchestrations by Phil Lang; musical direction by Jay Blackton; hair styles by Ernie Adler; associate conductor, Sam Farber; associate producer, Ben Frye; production stage manager, Charles Atkin; stage manager, Fred Smith; press representatives, Frank Goodman, Ben Washer and Leo Stern.

Musical numbers—

ACT I

```
"Welcome Song" ....Auntie, Uncle, Rainath, Children and Chorus
"My Indian Family" ...................................Christine
"A Doctor's Soliloquy" ................................Rashil
```

"UNICEF Song" ....The Children
"My Little Lost Girl" ....Christine and Rashil
"I'm Just a Little Sparrow" ......Jaya, Auntie, Rainath, Servants
and Children
"We're Just a Pair of Sparrows" ....Christine and Jaya
Cobra Ritual Dance ....Rainath and Dancers
"How to Pick a Man a Wife" ....Auntie and Uncle
"The Lovely Girls of Akbarabad" ....The Matchmaker and Chorus
"Room in My Heart" ....Christine
"The Divali Festival" ....Rainath, Dancers and Singers
"I Never Meant to Fall in Love" (Reprise) ....Christine and Rashil

ACT II

"Freedom Can Be a Most Uncomfortable Thing" ....Auntie
and Friends
"Ireland Was Never Like This" ....Christine and Dancers
"He Loves Her" ....Sita
"Christine" ....Rashil
"Room in My Heart" (Reprise) ....Christine
"Freedom Can Be a Most Uncomfortable Thing"
(Reprise) ....Auntie and Uncle
Dance
Kathak (Plate Dance) ....Rainath and Girls
Kathakali ....Dancing Boys
Bharatha Natyan ......Rainath, Dancing Girls and Dancing Boys
"The Woman I Was Before" ....Christine
"A Doctor's Soliloquy" (Reprise) ....Christine and Rashil
"I Never Meant to Fall in Love" ....Rashil and Christine

(Closed May 8, 1960)

THE KING AND I

(24 performances)

Musical in two acts, with music by Richard Rodgers; book and lyrics by Oscar Hammerstein II; based on the novel "Anna and the King of Siam" by Margaret Landon. Revived by the New York City Center Light Opera Company (Jean Dalrymple, Director) at the New York City Center of Music and Drama, May 11, 1960.

Cast of characters—

Captain Orton ....Sam Kirkham
Louis Leonowens ....Richard Mills
Anna Leonowens ....Barbara Cook
The Interpreter ....Murray Gitlin
The Kralahome ....Ten Beniades
The King ....Farley Granger
Phra Alack ....Mark Satow
Lun Tha ....Seth Riggs
Tuptim ....Joy Clements
Lady Thiang ....Anita Darian
Prince Chululongkorn ....Miki Lamont
Princess Ying Yoawalak ....Susan Lynn Kikuchi
Sir Edward Ramsay ....Claude Horton
Princes and Princesses: Alfred De Arco, Delfino De Arco, Evelyn Eng, Vivian Hernandez, Lauretta Lee, Roger Mahabirshingh, Richard Mills, Paul Petrillo, Ado Sato, Claudia Satow.
The Royal Dancers: Diane Adler, Fumi Akimoto, Ted August, Ethel Bell, Paula Chin, Barbara Creed, Bettina Dearborn, Barrie Duffus, Victor Duntiere, Jan Goldin, Marion Jim, Wonci Lui, Julie Oser, Wintress Perkins, Joysanne Sidimus, Nancy Stevens, Roland Vazquez.

The Singers (Wives, Priests, Amazons and Slaves): Jyll Alexander, Jennie Andrea, Irving Barnes, Ellen Berse, Jim Connor, Marvin Goodis, Ann Marisse, Claire Richard, Beatrice Ruth.

Staged by John Fearnley; choreography by Jerome Robbins, reproduced by Yuriko; settings by Joe Mielziner; costumes by Irene Sharaff, supervised by Stanley Simmons; lighting by Klaus Holm; musical director, Pembroke Davenport; orchestrations by Robert Russell Bennett; stage manager, Bill Field; press representative, Tom Trenkle.

The King and I was first produced by Rodgers and Hammerstein at the St. James Theatre, March 29, 1951, for 1,246 performances; and was revived by the New York City Center of Music and Drama April 18, 1956, for 23 performances.

(Closed May 29, 1960)

PLAYS PRODUCED OFF BROADWAY

Excerpts from THE CONNECTION

A Play in Two Acts

By Jack Gelber

[Jack Gelber *was born in Chicago in 1932. He has a degree in Journalism from the University of Illinois and lived for several years in the beatnik colony in San Francisco before coming to New York. He wrote "The Connection" while on vacation in Haiti and has finished a second play titled "The Apple."*]

THE entire action of *The Connection* takes place in Leach's pad, a hangout for a group of heroin users, whom we see sitting about waiting resignedly and irritably for their fix (the slang term for the hypodermic injection of dope which will allow them to face the world for another day).

The play formally begins with a speech to the audience by "producer" Jim Dunn, who introduces us to Jaybird, the playwright. Dunn and Jaybird immediately get into a disagreement about the play we are about to see, and thereby reveal to us the myriad of unreal conventions that the theatre applies to the way things really are. But they also prepare the audience to accept what follows as merely an attempt to explore the interrelation of ordinary people at bedrock level.

Then we watch a series of pre-arranged verbal improvisations, interspersed with some spontaneous jazz improvisation by a trio at various points in the play. First we hear from Leach, the tense landlord.

LEACH—I'm not a Bowery bum. Look at my room. It's clean. Except for the people who come here and call themselves my friends. My friends? Huh! They come here with a little money and they expect me to use my hard earned connections to supply them with heroin. And when I take a little for myself they cry, they scream.

The bastards. They wait here and make me nervous. Sleeping.
That's all they can do. Sleep. Last night I dreamt I was on a
ladder . . . There were a hundred clowns dangling on this rope
ladder, laughing to someone. You know what I mean? Then it
was all a painting and the name psychology was written at the
bottom.

Dunn brings in some photographers to film the action. They
have a morbid curiosity about dope-addiction, and Sam, a sleepy
Negro, explains it to them.

SAM—We swore off of swearing anything off. That's the way it
is—you know something in your mind for so long and you know
that talking nonsense is just that and nothing more. Yeah, man,
we were going to stay clean. Clean, man, clean. We collared the
first connection we could find. I said, "What am I doing?" Just
one fix won't hurt anything. What is this thing I'm fighting? That
taste come back to your mouth. And that's what you want. That
taste, that little taste. If you don't find it there you look some
place else. And you're running, man. Running. It doesn't matter
how or why it started. You don't think about anything and you
start going back, running back. I used to think that the people who
walk the streets, the people who work every day, the people who
worry so much about the next dollar, the next new coat, the chloro-
phyll addicts, the aspirin addicts, the vitamin addicts, those people
are hooked worse than me. Worse than me. Hooked.

There is a knock on the door and Harry enters carrying a portable
phonograph which he plugs into an overhead connection. He listens
ecstatically to a Charlie Parker record, unplugs the phonograph and
leaves. Jaybird stops the proceedings with the complaint that it is
too much "slice-of-life." From now on he wants them to be not
just themselves, but "part of something infinitely larger." One of
the photographers asks if by any chance the big connection might
show up. Sam replies that there is no big connection. "I am your
man if you come to me, and you are my man if I go to you." Now
Solly, a wise and placid Jew, proceeds to expound.

SOLLY—As you have gathered, we are, as they say in the tabloids,
dope fiends. We are waiting. We have waited before. The connection is coming. He is always coming. But so is education,
for example. The man who will whisper the truth in your ear. Or
the one who will shout it out among the people. I can't generalize

and believe it. I'm not made that way. Perhaps Jaybird has chosen this petty and miserable microcosm because of its self-annihilating aspects. This tells us something about Jaybird, but nothing about me. Hurry, hurry, hurry. The circus is here. Suicide is not uncommon among us. The seeking of death is at once fascinating and repellent. The overdose of heroin is where that frail line of life and death swings in the silent breeze of ecstatic summer. The concept of this limbo you can hold in your palsied hand. Who else can make so much out of passing out? But existence on another plane is sought, whether to alleviate the suffering from this one, or to wish for death, it doesn't matter. I hate over-simplification. Sam! Sam is simple. Sam, someone, say something. Say something to the customers.

SAM—Okay. What does Jaybird want? A soft shoe dance? I don't need any burnt cork, you know. Now, Solly, you know Leach . . . Leach is a queer without being queer. He thinks like a chick. You wouldn't live like that. I certainly wouldn't. Sometimes I wish he would stop fighting it and make the homosexual scene. It would be easier on all of us. Besides, he would swing more himself . . . And there's Solly. Man, he's hard to figure. Educated, shit, he knows an awful lot. But then he's here waiting on the same stuff I am. And he ain't rich. He don't get high unless he's happy. I can never figure that out. Most cats get high when they're down . . . Always with a book . . . He's always telling me what I do is got to do with the Africans or the Navahos. He breaks me up. A stand up cat. I like him. Ernie? As long as Ernie is straight with me, I am with him. But I don't like him. I hold back, you know? He has no will power when it comes to not having anything to get high with . . . I can't put Ernie down too hard. I steal. But I steal from people I don't like, and I wouldn't touch a match stick of a friend of mine.

ERNIE—Trust me? Man, I don't care one way or the other . . . I'm lonely! Not for you or anybody on this stage. I know these people. I've known them a long time. Too long . . . Get this straight. I admit when I've sinned. That's more than you'll get from most . . . Solly and Sam are very much alike . . . In this way. They swing with being high. Sam has been around junk and junkies all his life and no one is more familiar with that peculiar code that goes with it, you dig? He learned the hard way. Solly knows instinctively. I mean he was born hip . . . Which brings us to Cowboy. He's a good businessman. Some cats think he is a sweetheart. I mean he's noted for his honesty. I mean I hope he gets here soon, but he is the guy who will not run out. I think it's good business. Not a kind heart. After all, cross country gossip travels at high speed in my world. And nobody cheats him . . . I don't trust one son of a bitch here or in the audience. Why? Because I really don't believe any of you understand what this is about. You're stupid. You're stupid. Why are you here? Because you want to see someone suffer? You want to laugh at me? You don't want to know me.

At this point, Ernie becomes worried about the Cowboy who has his money, but who has not yet returned with the heroin. He also asks Jaybird to give him his pay for allowing the public to see him expose his misery to them and threatens to kill him, thus driving Jaybird and the photographers out. Leach has a boil on his neck which suddenly begins to pain him. He asks Ernie to look at it, but Ernie accidentally causes it to burst. As soon as Leach recovers he and Ernie get into an argument about money. Leach asks Ernie to leave, but Ernie refuses to go until Cowboy returns. Through the window Solly sees Cowboy approaching, accompanied by an elderly Salvation Army Sister. Before we can meet them, Dunn declares an intermission, promising that in the next act the boys will be turned on with a scientifically accurate amount of heroin.

ACT II

In Act II we meet Cowboy, a softspoken Negro, and Sister Salvation, an elderly woman of a trusting nature. It turns out that it was the innocent help of Sister Salvation that enabled the Cowboy to evade the police with the supply of heroin he is carrying. The junkies entertain Sister Salvation with hymns and kidding about their own redemption and the failure of old-time religion to deal with the problems of our expanded scientific universe. Cowboy provides individual fixes in the bathroom. Then one of the photographers asks to try an injection of heroin. Jaybird protests. Leach challenges him with "Hey, Jaybird, you've never made it. Why don't you find out what it's all about before you put it down." Jaybird reluctantly goes off with Cowboy to be turned on. Meanwhile, Sister Salvation seems to be getting wise to what is going on. She returns from the bathroom and accuses them all of being drinkers because she has found empty wine bottles there. She leaves. Jaybird and the photographers are feeling sick from their injections. Jaybird mumbles to Dunn, "There is this wall between you and me, Jim. So that's what it does!" Leach complains that he is not feeling high from his fix, and berates his companions for

talking about baseball, which marks them as "square daytime bastards." Cowboy replies.

Cowboy—What's wrong with day jobs? Or being square? Man,
I haven't anything against them. There are lousy hipsters and
lousy squares. Personally I couldn't make the daily work scene.
I like my work hours as they are. But it doesn't make me any
better.

Sam tells a long story about Cowboy and Leach and a brush
with the police. Afterwards Jaybird complains that his play is
disintegrating into just babbling and challenges Cowboy to act like
a hero, because "It's the basis of Western drama."

Cowboy—It's too much risk going out and scoring every night.
I mean I'm followed every night and I have to scheme a way of
getting back here. I'm tired. Man, I've been moving my whole
life. You think I enjoy leaving love behind? . . . Sit down and
quit worrying about your precious play . . . You can't find out
anything by flirting with people. What do you think we live in, a
freak show? You be the hero. Relax, we won't run out on you.

While this is going on, Leach gives himself an overdose of heroin
and passes out. He is revived by the ministrations of the Cowboy,
and we are left at the end of the evening just about where we
began, or as Jaybird says: "How did I ever get into this? Oh,
yes . . . I wanted to do something far out . . . It was my fault.
I thought perhaps the doctors would take over . . . Well . . .
No doctors, no heroes, no martyrs, no Christs. That's a very good
score. I didn't get burned. Maybe short counted, but not burned."
The play ends with the reappearance of Harry, who enters and
repeats the ritual with the phonograph and the Charlie Parker
record. One is left with the feeling that this religious ritual, which
involves the simple connection of plug to socket, is about as far
as this group of junkies can go towards the affirmation of life without feeling phony.

A SELECTION OF PLAYS PRODUCED OFF BROADWAY

THE CONNECTION

(239 performances)
(Continued)

Play in two acts by Jack Gelber. Produced by Living Theatre Productions, Inc. at the Living Theatre, July 15, 1959.

Cast of characters—

Jim Dunn ....Leonard Hicks
Jaybird ....Ira Lewis
Leach ....Warren Finnerty
Solly ....Jerome Raphel
Sam ....John McCurry
Ernie ....Garry Goodrow
First Photographer ....Louis McKenzie
Second Photographer ....Jamil Zakkai
Harry ....Henry Proach
Sister Salvation ....Barbara Winchester
Cowboy ....Carl Lee

Act I.—Leach's pad. Act II.—The same; a few minutes later.
Staged by Judith Malina; setting by Julian Beck; lighting by Nikola Cernovich; original tunes by Freddie Redd; stage manager, Peter Feldman.

U. S. A.

(237 performances)
(Continued)

Play in two acts by John Dos Passos and Paul Shyre, based on Mr. Dos Passos' novel "U. S. A." Produced by Howard Gottfried and Nick C. Spanos at the Martinique Theatre, October 28, 1959.

Principals—

William Windom   Joan Tetzel
Peggy McCay   William Redfield
Lawrence Hugo   Sada Thompson

The action of the play takes place between the turn of the century and 1930.
Staged by Paul Shyre; setting and costumes by Robert L. Ramsey; lighting by Lee Watson; orchestrations by Robert Cobert; musical direction and continuity by Herbert Harris; stage manager, Mary Ellen Hecht; press representatives, Frank Goodman and Ben Washer.

LITTLE MARY SUNSHINE

(224 performances)
(Continued)

Musical comedy in two acts, with book, music and lyrics by Rick Besoyan. Produced by Howard Barker, Cynthia Baer and Robert Chambers at the Orpheum Theatre, November 18, 1959.

Cast of characters—

Chief Brown Bear, Chief of the Kadota Indians ......John Aniston
Cpl. "Billy" Jester, a forest ranger ....John McMartin
Capt. "Big Jim" Warington, captain of the forest
  rangers ....William Graham
"Little Mary Sunshine" (Mary Potts), proprietress of
  the Colorado Inn ....Eileen Brennan
Mme. Ernestine Von Liebedich, an opera singer ...Elizabeth Parrish
Nancy Twinkle, Little Mary's maid ....Elmarie Wendel
Fleet Foot, an Indian guide ....Robert Chambers
Yellow Feather, Chief Brown Bear's son ....Ray James
Gen'l Oscar Fairfax, Ret., a Washington diplomat ......Mario Siletti
The young ladies of the Eastchester Finishing School
  Cora ....Floria Mari
  Maud ....Jana Stuart
  Gwendolyn ....Elaine Labour
  Henrietta ....Rita Howell
  Mabel ....Sally Bramlette
The young gentlemen of the United States Forest Rangers
  Pete ....Jerry Melo
  Tex ....Joe Warfield
  Slim ....Arthur Hunt
  Buster ....Ed Riley
  Hank ....Mark Destin
  The action takes place at the Colorado Inn, high in the Rocky Mountains. The time is early in this century. The Prologue—Cynthia Baer. Act I.—Scene 1—Exterior of the Colorado Inn. Scene 2—Point Look Out. Scene 3—Exterior of the Colorado Inn. Scene 4—Primrose path. Scene 5—Exterior of the Colorado Inn. Act II.—Scene 1—Exterior of the Colorado Inn. Scene 2—Point Look Out. Scene 3—In front of Chief Brown Bear's teepee. Scene 4—Cora's bedroom. Scene 5—Primrose path. Scene 6—Exterior of the Colorado Inn.
  Staged and choreographed by Ray Harrison; sets and costumes by Howard Barker; book direction and vocal arrangements by Rick Besoyan; musical direction and dance music arrangements by Jack Holmes; stage manager, Ed Royce; press representative, Bob Ullman.

Musical numbers—

ACT I

"The Forest Rangers" ....Captain Jim and Forest Rangers
"Little Mary Sunshine" ....Little Mary and Rangers
"Look for a Sky of Blue" ....Little Mary and Rangers
"You're the Fairest Flower" ....Captain Jim
"In Izzenschnooken on the Lovely Essenzook Zee" ...Mme. Ernestine
"Playing Croquet" ....The Young Ladies
"Swinging and Playing Croquet" ....The Young Ladies
"How Do You Do?" ....Forest Rangers and Young Ladies
"Tell a Handsome Stranger" ....Pete, Cora, Tex, Mabel, Slim
                                                  and Henrietta
"Once in a Blue Moon" ....Billy and Nancy
"Colorado Love Call" ....Captain Jim and Little Mary
"Every Little Nothing" ....Mme. Ernestine and Little Mary
"What Has Happened?" (Finale, Act I) ....Tutti

ACT II

"Such a Merry Party" ....Nancy, Rangers and Young Ladies
"Say, 'Uncle' " ....Oscar and Young Ladies
"The Forest Rangers" (Reprise) ....The Rangers
"Me, a Big Heap Indian" ....Billy
"Naughty, Naughty Nancy" ....Little Mary and Young Ladies
"Mata Hari" ....Nancy and Young Ladies
"Do You Ever Dream of Vienna?" ......Mme. Ernestine and Oscar
"A 'Shell Game' " ....Billy, Yellow Feather and Nancy
"Coo Coo" ....Little Mary
"Colorado Love Call" (Reprise) ....Captain Jim and Little Mary
Finale, Act II ....Tutti

DINNY AND THE WITCHES

(29 performances)

Play in three acts by William Gibson. Produced by Jess Kimmel
and Alfred Stern at the Cherry Lane Theatre, December 9, 1959.

Cast of characters—

Dawn ....Ellen Bogan Engel
Chloe ....Sylvia Shay
Bubbles ....Renee Taylor
Ben ....Harry Fritzius
Jake ....Wil Albert
Stonehenge ....Dean Lyman Almquist
Tom ....Robert Leland
Dick ....Jesse Jacobs
Harry ....E. Francis Simon
Amy ....Kay Doubleday
Dinny ....Bill Heyer
Luella ....Julie Bovasso
Ulga ....Bernard Reed
Zenobia ....Avril Gentles

The action of the play takes place in Central Park. The time is
now, and again. Act I.—The throne; "in which our hero inherits the
world and sees You Can Have Everything; then what?" Act II.—
The altar; "in which our hero, turning to the spirit, essays a more
Perfect union, and finds that Nothing Is." Act III.—The book; "in
which our hero pays for a peek at unholy scripture, and learns
What It is All About."

Staged by Jess Kimmel; production designed by John Robert Lloyd;
songs by William Gibson; musical arrangements by Bobby Scott;
dance movement by Ted Cappy; stage manager, George Thorn; press
representative, Bernard Simon.

(Closed January 3, 1960)

KRAPP'S LAST TAPE
and
THE ZOO STORY

(174 performances)
(Continued)

Two one-act plays by Samuel Beckett and Edward Albee. Produced by Theatre 1960 (Richard Barr and H. B. Lutz) and Harry
Joe Brown, Jr. at the Provincetown Playhouse, January 14, 1960.

KRAPP'S LAST TAPE

By Samuel Beckett

Krapp ....Donald Davis
    The action of the play takes place in Krapp's den. The time is a
late evening in the future.
    Staged by Alan Schneider.

THE ZOO STORY

By Edward Albee

Cast of characters—

Jerry ....George Maharis
Peter ....William Daniels
    The action of the play takes place on a Sunday afternoon in Cen-
tral Park.
    Staged by Milton Katselas.
    Settings and lighting by William Ritman; stage manager, Mark
Wright; press representative, Howard Atlee.

THE PRODIGAL

(126 performances)
(Continued)

Play in two acts by Jack Richardson. Produced by William
Landis at the Downtown Theatre, February 11, 1960.

Cast of characters—

Penelope ....Doreen Richards
Electra ....Carole Macho
Orestes ....Dino Narizzano
Phylades ....Del Tenney
Aegisthus ....William Landis
First Priest ....Harold Herman
Second Priest ....Fred Hodges
Third Priest ....Peter Burbage-Bell
Clytemnestra ....Tani Seitz
Agamemnon ....Russell Gold
Cassandra ....Josephine Nichols
First Soldier ....Fred Hodges
Second Soldier ....Art Wolff
Third Soldier ....Peter Burbage-Bell
Praxithia ....Michela Eisen
    The action of the play takes place in the cities of Argos and Athens
during the pre-history time of legend. Act I.—Scene 1—Early morning.   Scene 2—Afternoon.   Act II.—Scene 1—The beginning of
evening.   Scene 2—Morning in Athens; six months later.
    Staged by Rhodelle Heller; settings and lighting by Robin Wagner;
costumes by Liz Landis; production stage manager, Art Wolff; press
representative, Dave Lipsky.

THE CRYSTAL HEART

(9 performances)

Musical in two acts, with book and lyrics by William Archibald; music by Baldwin Bergersen. Produced by Charles Kasher at the East Seventy-fourth Street Theatre, February 15, 1960.

Cast of characters—

Ted	John Baylis
Jeremy John	John Sewart
Wellington Marchmount	Joe Ross
Herbert	Bob Fitch
Percy	Byron Mitchell
Donald	Vincent Warren
Prudence	Jeanne Shea
Virtue	Katherine Litz
Hope	Barbara Janezic
Charity	Margot Harley
Mistress Phoebe Ricketts	Mildred Dunnock
Alexandra Crowley	Virginia Vestoff
The Captain	Robert Penn

The time is somewhere between 1830 and 1840. Act I.—Scene 1—Aboard the ship; an hour before dawn. Scene 2—The house and garden of Rickett's Folly; immediately following. Scene 3—The following afternoon. Scene 4—The following afternoon. Act II.—Scene 1—A few hours later. Scene 2—The following morning. Scene 3—The following afternoon. Scene 4—Aboard the ship; later that night.

Staged and choreographed by William Archibald; settings and lighting by Richard Casler; costumes by Ted Van Griethuysen; musical director, Baldwin Bergersen; associate producer, Charles Saltz; production stage manager, Lincoln John Stulik; press representative, Joe Lustig.

Musical numbers—

ACT I

"A Year Is a Day"	Ted
"A Monkey When He Loves"	Ted, Herbert, Donald and Percy
"Handsome Husbands"	Mrs. Ricketts, Prudence, Virtue, Hope and Charity
"Yes, Aunt"	Alexandra
"A Girl with a Ribbon"	Ted, Maids and Sailors
"I Must Paint"	Alexandra
"I Wanted to See the World"	Jeremy and Virtue
"Fireflies"	Charity, Hope, Percy and Donald
"How Strange the Silence"	Prudence
"When I Drink with My Love"	Mrs. Ricketts
"Desperate"	Mr. Marchmount and Jeremy
"Lovely Island"	Virtue, Hope, Charity, Jeremy and Alexandra
"Bluebird"	Mrs. Ricketts

ACT II

"Agnes and Me"	Herbert
"Madam, I Beg You!"	Mrs. Ricketts and Mr. Marchmount
"My Heart Won't Learn"	Prudence
"Tea Party"	Mrs. Ricketts, Jeremy, Ted and Sailors
"Lovely Bridesmaids"	Virtue, Hope and Charity
"It Took Them"	Virtue, Hope, Charity, Herbert, Donald and Percy
"D-O-G"	Jeremy
"A Year Is a Day" (Reprise)	Ted

(Closed February 21, 1960)

THE BALCONY

(102 performances)
(Continued)

Play in two acts by Jean Genet, translated by Bernard Frecht-
man. Produced by Lucille Lortel and Circle in the Square at the
Circle in the Square Theatre, March 3, 1960.

Cast of characters—

The Bishop	F. M. Kimball
Irma	Nancy Marchand
Penitent	Grayson Hall
The Thief	Sylvia Miles
The Judge	Arthur Malet
The Executioner	John Perkins
The General	John S. Dodson
The Girl	Salome Jens
Carmen	Betty Miller
The Chief of Police	Roy Poole
The Envoy	Jock Livingston
Roger	Joseph Daubenas
The Slave	William Goodwin

Act I.—Scene 1—A studio. Scene 2—A studio. Scene 3—A
studio. Scene 4—Irma's room. Act II.—Scene 5—The funeral
studio. Scene 6—The council studio. Scene 7—The mausoleum
studio.

Staged by José Quintero; scenery and lighting by David Hays;
costumes by Patricia Zipprodt; stage manager, Thomas Burrows;
press representative, Harvey Sabinson.

UNDER THE SYCAMORE TREE

(41 performances)

Play in two acts by Sam Spewack. Produced by Stuart Duncan,
Hilary Lipsitz and David Sawyer, by arrangement with Jerry Leider,
at the Cricket Theatre, March 7, 1960.

Cast of characters—

The Queen	Margaret Phillips
The Chief Statistician	Thomas Barbour
The Scientist	David Hurst
The General	David Doyle
The Boy	Wayne Tippit
The Girl	Gaby Rodgers
The Nurse	Mary Grant
Brown Ant	Sam Lloyd
Worker	Jim Carruthers
Worker	Alfred De Graaff

The action of the play takes place in the Queen's throne room.
Act I.—Scene 1—The present. Scene 2—Three weeks later. Scene
3—Several months later. Act II.—Scene 1—Later. Scene 2—Some
years later.

Staged by Philip Minor; settings and lighting by Hugh Hardy;
costumes by Sonia Lowenstein; stage manager, John Priest; press representatives, Sol Jacobson and Lewis Harmon.

(Closed April 10, 1960)

THE SECRET CONCUBINE

(6 performances)

Play in two acts by Aldyth Morris. Produced by Terese Hayden, Ira J. Bilowit and Elaine Aiken at the Carnegie Hall Playhouse, March 21, 1960.

Cast of characters—

Chung	Donald Somers
Yuan-Ming	Pieter Bergema
Lumeng	Eva Stern
The Old Couple	Carolyn Gaines and Don Page
Yu-Ho	Dorothy Dill
Chao	Marc Howard
General Mu Chi	Jerry Stiller
First Soldier	Jack Waltzer
Second Soldier	Ben Hayeem
The Emperor	Michael Shillo
Rama	Andreas Voutsinas
Little Brother	Ernesto Gonzalez
Hu-Nang	Ruth Kaner
Grand Eunuck	Delos V. Smith, Jr.
The Empress	Myra Carter
Palace Midwife	Adelaide Klein
Court Drummers	Robert Levy, David Burns
Attendants	Eli Ask, Alex Gregory, Louis Whitehill
Concubines	Jo Ann Brier, Gaye Glaeser, Marni Holbrook, Cynthia Lasky, Kathryn Loder, Jamie Pastor

The action of the play takes place a long time ago, in a small village in China, near the India Border. Act I.—Scene 1—Courtyard of the Chung cottage; late afternoon. Scene 2—A cypress grove; early next morning. Scene 3—A mountain cabin; late that evening. Act II.—Scene 1—The cabin; morning, several days later. Scene 2—The palace; two months later. Scene 3—The cabin; afternoon, a few days later.

Staged by Terese Hayden; settings and lighting by Wolfgang Roth; incidental music by Sol Kaplan; production stage manager, Elizabeth Stern; press representatives, Max Eisen, Lorella Val-Mery and Robert Larkin.

(Closed March 26, 1960)

THE KILLER

(16 performances)

Play in three acts by Eugene Ionesco, translated by Donald Watson. Produced by Theatre 1960 (Richard Barr and H. B. Lutz) at the Seven Arts Theatre, March 22, 1960.

Cast of characters—

Berenger	Hiram Sherman
The Architect	Louis Edmonds
Miss Darnley	Lynne Lyons
The Drunken Man	James Pritchett
The Bartender	Ian Guthrie
Mrs. Peep	Georgia Burke
An Elderly Gentleman	Horace Cooper

A Young Man ....John Mandia
Edwards ....John Lovelady
First Policeman .... Ian Guthrie
Second Policeman ....John Mandia
The Soldier ....James McMillan
    Act I.—The Radiant City. Act II.—Berenger's room. Act III.—
A New York street.
    Interpretation, Richard Barr; movement, Todd Bolender; elec-
tronic sound by Allan Kaprow; settings and lighting by William Rit-
man; costumes by Nilo; collage painting by Ilse Getz; production
stage manager, Mark Wright; stage manager, Page Camp; press representative, Howard Atlee.

(Closed April 3, 1960)

JEANNETTE

(4 performances)

Play in three acts by Jean Anouilh, translated by Miriam John.
Produced by Myron Weinberg at the Maidman Playhouse, March
24, 1960.

Cast of characters—

Julia ....Patricia Bosworth
The Mother (of Frederic) ....Joan Croydon
Frederic ....Geoffrey Horne
Lucien ....Paul Stevens
The Father (of Julia, Lucien and Jeannette) ....Sorrell Booke
Jeannette ....Juleen Compton
Postman ....Pierre Epstein
    The action of the play takes place in a village in France during
a summer between the World Wars. Act I.—Scene 1—A room
in the Father's house; noon. Scene 2—The same; after dinner.
Act II.—A summerhouse in the woods. Act III.—Same as Act I;
late afternoon a week later.
    Staged by Harold Clurman; settings and lighting by Paul Morri-
son; costumes by Barbara Roberts; production stage manager, Pierre
Epstein; press representatives, Max Eisen, Lorella Val-Mery and
Robert Larkin.

(Closed March 26, 1960)

THE DEATH OF SATAN

(31 performances)

Play in three acts by Ronald Duncan. Produced by Marilyn
Shapiro, Walter Ernst and Geraldine Lust at the St. Mark's Playhouse, April 5, 1960.

Cast of characters—

Don Juan ....Robert Mandan
Satan ....Gerald E. McGonagill
Catalion ....Josip Elic
Wilde ....Roger C. Carmel
Byron ....Frederick W. Young
Shaw ....Leigh Wharton

A Bishop ....Bjorn Koefoed
Lionel ....Alex Reed
Evelyn ....Beverly McFadden
Anthony ....Donald Symington
Marcia ....Susan Brown
Baptista ....Muriel Gold
    Act I.—Scene 1—Hell; late afternoon. Scene 2—The cocktail
patio of a hotel in Spain; one hour later. Scene 3—A hotel bed-
room; immediately after. Act II.—Scene 1—The cocktail patio; a
half-hour later. Scene 2—The hotel garden; three A.M. Act III.—
Hell again; four A.M.
    Staged by Geraldine Lust; settings, lighting and costumes by
Robert L. Ramsey; production stage manager, Robert Keegan; press
representatives, Samuel J. Friedman and Maurice Turret.

(Closed May 2, 1960)

THE FANTASTICKS

(31 performances)
(Continued)

Musical in two acts, suggested by the play "Les Romantiques"
by Edmund Rostand; book and lyrics by Tom Jones; music by
Harvey Schmidt. Produced by Lore Noto at the Sullivan Street
Playhouse, May 3, 1960.

Cast of characters—

The Narrator ....Jerry Orbach
The Girl ....Rita Gardner
The Boy ....Kenneth Nelson
The Boy's Father ....William Larsen
The Girl's Father ....Hugh Thomas
The Actor ....Thomas Bruce
The Man Who Dies ....George Curley
The Mute ....Richard Stauffer
The Handyman ....Jay Hampton
    Staged by Word Baker; production designed by Ed Wittstein; mu-
sical direction and arrangements by Julian Stein; production stage
manager, Geoffry Brown; press representatives, Harvey Sabinson,
David Powers and Ted Goldsmith.

Musical numbers—

ACT I

Overture ....The Company
"Try to Remember" ....The Narrator
"Much More" ....The Girl
"Metaphor" ....The Boy and The Girl
"Never So No" ....The Fathers
"It Depends on What You Pay" ......The Narrator and the Fathers
"Soon It's Gonna Rain" ....The Boy and the Girl
"Rape Ballet" ....The Company
"Happy Ending" ....The Company

ACT II

"This Plum Is Too Ripe" ....The Boy, the Girl, the Fathers
"I Can See It" ....The Boy and the Narrator
"Plant a Radish" ....The Fathers
"Round and Round" ....The Narrator, the Girl and Company
"They Were You" ....The Boy and the Girl
"Try to Remember" (Reprise) ....The Narrator

ERNEST IN LOVE

(30 performances)
(Continued)

Musical comedy in two acts, based on Oscar Wilde's "The Importance of Being Ernest"; book and lyrics by Anne Croswell; music by Lee Pockriss. Produced by Noel Behn and Robert Kamlot at the Gramercy Arts Theatre, May 4, 1960.

Cast of characters—

Lane ....Alan Shayne
Perkins ....George Hall
Greengrocer ....John Hays
Bootmaker ....Frank Simpson
Piano Teacher ....Hal Buckley
Tobacconist ....Sam Stoneburner
Dancing Master ....D. P. Smith
John Worthing ....John Irving
Alice ....Margot Harley
Gwendolen Fairfax ....Leila Martin
Algernon Moncrieff ....Louis Edmonds
Lady Bracknell ....Sara Seegar
Cecily Cardew ....Gerrianne Raphael
Miss Prism ....Lucy Landau
Effie ....Christina Gillespie
Dr. Chasuble ....George Hall

Act I.—Scene 1—A London street; a summer afternoon at the turn of the century. Scene 2—Jack's flat; immediately following. Scene 3—Gwendolen's dressing room; about the same time. Scene 4—Algy's flat in Half-Moon Street; shortly before five o'clock. Scene 5—The garden of the Manor House in Hertfordshire; shortly before noon the following day. Act II.—Scene 1—One of the guest rooms in the Manor House; early afternoon. Scene 2—The garden; immediately following. Scene 3—The morning-room of the Manor House; immediately following. Scene 4—The lawn in front of the church; a few minutes later.

Staged by Harold Stone; settings and lighting by Peter Dohanos; costumes by Ann Roth; choreography by Frank Derbas; musical direction by Liza Redfield; arranged and orchestrated by Gershon Kingsley; production stage manager, Kenneth Paine; stage manager, James N. Clark; press representatives, Sol Jacobson and Lewis Harmon.

Musical numbers—

ACT I

"Come Raise Your Cup" ....Creditors and Valets
"How Do You Find the Words?" ....Jack
"The Hat" ....Gwendolen and Alice
"Mr. Bunbury" ....Algy and Jack
"Perfection" ....Jack and Gwendolen
"A Handbag Is Not a Proper Mother" ....Lady Bracknell and Jack
"A Wicked Man" ....Cecily
"Metaphorically Speaking" ....Prism and Chasuble

ACT II

"You Can't Make Love" ....Effie and Lane
"Lost" ....Algy and Cecily
"My First Impression" ....Gwendolen and Cecily
"The Muffin Song" ....Jack and Algy
"My Eternal Devotion" ....Gwendolen, Cecily, Algy and Jack
"Ernest in Love" ....Jack, Gwendolen, Cecily, Algy, Lane, Effie, Prism and Chasuble

A COUNTRY SCANDAL

(29 performances)
(Continued)

Play in four acts by Anton Chekhov, translated and adapted by Alex Szogyi. Produced by Lois Bianchi and Amnon Kabatchnik at the Greenwich Mews Theatre, May 5, 1960.

Cast of characters—

Yakov, a servant .... Sim Landres
Katya, a servant .... Patricia Davies
Mikhail Vassilievich Platonov, a schoolteacher .... Mark Lenard
Nicholas Ivanovich Triletski, Platonov's brother-in-law . Conrad Bain
Porfiry Semeonovich Glagolaev, a rich neighbor of
   the Voinitzev's .... Max Gulack
Anna Petrovna Voinitzev, widow of the late
   Gen. Voinitzev .... Beatrice Bakalyar
Sergey Pavlovich Voinitzev, Anna Petrovna's stepson .. Willy Switkes
Alexandra Ivonovna (Sacha) Platonov,
   Platonov's wife .... Carol Teitel
Ivan Ivanovich Triletski, father of Nicholas and Sacha .. Paul Andor
Petrin, a money-lender .... Earle Rankin
Abram Abramovich Vengerovich, a money-lender ...... Bruce Kimes
Sofia Egorovna Voinitzev, Sergey's wife .... Roberta Royse
Ossip, a horse thief .... Ronald Weyand
Maria Efimova Grekova, a young woman scientist ...... Crystal Field
Kiryl Porfiryevich Glagolaev, old Glagolaev's son ..... Jack Johnson
Markov, a court clerk .... Sim Landres

The action of the play takes place in Voinitzeva, a Russian town. The time is around 1880. Act I.—A garden outside the home of Anna Petrovna Voinitzev; soon after dusk on a summer's evening. Act II.—A yard of the schoolhouse, which is also Platonov's home; later that night. Act III.—A room in the schoolhouse; two weeks later. Act IV.—The late general's study in the Voinitzev house; the following day.

Staged by Amnon Kabatchnik; production designed by Richard Bianchi; costumes by Mary Ann Reed; stage manager, Robert Stevenson; press representatives, Bernard Simon and Ann Sloper.

FACTS AND FIGURES

VARIETY'S TABULATION OF FINANCIAL HITS AND FLOPS

HITS

The Best Man
Dear Liar
Fiorello!
Five Finger Exercise
Goodbye Charlie

Much Ado About Nothing
Once Upon A Mattress
The Tenth Man
Toys in the Attic
The Warm Peninsula

STATUS NOT YET DETERMINED

The Miracle Worker
The Andersonville Trial
Bye Bye Birdie
Finian's Rainbow

The Sound of Music
Take Me Along
A Thurber Carnival

FAILURES

At the Drop of a Hat
Beg, Borrow or Steal
Billy Barnes Revue
Caligula
Chéri
Christine
The Cool World
A Cut of the Axe
The Deadly Game
A Distant Bell
Duel of Angels
The Fighting Cock
Flowering Cherry
From A to Z
The Gang's All Here
The Girls Against the Boys
Golden Fleecing
The Good Soup
The Great God Brown
Greenwillow

Happy Town
Heartbreak House
The Highest Tree
Jolly's Progress
The Long Dream
A Loss of Roses
A Lovely Light
A Mighty Man Is He
Moonbirds
One More River
Only In America
Roman Candle
Saratoga
A Second String
Semi-Detached
Silent Night, Lonely Night
There Was a Little Girl
The Tumbler
Viva Madison Avenue!

SPECIAL, MISCELLANEOUS (UNRATED)

The King and I
Piccolo Teatre de Milano

The Visit
West Side Story

CLOSED DURING TRYOUT TOUR

Free and Easy
Goodwill Ambassador
Hilary
Juniper and the Pagans
Lock Up Your Daughters
Mad Avenue

The Midnight Sun
Motel
Odd Man In
One for the Dame
The Pink Jungle
Sweet Love Remembered

Holdovers from 1958-1959 Season, Since Clarified

HITS

Flower Drum Song
Gypsy

Redhead

STATUS NOT YET DETERMINED

Destry

FAILURES

The Gazebo
Make a Million

Rashomon

STATISTICAL SUMMARY

(Last Season Plays Which Ended Runs After June 1, 1959)

Plays	Number Performances	Closing Date
Once More, With Feeling	263	June 6, 1959
Rashomon	159	June 13, 1959
A Touch of the Poet	284	June 13, 1959
The Gazebo	218	June 20, 1959
West Side Story	732	June 27, 1959
Make a Million	308	July 18, 1959
J. B.	364	October 24, 1959
Two for the Seesaw	750	October 31, 1959
The Pleasure of His Company	474	November 21, 1959
The World of Suzie Wong	508	January 2, 1960
Sweet Bird of Youth	375	January 30, 1960
The Marriage-Go-Round	431	February 13, 1960
Redhead	452	March 19, 1960
Flower Drum Song	600	May 7, 1960

LONG RUNS ON BROADWAY

To June 1, 1960

(Plays marked with asterisk were still playing June 1, 1960)

Plays	Number Performances	Plays	Number Performances
Life with Father	3,224	Fanny	888
Tobacco Road	3,182	Follow the Girls	882
Abie's Irish Rose	2,327	The Bat	867
Oklahoma!	2,248	My Sister Eileen	865
South Pacific	1,925	White Cargo	864
Harvey	1,775	Song of Norway	860
* My Fair Lady	1,757	A Streetcar Named Desire	855
Born Yesterday	1,642	Comedy in Music	849
The Voice of the Turtle	1,557	You Can't Take It with You	837
Arsenic and Old Lace	1,444	Three Men on a Horse	835
Hellzapoppin	1,404	Inherit the Wind	806
Angel Street	1,295	No Time for Sergeants	796
Lightnin'	1,291	Where's Charlie?	792
The King and I	1,246	The Ladder	789
Guys and Dolls	1,200	State of the Union	765
Mister Roberts	1,157	The First Year	760
Annie Get Your Gun	1,147	Two for the Seesaw	750
The Seven Year Itch	1,141	Death of a Salesman	742
Pins and Needles	1,108	Sons o' Fun	742
Kiss Me, Kate	1,070	Gentlemen Prefer Blondes	740
Pajama Game	1,063	The Man Who Came to Dinner	739
The Teahouse of the August Moon	1,027	Call Me Mister	734
* The Music Man	1,022	West Side Story	732
Damn Yankees	1,019	High Button Shoes	727
Anna Lucasta	957	Finian's Rainbow	725
Kiss and Tell	957	Claudia	722
The Moon Is Blue	924	The Gold Diggers	720
Bells Are Ringing	924	The Diary of Anne Frank	717
Can-Can	892	I Remember Mama	714
Carousel	890	Tea and Sympathy	712
Hats Off to Ice	889		

Plays	Number Performances	Plays	Number Performances
Junior Miss	710	Blossom Time	592
Seventh Heaven	704	The Two Mrs. Carrolls	585
Cat on a Hot Tin Roof	694	Kismet	583
Li'l Abner	693	Detective Story	581
Peg o' My Heart	692	Brigadoon	581
The Children's Hour	691	Brother Rat	577
Dead End	687	Show Boat	572
The Lion and the Mouse	686	The Show-Off	571
Dear Ruth	683	Sally	570
East Is West	680	One Touch of Venus	567
The Most Happy Fella	676	Happy Birthday	564
The Doughgirls	671	Look Homeward, Angel	564
Irene	670	The Glass Menagerie	561
Boy Meets Girl	669	Wonderful Town	559
Blithe Spirit	657	Rose Marie	557
The Women	657	Strictly Dishonorable	557
A Trip to Chinatown	657	Sunrise at Campobello	556
Bloomer Girl	654	Jamaica	555
The Fifth Season	654	Ziegfeld Follies	553
Rain	648	Floradora	553
Witness for the Prosecution	645	Dial "M" for Murder	552
Call Me Madam	644	Good News	551
Janie	642	Let's Face It	547
The Green Pastures	640	Within the Law	541
Auntie Mame	639	The Music Master	540
The Fourposter	632	Pal Joey	540
Is Zat So?	618	What a Life	538
* La Plume de Ma Tante	617	* A Majority of One	538
Anniversary Waltz	615	The Red Mill	531
The Happy Time	614	The Solid Gold Cadillac	526
Separate Rooms	613	The Boomerang	522
Affairs of State	610	Rosalinda	521
Star and Garter	609	Chauve Souris	520
The Student Prince	608	Blackbirds	518
Broadway	603	Sunny	517
Adonis	603	Victoria Regina	517
Street Scene	601	* A Raisin in the Sun	512
Kiki	600	The Vagabond King	511
Flower Drum Song	600	The New Moon	509
Wish You Were Here	598	The World of Suzie Wong	508
A Society Circus	596	Shuffle Along	504
		Up in Central Park	504

Plays	*Number* Performances	Plays	*Number* Performances
Carmen Jones	503	Bird in Hand	500
The Member of the Wedding	501	Sailor, Beware!	500
Personal Appearance	501	Room Service	500
Panama Hattie	501	Tomorrow the World	500

NEW YORK DRAMA CRITICS CIRCLE AWARDS

At their annual meeting, the New York Drama Critics Circle chose Lillian Hellman's *Toys in the Attic* as the best play of the season. As the best foreign play, it chose Peter Shaffer's *Five Finger Exercise*, and as the best musical, *Fiorello!*

Circle awards have been—

1935-36—Winterset, by Maxwell Anderson
1936-37—High Tor, by Maxwell Anderson
1937-38—Of Mice and Men, by John Steinbeck
1938-39—No award.
1939-40—The Time of Your Life, by William Saroyan
1940-41—Watch on the Rhine, by Lillian Hellman
1941-42—No award.
1942-43—The Patriots, by Sidney Kingsley
1943-44—No award.
1944-45—The Glass Menagerie, by Tennessee Williams
1945-46—No award.
1946-47—All My Sons, by Arthur Miller
1947-48—A Streetcar Named Desire, by Tennessee Williams
1948-49—Death of a Salesman, by Arthur Miller
1949-50—The Member of the Wedding, by Carson McCullers
1950-51—Darkness at Noon, by Sidney Kingsley
1951-52—I Am a Camera, by John van Druten
1952-53—Picnic, by William Inge
1953-54—The Teahouse of the August Moon, by John Patrick
1954-55—Cat on a Hot Tin Roof, by Tennessee Williams
1955-56—The Diary of Anne Frank, by Frances Goodrich and
         Albert Hackett
1956-57—Long Day's Journey into Night, by Eugene O'Neill
1957-58—Look Homeward, Angel, by Ketti Frings
1958-59—A Raisin in the Sun, by Lorraine Hansberry
1959-60—Toys in the Attic, by Lillian Hellman

PULITZER PRIZE WINNERS

The Pulitzer Prize was awarded to the musical *Fiorello!*, for which Jerome Weidman and George Abbott wrote the book, Jerry Bock the music, and Sheldon Harnick the lyrics.

Pulitzer awards have been—

1917-18—Why Marry?, by Jesse Lynch Williams
1918-19—No award.
1919-20—Beyond the Horizon, by Eugene O'Neill
1920-21—Miss Lulu Bett, by Zona Gale
1921-22—Anna Christie, by Eugene O'Neill
1922-23—Icebound, by Owen Davis
1923-24—Hell-bent for Heaven, by Hatcher Hughes
1924-25—They Knew What They Wanted, by Sidney Howard
1925-26—Craig's Wife, by George Kelly
1926-27—In Abraham's Bosom, by Paul Green
1927-28—Strange Interlude, by Eugene O'Neill
1928-29—Street Scene, by Elmer Rice
1929-30—The Green Pastures, by Marc Connelly
1930-31—Alison's House, by Susan Glaspell
1931-32—Of Thee I Sing, by George S. Kaufman, Morrie Ryskind, Ira and George Gershwin
1932-33—Both Your Houses, by Maxwell Anderson
1933-34—Men in White, by Sidney Kingsley
1934-35—The Old Maid, by Zoë Akins
1935-36—Idiot's Delight, by Robert E. Sherwood
1936-37—You Can't Take It with You, by Moss Hart and George S. Kaufman
1937-38—Our Town, by Thornton Wilder
1938-39—Abe Lincoln in Illinois, by Robert E. Sherwood
1939-40—The Time of Your Life, by William Saroyan
1940-41—There Shall Be No Night, by Robert E. Sherwood
1941-42—No award.
1942-43—The Skin of Our Teeth, by Thornton Wilder
1943-44—No award.
1944-45—Harvey, by Mary Coyle Chase
1945-46—State of the Union, by Howard Lindsay and Russel Crouse

1946-47—No award.
1947-48—A Streetcar Named Desire, by Tennessee Williams
1948-49—Death of a Salesman, by Arthur Miller
1949-50—South Pacific, by Richard Rodgers, Oscar Hammerstein II and Joshua Logan
1950-51—No award.
1951-52—The Shrike, by Joseph Kramm
1952-53—Picnic, by William Inge
1953-54—The Teahouse of the August Moon, by John Patrick
1954-55—Cat on a Hot Tin Roof, by Tennessee Williams
1955-56—The Diary of Anne Frank, by Frances Goodrich and Albert Hackett
1956-57—Long Day's Journey into Night, by Eugene O'Neill
1957-58—Look Homeward, Angel, by Ketti Frings
1958-59—J. B., by Archibald MacLeish
1959-60—Fiorello!, by Jerome Weidman and George Abbott

BOOKS ON THE THEATRE

1959-1960

Anderson, Maxwell. *Four Verse Plays.* (*Elizabeth the Queen, Mary of Scotland, Winterset, High Tor.*) Harcourt, Brace. $2.25 (paperback).

Auden, W. H., and Isherwood, Christopher. *Two Great Plays.* (*The Dog Beneath the Skin, The Ascent of F6.*) Modern Library. $0.95 (paperback).

Anouilh, Jean. *The Fighting Cock.* (Translated and adapted by Lucienne Hill.) Coward-McCann. $3.00.

Behan, Brendan. *The Hostage.* Grove. $3.50; $1.45 (paperback).

Bentley, Eric (Editor). *The Classic Theatre: Volume III—Six Spanish Plays.* (Lope de Vega, Calderon, Cervantes, de Rojas, de Molina.) Anchor. $1.45 (paperback).

Blum, Daniel. *Theatre World: 1958-59.* Chilton. $6.00.

Campbell, Lily B. *Shakespeare's Tragic Heroes.* Barnes & Noble. $1.95 (paperback).

Campbell, Roy. *Federico Garcia Lorca.* Yale. $0.95 (paperback).

Camus, Albert. *The Possessed.* (Translated by Justin O'Brien.) Knopf. $3.50.

Cawley, A. C. (Editor). *Everyman, and Medieval Miracle Plays.* Dutton. $1.35 (paperback).

Chaplin, Charles, Jr. *My Father, Charlie Chaplin.* Random House. $4.95.

Chapman, John (Editor). *Broadway's Best.* Doubleday. $4.50.

Chayefsky, Paddy. *The Tenth Man.* Random House. $2.95.

Clurman, Harold (Editor). *Famous American Plays of the 1930s.* (*The Time of Your Life, Idiot's Delight, Of Mice and Men, Awake and Sing, End of Summer.*) Dell. $0.75 (paperback).

Cole, Toby. *Playwrights on Playwriting.* Hill & Wang. $3.95.

Cotes, Peter. *Handbook for the Amateur Theatre.* Philosophical Library. $12.00.

Crowley, Alice Lewisohn. *The Neighborhood Playhouse.* Theatre Arts. $5.00.

Delaney, Shelagh. *A Taste of Honey.* Grove. $3.50.

Draper, Ruth. *The Art of Ruth Draper: Her Dramas and Characters.* (With a Memoir by Morton Dauwen Zabel.) Doubleday. $4.95.

Eliot, T. S. *The Elder Statesman.* Farrar, Straus & Cudahy. $3.75.

Esslin, Martin. *Brecht:* The Man and His Work. Doubleday. $4.50.

Farquhar, George. *Four Plays.* (*The Constant Couple, The Twin-Rivals, The Recruiting Officer, The Beaux Stratagem.*) Hill & Wang. $1.75 (paperback).

Forsyth, James. *Héloïse.* Theatre Arts. $1.50 (paperback).

Fuchs, George. *Revolution in the Theatre.* (Editor and translator, Constance Kuhn.) Cornell. $4.75.

Garrett, John (Editor). *More Talking of Shakespeare.* Theatre Arts. $4.25.

Garten, H. F. *Modern German Drama.* Oxford. $6.00.

Genet, Jean. *The Blacks:* A Clown Show. Grove. $3.50.

Gillette, A. S. *Stage Scenery: Its Construction and Rigging.* Harper. $8.00.

Gorky, Maxim. *The Lower Depths and Other Plays.* (*Enemies, The Zykovs.*) Yale. $1.25 (paperback).

Greenberg, Noah (Editor). *The Play of Daniel.* Oxford. $5.00.

Grene, David, and Lattimore, Richmond (Editors). *The Complete Greek Tragedies.* (4 vols.) University of Chicago. $20.00.

Guthrie, Tyrone. *A Life in the Theatre.* McGraw-Hill. $5.95.

Hart, Moss. *Act One.* Random House. $5.00.

Heffner, Hubert. *The Nature of Drama.* Houghton Mifflin. $2.00.

Hewes, Henry (Editor). *Famous American Plays of the 1940s.* (*The Skin of Our Teeth, Home of the Brave, All My Sons, Lost in the Stars, The Member of the Wedding.*) Dell. $0.75 (paperback).

Hewitt, Barnard (Editor). *The Renaissance Stage.* University of Miami. $5.50.

Holland, Norman N. *The First Modern Comedies.* Harvard. $5.50.

Houseman, John, and Landau, Jack. *The American Shakespeare Festival.* Simon & Schuster. $3.95.

Inge, William. *A Loss of Roses.* Random House. $2.95.

Joyce, James. *Ulysses in Nighttown.* Modern Library. $0.95 (paperback).

Kallen, Horace M. *The Book of Job as a Greek Tragedy.* Hill & Wang. $1.25 (paperback).

Kanin, Fay and Michael. *Rashomon.* Random House. $2.95.

Kronenberger, Louis (Editor). *The Best Plays of 1958-59.* Dodd, Mead. $6.00.

Laurents, Arthur. *Gypsy.* (Music by Jule Styne, lyrics by Stephen Sondheim.) Random House. $2.95.

Lawrence, Jerome, and Lee, Robert E. *The Gang's All Here.* World. $2.95.

Lewis, D. B. Wyndham. *Molière, the Comic Mask.* Coward-McCann. $4.00.

Lockert, Charles Lacy (Editor). *The Moot Plays of Corneille.* Vanderbilt University. $6.50.

Lockert, Charles Lacy. *Studies in French Classical Tragedy.* Vanderbilt University. $6.50.

Loftis, John. *Comedy and Society from Congreve to Fielding.* Stanford University. $4.00.

Macgowan, Kenneth (Editor). *Famous American Plays of the 1920s.* (*The Moon of Caribbees, What Price Glory?, They Knew What They Wanted, Porgy, Street Scene, Holiday.*) Dell. $0.75 (paperback).

Mayorga, Margaret (Editor). *The Best Short Plays, 1958-1959.* Beacon. $1.75 (paperback).

O'Casey, Sean. *Five One-Act Plays.* (*The End of the Beginning, A Pound on Demand, Hall of Healing, Bedtime Story, Time to Go.*) St. Martin's Press. $0.95 (paperback).

Paterek, Josephine D. *Costuming for the Theatre.* Crown. $3.50.

Peacock, Ronald. *Goethe's Major Plays.* Hill & Wang. $3.95.

Rice, Elmer. *The Living Theatre.* Harper. $3.50.

Rodgers, Richard, and Hammerstein, Oscar. *Six Plays.* (*Oklahoma, Carousel, Allegro, South Pacific, The King and I, Me and Juliet.*) Modern Library. $1.65.

Rossiter, A. P. *English Drama from Early Times to the Elizabethans.* Barnes & Noble. $4.50.

Sartre, Jean-Paul. *The Devil and the Good Lord, and Two Other Plays* (*Kean, Nekrassov*). (Translated by various people.) Knopf. $5.00.

Schary, Dore. *The Highest Tree.* Random House. $2.95.

Schildkraut, Joseph. *My Father and I.* (As told to Leo Lania.) Viking. $3.95.

Shaffer, Peter. *Five Finger Exercise.* Harcourt, Brace. $3.00.

Southern, Richard. *Changeable Scenery.* Hill & Wang. $10.00.

Southern, Richard. *The Open Stage.* Theatre Arts. $3.00.

Strindberg, August. *Letters of Strindberg to Harriet Bosse.* (Translated by Arvid Paulson.) Nelson. $5.00.

Thomas, Dylan. *Under Milk Wood.* New Directions. $1.85 (paperback).

Turgenev, Ivan. *Three Famous Plays.* (*A Month in the Country, A Provincial Lady, A Poor Gentleman.*) Hill & Wang. $1.25 (paperback).

Valéry, Paul. *Plays: Volume III.* (Translated by David Paul and Robert Fitzgerald.) Pantheon Books. $4.50.

Vinaver, Eugene. *Racine and Poetic Tragedy.* (Translated by M. P. Jones.) Hill & Wang. $3.00.

Warren, Robert Penn. *All the King's Men.* Random House. $2.95.

Weidman, Jerome, and Abbott, George. *Fiorello!* (Music by Jerry Bock, lyrics by Sheldon Harnick.) Random House. $2.95.

Willett, John. *The Theatre of Berthold Brecht.* New Diretcions. $8.00.

Williams, Tennessee. *Sweet Bird of Youth.* New Directions. $3.25.

Wynn, Keenan. *Ed Wynn's Son.* (As told to James Brough.) Doubleday. $3.95.

PREVIOUS VOLUMES OF BEST PLAYS

Plays chosen to represent the theatre seasons from 1899 to 1958 are as follows:

1899-1909

BARBARA FRIETCHIE, by Clyde Fitch. Life Publishing Co.
THE CLIMBERS, by Clyde Fitch. Macmillan.
IF I WERE KING, by Justin Huntly McCarthy. Samuel French.
THE DARLING OF THE GODS, by David Belasco. Little, Brown.
THE COUNTY CHAIRMAN, by George Ade. Samuel French.
LEAH KLESCHNA, by C. M. S. McLellan. Samuel French.
THE SQUAW MAN, by Edwin Milton Royle.
THE GREAT DIVIDE, by William Vaughn Moody. Samuel French.
THE WITCHING HOUR, by Augustus Thomas. Samuel French.
THE MAN FROM HOME, by Booth Tarkington and Harry Leon Wilson. Samuel French.

1909-1919

THE EASIEST WAY, by Eugene Walter. G. W. Dillingham and Houghton Mifflin.
MRS. BUMPSTEAD-LEIGH, by Harry James Smith. Samuel French.
DISRAELI, by Louis N. Parker. Dodd, Mead.
ROMANCE, by Edward Sheldon. Macmillan.
SEVEN KEYS TO BALDPATE, by George M. Cohan. Published by Bobbs-Merrill as a novel by Earl Derr Biggers; as a play by Samuel French.
ON TRIAL, by Elmer Reizenstein. Samuel French.
THE UNCHASTENED WOMAN, by Louis Kaufman Anspacher. Harcourt, Brace and Howe.
GOOD GRACIOUS ANNABELLE, by Clare Kummer. Samuel French.
WHY MARRY?, by Jesse Lynch Williams. Scribner.
JOHN FERGUSON, by St. John Ervine. Macmillan.

1919-1920

ABRAHAM LINCOLN, by John Drinkwater. Houghton Mifflin.
CLARENCE, by Booth Tarkington. Samuel French.
BEYOND THE HORIZON, by Eugene G. O'Neill. Boni & Liveright.

Déclassée, by Zoë Akins. Liveright, Inc.
The Famous Mrs. Fair, by James Forbes. Samuel French.
The Jest, by Sem Benelli. (American adaptation by Edward Sheldon.)
Jane Clegg, by St. John Ervine. Henry Holt.
Mamma's Affair, by Rachel Barton Butler. Samuel French.
Wedding Bells, by Salisbury Field. Samuel French.
Adam and Eva, by George Middleton and Guy Bolton. Samuel French.

1920-1921

Deburau, adapted from the French of Sacha Guitry by H. Granville Barker. Putnam.
The First Year, by Frank Craven. Samuel French.
Enter Madame, by Gilda Varesi and Dolly Byrne. Putnam.
The Green Goddess, by William Archer. Knopf.
Liliom, by Ferenc Molnar. Boni & Liveright.
Mary Rose, by James M. Barrie. Scribner.
Nice People, by Rachel Crothers. Scribner.
The Bad Man, by Porter Emerson Browne. Putnam.
The Emperor Jones, by Eugene G. O'Neill. Boni & Liveright.
The Skin Game, by John Galsworthy. Scribner.

1921-1922

Anna Christie, by Eugene G. O'Neill. Boni & Liveright.
A Bill of Divorcement, by Clemence Dane. Macmillan.
Dulcy, by George S. Kaufman and Marc Connelly. Putnam.
He Who Gets Slapped, adapted from the Russian of Leonid Andreyev by Gregory Zilboorg. Brentano's.
Six Cylinder Love, by William Anthony McGuire.
The Hero, by Gilbert Emery.
The Dover Road, by Alan Alexander Milne. Samuel French.
Ambush, by Arthur Richman.
The Circle, by William Somerset Maugham.
The Nest, by Paul Geraldy and Grace George.

1922-1923

Rain, by John Colton and Clemence Randolph. Liveright, Inc.
Loyalties, by John Galsworthy. Scribner.
Icebound, by Owen Davis. Little, Brown.
You and I, by Philip Barry. Brentano's.
The Fool, by Channing Pollock. Brentano's.

MERTON OF THE MOVIES, by George Kaufman and Marc Connelly, based on the novel of the same name by Harry Leon Wilson.
WHY NOT? by Jesse Lynch Williams. Walter H. Baker Co.
THE OLD SOAK, by Don Marquis. Doubleday, Page.
R.U.R., by Karel Capek. Translated by Paul Selver. Doubleday, Page.
MARY THE 3D, by Rachel Crothers. Brentano's.

1923-1924

THE SWAN, translated from the Hungarian of Ferenc Molnar by Melville Baker. Boni & Liveright.
OUTWARD BOUND, by Sutton Vane. Boni & Liveright.
THE SHOW-OFF, by George Kelly. Little, Brown.
THE CHANGELINGS, by Lee Wilson Dodd. Dutton.
CHICKEN FEED, by Guy Bolton. Samuel French.
SUN-UP, by Lula Vollmer. Brentano's.
BEGGAR ON HORSEBACK, by George Kaufman and Marc Connelly. Boni & Liveright.
TARNISH, by Gilbert Emery. Brentano's.
THE GOOSE HANGS HIGH, by Lewis Beach. Little, Brown.
HELL-BENT FER HEAVEN, by Hatcher Hughes. Harper.

1924-1925

WHAT PRICE GLORY? by Laurence Stallings and Maxwell Anderson. Harcourt, Brace.
THEY KNEW WHAT THEY WANTED, by Sidney Howard. Doubleday, Page.
DESIRE UNDER THE ELMS, by Eugene G. O'Neill. Boni & Liveright.
THE FIREBRAND, by Edwin Justus Mayer. Boni & Liveright.
DANCING MOTHERS, by Edgar Selwyn and Edmund Goulding.
MRS. PARTRIDGE PRESENTS, by Mary Kennedy and Ruth Hawthorne. Samuel French.
THE FALL GUY, by James Gleason and George Abbott. Samuel French.
THE YOUNGEST, by Philip Barry. Samuel French.
MINICK, by Edna Ferber and George S. Kaufman. Doubleday, Page.
WILD BIRDS, by Dan Totheroh. Doubleday, Page.

1925-1926

CRAIG'S WIFE, by George Kelly. Little, Brown.
THE GREAT GOD BROWN, by Eugene G. O'Neill. Boni & Liveright.
THE GREEN HAT, by Michael Arlen.
THE DYBBUK, by S. Ansky, Henry G. Alsberg-Winifred Katzin translation. Boni & Liveright.
THE ENEMY, by Channing Pollock. Brentano's.
THE LAST OF MRS. CHEYNEY, by Frederick Lonsdale. Samuel French.
BRIDE OF THE LAMB, by William Hurlbut. Boni & Liveright.
THE WISDOM TOOTH, by Marc Connelly. George H. Doran.
THE BUTTER AND EGG MAN, by George Kaufman. Boni & Liveright.
YOUNG WOODLEY, by John van Druten. Simon & Schuster.

1926-1927

BROADWAY, by Philip Dunning and George Abbott. George H. Doran.
SATURDAY'S CHILDREN, by Maxwell Anderson. Longmans, Green.
CHICAGO, by Maurine Watkins. Knopf.
THE CONSTANT WIFE, by William Somerset Maugham. George H. Doran.
THE PLAY'S THE THING, by Ferenc Molnar and P. G. Wodehouse. Brentano's.
THE ROAD TO ROME, by Robert Emmet Sherwood. Scribner.
THE SILVER CORD, by Sidney Howard. Scribner.
THE CRADLE SONG, translated from the Spanish of G. Martinez Sierra by John Garrett Underhill. Dutton.
DAISY MAYME, by George Kelly. Little, Brown.
IN ABRAHAM'S BOSOM, by Paul Green. McBride.

1927-1928

STRANGE INTERLUDE, by Eugene G. O'Neill. Boni & Liveright.
THE ROYAL FAMILY, by Edna Ferber and George Kaufman. Doubleday, Doran.
BURLESQUE, by George Manker Watters and Arthur Hopkins. Doubleday, Doran.
COQUETTE, by George Abbott and Ann Bridgers. Longmans, Green.
BEHOLD THE BRIDEGROOM, by George Kelly. Little, Brown.
PORGY, by DuBose Heyward. Doubleday, Doran.
PARIS BOUND, by Philip Barry. Samuel French.
ESCAPE, by John Galsworthy. Scribner.

THE RACKET, by Bartlett Cormack. Samuel French.
THE PLOUGH AND THE STARS, by Sean O'Casey. Macmillan.

1928-1929

STREET SCENE, by Elmer Rice. Samuel French.
JOURNEY'S END, by R. C. Sherriff. Brentano's.
WINGS OVER EUROPE, by Robert Nichols and Maurice Browne. Covici-Friede.
HOLIDAY, by Philip Barry. Samuel French.
THE FRONT PAGE, by Ben Hecht and Charles MacArthur. Covici-Friede.
LET US BE GAY, by Rachel Crothers. Samuel French.
MACHINAL, by Sophie Treadwell.
LITTLE ACCIDENT, by Floyd Dell and Thomas Mitchell.
GYPSY, by Maxwell Anderson.
THE KINGDOM OF GOD, by G. Martinez Sierra; English version by Helen and Harley Granville-Barker. Dutton.

1929-1930

THE GREEN PASTURES, by Marc Connelly (adapted from "Ol' Man Adam and His Chillun," by Roark Bradford). Farrar & Rinehart.
THE CRIMINAL CODE, by Martin Flavin. Horace Liveright.
BERKELEY SQUARE, by John Balderston.
STRICTLY DISHONORABLE, by Preston Sturges. Horace Liveright.
THE FIRST MRS. FRASER, by St. John Ervine. Macmillan.
THE LAST MILE, by John Wexley. Samuel French.
JUNE MOON, by Ring W. Lardner and George S. Kaufman. Scribner.
MICHAEL AND MARY, by A. A. Milne. Chatto & Windus:
DEATH TAKES A HOLIDAY, by Walter Ferris (adapted from the Italian of Alberto Casella). Samuel French.
REBOUND, by Donald Ogden Stewart. Samuel French.

1930-1931

ELIZABETH THE QUEEN, by Maxwell Anderson. Longmans, Green.
TOMORROW AND TOMORROW, by Philip Barry. Samuel French.
ONCE IN A LIFETIME, by George S. Kaufman and Moss Hart. Farrar & Rinehart.
GREEN GROW THE LILACS, by Lynn Riggs. Samuel French.
AS HUSBANDS GO, by Rachel Crothers. Samuel French.

ALISON'S HOUSE, by Susan Glaspell. Samuel French.
FIVE-STAR FINAL, by Louis Weitzenkorn. Samuel French.
OVERTURE, by William Bolitho. Simon & Schuster.
THE BARRETTS OF WIMPOLE STREET, by Rudolf Besier. Little, Brown.
GRAND HOTEL, adapted from the German of Vicki Baum by W. A. Drake.

1931-1932

OF THEE I SING, by George S. Kaufman and Morrie Ryskind; music and lyrics by George and Ira Gershwin. Knopf.
MOURNING BECOMES ELECTRA, by Eugene G. O'Neill. Horace Liveright.
REUNION IN VIENNA, by Robert Emmet Sherwood. Scribner.
THE HOUSE OF CONNELLY, by Paul Green. Samuel French.
THE ANIMAL KINGDOM, by Philip Barry. Samuel French.
THE LEFT BANK, by Elmer Rice. Samuel French.
ANOTHER LANGUAGE, by Rose Franken. Samuel French.
BRIEF MOMENT, by S. N. Behrman. Farrar & Rinehart.
THE DEVIL PASSES, by Benn W. Levy. Martin Secker.
CYNARA, by H. M. Harwood and R. F. Gore-Browne. Samuel French.

1932-1933

BOTH YOUR HOUSES, by Maxwell Anderson. Samuel French.
DINNER AT EIGHT, by George S. Kaufman and Edna Ferber. Doubleday, Doran.
WHEN LADIES MEET, by Rachel Crothers. Samuel French.
DESIGN FOR LIVING, by Noel Coward. Doubleday, Doran.
BIOGRAPHY, by S. N. Behrman. Farrar & Rinehart.
ALIEN CORN, by Sidney Howard. Scribner.
THE LATE CHRISTOPHER BEAN, adapted from the French of René Fauchois by Sidney Howard. Samuel French.
WE, THE PEOPLE, by Elmer Rice. Coward-McCann.
PIGEONS AND PEOPLE, by George M. Cohan.
ONE SUNDAY AFTERNOON, by James Hagan. Samuel French.

1933-1934

MARY OF SCOTLAND, by Maxwell Anderson. Doubleday, Doran.
MEN IN WHITE, by Sidney Kingsley. Covici-Friede.
DODSWORTH, by Sinclair Lewis and Sidney Howard. Harcourt, Brace.

AH, WILDERNESS, by Eugene O'Neill. Random House.
THEY SHALL NOT DIE, by John Wexley. Knopf.
HER MASTER'S VOICE, by Clare Kummer. Samuel French.
NO MORE LADIES, by A. E. Thomas.
WEDNESDAY'S CHILD, by Leopold Atlas. Samuel French.
THE SHINING HOUR, by Keith Winter. Doubleday, Doran.
THE GREEN BAY TREE, by Mordaunt Shairp. Baker International
    Play Bureau.

1934-1935

THE CHILDREN'S HOUR, by Lillian Hellman. Knopf.
VALLEY FORGE, by Maxwell Anderson. Anderson House.
THE PETRIFIED FOREST, by Robert Sherwood. Scribner.
THE OLD MAID, by Zoë Akins. Appleton-Century.
ACCENT ON YOUTH, by Samson Raphaelson. Samuel French.
MERRILY WE ROLL ALONG, by George S. Kaufman and Moss Hart.
    Random House.
AWAKE AND SING, by Clifford Odets. Random House.
THE FARMER TAKES A WIFE, by Frank B. Elser and Marc Connelly.
LOST HORIZONS, by John Hayden.
THE DISTAFF SIDE, by John van Druten. Knopf.

1935-1936

WINTERSET, by Maxwell Anderson. Anderson House.
IDIOT'S DELIGHT, by Robert Emmet Sherwood. Scribner.
END OF SUMMER, by S. N. Behrman. Random House.
FIRST LADY, by Katharine Dayton and George S. Kaufman. Random House.
VICTORIA REGINA, by Laurence Housman. Samuel French.
BOY MEETS GIRL, by Bella and Samuel Spewack. Random House.
DEAD END, by Sidney Kingsley. Random House.
CALL IT A DAY, by Dodie Smith. Samuel French.
ETHAN FROME, by Owen Davis and Donald Davis. Scribner.
PRIDE AND PREJUDICE, by Helen Jerome. Doubleday, Doran.

1936-1937

HIGH TOR, by Maxwell Anderson. Anderson House.
YOU CAN'T TAKE IT WITH YOU, by Moss Hart and George S. Kaufman. Farrar & Rinehart.
JOHNNY JOHNSON, by Paul Green. Samuel French.
DAUGHTERS OF ATREUS, by Robert Turney. Knopf.

STAGE DOOR, by Edna Ferber and George S. Kaufman. Doubleday, Doran.

THE WOMEN, by Clare Boothe. Random House.

ST. HELENA, by R. C. Sherriff and Jeanne de Casalis. Samuel French.

YES, MY DARLING DAUGHTER, by Mark Reed. Samuel French.

EXCURSION, by Victor Wolfson. Random House.

TOVARICH, by Jacques Deval and Robert E. Sherwood. Random House.

1937-1938

OF MICE AND MEN, by John Steinbeck. Covici-Friede.

OUR TOWN, by Thornton Wilder. Coward-McCann.

SHADOW AND SUBSTANCE, by Paul Vincent Carroll. Random House.

ON BORROWED TIME, by Paul Osborn. Knopf.

THE STAR-WAGON, by Maxwell Anderson. Anderson House.

SUSAN AND GOD, by Rachel Crothers. Random House.

PROLOGUE TO GLORY, by E. P. Conkle. Random House.

AMPHITRYON 38, by S. N. Behrman. Random House.

GOLDEN BOY, by Clifford Odets. Random House.

WHAT A LIFE, by Clifford Goldsmith. Dramatists' Play Service.

1938-1939

ABE LINCOLN IN ILLINOIS, by Robert E. Sherwood. Scribner.

THE LITTLE FOXES, by Lillian Hellman. Random House.

ROCKET TO THE MOON, by Clifford Odets. Random House.

THE AMERICAN WAY, by George S. Kaufman and Moss Hart. Random House.

NO TIME FOR COMEDY, by S. N. Behrman. Random House.

THE PHILADELPHIA STORY, by Philip Barry. Coward-McCann.

THE WHITE STEED, by Paul Vincent Carroll. Random House.

HERE COME THE CLOWNS, by Philip Barry. Coward-McCann.

FAMILY PORTRAIT, by Lenore Coffee and William Joyce Cowen. Random House.

KISS THE BOYS GOOD-BYE, by Clare Boothe. Random House.

1939-1940

THERE SHALL BE NO NIGHT, by Robert E. Sherwood. Scribner.

KEY LARGO, by Maxwell Anderson. Anderson House.

THE WORLD WE MAKE, by Sidney Kingsley.

LIFE WITH FATHER, by Howard Lindsay and Russel Crouse. Knopf.

THE MAN WHO CAME TO DINNER, by George S. Kaufman and Moss
  Hart. Random House.
THE MALE ANIMAL, by James Thurber and Elliott Nugent. Ran-
  dom House, New York, and MacMillan Co., Canada.
THE TIME OF YOUR LIFE, by William Saroyan. Harcourt, Brace.
SKYLARK, by Samson Raphaelson. Random House.
MARGIN FOR ERROR, by Clare Boothe. Random House.
MORNING'S AT SEVEN, by Paul Osborn. Samuel French.

1940-1941

NATIVE SON, by Paul Green and Richard Wright. Harper.
WATCH ON THE RHINE, by Lillian Hellman. Random House.
THE CORN IS GREEN, by Emlyn Williams. Random House.
LADY IN THE DARK, by Moss Hart. Random House.
ARSENIC AND OLD LACE, by Joseph Kesselring. Random House.
MY SISTER EILEEN, by Joseph Fields and Jerome Chodorov. Ran-
  dom House.
FLIGHT TO THE WEST, by Elmer Rice. Coward-McCann.
CLAUDIA, by Rose Franken Meloney. Farrar & Rinehart.
MR. AND MRS. NORTH, by Owen Davis. Samuel French.
GEORGE WASHINGTON SLEPT HERE, by George S. Kaufman and
  Moss Hart. Random House.

1941-1942

IN TIME TO COME, by Howard Koch. Dramatists' Play Service.
THE MOON IS DOWN, by John Steinbeck. Viking.
BLITHE SPIRIT, by Noel Coward. Doubleday, Doran.
JUNIOR MISS, by Jerome Chodorov and Joseph Fields. Random
  House.
CANDLE IN THE WIND, by Maxwell Anderson. Anderson House.
LETTERS TO LUCERNE, by Fritz Rotter and Allen Vincent. Samuel
  French.
JASON, by Samson Raphaelson. Random House.
ANGEL STREET, by Patrick Hamilton. Constable & Co., under the
  title "Gaslight."
UNCLE HARRY, by Thomas Job. Samuel French.
HOPE FOR A HARVEST, by Sophie Treadwell. Samuel French.

1942-1943

THE PATRIOTS, by Sidney Kingsley. Random House.
THE EVE OF ST. MARK, by Maxwell Anderson. Anderson House.

THE SKIN OF OUR TEETH, by Thornton Wilder. Harper.

WINTER SOLDIERS, by Dan James.

TOMORROW THE WORLD, by James Gow and Arnaud d'Usseau. Scribner.

HARRIET, by Florence Ryerson and Colin Clements. Scribner.

THE DOUGHGIRLS, by Joseph Fields. Random House.

THE DAMASK CHEEK, by John van Druten and Lloyd Morris. Random House.

KISS AND TELL, by F. Hugh Herbert. Coward-McCann.

OKLAHOMA!, by Oscar Hammerstein 2nd and Richard Rodgers. Random House.

1943-1944

WINGED VICTORY, by Moss Hart. Random House.

THE SEARCHING WIND, by Lillian Hellman. Viking.

THE VOICE OF THE TURTLE, by John van Druten. Random House.

DECISION, by Edward Chodorov.

OVER 21, by Ruth Gordon. Random House.

OUTRAGEOUS FORTUNE, by Rose Franken. Samuel French.

JACOBOWSKY AND THE COLONEL, by S. N. Behrman. Random House.

STORM OPERATION, by Maxwell Anderson. Anderson House.

PICK-UP GIRL, by Elsa Shelley.

THE INNOCENT VOYAGE, by Paul Osborn.

1944-1945

A BELL FOR ADANO, by Paul Osborn. Knopf.

I REMEMBER MAMA, by John van Druten. Harcourt, Brace.

THE HASTY HEART, by John Patrick. Random House.

THE GLASS MENAGERIE, by Tennessee Williams. Random House.

HARVEY, by Mary Chase.

THE LATE GEORGE APLEY, by John P. Marquand and George S. Kaufman.

SOLDIER'S WIFE, by Rose Franken. Samuel French.

ANNA LUCASTA, by Philip Yordan. Random House.

FOOLISH NOTION, by Philip Barry.

DEAR RUTH, by Norman Krasna. Random House.

1945-1946

STATE OF THE UNION, by Howard Lindsay and Russel Crouse. Random House.

HOME OF THE BRAVE, by Arthur Laurents. Random House.

DEEP ARE THE ROOTS, by Arnaud d'Usseau and James Gow. Scribner.

THE MAGNIFICENT YANKEE, by Emmet Lavery. Samuel French.

ANTIGONE, by Lewis Galantière (from the French of Jean Anouilh). Random House.

O MISTRESS MINE, by Terence Rattigan. Published and revised by the author.

BORN YESTERDAY, by Garson Kanin. Viking.

DREAM GIRL, by Elmer Rice. Coward-McCann.

THE RUGGED PATH, by Robert E. Sherwood. Scribner.

LUTE SONG, by Will Irwin and Sidney Howard. Published version by Will Irwin and Leopoldine Howard.

1946-1947

ALL MY SONS, by Arthur Miller. Reynal & Hitchcock.

THE ICEMAN COMETH, by Eugene G. O'Neill. Random House.

JOAN OF LORRAINE, by Maxwell Anderson. Published by Maxwell Anderson.

ANOTHER PART OF THE FOREST, by Lillian Hellman. Viking.

YEARS AGO, by Ruth Gordon. Viking.

JOHN LOVES MARY, by Norman Krasna. Copyright by Norman Krasna.

THE FATAL WEAKNESS, by George Kelly. Samuel French.

THE STORY OF MARY SURRATT, by John Patrick. Dramatists' Play Service.

CHRISTOPHER BLAKE, by Moss Hart. Random House.

BRIGADOON, by Alan Jay Lerner and Frederick Loewe. Coward-McCann.

1947-1948

A STREETCAR NAMED DESIRE, by Tennessee Williams. New Directions.

MISTER ROBERTS, by Thomas Heggen and Joshua Logan. Houghton Mifflin.

COMMAND DECISION, by William Wister Haines. Random House.

THE WINSLOW BOY, by Terence Rattigan.

THE HEIRESS, by Ruth and Augustus Goetz.

ALLEGRO, by Richard Rodgers and Oscar Hammerstein 2d. Knopf. Music published by Williamson Music, Inc.

EASTWARD IN EDEN, by Dorothy Gardner. Longmans, Green.

SKIPPER NEXT TO GOD, by Jan de Hartog.

AN INSPECTOR CALLS, by J. B. Priestley.
ME AND MOLLY, by Gertrude Berg.

1948-1949

DEATH OF A SALESMAN, by Arthur Miller. Viking.
ANNE OF THE THOUSAND DAYS, by Maxwell Anderson. Sloane.
THE MADWOMAN OF CHAILLOT, by Maurice Valency, adapted from
the French of Jean Giraudoux. Random House.
DETECTIVE STORY, by Sidney Kingsley. Random House.
EDWARD, MY SON, by Robert Morley and Noel Langley. Random
House, New York, and Samuel French, London.
LIFE WITH MOTHER, by Howard Lindsay and Russel Crouse.
Knopf.
LIGHT UP THE SKY, by Moss Hart. Random House.
THE SILVER WHISTLE, by Robert Edward McEnroe. Dramatists'
Play Service.
TWO BLIND MICE, by Samuel Spewack. Dramatists' Play Service.
GOODBYE, MY FANCY, by Fay Kanin. Samuel French.

1949-1950

THE COCKTAIL PARTY, by T. S. Eliot. Harcourt, Brace.
THE MEMBER OF THE WEDDING, by Carson McCullers. Houghton
Mifflin.
THE INNOCENTS, by William Archibald. Coward-McCann.
LOST IN THE STARS, by Maxwell Anderson and Kurt Weill. Sloane.
COME BACK, LITTLE SHEBA, by William Inge. Random House.
THE HAPPY TIME, by Samuel Taylor. Random House.
THE WISTERIA TREES, by Joshua Logan. Random House.
I KNOW MY LOVE, by S. N. Behrman. Random House.
THE ENCHANTED, by Maurice Valency, adapted from a play by Jean
Giraudoux. Random House.
CLUTTERBUCK, by Benn W. Levy. Dramatists' Play Service.

1950-1951

GUYS AND DOLLS, by Jo Swerling, Abe Burrows and Frank Loesser.
DARKNESS AT NOON, by Sidney Kingsley and Arthur Koestler. Ran-
dom House.
BILLY BUDD, by Louis O. Coxe and Robert Chapman. Princeton
University Press.
THE AUTUMN GARDEN, by Lillian Hellman. Little, Brown & Co.

BELL, BOOK AND CANDLE, by John van Druten. Random House.
THE COUNTRY GIRL, by Clifford Odets. Viking Press.
THE ROSE TATTOO, by Tennessee Williams. New Directions.
SEASON IN THE SUN, by Wolcott Gibbs. Random House.
AFFAIRS OF STATE, by Louis Verneuil.
SECOND THRESHOLD, by Philip Barry. Harper & Bros.

1951-1952

MRS. MCTHING, by Mary Coyle Chase.
THE SHRIKE, by Joseph Kramm. Random House.
I AM A CAMERA, by John van Druten. Random House.
THE FOURPOSTER, by Jan de Hartog.
POINT OF NO RETURN, by Paul Osborn. Random House.
BAREFOOT IN ATHENS, by Maxwell Anderson. Sloane.
VENUS OBSERVED, by Christopher Fry. Oxford.
JANE, by S. N. Behrman and Somerset Maugham. Random House.
GIGI, by Anita Loos and Colette. Random House.
REMAINS TO BE SEEN, by Howard Lindsay and Russel Crouse.
   Random House.

1952-1953

THE TIME OF THE CUCKOO, by Arthur Laurents. Random House.
BERNARDINE, by Mary Coyle Chase.
DIAL "M" FOR MURDER, by Frederick Knott. Random House.
THE CLIMATE OF EDEN, by Moss Hart. Random House.
THE LOVE OF FOUR COLONELS, by Peter Ustinov.
THE CRUCIBLE, by Arthur Miller. Viking.
THE EMPEROR'S CLOTHES, by George Tabori. Samuel French.
PICNIC, by William Inge. Random House.
WONDERFUL TOWN, by Joseph Fields, Jerome Chodorov, Betty
   Comden and Adolph Green. Random House.
MY 3 ANGELS, by Sam and Bella Spewack.

1953-1954

THE CAINE MUTINY COURT-MARTIAL, by Herman Wouk. Double-
   day & Company, Inc.
IN THE SUMMER HOUSE, by Jane Bowles. Random House.
THE CONFIDENTIAL CLERK, by T. S. Eliot. Harcourt, Brace and
   Company, Inc.
TAKE A GIANT STEP, by Louis Peterson.
THE TEAHOUSE OF THE AUGUST MOON, by John Patrick. G. P.
   Putnam's Sons.

THE IMMORALIST, by Ruth and Augustus Goetz. Dramatists' Play Service.

TEA AND SYMPATHY, by Robert Anderson. Random House.

THE GIRL ON THE VIA FLAMINIA, by Alfred Hayes.

THE GOLDEN APPLE, by John Latouche and Jerome Moross. Random House.

THE MAGIC AND THE LOSS, by Julian Funt. Samuel French.

1954-1955

THE BOY FRIEND, by Sandy Wilson.

THE LIVING ROOM, by Graham Greene. Viking.

BAD SEED, by Maxwell Anderson. Dodd, Mead.

WITNESS FOR THE PROSECUTION, by Agatha Christie.

THE FLOWERING PEACH, by Clifford Odets.

THE DESPERATE HOURS, by Joseph Hayes. Random House.

THE DARK IS LIGHT ENOUGH, by Christopher Fry. Oxford.

BUS STOP, by William Inge. Random House.

CAT ON A HOT TIN ROOF, by Tennessee Williams. New Directions.

INHERIT THE WIND, by Jerome Lawrence and Robert E. Lee. Random House.

1955-1956

A VIEW FROM THE BRIDGE, by Arthur Miller. Viking.

TIGER AT THE GATES, by Jean Giraudoux, translated by Christopher Fry. Oxford.

THE DIARY OF ANNE FRANK, by Frances Goodrich and Albert Hackett. Random House.

NO TIME FOR SERGEANTS, by Ira Levin. Random House.

THE CHALK GARDEN, by Enid Bagnold. Random House.

THE LARK, by Jean Anouilh, adapted by Lillian Hellman. Random House.

THE MATCHMAKER, by Thornton Wilder. Harper.

THE PONDER HEART, by Joseph Fields and Jerome Chodorov. Random House.

MY FAIR LADY, by Alan Jay Lerner and Frederick Loewe. Coward-McCann.

WAITING FOR GODOT, by Samuel Beckett. Grove.

1956-1957

SEPARATE TABLES, by Terence Rattigan. Random House.

LONG DAY'S JOURNEY INTO NIGHT, by Eugene O'Neill. Yale University Press.

A VERY SPECIAL BABY, by Robert Alan Aurthur. Dramatists Play Service.

CANDIDE, by Lillian Hellman, Richard Wilbur, John Latouche, Dorothy Parker and Leonard Bernstein. Random House.

A CLEARING IN THE WOODS, by Arthur Laurents. Random House.

THE WALTZ OF THE TOREADORS, by Jean Anouilh, translated by Lucienne Hill. Coward-McCann.

THE POTTING SHED, by Graham Greene. Viking.

VISIT TO A SMALL PLANET, by Gore Vidal. Little, Brown.

ORPHEUS DESCENDING, by Tennessee Williams. New Directions.

A MOON FOR THE MISBEGOTTEN, by Eugene O'Neill. Random House.

1957-1958

LOOK BACK IN ANGER, by John Osborne. Criterion Books.

UNDER MILK WOOD, by Dylan Thomas. New Directions.

TIME REMEMBERED, by Jean Anouilh, adapted by Patricia Moyes. Coward-McCann.

THE ROPE DANCERS, by Morton Wishengrad. Crown.

LOOK HOMEWARD, ANGEL, by Ketti Frings. Scribner's.

THE DARK AT THE TOP OF THE STAIRS, by William Inge. Random House.

SUMMER OF THE 17TH DOLL, by Ray Lawler. Random House.

SUNRISE AT CAMPOBELLO, by Dore Schary. Random House.

THE ENTERTAINER, by John Osborne. Criterion Books.

THE VISIT, by Friedrich Duerrenmatt, adapted by Maurice Valency. Random House.

1958-1959

A TOUCH OF THE POET, by Eugene O'Neill. Yale University Press.

THE PLEASURE OF HIS COMPANY, by Samuel Taylor with Cornelia Otis Skinner. Random House.

EPITAPH FOR GEORGE DILLON, by John Osborne and Anthony Creighton. Criterion Books.

THE DISENCHANTED, by Budd Schulberg and Harvey Breit. Random House.

THE COLD WIND AND THE WARM, by S. N. Behrman. Random House.

J. B., by Archibald MacLeish. Houghton Mifflin.

REQUIEM FOR A NUN, by William Faulkner and Ruth Ford. Random House.

SWEET BIRD OF YOUTH, by Tennessee Williams. New Directions.

A RAISIN IN THE SUN, by Lorraine Hansberry. Random House.

KATAKI, by Shimon Wincelberg.

WHERE AND WHEN THEY WERE BORN

(Compiled from the most authentic records available)

Abbott, George .... Forestville, N. Y. 1889
Abel, Walter .... St. Paul, Minn. 1898
Addy, Wesley .... Omaha, Neb. 1912
Adler, Luther .... New York City 1903
Aherne, Brian .... King's Norton, England 1902
Aldrich, Richard .... Boston, Mass. 1902
Anderson, Judith .... Australia 1898
Anderson, Maxwell .... Atlantic City, Pa. 1888
Anderson, Robert .... New York City 1917
Andrews, Julie .... London, England 1935
Anouilh, Jean .... Bordeaux, France 1910
Arlen, Harold .... Buffalo, N. Y. 1905
Arthur, Jean .... New York City 1905
Ashcroft, Peggy .... Croydon, England 1907
Atkinson, Brooks .... Melrose, Mass. 1894

Bainter, Fay .... Los Angeles, Cal. 1892
Bancroft, Anne .... New York City 1931
Bankhead, Tallulah .... Huntsville, Ala. 1902
Barrymore, Ethel .... Philadelphia, Pa. 1879
Barton, James .... Gloucester, N. J. 1890
Beaton, Cecil .... London, England 1904
Begley, Ed .... Hartford, Conn. 1901
Behrman, S. N. .... Worcester, Mass. 1893
Bellamy, Ralph .... Chicago, Ill. 1904
Bergman, Ingrid ... ... Stockholm, Sweden 1917
Bergner, Elisabeth .... Vienna, Austria 1900
Berlin, Irving .... Russia 1888
Bernstein, Leonard .... Brookline, Mass. 1918
Best, Edna .... Hove, England 1900
Blackmer, Sidney .... Salisbury, N. C. 1898
Blaine, Vivian .... Newark, N. J. 1923
Bloom, Claire .... London, England 1931
Bloomgarden, Kermit ...... Brooklyn, N. Y. 1904
Bolger, Ray .... Dorchester, Mass. 1904

Francis, Arlene .... Boston, Mass. 1908
Fry, Christopher .... England 1907

Gahagan, Helen .... Boonton, N. J. 1900
Gaxton, William .... San Francisco, Cal. 1893
Gazzara, Ben .... New York City 1930
Geddes, Barbara Bel .... New York City 1922
Geddes, Norman Bel .... Adrian, Mich. 1893
George, Grace .... New York City 1879
Gershwin, Ira .... New York City 1896
Gielgud, Sir John .... London, England 1904
Gillmore, Margalo .... England 1901
Gilmore, Virginia .... El Monte, Cal. 1919
Gingold, Hermione .. .. London, England 1897
Gish, Dorothy .... Massillon, Ohio 1898
Gish, Lillian .... Springfield, Ohio 1896
Gordon, Ruth .... Wollaston, Mass. 1896
Green, Adolph .... New York City 1918
Green, Martyn .... London, England 1899
Greenwood, Joan .... London, England 1921
Guinness, Alec .... London, England 1914
Guthrie, Tyrone .... Tunbridge Wells, England 1900
Gwenn, Edmund .... Glamorgan, Wales 1875

Hagen, Uta .... Göttingen, Germany 1919
Hammerstein, Oscar, II ..... New York City 1895
Haney, Carol .... New Bedford, Mass. 1924
Hardie, Russell .... Griffin Mills, N. Y. 1906
Hardwicke, Sir Cedric .... Lye, Stourbridge, England 1893
Harris, Julie .... Grosse Point, Mich. 1925
Harrison, Rex .... Huyton, Lancashire, England .. 1908
Hart, Moss .... New York City 1904
Harvey, Lawrence .... Lithuania 1928
Havoc, June .... Seattle, Wash. 1916
Haydon, Julie .... Oak Park, Ill. 1910
Hayes, Helen .... Washington, D. C. 1900
Hayward, Leland .... Nebraska City, Neb. 1902
Heflin, Frances .... Oklahoma City, Okla. 1924
Hellman, Lillian .... New Orleans, La. 1905
Helmore, Tom .... London, England 1912
Helpmann, Robert .... South Australia 1911
Henie, Sonja .... Oslo, Norway 1913
Hepburn, Audrey .... Brussels, Belgium 1929
Hepburn, Katharine .... Hartford, Conn. 1909

Herlie, Eileen .... Glasgow, Scotland 1920
Hiller, Wendy .... Bramhall, England 1912
Holliday, Judy .... New York City 1924
Holloway, Stanley .... London, England 1890
Holm, Celeste .... New York City 1919
Homolka, Oscar .... Vienna, Austria 1898
Hull, Henry .... Louisville, Ky. 1890
Hunt, Martita .... Argentine Republic 1900
Hunter, Kim .... Detroit, Mich. 1922
Hussey, Ruth .... Providence, R. I. 1917

Inge, William .... Independence, Kan. 1913
Ives, Burl .... Hunt Township, Ill. 1909

Johnson, Harold J. (Chic) ... Chicago, Ill. 1891
Joy, Nicholas .... Paris, France 1889

Kanin, Garson .... Rochester, N. Y. 1912
Karloff, Boris .... Dulwich, England 1887
Kaufman, George S. .... Pittsburgh, Pa. 1889
Kaye, Danny .... New York City 1914
Kazan, Elia .... Constantinople 1909
Keith, Robert .... Fowler, Ind. 1898
Kennedy, Arthur .... Worcester, Mass. 1914
Kerr, Deborah .... Helensburgh, Scotland 1921
Kerr, John .... New York City 1931
Kidd, Michael .... Brooklyn, N. Y. 1920
Killbride, Percy .... San Francisco, Cal. 1880
King, Dennis .... Coventry, England 1897
Kingsley, Sidney .... New York City 1906
Kirkland, Patricia .... New York City 1927
Knox, Alexander .... Ontario 1907
Kruger, Otto .... Toledo, Ohio 1885

Lahr, Bert .... New York City 1895
Landis, Jessie Royce .... Chicago, Ill. 1904
Laughton, Charles .... Scarborough, England 1899
Laurents, Arthur .... New York City 1920
LeGallienne, Eva .... London, England 1899
Leigh, Vivien .... Darjeeling, India 1913
Leighton, Margaret .... Barnt Green, England 1922
Lerner, Alan Jay .... New York City 1918
Lewis, Robert .... Brooklyn, N. Y. 1909
Lillie, Beatrice .... Toronto, Canada 1898

Lindsay, Howard ....Waterford, N. Y. 1899
Linn, Bambi ....Brooklyn, N. Y. 1926
Loesser, Frank ....New York City 1910
Loewe, Frederick .... Vienna, Austria 1904
Logan, Joshua ....Texarkana, Tex. 1908
Lukas, Paul ....Budapest, Hungary 1891
Lunt, Alfred ....Milwaukee, Wis. 1893

MacGrath, Leueen ....London, England 1914
MacMahon, Aline ....McKeesport, Pa. 1899
Mamoulian, Rouben ....Tiflis, Russia 1898
Mann, Iris ....Brooklyn, N. Y. 1939
Marceau, Marcel ....Near Strasbourg, France 1923
March, Fredric ....Racine, Wis. 1897
Martin, Mary ....Weatherford, Texas 1913
Mason, James ....Huddersfield, England 1909
Massey, Raymond ....Toronto, Canada 1896
Maugham, W. Somerset .....England 1874
McClintic, Guthrie ....Seattle, Wash. 1893
McCormick, Myron ....Albany, Ind. 1907
McCracken, Joan ....Philadelphia, Pa. 1923
McDowall, Roddy ....London, England 1928
McGrath, Paul ....Chicago, Ill. 1900
McGuire, Dorothy ....Omaha, Neb. 1918
McKenna, Siobhan ....Belfast, Ireland 1923
Menotti, Gian-Carlo ....Italy 1912
Mercer, Johnny ....Savannah, Ga. 1909
Meredith, Burgess ....Cleveland, Ohio 1908
Merkel, Una ....Covington, Ky. 1903
Merman, Ethel ....Astoria, L. I. 1909
Middleton, Ray ....Chicago, Ill. 1907
Mielziner, Jo ....Paris, France 1901
Miller, Arthur ....New York City 1915
Miller, Gilbert ....New York City 1884
Mitchell, Thomas ....Elizabeth, N. J. 1892
Moore, Victor ....Hammonton, N. J. 1876
Moorehead, Agnes ....Clinton, Mass. 1906
Morgan, Claudia ....New York City 1912
Morley, Robert ....Semley, England 1908
Moss, Arnold ....Brooklyn, N. Y. 1910
Muni, Paul ....Lemberg, Austria 1895

Nagel, Conrad ....Keokuk, Iowa 1897
Natwick, Mildred ....Baltimore, Md. 1908

Schildkraut, Joseph .... Vienna, Austria 1895
Scott, Martha .... Jamesport, Mo. 1914
Segal, Vivienne .... Philadelphia, Pa. 1897
Sherman, Hiram .... Boston, Mass. 1908
Shumlin, Herman .... Atwood, Colo. 1898
Silvers, Phil .... Brooklyn, N. Y. 1911
Simms, Hilda .... Minneapolis, Minn. 1920
Skinner, Cornelia Otis ...... Chicago, Ill. 1902
Slezak, Walter .... Vienna, Austria 1902
Smith, Kent .... Smithfield, Me. 1910
Smith, Oliver .... Wawpaun, Wis. 1918
Sondheim, Stephen .... New York City 1930
Stanley, Kim .... Tularosa, N. M. 1921
Stapleton, Maureen .... Troy, N. Y. 1926
Starr, Frances .... Oneonta, N. Y. 1886
Stickney, Dorothy .... Dickinson, N. D. 1903
Stone, Carol .... New York City 1917
Stone, Dorothy .... New York City 1905
Stone, Ezra .... New Bedford, Mass. 1918
Stone, Fred .... Denver, Colo. 1873
Straight, Beatrice .... Old Westbury, N. Y. 1918
Sullavan, Margaret .... Norfolk, Va. 1910

Tandy, Jessica .... London, England 1909
Tetzel, Joan .... New York City 1923
Thorndike, Sybil .... Gainsborough, England 1882
Tone, Franchot .... Niagara Falls, N. Y. 1906
Tozere, Frederick .... Brookline, Mass. 1901
Tracy, Lee .... Atlanta, Ga. 1898
Treacher, Arthur .... Sussex, England 1900
Truex, Ernest .... Red Hill, Mo. 1890

Ustinov, Peter .... London, England 1921

van Druten, John .... London, England 1902
Van Patten, Dick .... New York City 1929
Varden, Evelyn .... Venita, Okla. 1893
Verdon, Gwen .... Culver City, Cal. 1926

Walker, June .... New York City 1904
Walker, Nancy .... Philadelphia, Pa. 1922
Wallach, Eli .... Brooklyn, N. Y. 1915
Wanamaker, Sam .... Chicago, Ill. 1919
Waring, Richard .... Buckinghamshire, England 1912

NECROLOGY

June 1, 1959—May 31, 1960

Archer, Harry, 72, composer. He was taught by his mother and worked his way through Michigan Military Academy. After attending Knox College he studied music at Princeton. He was most widely known for "Little Jesse James" (produced in London as "Lucky Break"). His first New York show was "Pearl Maiden" in 1912. Other shows included "Love for Sale," "Just a Minute" and "Shoot the Works." Born Creston, Iowa; died New York, April 23, 1960.

Barrymore, Diana, 38, actress. She attended private schools in New York, Baltimore and Paris, studied at the American Academy of Dramatic Arts and made her Broadway debut in "Romantic Mr. Dickens" in 1940. She then went to Hollywood for several films. Later, on Broadway, she was in "The Happy Days," "Rebecca" and "Hidden Horizon." Among her films were "Eagle Squadron," "Nightmare" and "Frontier Badman." She was the daughter of actor John Barrymore and poet Michael Strange. Born New York, March 3, 1921; died New York, Jan. 25, 1960.

Barrymore, Ethel, 79, actress. She was the last of a famous trio that included her brothers Lionel and John. At the age of 14 she left the Convent of the Sacred Heart in Philadelphia to join her grandmother, Mrs. John Drew, Sr. She made her debut in New York as Julia in "The Rivals" on Jan. 25, 1894. After roles in such plays as "The Bauble Shop," she rose to stardom in 1901, when Charles Frohman gave her the lead in "Captain Jinks of the Horse Marines." For the next ten years or more she appeared in many of the hits of the day: "Cousin Kate," "Sunday," "A Doll's House," "Alice-Sit-by-the-Fire," "The Silver Box." Her later notable roles were in such plays as "The Constant Wife," "The School for Scandal," "The Corn Is Green" and "Whiteoaks." She made many pictures, winning an Academy Award for her role in "None But the Lonely Heart." She took her final acting role on television in a "Playhouse 90" production in 1956. Born Philadelphia, Pa.; died Hollywood, June 18, 1959.

Boyne, Eva Leonard, 74, actress. After a successful stage career in England, she came to New York in Shaw's "Fanny's First Play." Winthrop Ames brought her back for her second New York appearance in his production of "A Pair of Silk Stockings." Later she was in "Little Miss Bluebeard," "Shanghai Gesture," "The Letter," "The Apple Cart," "Victoria Regina," "The Corn Is Green," "O Mistress Mine" and others. Born England; died New York, April 12, 1960.

Broderick, Helen, 68, actress. She started her career as a chorus girl in the Ziegfeld Follies. Later she was in "Jumping Jupiter," "The Kiss Burglar," "Nifties of 1923," "Oh, Please," "Fifty Million Frenchmen" and had a starring role in "The Band Wagon." She was prominent in vaudeville, radio and motion pictures. Born Philadelphia; died Beverly Hills, Calif., Sept. 25, 1959.

Brown, Gilmore, 73, producer. He guided the careers of many of the theatrical profession's most famous personalities during his 31 years as president of the Pasadena Playhouse. He began his career in the Middle West as an actor and pageant director and went to Pasadena in 1917 as head of a small stock company. Under his leadership the Pasadena Community Playhouse was founded the same year. In 1936 and 1937 he also served as state supervisor of the Federal Theatre Project. In 1938 the University of Southern California made him a Doctor of Letters. Born New Salem, N.D.; died Palm Springs, Calif., Jan. 10, 1960.

Camus, Albert, 46, playwright and novelist. His essays, novels, plays and other works in the decade after World War II established him in the front rank of the world's writers. His early fiction includes "The Plague" and "The Fall." He won the Nobel Prize in 1957. His play "Caligula" was produced on Broadway during 1959-60. His last work was a four-hour stage adaptation of Dostoevsky's "The Possessed." Birthplace not given; died Sens, France, Jan. 4, 1960.

Clark, Bobby, 71, actor. As a boy he attended the Springfield, Ohio grammar school, delivered papers, and sang in the church choir. While in school he became a friend of Paul McCullough and they taught themselves to play the bugle and joined a class in tumbling at the local Y.M.C.A. Later they joined a minstrel troupe as tumblers, buglers and handymen. In Springfield in 1902 Mr. Clark made his first stage appearance in "Mrs. Jarley's Waxworks." Later he and McCullough were hired by the Hagenbeck-Wallace Circus, and in 1906 they joined Ringling Brothers. In 1912 they entered vaudeville. They were in the London production of "Chuckles of 1922" and that same year were a real triumph in New York's "Music Box Revue." They achieved stardom in 1926 in "The Ramblers." The next several years they made films and were in Earl Carroll's "Vanities" and the "Ziegfeld Follies." After Mr. McCullough's death, Mr. Clark starred in "Streets of Paris," "Love for Love," "Mexican Hayride" and a number of other productions. Born Springfield, Ohio; died New York, Feb. 12, 1960.

Derwent, Clarence, 75, actor. Son of a diamond trader, he trained on the English stage and after appearing in London with Sir Herbert Tree in "Henry VIII" came to this country in 1915. He made his debut here in "Major Barbara." Since then he had appeared in nearly 500 plays, among them "The Woman of Bronze," "Serena Blandish," "Kind Lady," "Rebecca," "Lute Song," and all but three of Shakespeare's. Since 1952, he had been President of ANTA; earlier he served two three-year terms as president of Actors' Equity. He established a two-year scholarship at the Dramatic Workshop and Technical Institute, of which he was president. In 1945 he established the annual Clarence Derwent Awards in London and New York for the best performers in supporting roles. He was a member of the board of the American Theatre Wing. Born London; died New York, Aug. 6, 1959.

Douglas, Paul, 52, actor. He went to school in Philadelphia, later acting in various stock companies. In 1936 he was on Broadway in "Double Dummy." He was a top sports announcer on radio, where he also worked with Jack Benny, and Burns and Allen. In 1946 he gained prominence on Broadway in "Born Yesterday." His last Broadway appearance was in "A Hole in the Head" in 1957. He made many movies, including "Clash by Night," "Solid Gold Cadillac" and "The Mating Game." Born Philadelphia; died Hollywood, Sept. 11, 1959.

Duncan, Rosetta, 58, actress. Together with her sister, Vivian, she did a song-and-dance act, "Topsy and Eva." Rosetta played the blackface Topsy. This went on for years and developed into a full-scale musical which also played for years. She and her sister were also in "Doing Our Bit," "She's a Good Fellow" and "Tip-Top." In 1927 they made a movie of "Topsy and Eva" and in 1936 were signed for starring roles in "New Faces." Born Los Angeles; died Chicago, Dec. 4, 1959.

Emerson, Hope, 62, actress. She first made an impression in 1930 in "Lysistrata." In 1932 she was in the Fred Stone musical "Smilin' Faces." Other plays include "Swing Your Lady," "Chicken Every Sunday" and "The Cup of Trembling." In

1949 she was nominated for an Oscar for her supporting performance in the film "Caged." She made several other pictures and was a popular night-club entertainer. Born Hawarden, Iowa; died Hollywood, April 24, 1960.

Eyre, Laurence, 78, playwright. He began his career as an actor in 1907. Two years later he was in the original company at the New Theatre in New York. He wrote such plays as "The Things That Count" for Alice Brady, "Miss Nelly of N'Orleans" for Mrs. Fiske, "The Merry Wives of Gotham" for Grace George and Laura Hope Crews. Born Chester, Pa.; died The Bronx, New York, June 6, 1959.

Fields, Benny, 65, singer. He began his career at five and 20 years later was "discovered" by the vaudeville star Blossom Seely whom he afterward married. Together they were one of the biggest headliner acts in vaudeville. In 1944 he appeared in the movie "Minstrel Man" in which he sang some of his most popular numbers, including "Remember Me to Caroline," "Candy" and "Melancholy Baby." That year he was also back on Broadway in "Star Time." He appeared in many night clubs and on radio and television. Born Milwaukee, Wis.; died New York, Aug. 16, 1959.

Flynn, Errol, 50, actor. Before becoming a Hollywood glamour boy, he was a sailor, a novelist, a prize-fighter, a newspaper correspondent, a soldier of fortune and a world traveler. He attended schools in Paris, London, Australia and Ireland. He made a picture in Australia before joining the Northhampton Repertory Company in England. Warner Bros. brought him to Hollywood, where his first picture of any consequence was "Captain Blood." After this he starred in many films, among them "Robin Hood," "The Sea Hawk" and "Objective Burma." Not long before his death he starred on the stage in a tour of "Jane Eyre." Born Hobart, Tasmania; died Vancouver, B. C., Oct. 14, 1959.

Goldstein, Jennie, 63, actress. She made her debut at the age of six on the Lower East Side. At 18 she was managing her own theatre, a small playhouse on the Bowery. During the twenties she played various theatres on the Lower East Side and became known as the "Ethel Barrymore of Second Avenue." On Broadway in 1951 she was in "The Number" and two years later in "Camino Real." Born New York; died New York, Feb. 9, 1960.

Gorden, Leon, 64, writer and actor. After studying at St. John's College in London, he became an actor in 1920. A year later he was leading man with the Boston Repertory Company, and his play "The Poppy God" was produced there. He also wrote "Watch Your Neighbor" and "Garden of Weeds," and for Lionel Barrymore "The Piker." His outstanding play was "White Cargo," which played on Broadway for several seasons and was acted in many parts of the world. Born London; died Hollywood, Jan. 4, 1960.

Gray, Gilda, 58, singer and dancer. She did her first professional work in Chicago and introduced the "shimmy dance" into New York about 1919. She was in the "Ziegfeld Follies" and "George White's Scandals," singing many top songs of the era. Born Poland; died Hollywood, Dec. 22, 1959.

Gwenn, Edmund, 83, actor. He toured the provinces in England and was with Edmund Tearle in a Shakespearean repertoire. He played in Australia for three years, after which he returned to England in 1904 and appeared in several Shaw plays. He made his first New York appearance in 1921 in "A Voice from the Minaret." Back in England, he made several films. He returned to Broadway in "Laburnum Grove." He was also seen in "The Wookey" and in Katharine Cornell's 1942 revival of "The Three Sisters." Hollywood claimed him, and he became one of the film's best-loved character men, winning the 1948 Oscar at the age of 72 for his performance in "Miracle on 34th Street." Born London; died Hollywood, Sept. 6, 1959.

Hale, Sonnie, 57, actor. He first appeared on the London stage in 1921 in the chorus of "Fun of the Fayre." He was soon playing leading roles in such shows as "This Year of Grace" and "Ever Green." Just before his death he wrote "The French Mistress." He also appeared in several motion pictures. Born London; died London, June 9, 1959.

Harvey, Georgia, 85, actress. She attended Canadian schools and Boston's Emerson College before making her first stage appearance in Boston. She played New England as a monologuist before making her Broadway debut. For over ten years she was in musicals, including "The Pink Lady," and spent eight years trouping in Australia. She supported such actresses as Ethel Barrymore, Cornelia Otis Skinner, Lillian Gish, Helen Hayes and Tallulah Bankhead. Her more recent plays include "Ten Little Indians," "Mrs. McThing" and "The Chalk Garden." Born Nova Scotia; died New York, May 7, 1960.

Helburn, Theresa, 72, producer. She was educated at Bryn Mawr, the Sorbonne and Professor George Baker's "47 Workshop" at Yale. She became drama critic for *The Nation* and wrote plays. She was among the founders of the Theatre Guild and remained one of its guiding lights up to her death. She directed two plays and once acted briefly in "Suzanna and the Elders." She created the Theresa Helburn Human Freedom Award. Tufts College, Franklin and Marshall College, and Columbia University conferred honorary degrees upon her. Born New York; died Weston, Conn., Aug. 18, 1959.

Heydt, Louis, Jr., 54, actor. He began his career in journalism but turned to the stage to portray a role in "The Trial of Mary Dugan." He was also in "Strictly Dishonorable," "Nikki," "Thunder on the Left" and others, as well as in over 150 movies. At the time of his death, he was in the tryout of "There Was a Little Girl." Born Montclair, N. J.; died Boston, Jan. 29, 1960.

Holmes, Taylor, 80, actor. He began his career in 1899 in vaudeville but quickly became popular on Broadway. He was in Olga Nethersole's company for a time and was the first American Marchbanks in Shaw's "Candida." He supported E. H. Sothern, Robert Edeson and David Warfield before becoming a star in his own right in "His Majesty, Bunker Bean" in 1916. He played in both silent and talking pictures. His other Broadway plays include "The Hotel Mouse," "The Great Necker" and "I'd Rather Be Right." Born Newark, N. J.; died Hollywood, Sept. 30, 1959.

Hopper, Edna Wallace, age unknown but reputed to be 95, actress. Her first New York appearance was in 1891 in "The Club Friend." She was in Charles Frohman's opening production at the Empire Theatre—"The Girl I Left Behind Me." She was Lady Holyrood in the original "Florodora" in 1900. She played in musical after musical on Broadway, on tour and in London, among them "Wang," "El Capitan" and "Dr. Syntax." She was also known for her perpetual youth. Born San Francisco; died New York, Dec. 14, 1959.

Huber, Harold, 49, actor. A graduate of New York University, he also attended Columbia Law School before making his Broadday debut in "A Farewell to Arms" in 1930. Other plays in which he was seen were "First Night," "Two Seconds" and "Merry-Go-Round." He became famous as a villain in more than a hundred Hollywood films in the 1930s. He appeared on radio for years as Hercule Poirot, Agatha Christie's famous sleuth, and was the author of many radio and TV scripts. Birthplace not given; died Sept. 29, 1959.

Jerome, Edwin, 73, actor. He began his career as a boy basso, and at the age of nineteen he sang at the Paris Opera House. After taking leading roles in Milan, Brussels, Lisbon and Madrid, he returned to this country and appeared on the stage. He also appeared in several pictures, such as "Gigi" and "Death of a Salesman," and in over a thousand radio shows as well as on TV. Birthplace not given; died Sept. 10, 1959.

Keith, Ian, 61, actor. He came to Broadway in 1921 and appeared with William Faversham in "The Silver Fox." His more than 350 roles in his 43 years in the theatre were in such plays as "The Czarina," "Saint Joan," "Laugh, Clown, Laugh," "Volpone" and many of Shakespeare's works. He was prominent in both silent and talking pictures. At the time of his death, he was appearing in "The Andersonville Trial." Born Boston; died New York, March 26, 1960.

Kendall, Kay, 33, actress. She was educated in Wales, Scotland and London. She began her career on tour in a revue, "Wild Violets." She entertained occupation troops in Germany, Austria and Italy. After small parts in repertory, television and movies, she made a real hit in a film, "Lady Godiva Rides Again." She was a great success in the films "Les Girls" and "The Reluctant Debutante." One of her final stage appearances was December, 1958, in "The Bright One." She was married to Rex Harrison. Born Withensea, Yorkshire, England; died London, Sept. 6, 1959.

Kershaw, Wilette, 78, actress. She first appeared on the stage at age nine in a Sarah Bernhardt play. She played Ophelia at 15 and was a show girl in "The Country Boy." As the star of "The Crowded Hour," she made a big hit in Chicago in the role Jane Cowl played in New York. She made her London debut in 1921 in "The Bird of Paradise" and also won acclaim there in "Women to Women." Born St. Louis, Mo.; died Honolulu, May 4, 1960.

Kruger, Alma, 88, actress. Early in her career she played many Shakespearean roles, some of them with Louis James and Sothern and Marlowe. She was in George Kelly's "Daisy Mayme" and was with Eva Le Gallienne's Civic Repertory Company. Among her films were the Dr. Kildare series, and she was in countless radio dramas. Born Pittsburgh; died Seattle, April 7, 1960.

Lane, Lupino, 67, actor. A member of the famous Lupino theatrical family of England, he appeared in New York in 1924 in "The Ziegfeld Follies" and the following year in "The Mikado." His greatest London success was "Me and My Girl," of which he was producer, director and star. It opened in 1937 and ran for 1,646 performances. He also directed several British pictures. Born London; died London, Nov. 10, 1959.

Lonergan, Lester, Jr., 65, actor. He made his stage debut at the age of five in "The Heart of the Klondike." He appeared in vaudeville and was stage manager and director in stock companies throughout the country. His Broadway debut was in 1932 in "The Good Earth." Other appearances on Broadway were in "Mother Lodi" and "Live Life Again." He also played a number of roles in films and television. Birthplace not given; died New York, Dec. 23, 1959.

McCarthy, Lillah, 84, actress. A British actress who was famous for her roles in many of George Bernard Shaw's plays. Mr. Shaw wrote "Fanny's First Play" for her. The wife of Granville Barker, she appeared in this country in his repertory company. After her retirement, she wrote a book of reminiscences entitled "Myself and My Friends." Born Chiltenham, Eng.; died London, April 15, 1960.

McLaglen, Victor, 72, actor. He ran away from home to enlist in the London Life Guards for service in the Boer War. He toured Canada with a traveling side show as a boxer. After service in World War I, he started his acting career in a British movie, "Call of the Road." He went to Hollywood in 1924 and became a popular film star, winning an Oscar in 1935 for his performance in "The Informer." He was in nearly 150 films, among them "What Price Glory?" Born Tunbridge Wells, Eng.; died Hollywood, Nov. 1959.

Martin, Owen, 71, actor. He appeared in such plays as "Three Men on a Horse," "Room Service" and "The Boys from Syracuse." He is best remembered for having virtually made a career out of "Oklahoma." He was the only principal member of the original cast to play the entire Broadway run of five years and two months. He ran up another two thousand performances on tour. At different times he appeared as Cord Elam, Pop Carnes and Ali Hakim in this musical. Birthplace not given; died Saranac Lake, N. Y., May 4, 1960.

Morris, Wayne, 45, actor. He attended school in Los Angeles and at the Pasadena Playhouse. A 1937 film, "Kid Galahad," brought him stardom and he appeared in a number of other films. He starred on the stage in touring companies of "The Tender Trap" and "Mr. Roberts." In 1957 he starred on Broadway in William Saroyan's "The Cave Dwellers." Born Los Angeles; died Oakland, Calif., Sept. 14, 1959.

Norworth, Jack, 80, actor and composer. He began his stage career in his teens as a blackface comedian. He was in the "Ziegfeld Follies of 1907," where he met and married Nora Bayes. For several years they toured together in vaudeville and starred in their own show, "Little Miss Fix-It." He was last seen on Broadway in "The Fabulous Invalid." His more than three thousand songs include the popular "Take Me Out to the Ball Game," "Shine on Harvest Moon," "Meet Me in Apple Blossom Time" and "Come Along, My Mandy." Born Philadelphia; died Laguna Beach, Calif., Sept. 1, 1959.

Philipe, Gerard, 36, actor. He made his debut in Nice and then, in Paris in "Sodom et Gomorrhe," he was acclaimed a star after one performance. At the age of 21, he started a film career that included "Devil in the Flesh," "Riptide," "Beauty and the Beast" and "La Ronde." Broadway saw him in 1958 as star of the Théâtre National Populaire in "Lorenzaccio" and "Le Cid." Born Cannes, France; died Paris, Nov. 25, 1959.

Pickard, Helena, 59, actress. She studied for the stage at the Royal Academy of Dramatic Art in London and made her first appearance in 1915 at the Repertory Theatre in Birmingham. She played leading roles in many London productions and was seen on Broadway in "The Country Wife," "Time and the Conways" and "Flare Path." Born Yorkshire, Eng.; died Reading, Eng., Sept. 22, 1959.

Reese, James W., 62, actor. He made his Broadway debut in 1955 in "Festival" before which he had appeared in more than two hundred plays in his native Georgia. His last Broadway role was in "Sunrise at Campobello." He also appeared on the screen and television. Born Buena Vista, Ga.; died New York, Feb. 17, 1960.

Relph, George, 72, actor. He began acting at 17 in "Othello" and acquired a reputation in Shakespearean roles. He came to the U. S. in 1911 in "Kismet." He was in Barrymore's London production of "Hamlet" and with George Arliss in "The Green Goddess." His last New York appearance was with Sir Laurence Olivier in "The Entertainer" in 1958, and his last role was in the film "Ben Hur." Born Cullercoats, Eng.; died London, April 24, 1960.

Ross, Thomas, 86, actor. He began his career with the old Boston Museum Company. He was featured in such Broadway hits as "Soldiers of Fortune," "Checkers," "Polly Preferred," "Laff That Off," "The Gossipy Six" and "Our Town." Born Boston; died Torrington, Conn., Nov. 14, 1959.

Schwartz, Maurice, 69, actor. His parents brought him to New York in 1901 and he made his first stage appearance in 1905 in Baltimore with a Yiddish stock company. He subsequently played in stock in Cincinnati, Chicago and Philadelphia. In 1912 he was engaged by David Kessler for the opening of the Second

Avenue Theatre in New York and remained there until he founded the Yiddish Art Theatre in 1918. This was a Mecca for Jewish theatregoers on New York's Lower East Side until it was disbanded in 1950. Mr. Schwartz was a frequent performer in Yiddish Theatres throughout the world and was often called the "John Barrymore of the Yiddish Theatre." Born Sedikor, Russia; died Petah Tikva, Israel, May 10, 1960.

Selwyn, Arch, 82, producer. He worked as errand boy, bellhop, usher and laundry operator before becoming box-office attendant at the old Herald Square Theatre in New York. With his brother Edgar he entered the play brokerage business and later merged with Elizabeth Marbury and John Ramsay, forming the American Play Company. Beginning with "Within the Law," the Selwyns had a long string of hits, including "Fair and Warmer" and "Smilin' Through." Later Selwyn produced Noel Coward's "Private Lives" and "Bittersweet." In 1916 the Selwyns, together with Sam Goldwyn, organized the Goldwyn Film Company, afterward sold to Metro-Goldwyn-Mayer. Arch Selwyn built three New York theatres on 42nd Street: the Selwyn, the Apollo and the Times Square, and two theatres in Chicago, the Selwyn and the Harris. Birthplace not given; died Hollywood, June 21, 1959.

Smith, G. Albert, 61, actor. He made his stage debut in 1914 with Pauline Frederick in "Joseph and His Brethren." He was with Marjorie Rambeau in "As You Like It," with Walter Hampden in "Cyrano de Bergerac" and with Francine Larrimore in "Chicago." Perhaps his greatest success was with Helen Hayes in "Coquette." He played in both television and motion pictures. Born Louisville, Ky.; died New York, Sept. 3, 1959.

Sturges, Preston, 60, director, producer, writer. He spent much of his early life in Paris and at the age of 16 became manager of his mother's beauty salon in Deauville, France. He invented a kiss-proof lipstick which helped keep the business solvent. He wrote his first play, "The Guinea Pig," in Chicago, Illinois, and produced it himself on Broadway in the mid 1920s. He attained fame in 1929 with his play "Strictly Dishonorable," which ran on Broadway for two years and earned him a contract as a Hollywood screen writer. He either wrote or directed "Christmas in July," "The Lady Eve," "The Miracle of Morgan's Creek," "Sullivan's Travels" and others. In 1940 he won an Academy Award for his script of "The Great McGinty." Later he wrote and directed a film in France called "The French They Are a Funny Race." Born Chicago; died New York, Aug. 6, 1959.

Sullavan, Margaret, 48, actress. She attended three private schools and Sullins College in Bristol, Va. Later she studied dancing in Boston and enrolled in the E. E. Clive Dramatic School. In 1928 she joined the University Players Guild in Falmouth, Mass., and later toured the South in "Strictly Dishonorable." Her first four Broadway plays were failures. She went to Hollywood and was starred in "Only Yesterday." This led to many other films and she became a popular screen star. She returned to Broadway in 1936 to appear in "Stage Door." Perhaps her greatest success was in 1943 in "The Voice of the Turtle." Other plays include "The Deep Blue Sea," "Sabrina Fair" and "Janus." She also appeared on television. At the time of her death she was trying out a play, "Sweet Love Remembered," on tour. Born Norfolk, Va.; died New Haven, Conn., Jan. 1, 1960.

Thropp, Clara, 88, actress. Her stage debut was made at the age of eight in "Rip Van Winkle" in Washington, D. C. She acted with many of the great personalities of her day. Her plays include "Little Johnnie Janes," "The Field God," "Get Me in the Movies," "Jonica" and "The Mountain." Birthplace not given; died New York, Feb. 29, 1960.

Vanderbilt, Gertrude, 60, actress. She went on the stage at 14 and was in many shows during the twenties. She replaced Ina Claire in "The Gold Diggers," and was a star of the "Ziegfeld Follies." She was president of the Ziegfeld Alumni Association and of Show Folks, Inc. Birthplace not given; died New York, Feb. 18, 1960.

Windust, Bretaigne, 54, actor, director. As an undergraduate at Princeton he became a member of Theatre Intime and played in a modern-dress version of "Much Ado About Nothing." He was assistant stage manager for "Strange Interlude" and was active in "Elizabeth the Queen." He directed the Lunts in "Idiots Delight," "The Taming of the Shrew," "Amphitryon 38" and "The Great Sebastians." He acted in "Oliver Oliver" and "The Distaff Side." He directed an impressive array of hits: "Life with Father," "Arsenic and Old Lace," "State of the Union" and "Finian's Rainbow." Recently he directed "The Girls in 509." Born Paris; died New York, March 18, 1960.

THE DECADES' TOLL

(Prominent Theatrical Figures Who Have Died
in Recent Years)

	Born	Died
Adams, Maude	1872	1953
Anderson, John Murray	1886	1954
Anderson, Maxwell	1888	1959
Anglin, Margaret	1877	1958
Arliss, George	1869	1946
Bennett, Richard	1873	1944
Bernstein, Henri	1876	1953
Buchanan, Jack	1891	1957
Calhern, Louis	1895	1956
Carroll, Earl	1893	1948
Carte, Rupert D'Oyly	1876	1948
Christians, Mady	1900	1951
Cochran, Charles B.	1872	1951
Collier, Willie	1866	1943
Cowl, Jane	1884	1950
Craven, Frank	1890	1945
Crosman, Henrietta	1865	1944
Crothers, Rachel	1878	1958
Davis, Owen	1874	1956
De Mille, Cecil B.	1882	1959
Digges, Dudley	1879	1947
Duncan, Augustin	1872	1954
Errol, Leon	1881	1951
Fields, W. C.	1879	1946
Gaige, Crosby	1883	1949
Garfield, John	1913	1952
Geddes, Norman Bel	1893	1958
Golden, John	1874	1955
Guitry, Sacha	1885	1957
Hampden, Walter	1879	1955
Hart, Lorenz	1895	1943
Hart, William S.	1870	1946
Hooker, Brian	1881	1947

	Born	*Died*
Howard, Willie	1883	1949
Jolson, Al	1886	1950
Jouvet, Louis	1887	1951
Kane, Whitford	1882	1956
Kern, Jerome D.	1885	1945
Lawrence, Gertrude	1898	1952
Lehar, Franz	1870	1948
Loftus, Cecilia	1876	1943
Lord, Pauline	1890	1950
Mantle, Burns	1873	1948
Marlowe, Julia	1866	1950
Merivale, Philip	1886	1946
Molnar, Ferenc	1878	1952
Moore, Grace	1901	1947
Nathan, George Jean	1882	1958
Nazimova, Alla	1879	1945
Nethersole, Olga	1870	1951
O'Neill, Eugene	1888	1953
Patterson, Joseph Medill	1879	1946
Perry, Antoinette	1888	1946
Pinza, Ezio	1895	1957
Powers, James T.	1862	1943
Reinhardt, Max	1873	1943
Romberg, Sigmund	1887	1951
Scheff, Fritzi	1879	1954
Selwyn, Edgar	1875	1944
Shaw, G. B.	1856	1950
Sheldon, Edward	1886	1946
Sherwood, Robert E.	1896	1955
Shubert, Lee	1875	1953
Stone, Fred	1873	1959
Tarkington, Booth	1869	1946
Tauber, Richard	1890	1948
Todd, Mike	1909	1958
Tyler, George C.	1867	1946
van Druten, John	1902	1957
Ward, Fannie	1872	1952
Warfield, David	1866	1951
Webster, Ben	1864	1947
Whitty, Dame May	1865	1948
Woods, Al H.	1870	1951
Woollcott, Alexander	1887	1943
Youmans, Vincent	1899	1946

INDEX OF AUTHORS AND PLAYWRIGHTS

INDEX OF PLAYS AND CASTS

Bold face page numbers refer to pages on which
Cast of Characters may be found.

INDEX OF PRODUCERS, DIRECTORS, DESIGNERS, STAGE MANAGERS, COMPOSERS, LYRICISTS AND CHOREOGRAPHERS